INTO THE NIGHT SKY

RAF MIDDLETON ST GEORGE: A BOMBER AIRFIELD AT WAR

PAUL TWEDDLE

SUTTON PUBLISHING

First published in 2007 by
Sutton Publishing, an imprint of NPI Media Group Limited
Cirencester Road · Chalford · Stroud · Gloucestershire · GL6 8PE

British Library Cataloguing in Publication Data
A catalogue record for this book is available from the British Library.

ISBN 978-0-7509-4596-7

Typeset in Garamond 3.
Typesetting and origination by
Sutton Publishing.
Printed and bound in England.

Contents

Acknowledgements —
or 'Proud Words on a Dusty Shelf'

This book has taken an inordinately long time to write and I have run up many debts of gratitude along the way. I am particularly grateful to the many men and women who were stationed at Middleton St George and gave up their time to speak to or correspond with me, often at some length. Their recollections form the very heart of this book. I have also benefited from the help and advice given by the 76, 78, 419/420/428 Squadron Associations and the Bomber Command Association. The Kamloops Museum and Archives supplied me with much useful and interesting information and I am grateful to Dr David Milobar of Vancouver for putting me in touch with it.

I would also like to thank Hazel Arrandale, Joan Marshall and Gwen Griffiths for their help with the typing and computer work, and Jonathan Falconer at Sutton for giving me this opportunity. Thanks are due to Pauline Calvert of the *Northern Echo*, Caroline Archer and Penny Smith for supplying photographs. Many friends have taken a much appreciated positive interest, notably Dr James Pulle, Drs Andrew and Margaret Yacoot and Mr Willie Murdock. Several years' worth of boys and girls at Danes Hill School have also patiently endured snippets of modern military history popping up in their Latin lessons.

I have enjoyed unstinting support and encouragement from my mam Marjorie and my late dad Gordon, who, among other things, toiled patiently for countless hours on my behalf in Darlington library.

My wife Caroline has had to live with me and my bombers for far too long and has done so with amazing equanimity. She has made an incalculable contribution to this book and it is to her and to our little boy Benedict that I dedicate this work. Sine qua non.

Introduction

Large aircraft trundles along the perimeter track and turns to face the runway. It pauses briefly before, with engines screaming, it roars off down the tarmac, gathering speed until the wheels gently lift off the ground and it soars smoothly into the sky. On board a couple of hundred men and women, boys and girls, chatter excitedly on their way to a European holiday resort. They have just left an airfield once known as Middleton St George, commissioned in 1941 as a base for the Royal Air Force and later for the Royal Canadian Air Force. Back then, in the dark days of the Second World War, grim-faced young men hauled their Whitleys, Wellingtons, Halifaxes and Lancasters, heavily laden with bombs, into the deadly night skies over Occupied Europe and Nazi Germany.

Middleton St George was just one of dozens of Bomber Command bases but its contribution to the final victory and the efforts and sacrifices made by the men and women stationed there to achieve it deserve to be remembered. This book is intended to be a plain and straightforward operational history of Middleton St George's role in the war, no more, no less. It draws upon the recollections, published and unpublished, of men and women who were stationed there, supplemented by official records held at the National Archives, Kew (formerly known as the Public Record Office), and the Public Archives of Canada. I only hope the words do the deeds justice.

A BRAVE NEW WORLD

Middleton St George was one cog in the vast machine that was Bomber Command in the Second World War. It was a fairly typical, ordinary airfield where hundreds of ordinary men and women laboured around the clock to carry out extraordinary actions, taking the war right to the heart of one of the most evil regimes in history. As much of what was being attempted had never been tried before, it is not surprising that errors were made. At the very cutting edge of technology, confronted by the hostile natural elements of the skies and hunted by a well-equipped, skilful and determined enemy, it is testimony to the courage of the men concerned that they achieved as much as they did.

The Strategic Air Offensive, in essence a scheme to remove an opponent's capacity and, indeed, will to wage war effectively, grew out of the German Zeppelin and Gotha raids of the First World War and came to dominate both military and political thinking throughout the

The memorial stone on the lawn outside the former officers' mess commemorating the wartime role of 419, 420 and 428 Squadrons, RCAF, 6 Group, Bomber Command. (C.J. Archer)

1920s and 1930s. As Harold Macmillan wrote in his memoirs, 'We thought of air warfare in 1938 rather like people think of nuclear war today.' The public long remembered Prime Minister Stanley Baldwin's chilling statement made in the House of Commons on 10 November 1932: 'No power on earth can protect the man in the street from being bombed. Whatever people might tell him, the bomber will always get through.' Living in the shadow of the bomber, it became widely accepted that there were only two effective defences against such a 'knock-out blow': first, to disarm, and secondly, to out-stick and out-punch an opponent. Britain tried the former and after the inevitable failure, switched to the latter in the mid-1930s.

Plans were hurriedly drawn up for new, long-range heavy bombers and for their development, later codified as the Western Air Plans. This blueprint for the Strategic Air Offensive against Germany focused upon weakening the Luftwaffe and the German aircraft industry – thereby protecting Britain from aerial assault – and destroying Germany's heavy industry, oil industry, administrative and communication centres, transportation system, including shipping, and fatally undermining its willingness to fight. Target selection was by no means as random as it might first appear. Much of what the squadrons based at Middleton St George were doing must be placed within this historical context.

Plans are subject to revision and modification and the Air Ministry accepted that the day-to-day necessities and exigencies of war had to take precedence so that Bomber Command often found itself operating well beyond its original brief. It also had to admit that the Command initially lacked the technological means to carry out its own plans in any meaningful manner and, in many ways, its 6-year-long offensive is the story of the advances made by the boffins in the back rooms. The Bomber Command of May 1945 bore little resemblance to that of September 1939.

The men and women stationed at Middleton St George played their full part in that long offensive and the airfield's 'battle honours' chart the Command's and the war's progress – the Battle of the Atlantic, the Thousand Bomber Raids, the Battle of the Ruhr, the Battle of Hamburg, the Battle of Berlin, the Normandy Campaign, operations against shipping, the V-weapons and the final assault upon Germany.

After the war it became fashionable to criticise the Strategic Air Offensive and vilify those who participated in it. Only towards the end of the twentieth century was a more balanced, revisionist view promulgated. The actions of the Command, including those carried out by 76, 78, 419, 420 and 428 Squadrons based at Middleton St George, must be placed in and judged by their full historical context. The government, the armed forces and the man in the street fully expected that the bomber would be used in war, both against them and by them. It was acknowledged to be a blunt and horrifying weapon but few standing at the graveside of a loved one, or in the midst of the rubble that was once a cherished home, a school, a hospital, a church or cathedral in any number of towns and cities the length and breadth of Britain, voiced any qualms or concerns about Bomber Command's assault on Hitler's Reich. A handful did but theirs were merely feeble voices in the wilderness, overwhelmed by the powerful demands to hit back hard and bring the war to a speedy end. For the vast majority of the population of grim wartime Britain and of the many countries enduring German repression and occupation, the mighty roar of Lancasters, Halifaxes, Wellingtons, Whitleys and Hampdens thundering overhead was an immensely cheering and positive sound, pounding out an unmistakable message – Britain and her allies meant business. It is to their eternal credit that they did.

CHAPTER 1

The Building of a Bomber Station

The advent of the aeroplane marked the beginning of a whole new industry. Not only was there the manufacture of the aeroplane itself and all its components but there was all the paraphernalia that was necessary to fly it. As time went on and technology advanced, this paraphernalia became increasingly sophisticated and, like Topsy, just grew and grew. So did the space needed for the aircraft to take off and land, to be stored and maintained.

The first military airfield, or aerodrome as it was known, opened at Larkhill on Salisbury Plain in 1911. Amounting to little more than a reasonably flat field with a collection of wooden sheds and huts, it was the direct ancestor of the later and much larger airfields that followed. By the end of the First World War in November 1918, the fledgling RAF could boast around three hundred operational airfields, though many were not significantly better equipped than the original at Larkhill. Such was the monumental nature of the postwar scale-down that by 1924 there were only twenty-seven operational airfields left. Lincolnshire, one of the RAF heartlands, for example, was reduced to just three out of a wartime thirty-seven stations.

As a wave of anti-militarist views swept through postwar Britain, there were few who complained when the armed forces had their budgets slashed. All three services were consigned to a period of stagnation in which they were barely able to defend and maintain the empire, let alone wage a major war. With the Ten Year Rule, under which a full-scale war was not foreseen within a ten-year period, in operation until 1932, there was no increase in the defence budget until the Geneva Disarmament Conference finally gave up the ghost in 1934. Even then, with economic prudence still the order of the day, expenditure remained low and rearmament painfully and dangerously slow.

During this time the RAF, starved of investment, had made little progress in technological terms and the designs, capabilities and requirements of the bombers, for example, in the mid-1930s were little different from those in the mid-1920s. In airfield terms, all that was required was an adequate stretch of compacted grass for take-off and landing. All that, however, was about to change as the far sighted in the armed forces began to discern the uncertainties of the future a little more clearly and to make plans accordingly.

In the early 1930s, as the disturbing events in Germany were just beginning to unfold, an Air Ministry Works Directorate was formed to plan and oversee the development and construction of new airfields. These were an essential prerequisite for any expansion of the RAF and obviously had to be capable of handling the new generation of aircraft, which were finally making their way on to the designers' drawing-boards. On 26 May 1934 the Air Ministry Aerodromes Board was set up, under the guidance of the Works Directorate, to work alongside the Air Ministry Lands Branch in the selection and acquisition of suitable sites. The new Aerodromes Board, under the stewardship of two experienced retired officers, AVM C.A.H. Longcroft and Air Cdre the Hon. J.D. Boyle, did not have an easy time of it. Chronically short of staff and run on a shoestring budget, it lacked the power to compulsorily purchase or requisition land; indeed, for most things it was forced to rely on the powers afforded by a relic of the past, the Defence Act of 1842. Much time and effort was wasted upon long-winded and convoluted negotiations with recalcitrant landowners, local authorities and interested parties, such as the Society for the Preservation of Rural England. Indeed, matters were not substantially improved until the passing of the Emergency Powers (Defence) Act in 1939.

The Board did, however, know what it was looking for. The RAF Expansion Scheme A – the first of a long line of such schemes – was approved by Cabinet in July 1934 and set the general pattern for the future, proposing a new force of 28 fighter squadrons and, significantly, 41 bomber squadrons. In March 1935, by which time Germany was beginning to emerge as a realistic threat to Britain and her interests, Scheme C laid down that the RAF's bombers must be able to reach Berlin. This obviously pointed the Aerodromes Board towards the eastern fringes of England and it was there that the great expansion began.

Instructed to look for suitable sites at least 3 miles apart, the Board began its search by the simple but effective method of using 1-inch Ordnance Survey maps to find flat areas in open country with no obstructions within a circle of 1,100 yards in one direction and 800 yards in two others. The sites should also be some distance from any large town and, preferably, villages too. Areas below 50ft above sea level were discounted owing to the threat of flooding, as were those above 600ft owing to potential problems with low cloud base. Once a suitable location had been selected on a map, a preliminary on-the-spot inspection was made by Board officials, often retired officers paid only a small retainer – and the Air Ministry had to have its arm twisted to pay even that. It is said that the rough rule of thumb test for assessing the suitability of the surface applied by the inspectors was to drive an ordinary car across the site at 20mph and monitor the level of comfort of the passengers within! This simple and rudimentary method proved surprisingly effective.

The final decision rested with the President of the Board:

The President of the Aerodromes Board is personally responsible for the ultimate selection of every potential aerodrome site and this is a heavy responsibility. For example, the selection of a site with poor approaches might well result in accidents to aircraft, which might cost several hundreds of thousands of pounds, quite apart from the loss of human life. Further, when it is remembered that the average cost of an operational station is three quarters of a million pounds, it is clear that the responsibility for the ultimate selection of the site cannot be other than heavy.

In military terms, an airfield cost as much as a cruiser for the Royal Navy and, with an empire to defend, there were many calls to build ships and not airfields. Nevertheless, by the end of 1935 almost a hundred new airfields were either being planned or under construction, at a cost of just under £5 million out of a total RAF budget of £27.5 million. By 1939 the annual expenditure on works was running at over three times the entire RAF budget of 1934, eventually peaking in 1942 at an enormous £145 million.

The first of these new Expansion Scheme airfields began to be completed by late 1935 and 1936, and included such later distinguished names as Waddington, Stradishall, Dishforth, Driffield, Scampton and Wyton. In total seven stations were opened in 1935–6, eight in 1936–7 and six in 1937–8. The stations were not, however, slapdash affairs and much care and attention was put into the design of the buildings. Each of the designs had to be approved by the Fine Arts Commission, following a lengthy period of consultation with a variety of semi-official bodies, such as the Society for the Preservation of Rural England. After all, most of the stations covered in the region of 600 acres, usually of prime agricultural land.

During the war years, when the new and hurriedly built stations were, at best, somewhat spartan, many an envious eye was cast upon the understated elegance and comfort of the neo-Georgian, red-brick official buildings, residences and messes of the pre-war Expansion Scheme airfields. The main buildings followed a more or less standard format to a design by Sir Edwin Lutyens, who received 10 per cent of the value of each work as his fee – a very profitable contract.

Accommodation areas were centralised, with messes for the officers and sergeants enjoying secluded and often landscaped settings. The officers' mess at Middleton St George, now the very comfortable St George Hotel at Durham Tees Valley Airport, had a large formal dining room, four well appointed sitting rooms or anterooms and the inevitable bar. On the second storey were a number of bedrooms for the officers, giving an impression rather like that of a country hotel. The sergeants' mess, though less grand, was a comfortable and less formal place to eat, sleep and relax. The well furnished airmen's quarters were, as usual, near the technical buildings and hangars. Each of the barrack blocks was self-contained, equipped with its own ablution blocks. A handful of single rooms were available for corporals. The NAAFI was the hub of many an airman's life on the station. A place to meet and chat, and to try to satisfy the young men's constant craving for food, the NAAFI produced endless cups of strong tea and sandwiches, known throughout the RAF as 'wads'. The kitchens were fitted out with the latest catering equipment and the food, served cafeteria style, was, on occasion, rumoured to be quite edible. With the resuscitation of the WAAF in June 1939, provision had to be made for new and separate accommodation – Waaferies as they were affectionately known. It was often a sore point that this accommodation, created as it was in more hurried and straitened circumstances, was by no stretch of the imagination as well built or comfortable as that of their male counterparts.

The imposing statue of Plt Off Andrew Mynarski, who won a posthumous VC in June 1944 while serving at Middleton St George, stands outside what was the officers' mess, now the St George Hotel at Durham Tees Valley Airport. *(C.J. Archer)*

Even on the permanent stations there always seemed to be building work going on as attempts were made to keep pace with the ever-changing operational requirements and specifications laid down by the Air Ministry. There were also guardrooms, sick quarters, store rooms, wooden huts and brick-built huts of indeterminate origin and purpose, and from March 1941 the ubiquitous Nissen hut constructed of iron sheets fixed to a steel frame and concrete base. In total there were a couple of hundred buildings on site in Middleton St George.

Among the last batch of pre-war Expansion Scheme stations was RAF Middleton St George, the recently formed Bomber Command's most northerly station and the only one in County Durham. Work began on the site, known locally as Goosepool on account of a nearby farm, in 1938. The selected site was at just 115ft above sea level and about 5 miles east of the large market town of Darlington. Further east towards the coast were the industrial towns of Middlesbrough and Stockton; about 20 miles to the south-east lay the North Yorkshire Moors and about the same distance to the west lay the high ground of the Pennines; to the south lay the flat Vale of York which was already home for stations like Dishforth, Leeming and Catterick. In line with Air Ministry practice the construction contracts were put out to tender and it fell to the well established firm of Miskins Ltd, based over 250 miles away in St Albans, to act as main contractor, alongside the large national company Wimpey.

Progress was slow, partly due to the dreadful conditions on the site but mainly due to a shortage of materials. With the LNER railway line running alongside the airfield's perimeter fence and Dinsdale station barely a mile away, truck-loads of hard core taken from demolished brick kilns in the village of Howden-le-Wear, about 20 miles away, were delivered to the constructors. This was supplemented by tons of shale from the local small towns of Sacriston and Shildon and wagon-loads of ash and slag from the power stations and great steel works on Teesside. About 130,000 tons of such materials were needed to construct the foundations for the runways, taxiways, hardstandings, paths and roads on the station. Some eighty men were employed at Dinsdale railway station unloading the trucks, mostly by hand.

Jobs were in short supply in south Durham throughout the 1930s and there was initially no shortage of men ready to work on this sizeable construction site, in spite of the poor terms and conditions. With the outbreak of war, however, the position changed considerably as the manpower was rapidly siphoned off into the armed forces. Greater demands were also placed upon the national supply of materials and consequently progress slowed down considerably.

There were the usual problems with drainage – a result of so much building work, tarmac and concrete disturbing the natural drainage patterns – and attempts to improve the situation initially proved fruitless. After some time, and with the site showing little sign of improvement, Lawrence Logan, the site manager, came across an elderly local man who knew the area well. Upon having the problems explained to him, the old man showed little surprise. He told Logan to follow him and set off across the waterlogged morass to the south-west side of the site. A few hundred yards later he stopped and pointed out a half-hidden and thoroughly overgrown large ditch. It took several men 9 hours to clear away the debris and vegetation to reveal beneath a very large, and very blocked, brick-built drain, the previous owner's solution to the same problem. Once this drain was cleared, the water levels subsided considerably and allowed Middleton St George eventually to pass the standard rule of thumb test for suitable drainage – which involved driving a 3-ton lorry over the field without leaving appreciable tyre tracks.

Conditions, however, remained poor on the windswept field during the harsh winter of 1939/40 and four men died on site owing to a combination of the extreme cold, hard work and meagre supplies of food. When rumblings of severe discontent were heard emanating from the local union officials – war or no war – an application was made to the Air Ministry for additional clothing and boots, especially Wellington boots, to be made available to the workforce without the usual coupons. However, the conditions really only improved as the winter came to an end.

The amount of work to be completed kept on increasing as the Air Ministry requirements were updated, particularly with the planned introduction of the four-engined heavy Halifaxes. In the end, well behind the original time schedule, RAF Middleton St George comprised a full complement of brick-built buildings with full utility services and telephone communications, together with one 2,000ft (later extended again to 2,400ft) runway and another at 1,400ft, both linked by a 50ft-wide perimeter taxiway, built of concrete 6 inches thick, to the hardstandings, each of which was 125ft in diameter. All aerial activity was directed from a state-of-the-art control tower, the top storey of which was almost completely made of glass in order to provide an uninterrupted view of the airfield and the sky around.

There were several main hangars scattered around the station, although these were rarely used for the mere storage of aircraft as is often thought. Most of the main servicing of the aircraft took place in these vast, draughty and dimly lit enclosures, with most of the day-to-day maintenance work being carried out in the open, whatever the weather. Middleton St George boasted one C-type hangar, 152ft wide, mainly constructed in brick and steel in an attempt to match the other buildings, though there was some use of the cheaper asbestos; one J-type hangar, 300ft long and 150ft wide, again constructed of brick and with a curved roof made of ¼-inch steel sheets; one B1-type hangar, which had a much smaller span of 87ft and was made of steel, with large doors of the same material at each end; two T2 hangars, 240ft in length and with a span of 115ft, built with a pre-fabricated and rapidly constructed steel frame and skin. The T2 hangars had, in fact, been designed a few miles down the road in 1940, as a result of a collaboration between the Ministry of Defence and the Teesbridge and Engineering Works.

Brick-built offices and workshops were added externally along the length of the hangars. These were, in many ways, the nerve centres of the squadrons, providing workshops, store rooms, flight offices and crew rooms where the ubiquitous tea and wads were available for the aircrew who often hung around the offices, waiting to find out the latest 'gen'. An ever-increasing number of Nissen huts, Romney huts and a variety of other huts and sheds were dotted over the airfield, providing office space, storage space, workshops, rest areas and bolt-holes for ground staff and shelter for motor transport, tractors, trolleys, fuel bowsers and all the rest of the paraphernalia needed to run a busy airfield and service a community of well over a thousand men and women, and these completed the operational furniture of the station.

All of this was hard to disguise from the air, but camouflage was a necessity given the intruder attacks carried out by the Luftwaffe all over the country in 1940 and 1941. As a result the hangars were painted dull green and brown and had scrimmed netting fixed to the sides. Great efforts were made to break up the obvious layout and shape of the airfield by blending in with the surrounding field patterns, whether by ploughing, cutting the grass in the same direction or even planting crops. Several of the early arrivals at Middleton recall seeing a good crop of growing corn waving in the middle of the airfield in the summer of 1941.

The final additions to the plans came about as the result of hard-won battle experience. The pre-war plans had paid surprisingly little attention to airfield defence and the safety of the personnel stationed there, beyond placing the bomb dump and armoury some distance from the main areas. However, this major omission had been recognised and rectified by the time Middleton was nearing completion. Slit trenches were dug, and road blocks and pill boxes, protected by barbed-wire entanglements, were placed on all the entrances to the station, manned initially by elements of the local regiment, the Durham Light Infantry. Several light flak positions were added as defence against attack from the air. Air raid shelters, each capable of sheltering fifty people, were constructed and several open blast shelters, their walls submerged beneath earthen banks, were also built. The hangars too were protected to some extent against the effects of blast; an ingenious design allowed the doors to be filled with gravel up to a depth of 20ft. Fortunately the defences at Middleton St George were never called upon in earnest, though those at several of the airfields nearby were.

RAF Middleton St George finally opened as part of No. 4 Group, Bomber Command, on 15 January 1941, though building work continued well into 1942 and a station works flight of about eighty men, under the command of a warrant officer, was formed as 5007 Airfield Construction Squadron to work alongside the civilian contractors in putting the finishing touches to the project. In fact, new technology, constant expansion and new operational demands meant that the work never did really come to an end. Nevertheless, the station was ready enough to fulfil its basic function and become an operational cog in the giant machine that was Bomber Command. It was, however, also the home, for varying periods of time, to well over a thousand men and women. Although much of their time would be spent on the station itself, they were to have a considerable impact upon the small villages and communities nearby. Though radically changed in character, to a large extent the airfield – and its personnel – still does.

CHAPTER 2

First Steps

The first RAF personnel arrived at a windswept Middleton St George in the depths of the harsh northern winter a few days after Christmas in 1940. As they surveyed the desolate and unfinished airfield, still strewn with building equipment and ankle deep in semi-frozen mud, A/Flt Lt H. Dear and Flg Off S. Lockie, who opened the station on a care and maintenance basis, must have wondered just where they had been posted. The winter was especially fierce that year and the dire conditions made their task more taxing so that it would take much longer than expected. Although the station was formally accepted as part of No. 4 Group on 15 January 1941, under the overall command of AVM Arthur Coningham, then based at Heslington Hall near York, there was still much to be done before it could be declared operational.

When A/Sqn Ldr D.G. Singleton arrived to assume command the following day, he found more tradesmen than RAF personnel, as contractors battled to get the work roughly back on track and on schedule. Although the main buildings were complete, there was still much to be done to make them functional and inhabitable, such as the provision of running water, electricity cables, heaters, telephone lines, drains and a thousand and one little things needed to support and sustain the station and its sizeable future personnel. This was no easy task well over a year into the war, when pre-war supplies had long since run out and war economies meant shortages and delays, even for approved war work. Singleton did his best to create some order out of the chaos, riding roughshod over established working practices when necessary. He had no choice; the initial batch of airmen, some 305-strong, were due to arrive from Blackpool on the 17th. Almost as if on cue, the bleak northern winter closed in again on the day they arrived and welcomed the airmen with a chilly gale, freezing temperatures and a generous helping of snow and ice. The partially completed domestic heating and water systems were unable to cope with the semi-polar conditions and after just two days 253 of the airmen were sent home on 7 days' leave. Conditions for the skeleton staff left behind were bleak indeed, especially as there was little for them to do since the weather had brought most of the work to a standstill.

Towards the end of the month the weather relaxed its icy grip sufficiently for work to get under way once more and for a number of distinguished persons to visit the fledgling airfield.

Coningham, anxious to get the airfield operational and increase the fire-power of his Group, arrived at 11:30 on 4 February to see the situation for himself and to review the site of the proposed satellite airfield at nearby Croft on the Yorkshire side of the River Tees. Coningham's anxiety can be judged from the fact that he issued specific orders for all work to continue as normal throughout his visit. What he saw can scarcely have alleviated his fears as he saw at first hand how much there was still to do.

Little by little, however, things began to progress smoothly and gradually order came out of chaos as each part of the enormous jigsaw began to slot into place. Some time was even clawed back from the battered time schedule before the dreadful weather intervened once more. On 19 February it began to snow heavily and it did so without a break for over 36 hours. All work on the vital runways, roads, paths, buildings and services was brought to a dead stop. Everything remained buried beneath a thick white blanket until the 27th, when a rapid thaw set in. One hindrance was simply exchanged for another less picturesque one as several feet of snow quickly melted causing severe flooding; the whole airfield became a vast, glutinous sea of mud. It was early March before any serious construction work could begin again.

However, by 29 March the work was sufficiently completed for an Advance Working Party of 78 Squadron to be sent to Middleton from Dishforth, another 4 Group bomber airfield situated about 30 miles to the south in North Yorkshire, near Ripon. One of the first to arrive was AC2 Derek Beasley, who had volunteered for the RAF the day after his 19th birthday and had just completed his initial training at RAF Melksham in Wiltshire. Full of excitement and trepidation at his first posting, he was more than a little disappointed at what he found. Not for him a Biggin Hill, a Scampton, a Linton-on-Ouse or even a Dishforth, bustling with purposeful activity and actively participating in the air war. Instead, the scene that greeted him still greatly resembled a First World War battlefield. His dismay grew considerably more when he noticed that even the runways were still incomplete. It seemed possible that the war might be three parts won before the airfield was able to make a positive contribution to winning it. However, he had little time to reflect upon the vagaries of the posting system as he was quickly put to work preparing for the arrival of his new squadron under the guidance of the Station Engineering Officer, Flt Lt Lane. One of his first, yet abiding, memories of those early days was the bitter weather: 'One of the things I will always remember was the strong winds that seemed to blow all day and only die down in the evening, probably straight from the North Sea.' It was especially noticeable as much of the Advance Party's work had to be done outside.

By 30 March things were rapidly coming together. On that day the bomb store, a little way from the main site, began to receive and stockpile its deadly commodities and a delegation from 4 Group, headed by Lt Col Theobald, arrived to assess the station's readiness. The decision was made that it would be ready to receive 78 Squadron on 7 April 1941, subject to AVM Coningham's final approval. Coningham had to weigh up the situation at Middleton St George with his desire to get the station operational and the disruption that would inevitably be caused to 78 Squadron and 4 Group's operational strength for the period of the move. After due consideration Coningham gave the go-ahead for the 7th and on that day all ground personnel of 78 Squadron headed north by road. This was to be a very busy

A typical 'area load' is towed out from the bomb dump. In the foreground are two 4,000lb high-capacity bombs followed by trolleys of small bomb containers filled with incendiaries. *(Department of National Defence PL 26964)*

time for the ground staff who, working against the clock and under pressure to get everything ready to receive the aircraft and get them back into the war, immediately set to and laboured all hours in strange and still far from perfect conditions. Just two days later, on 9 April, sixteen Whitley Vs under the command of Wg Cdr Basil Robinson made the short journey from Dishforth and landed safely at Middleton St George.

The newly arrived aircrew were just as surprised by the appalling state of the airfield as the airmen had been a couple of weeks earlier. A.D. Barker, who later earned a DFC, recalls his first landing at the squadron's new home: 'The squadron flew from Dishforth on 9 April 1941 to Middleton and I remember very plainly workmen still working everywhere on the station. Dirt was piled high at either side of the runway and civil lorries were busy carting it away.' He, like many others, was mightily relieved to find that there was at least one oasis of comfort and warmth amid the muddy wastelands. The officers' mess, equipped with a well stocked bar, had been finally completed and fitted out. As the squadron settled in to its new surroundings, a congratulatory message was received from AVM Coningham, officially welcoming RAF Middleton St George into 4 Group as an operational – if slightly incomplete – bomber station. It was not long before the station was called upon to begin repaying the enormous amount of time, money and effort invested in it. Middleton St George was going to war.

FIRST OPERATIONS IN SUPPORT OF THE BATTLE OF THE ATLANTIC

The airfield was abuzz on the morning of 12 April 1941. The past few days had seen a great deal of frantic work by everyone on the station as each section sorted itself out and made ready for operations. If there had been any time left after that, there was enough to keep everyone busy adjusting to their new and not very homely surroundings. A certain degree of order was beginning to establish itself when the teleprinter rattled out its first operational directions from 4 Group Headquarters. The 'freshman' crews – those who were not yet fully operational and were generally given comparatively easy assignments in order to gain much-needed experience – were to attack targets in Ostend's dock area.

The ground crews and armourers immediately set to work preparing the slender Whitleys for the night's operation. Met. reports were prepared, flight plans put together, intelligence reports scrutinised and briefings held – only for the operation to be called off late in the day on account of inclement weather. On the next day, ominously the 13th, the same happened. It looked as if Bomber Command's newest and most northerly operational airfield was going to be a non-starter.

On the 14th Gp Capt T.C. Traill OBE, DFC, arrived from Bomber Command HQ at High Wycombe to take over command of Middleton St George from Wg Cdr Robinson. He arrived to find that eight aircraft were scheduled to attack Mannheim that night. However, the jinx held fast and the attack was called off owing to bad weather over the target area. A little later on further orders were received for an attack upon the German battlecruisers *Scharnhorst* and *Gneisenau* at Brest. New preparations were hurriedly made and take-off began at 21:30 hours. Although one of the aircraft was forced to return early owing to problems with its port engine, the remaining seven Whitleys pressed on to find between 2 and 5/10ths cloud cover at 4,000ft over the harbour and dock areas. This patchy cloud was enough to mask the major warships, though several other ships were seen lying alongside the quay. The crews noted a fair number of bomb bursts in the target area in spite of a considerable amount of heavy flak. All of Middleton's aircraft returned safely. Marked by nothing more than a few beers in the mess, the first operation to be carried out from RAF Middleton St George was over. A couple of days later the crews could read in the local newspaper, the *Northern Echo*, claims by the Vichy government that the raid had had little effect upon the dockyards but had caused the deaths of 76 Frenchmen and women living nearby. The paper also carried reports from German radio that Admiral Raeder had personally visited Brest and that 'he had inspected vessels that had been engaged in the Battle of the Atlantic and convinced himself of their readiness for renewed service'. Even if they took any notice of such comments, by then the crews had much more to think about.

Once the operational ball had started to roll it gathered a momentum of its own, a momentum that would carry on almost without pause for over four long years. On the 16th nine of 78 Squadron's Whitleys were made ready and bombed-up for a raid on the most prestigious and emotive target of them all – Berlin, the symbolic heart of the Nazi regime. But the crews were to be denied this popular line-shoot and were left feeling both let-down and relieved when, at 16:50 hours, orders were received from 4 Group switching the target from Berlin to Bremen. Only six of the aircraft that left the airfield that night actually reached and attacked Bremen; the remainder attacked either the alternative target or targets of opportunity at Wilhelmshaven, Oldenburg and Texel airfield. This was about par for the course on a night when widespread cloud and thick ground fog meant that only 74 of the 107 aircraft dispatched claimed to have hit Bremen and its environs. However unsatisfying the night's work may have been, at least all of 78 Squadron's aircraft came back safely.

The following night, 17 April, the name Berlin once again appeared on the briefing-room map. This time 78 Squadron was to provide just 4 of the 28 Whitleys that attacked the German capital that night out of a total force of 118 aircraft. Poor conditions on the ground

'Flak so thick you could get out and walk on it.' The kind of spectacular but lethal sight that regularly greeted crews from Middleton St George over the Port Militaire, Brest, early in 1941. *(Imperial War Museum C 1856)*

once more thwarted the raiders and only two dropped their deadly loads upon the designated target.

The duff weather lifted sufficiently on the 20th for a single freshman crew to attack the oil storage depot in Rotterdam. The inexperienced crew made a good job of their operational sortie, diving down from 10,000ft to below 3,000ft to ensure that their load fell on to what was by then a substantial concentration of fires. Such determination would be repeated many times in the years ahead.

German naval units in Brest were the target on the 23rd. Eight of 78 Squadron's aircraft dropped their bombs in and around the harbour area but the ninth, Z6484, piloted by the experienced Sqn Ldr Mercer, failed to identify the target clearly through the cloud, smoke and searchlight glare. Mindful of the French men, women and children beneath him and ignoring the sporadic bursts of flak and the probing searchlights, Mercer circled Brest for over an hour in the hope that conditions would improve sufficiently for him to make a successful attack. When it became obvious that this was not going to happen, Mercer set course for home and landed safely at Middleton, still carrying a full bomb-load.

The weather, which seemed to have dogged Middleton St George from the outset, closed in once again and only a single operation was able to be mounted before the end of the month – and that was not a conspicuous success. Of the four freshman crews detailed to attack Rotterdam, only one succeeded in finding the target through the murk and of the ten experienced crews detailed to attack the elusive Mannheim, itself a late target change from Hamburg on account of the conditions, only eight completed the sortie successfully. Of the other two, one was scrubbed at take-off when the pilot fell ill and the other sustained damage while taxiing and was forced to abort. The station's first month had been a bitty and largely unsatisfactory one, mainly on account of the weather. The saving grace had been a total absence of casualties, an all too rare occurrence in the months to come. At least a start had been made and much valuable experience had been gained, both by those on the ground and those in the air.

May began much as April had ended, with conditions doing much to belie the fact it was well into spring and causing the scrubbing of several sorties. On the 3rd fourteen crews, including, unusually, two freshman crews, were briefed for an attack on the major railway confluence at Cologne. For Wg Cdr Basil Robinson in Whitley Z6466 it was a long, hard night's work. His sortie to Cologne lasted from 22:05 to 07:15 hours, placing a tremendous strain upon pilot and crew both physically and mentally, especially as the rear gunner suffered shrapnel wounds over the target and was in need of proper medical attention. There was little anyone could do except wait for the old Whitley to plod its pedestrian way home through the dark and hostile skies, a fact that did little to ease the mental strain on the wounded gunner and crew.

For some the very length of time spent in the air could be a matter of life or death. Sgt Hatcher's aircraft successfully attacked Cologne from 15,000ft that night and had already turned for home when the W/Op reported his set U/S. In the pitch black and in poor weather and unable to pick up a fix on the airfield as he crossed the North Sea, Hatcher flew his aircraft up and down the east coast, hoping that conditions might improve enough for the crews' straining eyes to catch sight of a known landmark to enable them to pinpoint their position. Despairing of success and desperately short of fuel, Hatcher eventually headed inland. Almost immediately, both engines began to splutter. Using the last precious gallons of fuel, Hatcher dragged the Whitley to 3,000ft and ordered his crew to bale out. All of the crew landed safely but were amazed to find that they had landed in Hertfordshire, over 200 miles south of where they had expected. Their flight had lasted a nerve-shattering 9 hours and 45 minutes.

Two nights later 12 aircraft headed for Mannheim once again and a single freshman crew formed part of a 5-strong force to attack the port area of Boulogne. The raid on Mannheim was a large one by the standards of the day, with some 141 aircraft taking part. The 10/10ths cloud that greeted the bombers prevented about twenty crews from locating the target area but the remainder pressed home their attack as accurately as possible. German records show a depressingly small return for the gallantry and determination shown that night. City officials estimated just 25 bomb-loads fell on the city, causing 19 small fires that destroyed a house and a barn, badly damaged four more houses and slightly damaged a further 199. Four people and some fifty rabbits and chickens were killed. The effect upon industrial production was negligible, in spite of the demolition of an electricity pylon and the severing of a water main. Mercifully and unusually, all of Bomber Command's aircraft returned safely.

Fortunately hope springs eternal and on 7 May Middleton St George dispatched a total of 15 aircraft against the *Scharnhorst* and *Gneisenau*, still holed up in Brest. For the first time the weather behaved itself and visibility was excellent in the bright moonlight. The official records for 4 Group optimistically declared that 'although no actual hits on the warships are claimed, all the crews were satisfied that the great majority of bombs fell around the target'. Once again all the 78 Squadron crews returned safely. Unfortunately the tired crews found themselves awoken earlier than usual on the morning after an operation to prepare for an inspection visit. AVM Coningham arrived by air in mid-morning and made a formal inspection of the station before taking a more casual meal with many of the squadron's aircrews. The New Zealander overran his schedule and did not depart until 16:40 hours, having stayed on to watch the preparations for that night's operation against the dockyards of Bremen.

This was to be a big night for Bomber Command as a whole, with a record 364 sorties being made against not only Bremen but also Hamburg and the Kiel Canal. A maximum effort, codenamed 'Goodwood', was demanded from all stations and 78 Squadron worked hard to provide a full complement of 16 aircraft. The special effect was somewhat lessened when one aircraft was accidentally damaged on take-off and was forced to abort its sortie. However, the remainder pressed on through thick, solid cloud, which did not begin to break up until they crossed the enemy coast. By the time the aircraft reached the target area there was only a thin layer of haze covering the large Deutsche Schiff Werke. The crews returned home confident that a good job had been done. No. 4 Group noted: 'There is no doubt that it was hit by some aircraft and that all bombs fell within a fairly close radius of the Aiming Point. Large fires were seen, particularly oil fires, close to the target and there is no doubt that this Group's record attack up to date has caused very heavy damage in Bremen.' For Middleton St George the cost of this success was its first casualties. Sgt Thorpe and his crew, who took off at 22:25 hours in Whitley T4147 EY-D, probably sustained damage over the target area and crashed at Helsfelde, killing all on board.

On the ground at Middleton St George there was an increased level of tension and anxiety as strenuous efforts were made to improve the station's defences against air attack. The catalyst for this burst of activity was the attacks that took place on the night of the 12th against the airfields at Driffield and Linton-on-Ouse. At Driffield intruder aircraft scattered incendiary bombs across the station but fortunately caused little damage and only a few minor casualties. The situation was far more serious at Linton where sporadic attacks, using high explosive and incendiary bombs and machine-guns, took place over a period of two hours. Considerable damage was caused to the station and eleven people were killed, including the Station Commander, Gp Capt F.F. Garraway OBE. A further eight were injured, one seriously. Nevertheless Linton was fully operational again by the 15th. These attacks brought home the harsh realities of war to those serving on all the stations in 4 Group. Although other airfields in the Group did indeed later receive the lethal attentions of the Luftwaffe, as it turned out Middleton never did, though the threat was a real and onerous one.

With even the security of 'home' being threatened, the freshman crews must have wondered just what they had got themselves into. With one milk-run to Boulogne cancelled on account of poor weather over the target, Christopher Cheshire, whose brother Leonard was already carving out a formidable reputation in Bomber Command, was very relieved to get the green light for another crack at the French port on 15 May. Although he had flown as 'second dickey' on a couple of raids, this was to be his first as captain and he was all keyed up not to make a mess of it. Taking off in Z6625 L for Leather, Cheshire set course and headed south. Finding the target was dead easy: all he had to do was head towards the conglomeration of searchlights and flak on the far side of the Channel. Swallowing hard and concentrating upon his instruments, Cheshire worked hard to keep his lumbering Whitley steady and on track through the maelstrom of flak bursting all around. Well aware that his aircraft was taking a pounding from shrapnel from near-misses, Cheshire heartily welcomed the news that his bombs had been successfully dropped on the docks and turned away from this 'easy' target. He called for damage reports from his crew and each man wondered whether the mangled Whitley would make it back to British shores, each listening intently to the engines, straining to detect any extraneous and unusual noises. As it turned out, Cheshire was able to nurse the aircraft all the way back to Middleton where he landed safely. The faint light of dawn revealed a frightening scene. The Whitley closely resembled the proverbial colander, with whole chunks having being blown away by the flak. Seeing the airmen looking somewhat overwhelmed by the extent of the damage, and with a glance at the bomber which was looking very sorry for itself in the cold light of day, two soldiers of the Durham Light Infantry based at the airfield were heard to remark on their way to breakfast: 'Well, mate, ah dinnit mind sayin', they'll niver git me in one of them bloody things!' All in all, it had been an interesting night for the freshman crew.

The volatile meteorological situation only allowed 78 Squadron to put up two raids on Cologne before 27 May. On that date fourteen crews were already briefed and the aircraft bombed-up ready for an attack on Wilhelmshaven when word came through cancelling the operation, once again as the result of poor weather. However, before the crews could begin to relax and plan their evening's entertainment, fresh orders were received designating a new and important target: the mighty 42,900-ton battleship *Tirpitz*, then residing in the enormous southern floating dock at Kiel.

No. 78 Squadron was to provide the entire assault force of fourteen aircraft, and their task was to damage this naval goliath, which was almost ready for service. The bad weather that had caused the scrubbing of the Wilhelmshaven raid was just as prevalent over Kiel, and as the elderly Whitleys laboured to the north German port they encountered 10/10ths cloud and severe electrical storms. This resulted in both heavy icing and lightning strikes that played over the fuselage, wing tips, leading edges of the wings and airscrews, illuminating the whole aircraft and scaring the living daylights out of the already tense and anxious crews. Four of the aircraft were unable to make any sort of attack and only one succeeded in identifying the target through the murk. No. 4 Group records noted the desperate nature of the attack and matter-of-factly stated: 'Under these conditions definite pinpointing was impossible and the few observations made cannot be definitely positioned.' For the crews it had been a perilous and terrifying experience and for one crew, that of Sgt A.T. Copley, it was their last. Thankfully the futile nature of such raids was noted and a repeat sortie planned for 31 May was cancelled.

Things were changing apace at Middleton St George. On 4 June six Halifax four-engined bombers of 76 Squadron, complete with accompanying personnel, arrived from Linton under the command of Wg Cdr G.T. Jarman. Reformed from C Flight 35 Squadron at Linton on 12 April 1941 under the command of Wg Cdr S.O. Bufton – later to enjoy a successful and influential career in both Bomber Command and at the Air Ministry – 76 Squadron had only recently finished the conversion course to Halifaxes and had yet to make an operational flight against the enemy. For some of the crews, still recovering from their recent brush with the Luftwaffe, the move from Linton came as a bit of a surprise.

AC2 Cyril Tuckwell was posted to 76 Squadron following the completion of his Fitter II E course at Cosford. Informed that the squadron was at Linton,

> I arrived at York station and was taken by RAF transport to RAF Linton-on-Ouse only to find that it was now the home of 35 Squadron. My squadron had just left for RAF Middleton St George, near Darlington in Co. Durham. No. 76 Squadron, you see, had been re-formed from one of the flights from 35 Squadron. So, after eventually finding and spending the night in temporary accommodation at Linton, off I went again by RAF transport the next morning, kit and all.

Things had changed significantly at Middleton since the first arrivals in January and Cyril found it 'an extremely nice camp, with the usual brick-built two-storey sleeping accommodation'. He was by no means alone in having to learn the ropes in a new station, as a veritable stream of new recruits flowed into the expanding station to meet the number of ground personnel needed to maintain and support two front-line squadrons. Middleton St George was, at last, reaching its full operational capacity.

While the personnel of 76 Squadron were busy settling in and sorting themselves out, 78 Squadron carried on with the war, or rather would have done but for the weather which continued to frustrate the senior officers at Bomber Command and 4 Group. It lifted sufficiently on the 8th to allow ten of 78 Squadron's Whitleys to operate against Dortmund. On this occasion the crews were thwarted by the thick industrial haze hanging over the city and three of the aircraft were compelled to seek out and bomb alternative targets. On their return to Britain the crews found to their dismay that the weather had closed in considerably since their departure. Only five of the Whitleys managed to land at Middleton, with two others putting down at Linton and Silloth. Another force-landed, luckily without causing casualties, some 20 miles east of Lancaster, but the crew led by Sgt D.R. Simon was not so fortunate. All of them were killed as the aircraft crashed in very poor conditions into fields adjacent to the village of Ellingstring, near Masham, in North Yorkshire.

The fifth crew had a hair-raising time. Chris Cheshire lifted the resilient and patched-up Z6625 L for Leather from the runway at Middleton at 22:25 hours and set course for Dortmund. Having dropped his bomb-load over the target area, Cheshire set course for home and flew almost immediately into 10/10ths cloud. Unable to climb out of the cloud, the aircraft ploughed straight on, hoping to fly out of it nearer home. Unfortunately no gaps appeared and both Cheshire and his navigator, Slim Smalley, were forced to admit that they had only the sketchiest of ideas where they were. By this time they had been airborne for well over 6 hours and fuel was running dangerously low, and with the Pennines reaching up to almost 3,000ft the outlook seemed bleak. Cheshire gingerly dropped down through the cloud to 2,500ft, the crew's eyes standing out like organ stops as they searched desperately for somewhere to land, and suddenly green fields were spotted briefly through a small break in the cloud. Heaving the Whitley round in a tight turn and pushing her nose down towards the fast-disappearing patch of green, Z6625 emerged from the cloud and fog at 500ft. With the fuel gauges already resting on empty, Cheshire, praying that the field was relatively flat, managed to slam the wheels down on to the grass and stood hard on the brakes. A sturdy drystone wall loomed out of the gloom and the Whitley seemed magnetically drawn towards it. Everyone braced themselves for the crash but the Whitley came to a halt with a lurch 10 yards from the wall. As it did so the port engine cut out, the fuel tanks dry. Relieved to be alive, the crew set out to find help and in the process discovered that they were near the village of Clapham on the Cumberland/West Yorkshire border. They had landed in the largest field around. Such is the fine line between success and failure, life and death.

The night of 12 June proved to be an important one for Bomber Command, with some 339 sorties being made. It was also a big night for Middleton as 76 Squadron went to war for the first time. Three Halifaxes, piloted by Flt Lt Hillary, Plt Off Lewin and Plt Off Richards, formed part of the 18-strong force directed to attack the chemical works at Hüls. It was not to be the most auspicious of starts. Plt Off Lewin took off at 23:34, only to return within the hour with engine trouble. Flt Lt Hillary got as far as the German border before severe engine trouble forced him to set course for home; he landed at Middleton with a full bomb-load after being airborne for 5 hours. Although Plt Off Richards' engines did not let him down, he was unable to identify Hüls so attacked Essen as a worthwhile alternative.

The twelve aircraft of 78 Squadron fared little better on their raid to nearby Schwerte. Once again the Ruhr's inadvertent industrial defences thwarted the attackers and 4 Group noted: 'Over the target area thick haze made positive identification difficult . . . [and] obscured all ground detail and bombs must have been dropped over a wide area. Photos taken show that most of the bombs were dropped in open country.' The night's only saving grace was that all of Middleton's aircraft returned safely.

On 15 June the station saw its first, but by no means last, serious accidental crash, reminding the crews that flying was an inherently dicey business. With the station's aircraft detailed to attack targets in Düsseldorf and Hannover, a number of final air tests took place throughout the afternoon in order to iron out any last-minute problems. The gentle and routine order of things was rudely shattered when one aircraft of 76 Squadron, coming in to land, managed to collide with another Halifax already on the ground and taxiing. Both aircraft were seriously damaged but fortunately the crews received nothing worse than cuts and bruises – and an almighty fright. However, the twisted and tangled remains of the aircraft took some time to clear and, once removed, substantial damage to the runway itself was revealed. A frantic race against the clock began in an effort to enable the remaining aircraft to take off as planned that evening. In the end 4 Group solved the problem by scrubbing the operation on account of poor weather conditions over Germany.

Everything was shipshape once again for the next night when a total of fourteen aircraft from 78 Squadron and three from 76 Squadron were ordered to attack aiming point C in Cologne, which was smothered, as it turned out, by its protective industrial smog. For Sgt Geale's crew it was a nerve-wracking night spent watching their fuel gauges. A petrol cock had been wrongly assembled and only the wing tanks could be used for the starboard engine of the Whitley. The fuel eventually gave out over RAF Marham and, with one engine stopped and the other beginning to display signs of fuel starvation, Geale ordered his crew to bale out. The rear gunner did so promptly but the other crew members chose to stay with the aircraft and their captain and hastily took up crash positions. Geale carried out a textbook one-engine landing just as Marham switched on the flarepath lighting and only a little after the obedient rear gunner had touched down safely. Refuelled, the aircraft returned to Middleton the next morning. Plt Off D.S.W. Lake and crew in Whitley Z6492 EY-K, however, did not return and vanished without trace, having taken off at 22:32. The dread reaper was taking a steady toll.

The 20th also proved to be a hard night for the crews from Middleton. Ten aircraft from 78 Squadron and five from 76 Squadron set off for Kiel to try to locate and attack the *Tirpitz*. No aircraft succeeded in doing so amid the thick cloud and Kiel itself became the main focus of the attack. A wall of flak greeted the raiders and it was flak that damaged the port engine of Plt Off Cant's Whitley and blew its cowling clean off, forcing him to drop his bombs in one stick from 12,000ft over Emden and head for home on just one engine. Having been airborne for over 6 and a half hours, he arrived over the North Sea to find Middleton St George all but closed on account of the murky weather. With little option but to continue and make a direct approach, Cant ploughed on through the cloud, searching for the airfield. In fact he found it at the first attempt and set about landing straightaway, unaware that his aircraft's port tyre had been ripped to shreds by the flak and that the undercarriage itself was damaged. The weakened undercarriage collapsed on landing and the aircraft skidded to a halt on its belly. By great good fortune no one was seriously injured. Only one other aircraft landed at Middleton that night, with the remainder being diverted to Driffield, further south in the East Riding of Yorkshire.

For another aircraft operating from Middleton that night the danger began almost immediately after take-off. Sqn Ldr Tom Sawyer, an experienced campaigner, was still settling into his seat and happily flying on the course given to him by his navigator when, to his amazement and great consternation, he noticed what looked like a barrage balloon several hundred feet above him. A quick glance around him confirmed his worst fears. There were balloons bobbing gracefully on all sides. The next minute or so was spent carefully threading his way through the cables and balloons as they loomed out of the darkness before his straining eyes. The next few minutes after that were spent tearing a great strip off the navigator who had given him a course straight through the heart of Middlesbrough's air defences. Sawyer noted later: 'The rest of the trip was a piece of cake by comparison.'

On the 23rd eleven aircraft of 78 Squadron headed off into the darkening skies towards Cologne, while five Halifaxes from 76 Squadron turned further north and made for Kiel once again. Of these, Halifax L9492 piloted by Plt Off W.K. Stobbs became the first lost to enemy action when it was shot down by Oberleutnant R. Eckhardt in an Me110 of II/NJG1 near Eilendorf, 20km south-west of Hamburg, killing all the crew except Sgt J.S. Lipton, who spent the rest of the war as a prisoner. A loss such as this would have been keenly felt by the squadron and by the Inspector-General of the RAF, ACM Sir Edgar Ludlow-Hewitt, a former Commander in Chief of Bomber Command, who visited Middleton on the following afternoon, touring the sergeants' and airmen's messes, stores and workshops. He spent some time examining a Halifax and speaking to both aircrew and ground staff about this relatively new aircraft, before attending the briefing for the night's raid. A well respected airman, Ludlow-Hewitt left behind the impression that he knew what he was on about and was genuinely interested in what people had to say to him. Indeed, he served in the post with distinction.

The final raid of a busy but not wholly productive month took place on 29 June when four aircraft of 76 Squadron were detailed to attack Hamburg, though only one arrived and contributed to the raid, which caused considerable damage and destroyed a large food warehouse. Meanwhile twelve old Whitleys from 78 Squadron headed towards Bremen. Eight found their way to the port and, as the squadron record noted, 'in improved visibility the target was identified with more certitude than usual'. Having bombed the target, all eight headed for home but were diverted to Linton on account of fog at Middleton. One aircraft, that of Sgt R.S. Green, was tracked at about 65–100 miles due east of Alnmouth in Northumberland but failed to make it to the coast, consigning the crew to an unknown and watery grave in the North Sea.

July's campaign began on the second night of the month with an attack on the oft-visited city of Cologne. Having bombed virtually blind through the thick ground haze that blanketed the target like a protective umbrella, the thirteen aircraft of 78 Squadron turned

The crew of Armstrong Whitworth Whitley Z6743 of 78 Squadron awaiting take-off in July 1941. *(Imperial War Museum TR 105)*

for home. One aircraft, that piloted by Sgt A. Jepson, fell to the guns of Leutnant Reinhold Knacke of II/NJG1 and crashed at Ilteren in Holland shortly after 01:00, killing the whole crew. For another crew, captained by Sqn Ldr Williams, it was to prove a nerve-jangling return leg. Shortly after releasing its load on to the fires of Cologne, Whitley Z6655's rear turret went U/S, thereby leaving the aircraft vulnerable to attack from the prowling night-fighters known to be in the area. A few minutes later the starboard engine gave a splutter and a shudder and lapsed into silence. After some six minutes of frantic efforts in the cockpit, the engine restarted hesitatingly but it remained rough and juddered all the way across the sea. Williams did not fancy his chances of reaching Middleton and opted for Bircham Newton in Norfolk. Unsure of what other damage the Whitley might have sustained, Williams ordered his crew to bale out over the airfield before bringing in his aircraft for what turned out to be a smooth landing – a welcome end for what he described with an understatement characteristic of the day as 'an anxious trip'. It was clearly a night for drama as Sgt Dunlop, flying one of 76 Squadron's aircraft, fell seriously ill at the controls. The observer, Plt Off Jones, took command of the aircraft and made the brave decision to press on with the sortie and complete what the crew had set out to do. This success was topped by his pulling off a safe landing upon return to a Middleton shrouded in fog and mist several hours later.

By now several crews had either completed or were nearing completion of their tour of operations. New crews and crew members were arriving at the busy station on a regular basis. One of these men was Sgt Jack Moorfoot, who joined 78 Squadron at the beginning of

July 1941. The only one from his OTU course in Abingdon to be posted to Middleton St George, Jack, like so many men and women, approached his first operational posting with a mixture of excitement and trepidation. Fortunately, the night he arrived there was a large and boisterous party in the mess and Jack was quickly made to feel welcome. He later noted, 'I cannot recall a great deal more about the evening but I enjoyed it and slept very well after it!'

The next morning, 5 July, Moorfoot managed to stir himself, ate a hearty breakfast and set off to explore his new surroundings, fully expecting to have a few days to settle in before going on ops. Much to his surprise and delight, he found his name chalked up on one of the boards at the flights. He was to fly as second pilot to Sgt Jones, an Australian serving in the RAF, on operations that very night. No sooner had he been introduced to his captain and crew than he was airborne on a familiarisation and test flight. On a lovely summer's day Jack enjoyed a delightful 'Cook's Tour' of the beautiful northernmost counties of England, flying down the Vale of York, across the rugged Pennines and up over the Lake District before crossing the Pennines once more, cruising over Weardale and Teesdale and ending up circling the magnificent castle and cathedral in Durham, less than 20 miles north of Middleton.

With his aircraft, Whitley V6491, pronounced serviceable, the crew left the ground staff to make any final adjustments and preparations and headed for the briefing room at 14:00 hours. Armed guards were posted outside the room as the Station Commander, Squadron Commander, Squadron Navigator, Gunnery Officer, Meteorological Officer and Intelligence Officer all took their turn to brief the crews for their forthcoming raid on Münster. When the formal part of the briefing was over, the men of each crew huddled together to plan their individual route. Unsure of what was to come next, Moorfoot filled in his remaining time alternately lounging and pacing around. He found he had considerably more difficulty in forcing down his flying supper of eggs, bacon and baked beans than he had had in devouring his breakfast earlier that day.

Eventually the take-off time of 22:00 hours approached and the time came to don flying gear, draw a parachute and, in the gathering dusk, waddle towards the flight wagon and haul oneself into the back. It was only a short ride to Moorfoot's aircraft for the night. Various visual and mechanical checks were made both inside and outside the aircraft before, with all the crew in place, Sgt Jones sought permission to taxi for take-off. When the green light was given by the controller, the brakes were put hard on and the engines run up to full power in order to get the maximum length out of the runway for the heavily laden bomber. Climbing slowly into the darkening sky, Jones turned the Whitley south-east, crossing the coast at Flamborough Head. Cruising at 12,000ft and about 130mph, the aircraft flew serenely across the North Sea, the water shining brightly in the moonlight. As they crossed the Dutch coast Jack noticed some searchlight activity and some extensive anti-aircraft fire over to his right. An hour or so later the navigator announced that the target was coming up and Jack made his way to the nose of the aircraft to the bomb aimer's position. Jones put the aircraft into a shallow glide before dropping the incendiaries and then gave the Whitley some throttle as he turned to make a second run over the target. Putting the aircraft into a glide once more, Jack dropped the high explosive bombs smack into the sizeable fires blazing below. It was only when his job was over that Moorfoot, on his first operation, noticed the heavy flak bursting all over the sky. The return journey proved uneventful and Jack Moorfoot completed his initial sortie at 04:30 hours as he landed the aircraft at Middleton St George.

For Sgt Malet-Warden, however, the night's work was not so straightforward. He took off at 22:38 and successfully attacked the target from 11,000ft, calculating that his load had fallen about a mile and a half from the aiming point. Almost immediately his Whitley was coned by searchlights and was attacked by a night-fighter, which hit and holed the port wing with its opening burst. Return fire from the rear gunner forced the night-fighter to break off temporarily. Having repositioned himself, the German pilot made another pass a few minutes later, although this time his shots missed the weaving bomber. The rear gunner helped him on his way with another long burst but no hits were noted. With fuel slowly seeping out of the port wing tank, it would be touch and go whether the aircraft would reach Britain. It was a nerve-wracking return flight for Malet-Warden, alternately scanning the sky for another attack and keeping a close watch on the fuel gauges. An overwhelming feeling of relief washed over the crew as the Whitley came in to land at Middleton at 05:14, after a gruelling 6 and a half hours in the air.

The excellent visibility that night allowed the Intelligence Officers at 4 Group to conclude that 'the whole town appeared a mass of flames, the fiercest conflagration appearing to be in the south-west portion of the town'. One particular explosion was seen to have thrown smoke and debris up to 3,000ft in the air. When conditions allowed, Bomber Command could really do the business.

GERMANY AGAIN: ATTACKS ON MORALE AND THE INLAND TRANS-PORTATION SYSTEM

Sadly, 8 July was to prove an unusually eventful and costly one for the squadrons based at Middleton St George. Contributing six aircraft, 76 Squadron provided almost half of the strike force against the IG Farben Leuna synthetic oil plant at Merseburg. Flying through 10/10ths cloud over the North Sea, the thirteen Halifaxes and a single Stirling found a thick and almost impenetrable industrial smog shrouding the area containing the works. Nevertheless, the Intelligence report surmised: 'The majority of aircraft appear to have located the target and two sticks of bombs were seen to have burst in the north and south-west corners of the target, the former causing large showers of white sparks . . . [otherwise] no spectacular results were noted.' Some of the crews had more on their minds than careful observation. The Halifax of Sqn Ldr Bob Bickford was coned by searchlights over the target and treated to some rough treatment from a sustained barrage of heavy and accurate anti-aircraft fire, which ripped several chunks out of the aircraft. Hurling the Halifax about the sky, Bickford succeeded in losing the searchlights but almost immediately came under attack from a hitherto unseen night-fighter. Cannon shells smashed through the delicate nose area, wounding both Sgt Kenworthy, the flight engineer, and Bickford himself. Once again the battered Halifax was thrown around the sky in a successful attempt to shake off the attacker. Upon his return to England, Bickford thankfully put the Halifax down at Linton and both he and Kenworthy were rushed away to receive treatment for their wounds.

A Halifax B Mk II of 76 Squadron in the summer of 1941. *(Imperial War Museum CH 3396)*

For 78 Squadron the night's target was the large and important marshalling yards at Hamm and it proved to be a costly and heartbreaking attack for many of the young airmen involved. The heavily laden Whitleys rolled down the runway at Middleton a little after 23:00 hours and, passing over Filey on the North Yorkshire coast, set course for Hamm. The journey out passed uneventfully for Jack Moorfoot, flying once again as second dickey to Sgt Jones. For once the target was clearly visible from 12,000ft and the moderate levels of flak posed no great problems for the Whitley. As they turned for home, Moorfoot took over the controls. As he crossed the North Sea, steadily losing height as he did so, he flew into increasingly dense and volatile cloud. Trying to slip out beneath the murk, he lost more height but only ran into fog. To his horror, out of the gloom and darkness there loomed up an enormous barrage balloon and then another and another. Mindful of the need to avoid a stall, Moorfoot banked the aircraft as hard as he dared and climbed a little to avoid these deadly obstacles. On a sharp count of three Jones took over the controls and dispatched his still-trembling colleague to the nose to see if he could make out anything below. The crew did not know whether the barrage belonged to Hull, Teesside, Tyneside or Wearside but they all knew and understood the dangers posed by the high ground of the Wolds, Pennines, Moors and Cleveland Hills, the graveyards of numerous aircraft lost in conditions similar to these. Still flying through the airborne equivalent of cotton wool, Jones had little choice but to gradually lose height in the hope of coming out into clearer conditions. Each member of the crew was systematically scanning the cloud, straining their eyes to pick out any recognisable feature beneath them, when the engines gave a cough and stopped. Jones announced that the Whitley had run out of fuel and ordered the crew to take up crash positions as quickly as possible. Moorfoot, in the exposed nose of the aircraft, needed no second bidding but he had only got as far as the steps by the cockpit when there was a huge thump and the ear-splitting shriek of tearing metal as the nose section crumpled and disintegrated on impact. The aircraft seemed to tear its way along the earth for some time before it came to a halt and an eerie stillness fell. This brief period of calm was shattered as the crew members began shouting to one another and hurried to extricate themselves from the tangled wreckage. As the crew, miraculously suffering from nothing more serious than cuts and bruises, assembled at a respectable distance from the aircraft, it was found that the rear gunner was missing. The men ran back to the aircraft and discovered the gunner slumped unconscious in his turret. They managed to open the turret and heave him out and carried him well away from the crash site. In contrast to the ordeal the men had just suffered, the birds were singing and the sun was coming up, burning away the fog and revealing the picturesque hills above the market town of Thirsk. Jones and his navigator set off on a 6-mile walk to find a telephone and arrange transport back to Middleton.

Another aircraft of 78 Squadron made a forced-landing the same night. Plt Off Wright's port engine failed as he returned home over the North Sea. He limped back to RAF Bircham Newton in Norfolk, where at 04:05 he made a successful landing – only to overshoot the runway and become entangled with a rather inconveniently placed haystack. All the crew emerged unhurt. That is more than can be said for Whitley Z6555, piloted by Sgt O.W. McLean RAAF, which crashed into the North Sea just before 03:00, killing all on board.

Even after this loss, the cruel fates had not finished with 78 Squadron that night. Sgt W.M. McQuitty and crew took off from Middleton St George at 23:00 and enjoyed an uneventful flight to Hamm. On the bomb run the aircraft was hit by flak, which tore off part of the front turret, allowing the full force of the wind and slipstream to come howling in. The bombing run, in spite of this, was completed successfully. To add to their woes, the Whitley was picked up and held by a searchlight and the aircraft was badly buffeted by the bursts of flak that followed. The starboard engine was hit and burst into flames, blazing for several minutes before fizzling out. Having succeeded in escaping the dazzling and probing searchlight, McQuitty set course for home, shrouded in the welcoming embrace of darkness. However, on this occasion, even that offered little protection.

Losing height as it went, the Whitley limped homewards painfully slowly. As it crossed the Dutch coast near Texel at 03:00 it was attacked by an Me110, which had tracked the stricken bomber for several minutes before unleashing a deadly burst of cannon fire, further damaging the aircraft. Fortunately the German pilot made only one pass and then, helped on his way by prolonged bursts of machine-gun fire from the rear gunner, dived away into the night. McQuitty then asked Sgt J.F. Haffenden, the navigator, for the most direct course to Bircham Newton, one of the stations nearest the coast.

For a while it looked as if the Whitley would stay airborne long enough to reach the coast but the strain on the overworked remaining engine eventually proved too great. To everyone on board's dismay, if not surprise, it overheated and seized solid. At just 400ft, there was little anyone could do and the Whitley belly-flopped into the sea almost immediately. It plunged under the water with all on board, only to pop up to the surface once more before settling in a slightly nose-down position. With the fuselage filling fast and the cold sea water already chest high, McQuitty and Haffenden made their way to the tail turret where the gunner lay bleeding from a nasty wound to the head. Heaving him out of the confined space of the turret in icy water and pitch darkness was no easy task and matters were made worse when the gunner's mae west was found to have been holed. Haffenden gave him his own and the three men made their way through the choppy water towards the nose of the slowly sinking bomber, where the second pilot, Plt Off Scott, had managed to deploy the emergency dinghy. It too had been holed by the Me110's attack but still floated sufficiently to support the weight of one man. The wounded gunner was bundled into the semi-submerged dinghy and the rest of the crew clung on to its sides, supported by their mae wests – except for Haffenden.

Realising that the situation was desperate, Haffenden, a strong swimmer, voiced his intention to swim towards the first glimmers of the dawn and a coast line he could not even see. After some time he realised that he was not making much headway against the current and turned back towards the dinghy. When he eventually found it, it was empty, confirming his worst fears. Having called out repeatedly for his friends, and being unable to see any sign of them, he once more set out for the darkest part of the emerging horizon, hoping it was land. A short time later, between the rising and falling of the waves, he spotted the bright colour of a mae west floating in the water and struck out towards it as hard as he could in the hope that he had found one of the crew. It turned out to be empty. He managed to put it on and continued on his slow and painful way. Unfortunately he discovered that the life-jacket was holed, which was probably the reason why it had been discarded in the first place, and it was all he could do to extricate himself from it.

As it grew light he was able to see the coast, still several heartbreaking miles ahead of him. Suffering from severe cramp, hypothermia and plain exhaustion, Haffenden alternated between breast stroke and front crawl as he slowly and doggedly closed the gap between the coast and himself. Even when he eventually reached dry land his ordeal was not over for he discovered that he had come ashore on a deserted stretch of coast. Gathering all his remaining strength and determination, Haffenden had to walk 2 miles to find any sign of habitation. Luckily enough, he stumbled across a coastguard's cottage. After listening to the airman's desperate plea for someone to look for his friends, the coastguard was able to notify the authorities of the situation straightaway. Although a search was undertaken immediately, no trace of the other members of the crew was ever found: scant and undeserved reward for a truly remarkable feat of courage and endurance.

Even for those who made it home, the weather, even in high summer, could make routine events a matter of life or death. On 14 July eight Halifaxes of 76 Squadron formed part of a 97-strong force tackling three separate targets in Hannover. Assigned the main railway station, the Halifaxes were able to identify the target clearly, in spite of the considerable flak. Upon their return the aircraft found Middleton closed on account of fog and were diverted to Linton. Even there the visibility was poor. Sgt Harry Drummond located the runway a little late and landed too far down it to stop safely. Hammering on the brakes and with the perimeter fence rushing up to meet him, Drummond tried to turn off the runway, only to have his undercarriage collapse under the unaccustomed strain. The aircraft ploughed on and eventually ground to a halt only a minute or two before Plt Off Ireton in his battle-damaged aircraft repeated the procedure. The next aircraft to land was that of Chris Cheshire, who had been following the proceedings closely; though an experienced pilot, he was on his first operation after converting to the Halifax. In the event the perspiring pilot managed to put in a textbook landing, much to the relief of all concerned. Nevertheless, with another aircraft crash-landing at Bircham Newton, it had been another expensive night for Middleton St George's aircraft.

Routine training and testing flights were not without their dangers and 20 July brought what the station's operational logbook described as 'a severe loss'. The popular and experienced Plt Off L.R. Blackwell and his crew had just completed a routine cross-country exercise and, with his wheels down, he was coming into land as normal. Suddenly, without warning, a Hurricane flew directly across the bomber's path, forcing Blackwell to wrench the nose upwards to loop over the fighter. The inevitable stall swiftly followed and the Halifax plunged to the ground on the perimeter of the airfield, killing all five crewmen on board. The resultant explosion and enormous pall of smoke put paid to the station's lunchtime routine and brought home to all the risks faced on a daily basis by the aircrews. Blackwell and his crew were particularly well known on the station as they had served with both 76 and 78 Squadrons.

On the 23rd, however, there was a radical departure from normal operating procedures. Eight aircraft of 76 Squadron flew down to Stanton Harcourt in Oxfordshire, as part of a coordinated operation against the powerful German warship *Scharnhorst*, then berthed at La Pallice. That night attacks were made by various Bomber Command units and a further raid was planned for the next morning. The attack was to be three-pronged: 99 aircraft escorted by a large number of Spitfires were to attack the *Gneisenau* and the *Prinz Eugen* in Brest Harbour; 35 Blenheims, along with a heavy fighter escort, were to make a diversionary raid on Cherbourg; and 15 Halifaxes from 76 and 35 Squadrons were to bomb La Pallice. Significantly, they were to be unescorted. The success of the whole scheme depended upon timing, with the Brest and Cherbourg raids planned to be simultaneous. It was hoped that this would draw up all the German fighters, leaving La Pallice undefended against the Halifaxes. It was a considerable gamble.

The 24th dawned a beautiful summer's day and it was clear that conditions for the bombers – and the fighters – would be ideal. At the unaccustomedly civilised hour of 10:35, Wg Cdr Jarman led the first wave of three 76 Squadron Halifaxes and the whole of the 35 Squadron contingent into the sky and set course for the target. Unfortunately mechanical failure caused a delay of 12 minutes before Sqn Ldr Walter Williams was able to lead 76 Squadron's second wave of aircraft into the air. Over the radio Jarman and Williams agreed to rendezvous over Swindon but in the event the formations missed each other and were compelled to make for the target independently. Flying at just over 1,000ft to avoid German radar, the Halifaxes swept over the English Channel, only climbing to 14,000ft as they neared the French coast.

A little after 14:00 La Pallice came into view – and so did the German fighters, which climbed high above the lumbering bombers before swooping down to make repeated high-speed passes. Flt Lt Lewin of 76 Squadron was attacked by a pair of Me109s and was shot down near L'Aiguillon sur Mer. One of 35 Squadron's aircraft fared no better and was shot down only seconds later. Over the target the conditions, according to the official records, were excellent and 'bombs were seen to straddle the ship near the stern and our bombs appeared to have scored a direct hit. A column of black smoke was seen in the dock area. Several bombs were seen to drop in the dock area.' However, the defenders continued to take a heavy toll and several more Halifaxes were damaged, both by fighter attacks and by sustained and accurate flak, as they turned for home.

As the surviving Halifaxes battled their way out of the target area, the last section, now comprising just two aircraft from 76 Squadron as the third, piloted by Flt Lt Hillary, had been forced to turn back on account of severe engine trouble, was only now making its way into the maelstrom. Alone in the sky these two aircraft, flown by Sqn Ldr Williams and Plt Off McKenna, faced the full force of the very much alerted ground defences. The pair bravely held their course towards the target, now heavily shrouded in thick smoke, and began their bomb run, straight and level. When his bomb aimer shouted over the intercom that he was not satisfied that he could identify the target clearly, Williams made the courageous decision to go round again, still followed and supported by McKenna.

The inevitable happened. As the pair held steady for their second run over the target, McKenna's aircraft was blasted and badly damaged by flak and plunged almost immediately into the sea off La Rochelle. The bodies of only four of the seven men on board were recovered after the tides had brought them ashore. Williams' Halifax was now the only British aircraft in the area and it came under attack from all sides. One of the starboard engines was hit by flak and began to leak glycol and, as the bomber battled its way out to sea, an Me109 succeeded in putting the remaining starboard engine out of commission in spite of the best efforts of the gunners. Williams managed to maintain some sort of glide and the aircraft eventually ditched some 7 or 8 miles off the French coast. All the crew were able to get out of the aircraft before it sank and they were picked up from their dinghy by a French fishing boat almost immediately. Upon their return to port, the crew members were handed over to the German authorities. The remaining aircraft of the first wave eventually staggered back to Stanton Harcourt without suffering further loss.

The *Scharnhorst* had taken five hits from bombs but the damage caused by the relatively small bombs had inflicted little damage, especially as two of them had failed to explode and had passed through the ship quite harmlessly. Although messages of congratulations poured in from all sides, including from the AOC Bomber Command, whose remarks were trumpeted by the newspapers, especially the station's local, the *Northern Echo* – 'a magnificent day's work, executed with the characteristic dash and courage which the world knows is the tradition of Bomber Command, Well done!' – it had, in truth, been a hard and costly day's work. Unusually the names of the crew members taken prisoner on the raid were broadcast on German radio at 13:00 hours on 30 July, thereby providing a merciful release from anxiety for at least some of the worried families and friends.

There was an interesting and enjoyable distraction for aircrew and ground crew alike on the 29th. In the summer of 1941 the threat of invasion was still a serious one and suitable provision for it had to be made, even as far north as Middleton St George. After all, night raids had been made on stations like Pocklington, Driffield and Linton and the bombs dropped may just as well have been parachutists – as events in Crete had amply demonstrated. So, on a miserable and wet July day, a thousand troops from the Durham Light Infantry put in a mock attack on the airfield. The defenders, themselves partly drawn from the DLI, supplemented by an anti-aircraft detachment and RAF personnel, put up a spirited defence and bricks, hoses and 'sundry other novel forms of defence and offence were brought into play' in what was described as 'a good scrap'. Whether any real and valuable lessons were learned from the mêlée is debatable but the station log records that 'a very enjoyable morning was had by all'. Fortunately the youthful exuberance did not cause any serious injuries but the station Medical Officer and the sickbay attendants were kept busy patching up wounds and stitching a variety of lacerations. To top it all, the umpires concluded that the station's defences had been robust and had successfully seen off the offensive force. The high spirits were, however, soon dampened, at least temporarily. In the middle of the afternoon Sgt Turnbull RCAF set off on a routine training flight but crashed spectacularly just after take-off on account of a problem caused by jammed ailerons. The station rescue teams were scrambled and found all the crew, dazed but unhurt, sitting well away from the wreckage in the field adjacent to the station.

August began in operational terms on the 2nd with the arrival on the station of AVM C.R. Carr CB, CBE, DFC, AFC, the new AOC 4 Group. He arrived at 15:30 to be greeted by the Station Commander, Gp Capt Tommy Traill. Keen to see how a station under his command worked on an 'average day', Carr attended the briefing, watched the take-off and observed the interrogation of the crews upon their return before making his way back to York at 08:00 hours. Carr did, in fact, see a representative night's work. Four aircraft from 76 Squadron, led by Sqn Ldr Bickford, made the squadron's first attack upon the most prestigious and emotive target of them all – Berlin. As it turned out, the city was shrouded in a thick haze and none of the 53 attacking Halifaxes, Wellingtons and Stirlings was able to find their specified targets, the Air Ministry buildings and Friedrichstrasse railway station. Inevitably in such conditions the bombing was scattered and largely ineffectual, though the glow of the burning fires was still satisfyingly visible from 80 miles away. The situation was not much better for 78 Squadron, which dispatched nine aircraft to a cloud-shrouded Hamburg. For Jack Moorfoot, making one of his last trips as a second pilot, the operation taught him a valuable lesson – that concentration was a must at all times. Flying towards the target above a thick layer of cloud, Moorfoot noticed the bright moon on his right-hand side – due south. After bombing the target, the navigator gave the experienced pilot, Jock Calder, a course for home of 274 degrees – almost due west. A turn was duly made but after some time Moorfoot, sitting in the front turret scanning the sky anxiously for prowling night-fighters, noticed that the moon was still firmly fixed on his right-hand side. The aircraft was, he decided after some thought, still heading deeper into enemy territory. Not wishing to appear a fool or insubordinate, he called the pilot on the intercom and diplomatically asked him whether there was any good reason why the moon was still on the same side of the aircraft as when they flew out. There was a short but pregnant pause while the skipper looked out of the window and then studied the compass with some care. A muffled oath crackled through the intercom and the Whitley banked once again. No doubt tired and stressed, the skipper had put 'red on black' by turning the compass rose so that the needle was in a parallel line – but instead of the needle pointing north it was pointing south. By such slender threads men's lives hung each night.

Five aircraft from 76 Squadron headed to Karlsruhe on the 5th to destroy the railway workshops, which were unusually bathed in clear moonlight. The enthusiastic 4 Group scribes noted: 'Many bombs were seen to drop [including 4,000-pounders] and large fires were started, causing considerable damage in the target area. From observation made by aircraft there is no doubt that this was a most successful operation.' German records show that considerable damage was caused in the west of the city and some 34 people lost their lives that night beneath the bombs. Three aircraft were lost that night, including a Halifax from 76 Squadron captained by Sgt T.A. Byrne. His aircraft was brought down 8km north of Tienen in Belgium, though with only one fatality, Sgt R. Brown. The remainder of the crew were taken prisoner. Unusually for one crew, two men made separate recorded attempts to escape. Sgt C.B. Flockhart made a successful 'home run' from his prison camp, but Flt Lt T.B. Leigh, an Australian in the RAF, was shot by the Gestapo on 30 March 1944 for his part in the 'Great Escape' from Stalag Luft 3. His remains lie in the Old Garrison Cemetery in Poznan, Poland.

Once again 78 Squadron was in action the following night. Twelve aircraft set out towards the railway yards at Frankfurt but flew into almost solid banks of cloud. Only two crews claimed to have located the actual target while the remainder were forced to drop their loads on to the dull red glow of the fires beneath them. This was the first operation for Michael Renaut, who had arrived from OTU Kinloss on 18 July and now found his name on the operations board as second pilot to Plt Off Lowry, who already had twenty or so operations to his credit. It was to be a tough operational baptism for the young and nervous Renaut.

Buffeted by flak as it crossed the enemy coast, his Whitley flew into one of the most potent electrical storms bashing its way into Occupied Europe that night. The aircraft was rapidly icing up at only 14,000ft when there was an enormous bang, a blinding flash of light and all the dials on the instrument panel began to whirl madly as the lights went out. Lowry responded immediately and ordered the crew to prepare to bale out. However, the aircraft's trailing wireless aerial had been struck by lightning and once the crew discovered this, they realised that the aircraft was still just about in one piece and in almost full working order. However, the Whitley had consumed a significant amount of fuel in its laborious battle against the elements and there was little option but to jettison their bomb-load over the Franco-German border and turn for home. Three other aircraft that night were forced to do likewise. Climbing as high as possible to get clear of the storm and the icing, Renaut's Whitley made an anxiety-ridden and seemingly never-ending return journey, eventually touching down at 05:40 hours.

For Plt Off Atchinson there was a much more eventful return. Flak-damaged over the target, his Whitley wandered off course in the storm. Inevitably running short of fuel,

Atchinson tried to ditch the aircraft while he still had some measure of control, sending out repeated distress and position signals all the while. He put down safely into the sea 12km north of Dunkirk and all the crew managed to clamber out of the waterlogged aircraft and into the dinghy. Unfortunately the advent of the first rosy fingers of dawn spreading across the sky gave the German coastal batteries ample opportunity to practise their trade upon the downed airmen bobbing helplessly in their little dinghy. Only the timely arrival of the Dover Air Sea Rescue launch – itself under direct fire – prevented the inevitable. No crew was ever more thankful to be snatched from the sea.

A few night later the Deutsche Werke shipyards on the eastern side of the harbour in Kiel were chalked up as the target. Taking off from 22:00 hours onwards, the crews for once enjoyed excellent flying conditions and the clear moonlit skies extended all the way to Kiel itself where the layout of the docks was clearly visible from over 10,000ft, in spite of the extensive use of searchlights and a considerable amount of heavy flak. Many bombs were noted as falling in the harbour area and the attack was deemed to have been a successful one. Indeed, it was commented that 'a very enjoyable sortie was experienced by eleven of the crews'. The twelfth crew was not so fortunate.

Whitley Z6655 took off at 22:19 with Sgt J.W. Bell at the controls and duly dropped its bombs from 10,000ft at 01:30 on to a quay north of two square-shaped docks. Shortly thereafter the aircraft shuddered as it was hit by flak. With several punctures in the fuselage tank, the aircraft began to lose considerable amounts of both fuel and height and it soon became clear that the battered Whitley would not make it back to Britain. Having sent out repeated Mayday calls, Bell lowered the stricken Whitley into the sea as gently as he could some 78 miles north-east of Blyth in Northumberland. The aircraft remained afloat long enough for the crew to scramble out and into the dinghy, only to find to their dismay that it had been holed by the flak and was slowly settling into the sea. This, as it was later reported, 'made things far from comfortable', but things began to look a little brighter when it was discovered that steady baling would keep the dinghy just about afloat. A miserable couple of hours was spent bobbing up and down in the swell until 07:45 when a Hudson spotted the dinghy and dropped a bag of provisions within 20ft. The crew paddled frantically towards the floating bag but were unable to keep pace with it as it drifted away on the current. It was not until 10:30 that an Air Sea Rescue launch arrived on the scene and hauled aboard the exhausted and soaked crew. They were taken to Blyth where they enjoyed considerable and much appreciated hospitality at the naval station before returning to Middleton.

Unfortunately 12 August proved to be anything but glorious for the crewmen of 76 Squadron. Seven Halifaxes from the squadron were to form 10 per cent of the attacking force on the German capital Berlin, with the Air Ministry buildings in the Alexander Platz as the aiming point. Only 32 aircraft, of which two were from Middleton, were able to make it to and bomb the target in difficult flying conditions. Many were unhappy with the choice of route that night as it took the aircraft close to the heavy flak concentrations near Amsterdam and Rotterdam. They were right to be unhappy. Heavy flak greeted them and several aircraft sustained damage as they passed overhead. Sadly 76 Squadron lost three aircraft on this operation and it was noted in the squadron record as a 'bad night's work'.

Halifax L9530 in flight. This aircraft was the personal mount of Plt Off Christopher Cheshire. It was lost to flak on 12/13 August 1941, raiding Berlin. *(Imperial War Museum CH 3378)*

Flt Lt Chris Cheshire lifted his heavily laden Halifax off the runway at Middleton St George at 21:35 hours and as he crossed the enemy coast it became apparent that the aircraft, for some unknown reason, had already used almost half of its fuel. Clearly Berlin was out of the question, so course was set for Hamburg, a suitable alternative target for his 4,000-pounder. As the only aircraft over the heavily defended port, the Halifax endured the full and undivided attention of the impressive defences. Although blasted around the night sky, miraculously the aircraft remained intact during the bomb run. However, such good fortune was too good to last and when an almighty thump rocked the aircraft, it was time to bale out. Sgt A. Niven and Flt Sgt W. Woods were killed but the remaining five crew members survived to become prisoners.

Halifax L9531 MP-R, under the command of Sgt C.E. Whitfield, took off one minute earlier than Cheshire but was shot down near Wittstedt by Leutnant Hans Autenrieth of VI/NJG1. All the crew succeeded in baling out but tragically five of them drowned after coming down in marshy ground. The run of bad fortune continued when one of the survivors, Flt Sgt W. Bone, was killed on 19 April 1945 as an Allied fighter strafed a POW column by mistake, leaving Sgt K. Kenworthy the sole survivor of that ill-fated crew.

The night had still not finished with 76 Squadron. Sgt J. McHale's Halifax made it back to Middleton St George just as dawn was breaking. While making a gentle turn on the standard approach, the aircraft stalled and suddenly ploughed into the ground and erupted into flames, killing all on board. A later inspection of the wreckage suggested that the Halifax had sustained considerable battle damage. Such a terrible event, in sight of the airfield, brought home to the ground crews once again the full horrors of war and the dreadful risks the crews faced on each operation.

The wheels of war rolled on remorselessly and on the 16th Middleton St George suffered another dreadful night, losing three Whitleys on a raid to Cologne. It was a bad night from the outset as one aircraft failed to take off, four others returned early with mechanical problems, and another was forced to turn about over occupied territory and dropped its load over Rotterdam. Four more pressed on and bombed the fires visible underneath the usual industrial haze; German records report only a light raid with minimal damage and no casualties. It seems likely that the crews were misled by the decoy fires outside the oft-visited target. The remaining three aircraft, captained by Sgt T.A. Sherman RCAF, Sgt J.H. Malet-Warden and Flt Lt J.A. Cant, all came to grief over Holland in the small hours. Only three of the crewmen involved survived. There were many long faces and empty spaces in the mess that morning. The sixteen days of August 1941 had seen the loss of nine aircraft and crews.

At this point the weather clamped down over Europe, limiting operations. However, an inconclusive raid on a cloud-covered Düsseldorf cost two more crews from 78 Squadron. Sgt W.G. Rodgers, who had only recently been posted to the squadron, perished with the rest of his crew when his aircraft came down near Wavre. Plt Off Fransden's Whitley made it back to England and finally crashed to earth near Mistley in Essex, taking with it the second pilot Sgt D. Sinclair, who had selflessly and courageously volunteered to hold the damaged aircraft steady while the remainder of the crew baled out safely.

On the 27th it was Mannheim's turn to be paid a visit, by three aircraft from 78 Squadron. Two of these made it to the target and contributed their loads to the fires blazing beneath them. The third was badly shot up by flak as it crossed the enemy coast and was forced to turn for home after bombing the alternative target of Bruges. Sgt H.A. Woodhatch did a fine job in bringing his battered aircraft back to Middleton and carried out a successful, if somewhat hairy, crash-landing shortly before 01:00 hours. As the aircraft ground to a halt it burst into flames, adding mild burns to the minor injuries already sustained in the landing. Woodhatch himself had a miraculous escape, surviving, without serious injury, being hurled through the front turret. Heartened by the good fortune of this crew, those men and women waiting in the dim light of dawn were saddened by the news that Plt Off Davies and his crew were long overdue from a raid to the so-called easy target of Dunkirk. Their Whitley had crashed into the sea just off the port, with the loss of all on board. Middleton St George was having a hard time of it.

But the grim reaper had still not had his fill of young men's lives. On 29 August the first 100-plus raid on Frankfurt was carried out, with its important railway junctions and harbours as the aiming points. Three aircraft from 76 Squadron and eight from 78 Squadron battled their way through 10/10ths cloud only to find the target completely invisible. The crews were forced to bomb on ETA or on to the dull red glow of fires barely discernible beneath them. Several aircraft were damaged by flak. One of them was a Halifax flown by the experienced Sqn Ldr Bob Bickford DFC. He nursed the bomber home on three engines for much of the return journey, but a second engine cut out over North Yorkshire when the aircraft was at just 2,000ft. Bickford struggled to hold the wallowing Halifax as steady as he could while the crew baled out, before diving for the hatch himself. Unfortunately his parachute got caught in the slipstream and wound around the tail unit, dragging the courageous Bickford to his death. The body of the rear gunner, Sgt G.W. Duckmanton, was found near the crash site not far from Pocklington when daylight came; his parachute had not fully deployed before he hit the ground. The official squadron record states that the squadron leader's loss 'was a severe blow to the squadron and the station. His skill and experience as a pilot were of immense value to the squadron and his very pleasing personality made him genuinely popular and esteemed by his brother officers.' It is sad to note that no similar comment was made about the loss of Sgt Duckmanton, another mother's son.

August had been a devastating and frustrating month for the squadrons based at Middleton St George. Some fourteen of the aircraft dispatched – the best part of a whole squadron's establishment – had either been shot down or crashed, and yet there had been no really successful raids to balance the equation. Losses on this scale could not but affect the whole station, especially as several of the losses had occurred over the airfield itself. Things could only get better in September.

Both squadrons had hoped for some time to lick their wounds and recuperate but instead their depleted ranks were called upon on just the second night of the month. Three of 76 Squadron's aircraft were to attack Berlin. One swung off the runway on take-off and aborted but the other two pressed on to find, unusually, the German capital free from cloud. The official report noted the novelty of this and stated: 'The target was definitely identified. Bursts and several fires were seen to the east of the aiming point. Large explosions were observed. An excellent photo was taken which shows bombs bursting in the Berlin meat market, one mile east of the aiming point.' This upbeat assessment clearly shows the operational expectations in terms of accuracy in mid-1941 over Germany.

Berlin was the target again for 197 bombers on the 7th, five of them coming from Middleton St George. It was the first night that 76 Squadron had operated under the command of Wg Cdr J.J.A. Sutton DFC. Genuine damage was caused to the city that night as clear conditions and bright moonlight permitted much more accurate bombing of the main aiming point, the Schlesischer station. The crews were especially impressed by the scale of the fires and the effects of the new 50lb incendiary bomb. The official record notes: 'This operation was very successful and Berlin received the most severe attack it has yet encountered.' The 2,500 people bombed out of their homes that night may not have disagreed. To cap it all, all the men from Middleton survived the raid, though Sgt Simmonds was forced to crash-land his Whitley when it ran out of fuel over Houghton-le-Spring in County Durham, no more than 20 miles from home. A third attack on the Reich capital later in the month was called off on account of worsening weather only when the aircraft were airborne and heading east over the North Sea.

Four aircraft of 76 Squadron, flying from an advanced base at Stradishall in Suffolk, made the long journey to Turin on the 10th. This audacious and symbolic attack was aimed at the Royal Arsenal, the giant Fiat steelworks and the main railway station. Cruising serenely in bright moonlight, the crews were treated to magnificent and panoramic views of the Alps, stretching up almost as high as the heavily laden aircraft themselves. Unfortunately, and to the crews' frustration and dismay, the bombers flew into cloud sufficiently dense to make accurate bombing impossible. Nevertheless several large fire-glows began to spread over the earth beneath them and the anti-aircraft fire rapidly became wilder and more sporadic. It was still, however, sufficiently potent to seriously damage Flt Lt Leonard Smith's Halifax on the final operational sortie of his tour. No one was more pleased than Smith himself when he eventually lowered the straining aircraft safely on to the tarmac on the emergency runway at RAF Manston in Kent.

The major German surface raiders, the *Scharnhorst* and the *Gneisenau*, still ensconced in Brest harbour, were the target for four aircraft of 76 Squadron and nine of 78 Squadron on 13 September. Although patchy cloud and the customary heavy flak proved little problem for the airmen, many of whom were veterans on this target, the dense smokescreen certainly did, enveloping the warships entirely in thick, oily folds. Almost 150 aircraft were over Brest that night but none caught even so much as a glimpse of the quarry, releasing their loads instead over the general dock area. Sgt Bell, captaining Whitley Z6978 from 78 Squadron, had a narrow escape when, on the return journey at 16,000ft, he came under attack from an enemy night-fighter, unseen until it opened fire from just 150 yards astern and below. The burst caused only minor damage and, as the fighter hurtled beneath the lumbering Whitley, the rear gunner reacted swiftly enough to get in three or four good bursts. Fortunately that was the one and only pass the fighter made and Bell and his crew were able to resume their homeward journey, somewhat shaken by those few shattering seconds and the longer realisation of what might have been. They would have been more cheered to have heard the news of Plt Off Michael Renaut, who, on his first operation as captain, witnessed the awe-inspiring sight of 'this flaming, falling ball of fire hurtling through the cloud', as the night-fighter plunged to its doom. In the language of the day, the official records note this as 'a very good show' – a comparatively rare event at this stage of the war. Sgt Bell eased his Whitley on to the ground at Kirton in Lindsay for a check-over before returning to a triumphant reception at Middleton St George. There would be no return of any kind, however, for Plt Off R.E. Hutchin, who ordered his crew to bale out near Bedford on the outbound leg when his Halifax developed serious engine trouble. Minutes later, at 02:55 hours, Hutchin's short life came to an abrupt end as the aircraft plunged out of control and crashed.

The following day was a red-letter spit and polish day for everyone on the airfield. Shortly after midday one of the best-known figures in the RAF, and the acknowledged father of both it and Bomber Command, MRAF Viscount Trenchard GCB, GCVO, DSO arrived at Middleton St George by air. AOC 4 Group, AVM Carr, landed shortly after and joined Trenchard on a brief but thorough tour of the whole station. Having dined in the officers' mess, Trenchard inspected the hangars, maintenance and intelligence sections as well as the operations room before addressing the young crews, who had heard so much about this austere and yet revered figure, in the briefing room. Everything went well but it was no doubt with considerable relief that Gp Capt Traill watched his distinguished visitor's aircraft depart safely at 14:40 hours. Though not all personnel on the station were lovers of the 'bull' that accompanies such visits, the day did at least provide them with a welcome break from routine.

The foul weather continued and, apart from small-scale attacks on Hamburg, Stettin and Ostend, operations did not resume until the night of the 29th, when three aircraft from 76 Squadron and ten from 78 Squadron made the long and hazardous flight to Stettin once again. The basic conditions were surprisingly good, marred only by a slight haze, and considerable damage was again inflicted on the port and the city centre. Jack Moorfoot headed towards the docks at Warnemünde and almost immediately wished he hadn't as he was greeted by very heavy and uncomfortably accurate flak. This continued throughout his seemingly endless bomb run and he considered it only by the Grace of God that his aircraft came through it with only minor damage and a few holes. Michael Renaut, on his first incursion to Germany as captain, had a 21st birthday to remember in the skies over Stettin that night. As he turned for home he noticed that the flak had eased off considerably and immediately warned his crew to keep a sharp eye out for enemy fighters. Sure enough, a few minutes later the bomber came under determined attack from a fighter identified as an Me109. Fortunately free of its heavy bomb-load, Renaut hurled his elderly Whitley around the sky with a vigour born of desperation. After a considerable amount of gut-wrenching twists and turns Renaut succeeded in shaking off his assailant and sliding away into the darkness. A little later, however, over Denmark his gunner spotted a Junkers Ju88 and, with their hearts in their mouths, the entire crew watched this formidable night-fighter continue serenely on its way, completely unaware of the bomber's presence. Sgt R.W. Bird and his crew were not so fortunate. A call for help was received from his aircraft at 04:23 hours on a bearing near Sylt but nothing more was heard. The young men perished in the cold waters of the North Sea.

October was to see some major changes at the airfield but it began in an all too familiar way. A paltry total of five aircraft had managed to attack the ports of Brest and Dunkirk before bad weather intervened, preventing any further operations until the 10th, when the industrial city of Essen was the target. The operation went wrong at Middleton St George right from the start. Plt Off King in Z6048 was a non-starter, having swung off the runway on take-off and damaged his undercarriage. Shortly afterwards the airfield was rocked by the enormous blast of two entire bomb-loads exploding in a vast multicoloured ball of flame. Plt Off Leyland in Z9127 and Plt Off Fransden in Z6825 had collided in the gloom while taxiing along the flarepath. The Whitleys, heavily laden with both bombs and fuel, immediately burst into flames and rapidly turned into an inferno as the petrol tanks ignited. Incredibly as it seemed to those who witnessed the awesome fireball, only two men were injured, Sgts Dench and Taylor from Plt Off Leyland's crew. A number of surprised and shaken ground crew were treated for cuts caused by flying glass, and the force of the explosion unexpectedly shattered much of the glass on the station. The fire crews were rapidly on the scene and soon had the blaze under control. As soon as was possible, the charred remains of the aircraft were shunted off the taxiway and the large hole was filled in by an emergency working party in order to allow the rest of the strike force to take off. As it turned out, much of this Herculean effort was wasted as Essen was completely hidden beneath 10/10ths cloud and of the 78 British aircraft in German airspace that night only 13 claimed to have bombed the city. Middleton's aircraft were diverted to Dishforth on their return as the Station Armament Officer, Flt Lt Burke, and his team were still busy dealing with several unexploded bombs. It was not until the middle of the next day that the airfield was finally declared safe and the aircraft were able to return.

Two nights later twelve aircraft from Middleton St George were dispatched to the Siemens Schuckert works at Nuremburg as part of a strong force of 152 bombers. In clear conditions the crews reported seeing several large fires burning from their bombing altitude of 12–15,000ft. One aircraft flown by Sgt Thomas dodged well beneath the flak and crossed the target at just 3,000ft, clearly identifying the target and observing several hits as he went. Yet German records for that night note that only a few bombs fell in the city, killing just one unlucky soul and injuring a half a dozen more. However, many bombs were recorded as falling on Schwabach, some 10 miles south of Nuremburg, and over 200 high explosive and 700 incendiary bombs rained down on the hapless inhabitants of Lauingen some 65 miles from the home of the infamous Nazi rallies. Furthermore quite a bit of damage was caused that night in Lauffen, almost 100 miles from the intended target. The most likely explanation for this huge discrepancy lies in the fact that these towns, like Nuremburg, were situated on wide rivers, one of the features most easily spotted but not very easily identified from the air by night. Over such a long night flight as the one to Nuremburg – one of the longest undertaken by Bomber Command at this stage of the war – navigating only by dead reckoning meant that errors were almost inevitable, although not usually on this scale. Once the fires had been started, they tended to draw other aircraft to them like moths to a flame, thereby compounding the original error.

Indeed, the strain of concentrating throughout such long flights, significantly exacerbated by the very real fear of an unseen and deadly attack by a night-fighter, could play strange tricks on the overworked eyes of the pilot and crew, who spent their time constantly peering into the inky blackness. Flying back above a layer of stratus cloud that night, Michael Renaut jumped in his seat as he saw a night-fighter heading straight towards him with its wing lights full on. He reacted at once, pushing the Whitley's nose down into the cloud and shouting to the startled crew to keep their eyes peeled. A minute or two later he gently nosed up and out of the cloud only to find the fighter still in position and coming closer. Still the gunners had not spotted it and Renaut dipped back into the cloud immediately. Poking the Whitley's nose out of the cloud once more a couple of minutes later, he found his adversary still there and it began to dawn on him that his 'night-fighter' was nothing more hostile than the moon coming up over the cloud bank. He survived both the sortie and the embarrassment to make a successful landing at Abingdon, though very short on fuel. One aircraft, however, did not make it. Flt Sgt E.B. Muttart, flying Halifax L9561, was 76 Squadron's only representative that night on an attack against Bremen. At 21:49 the aircraft was shot down over Wons in Holland by Leutnant Leopold Fellerer of IV/NJG1. All except Muttart successfully baled out and were taken prisoner. It was not until over fifty years later, on 4 July 1993, that several members of the crew met up once again at a 76 Squadron reunion, held, fittingly, at the old officers' mess, now the St George Hotel.

An AEC Matador bowser refuels a Halifax B Mk I of 76 Squadron. In the background is the distinctive shape of a Whitley of 78 Squadron. *(Imperial War Museum CH 4462)*

Two nights later, on 14 October 1941, one Halifax of 76 Squadron and ten Whitleys of 78 Squadron made another attempt to damage the war industry in Nuremburg. The conditions that night were horrendous, with 10/10ths cloud and severe icing all the way to the distant target. Most crews were forced to bomb on ETA and only 13 of the 80 aircraft dispatched claimed to have actually hit the city. One of these was Sqn Ldr A.J.D. Snow, who added a positive identification of the Siemens factory and dropped six high explosive bombs. The city records show that the factory did receive one bomb hit that night, and it may well have been Snow's bomb. Nevertheless the official verdict on the operation was 'disappointing'.

The dreadful conditions caused additional problems for the crews, particularly excessive fuel use on an already very long flight. Plt Off D.S. King, a member of the RCAF though born in Buenos Aires, had taken off from Middleton St George at 22:52 and by 06:15, having battled against the elements throughout the night, the fuel gauges read empty. King and his crew baled out successfully and were relieved to find that they had cleared the English coast – just! They landed near Hythe in Kent.

Ostend was the target for four freshman crews of 78 Squadron on 16 October. Two of the aircraft brought their bombs back with them as 10/10ths cloud over the Belgian port prevented them from pinpointing their target accurately. All four returned safely to base. This was to be 78 Squadron's last offensive sortie from Middleton St George for almost eight months as a couple of days later, on the 20th, the squadron transferred to the mostly completed but spartan satellite airfield at Croft, a couple of miles away across the River Tees in North Yorkshire. But the gremlins had not quite finished with 78 Squadron and Middleton St George. What was described as 'an unfortunate accident' occurred at 20:10 on the 6th when Plt Off B.O. Smith and his crew were carrying out a local night-flying exercise. One of the engines packed up at low altitude and Smith made an immediate forced-landing not far from Croft. Three of the crew members were seriously burnt in the resultant blaze.

In spite of the depletion of Middleton St George's ranks, this small cog in the Bomber Command's wheel continued to turn, if at a rather slower pace than usual on account of the inclement weather.

On the 22nd it was Mannheim's turn and on the 26th Hamburg's, with a much more successful and destructive raid than usual, before a less successful return visit at the end of the month. Such a period provided some relief for the crews but did not release them entirely from the stresses of operations. Each day Middleton St George was allotted a target and the aircrews were notified, with each crew member suffering the strain of anticipation – itself often worse than the actual event – until they were eventually released by the stand-down order. This often left them no more than the evening to relax in before the whole procedure began all over again.

Little better could be expected as the winter progressed. Bad weather forced the cancellation of several operations before 7 November, when five aircraft of 76 Squadron formed part of a 169-strong attack on Berlin. In spite of the forecast of thick cloud, icing and electrical storms, the assault went ahead on the orders of the Air Officer Commanding in Chief Bomber Command himself, Sir Richard Peirse. It was a bad decision. The aircraft met with the weather predicted, causing their air speed indicators and compasses to go U/S and forcing two aircraft to jettison their loads and another, captained by the experienced Sqn Ldr Bouwens, to attack Flensburg as a more viable proposition. The remaining two aircraft, flown by Plt Off Calder and Sgt Herbert, dropped their bombs on what they thought was the general area of Berlin on ETA. Middleton St George was lucky not to share in the 21 aircraft lost that night – some 12.4 per cent of the force dispatched. In Berlin only 11 people were killed, 44 injured and some 637 people bombed-out. The scales of achievement against effort had tipped too far. There were to be no more major raids on the German capital until January 1943, by which time the tactical and operational situation had changed considerably.

This was also to be 76 Squadron's final raid under the command of Wg Cdr J.J.A. Sutton DFC, who was posted to Bomber Command HQ somewhat unexpectedly on the 9th. The official station record notes that 'both squadron and station took a poor view of the loss'. His successor was Sqn Ldr Bouwens DFC. The weather, however, did not prevent another distinguished visitor making his way to Bomber Command's most northerly operational airfield. On the 15th the Secretary of State for Air, Sir Archibald Sinclair, accompanied by AVM Carr and Gp Capt Sir Louis Greig KBE, CVO, arrived to inspect the facilities, crews and ground staff. The highlight was a tour of a Halifax complete with a full crew in place, and the visitors were thought to have been suitably impressed.

PAUSE FOR THOUGHT – HOLDING THE LINE AND ATTACKS ON NAVAL TARGETS

There was still no let-up in the weather and several more operations were scheduled, planned and then scrubbed. It was not until the 25th that conditions improved sufficiently to permit the offensive to be resumed. Eleven Halifaxes, four of them from 76 Squadron, and seven Stirlings were to make an early evening attack on the German warships lying at anchor in Brest harbour. The aircraft took off late in the afternoon. Flying through a cloudless sky, bathed in bright moonlight, they headed south over England and out over the Channel. The aim was to catch the defences unaware but the plan went astray, as the official summary describes:

> Orders were given for the synchronisation of this attack and the Group effort was concentrated within a period of 6 minutes. Aircraft from other groups, which were detailed to attack this target, arrived more than quarter of an hour before the specified time of attack and this resulted in the smokescreen being fully effective over the target by the time the 4 Group aircraft arrived. Bombs are believed to have fallen on to the docks but the smokescreen prevented any observation of results.

The pernicious weather again took a hand and no further operations could be mounted until the last day of the month. In good visibility and bright moonlight five Halifaxes from 76 Squadron joined a strong force making its way to the shipyards and city centre of Hamburg. For once the favourable conditions enabled the raiders to wreak considerable havoc in the target area, raising 22 large fires, killing 65 people, injuring another 176, and bombing-out in excess of 2,500 inhabitants.

The pattern continued, with few operations being scheduled and those that were being cancelled on account of poor winter weather. There were, however, a couple of changes in the command structure of the station. The popular Station Commander Gp Capt Traill fell ill and for most of the month Gp Capt J. Bradbury DFC was drafted in to take overall day-to-day charge of the airfield. On the 12th Sqn Ldr J.T. Bouwens DFC relinquished his temporary command of 76 Squadron and handed over to Wg Cdr David Young, later DSO, DFC, AFC, who was to have a profound effect on the squadron for the remainder of its time at Middleton St George. Michael Renaut recalls his first meeting with the new CO shortly after his return from exile with 78 Squadron at Croft on 22 December: 'What an incredible person he was – tall, good-looking, with iron grey hair, a devout Catholic, an experienced pilot with already 3,000 hours, mainly in civil flying, behind him. A man of extreme courage and a true commander. He oozed authority and the impact he made on the squadron and the station was electric.'

Wg Cdr Young was to need all of these special qualities on his first operation in charge of 76 Squadron on 18 December 1941. Having been ordered to carry out several days of intensive formation flying practice, the crews were rightly suspicious that something big was coming up. At a briefing held at 18:00 hours on the 17th it was announced that there was to be an attack upon the German warships in Brest harbour – in daylight! The station was sealed and maximum security enforced to minimise the risk of careless chatter in the locality. Six of Middleton's most experienced Halifax crews were to take part in the audacious operation alongside 41 other Halifaxes, Stirlings and Manchesters. To counter the swarms of German fighters that would inevitably come up to meet them, a complex plan had been devised for Spitfires and Hurricanes to provide strong cover.

The operation did not get off to an auspicious start. Flt Lt Jock Calder's Halifax suffered a severe brake problem while taxiing for take-off and was forced to head back to dispersal. Quick work by the ground crew enabled a spare aircraft to be made ready in time for Calder to rendezvous on time with the other 4 Group aircraft at 4,000ft over Linton in mid-morning. A course was set for Lundy Island and the aircraft from 35, 10 and 76 Squadrons headed south through patchy cloud. Then the gremlins woke up again and Sqn Ldr Packe was forced to land at Boscombe Down with a misfiring engine and instrument problems, reducing 76 Squadron's contingent to five aircraft.

On schedule the Manchesters of 97 Squadron and the Stirlings from several 3 Group bases joined the formation over the Channel; more reassuringly, so did the fighter escort. Shortly

A daylight attack upon the battlecruisers *Scharnhorst* and *Gneisenau* and the heavy cruiser *Prinz Eugen* in Brest harbour on 18 December 1941. *(Imperial War Museum C 2230)*

after midday, in clearing conditions, the French coast came into view. For the crews of 76 Squadron it was an awesome sight. Overhead the Spitfires and Hurricanes were fending off the attacks of the German Me109s, whirling and diving all over the blue sky, and intense flak from both the shore batteries and the ships themselves was hurtling upwards to greet the arrival of the Manchesters and Stirlings ahead. Wg Cdr Young held his aircraft steady in two vics and flew into the maelstrom straight and level from the west; 10 and 35 Squadrons adopted the line astern formation and released their bombs from 16,000ft. Such was the degree of surprise achieved that the smoke pots which had thwarted so many previous attacks had not been ignited, leaving the whole harbour and the great ships themselves exposed and open to view. Several sticks of bombs were seen to pound the dock area and thick black smoke was seen rising from the *Gneisenau*.

As the bombers turned for home, a wave of German fighters put in a determined attack and a total of six bombers fell to either the actions of the fighters or flak. Fortunately none of the aircraft lost came from 76 Squadron, though several were damaged and holed. Since they had left Middleton St George that morning the weather conditions had deteriorated considerably, compelling Wg Cdr Young to instruct his weary crews to land at Boscombe Down in Wiltshire.

The weather continued to be foul and unsuitable for operations, enabling the crews to enjoy a reasonably stress-free and extended Christmas break. When the weather cleared sufficiently to allow operations to resume the crews assembled amid tight security in the briefing room and were surprised to find that their target was once again the German warships in Brest harbour, once again in daylight. As all the gathered airmen had heard the stories of the aerial mayhem recounted by the crews from the first operation, many thoughtful and apprehensive young men left the room to make their preparations that afternoon. Sixteen Halifaxes, including six from 76 Squadron, were to make the attack, following much the same route as on the 18th. Surely, the crews thought, the Germans must guess that they would go back and thus would have prepared an even hotter reception for them. Such pessimistic views proved to be all too accurate.

The heavily loaded Halifaxes lumbered into the air over Middleton St George a little after 11:00 and once again there was a hitch. Sgt Morin's aircraft was found to have a defective rear turret. The crew disembarked as quickly as they could and boarded a reserve aircraft and managed to make up enough time to rendezvous with the aircraft from 10 and 35 Squadrons on schedule. Flying at 16,000ft over 10/10ths clouds, the bomber crews were cheered by the sight of long-range Spitfires from the Polish Wing sliding into place some 4,000ft above them.

As the bombers approached the target the cloud cleared a little – enough to give the waiting German gunners the chance they had been waiting for. While the Spitfires twisted and turned overhead and succeeded in heading off all but the most determined of the Luftwaffe attacks, the Halifaxes held a close line-astern formation over the target, thereby presenting an excellent target for the massed batteries below. The gunners made the most of the opportunity and every aircraft was hit and damaged to a greater or lesser degree. The Halifaxes made a direct run at the target but no results of their bombing were observed on account of the veritable barrage thrown up by the defending artillery and the plumes of smoke below, not to mention the vigorous evasive action being taken by the aircraft in the interests of survival. Shortly after turning for home Plt Off D.S. King, who had survived several dicey dos in the past, was observed to have had a near-miss that momentarily enveloped his aircraft in smoke. Gradually slipping out of the formation to starboard in a gentle glide with smoke pouring from his starboard outer engine, Plt Off King's aircraft fell further behind, still losing height. King pressed on, hoping to make it across the Channel but it was a hopeless task. Some 20 miles from the French coast the Halifax crashed into the sea. Two Spitfire pilots, who had escorted the crippled aircraft out of the target area, circled overhead for some time but saw no sign of any survivors. Two other bombers and three of the Spitfires went the same way as King, but the rest of 76 Squadron's aircraft limped home, Wg Cdr Young, Sqn Ldr Packe and Flt Sgt Whyte all on only three engines. As it turned out, no damage had been caused to either the *Gneisenau* or the *Prinz Eugen*, but it was not from want of trying.

In the event this was the final raid of the month, drawing Middleton St George's first year of service to a close. It had been a remarkable and busy year, with a steep learning curve for senior officers, aircrew and ground crew alike. The airfield was a hive of activity 24 hours a day, every day of the week. There was always another target to attack, another aircraft to service, another route to plot, another report to write, and, all too often, another letter of condolence to draft and dispatch. But the pace of events was only to quicken in the next twelve months as the Bomber Command offensive – and Middleton St George's part in it – gathered further momentum.

The new year began deceptively quietly at Middleton St George, with no operations being scheduled until the night of 5 January, when four Halifaxes were briefed for an attack on Brest. Once again the sizeable force of 154 aircraft was thwarted by the thick oily smokescreen that was pumped into the air above the harbour area by the ever-vigilant German defenders as the bombers approached. On the ground there had been 'bull' aplenty as AVM Carr drove up to Middleton St George, accompanied by Gen Ralph Royce USAAF. His country had only been at war with Germany for less than a month and Royce was keen to see what life was like at the sharp end. He left for York suitably impressed and well fed. Another distinguished and more unusual visitor to the airfield was Capt Ursal of the Turkish Embassy, the guest of Gp Capt A.H.H. MacDonald, who had assumed temporary command of Middleton St George while Gp Capt Traill was on leave. There is no record of Ursal's views or comments. A much more lasting impression was made by some visitors who arrived on 14 January. Six Russian officers under the command of Major Svetzov, a veteran of the early campaigns in the Soviet Union, arrived at Darlington station to be met by Sqn Ldr Burdett and Flt Lt Hanness, the Station Adjutant. The soldiers were taken on a tour of the airfield and given the opportunity to inspect a Halifax, a far more advanced and formidable bomber than anything the Soviet armoury could muster. They were suitably impressed. The cooks in the officers' mess really pushed the boat out that evening and put on an extraordinarily luxurious spread, but the result of their efforts was not the one the British officers had anticipated. Their guests, while tucking into the fine fare, began to berate their hosts for dining so well when their countrymen were starving. Had this unexpected and unwarranted viewpoint been thought of in advance, no doubt bully beef and stewed prunes would have

Low-level reconnaissance photograph of the *Tirpitz* in Aas Fjord on 15 February 1942. The attacks on the battleship mounted by 76 Squadron were among their most difficult and dangerous. *(Imperial War Museum C 2356)*

been the order of the day! Moreover, the Russians asked, why were these great bombers not in the sky, blasting away at Germany? The patient explanation that the weather was so lousy that even the birds were walking seemed to cut little ice with the bellicose Russians. Nevertheless, the atmosphere warmed up as the alcohol flowed and 'after dinner, light music and dancing were indulged in'. Slowly recovering from serious hangovers, the RAF men said their farewell to their allies at Darlington station the following day.

The real nitty-gritty continued whenever the weather permitted. Several small-scale attacks of limited penetration were mounted against the French ports of St Nazaire and Brest, but a raid on Emden on the 16th and another a few days later on Bremen were scrubbed on account of the same mechanical problem. The Halifaxes were found to have inadequate brake pressure, an unusual occurrence that was blamed on the extremely cold weather. A thought should be spared for the poor ground crew who worked on them day in day out, whatever the weather. However, things remained unusually quiet for 76 Squadron and the crews began to suspect that something big was in the offing. They were right.

On 29 January Plt Off Ron Waite, who had only recently arrived at Middleton St George, found the officers' mess strangely quiet when he returned that afternoon from a dinghy drill practice in Stockton swimming pool. Diffident questioning of one of the station's intelligence officers, Flt Lt Simpson, produced only the vague reply that several of the squadron's aircraft and ground crew had flown to somewhere in Scotland for some operation or other. The 'somewhere' turned out to be Lossiemouth and the 'some operation or other' turned out to be a raid against Germany's new and immensely powerful battleship *Tirpitz*, moored in the Aas Fjord near Trondheim in Norway.

This brand-new 42,900-ton battleship, launched at Wilhelmshaven on (of all days) April Fools' Day 1939, was the pride of the German Navy when it entered service in January 1941. With eight 15-inch guns and an impressive array of secondary armament and anti-aircraft provision, a speed of 31 knots and a range of 9,000 miles at 19 knots, the *Tirpitz* was more than a match for any ship in the Royal Navy. Any opportunity to damage or destroy her before she could get among the Atlantic convoys had to be grabbed with both hands. Once she was spotted in Norway, the Admiralty called in Bomber Command. The five Halifaxes of 76 Squadron headed north on the morning of the 29th to join a further six Halifaxes from 10 Squadron at Leeming under the command of Wg Cdr Tuck and ten Stirlings from 15 Squadron based at Wyton under the command of Wg Cdr MacDonald. Conditions at Lossiemouth that day were dreadful, with sub-zero temperatures and a chill wind not being at all conducive to the preparation and bombing-up of aircraft. The ground crews toiled all day and by 00:30 hours the first of the aircraft took to the night sky expecting severe icing and thick cloud on the outward leg but clear conditions over the target. Alas, the Met. office had miscalculated the rate of clearance and the aircraft flew through dense murk that stretched from sea level to 20,000ft. Thick layers of ice built up and lumps of it broke off and whacked against the aircrafts' fuselages with heart-stopping thumps. The heavy icing caused several aircraft to return to base on account of excessive fuel consumption.

No. 76 Squadron's contingent took off later than the others, a little after 02:00, and actually made it to the target area but in spite of the fact that the cloud was beginning to break up they were unable to find their target. Rather than bomb indiscriminately over friendly territory, they jettisoned their bombs over the sea and turned for home. Sgt Herbert, however, was the exception. Passing over the target area shortly after 06:00, his Halifax was greeted by a barrage of light flak and this helped him to pinpoint the battleship. He bombed from 8,000ft and reported seeing explosions between the ship and the shore. German records do not, however, mention this in their account of the attack that night.

The harsh conditions made even the return journey to safety a difficult and unpleasant one. For Sgt Harwood and his crew in Q for Queenie it was more than that. Blown a little off course and hampered by the adverse weather, Harwood's Halifax was considerably overdue and running very short of fuel. To cap it all the wireless set had packed up too. It was with great relief that the crew saw the Scottish coastline in the pale light of dawn. Just then one of the engines, the port inner, cut out and the others coughed and spluttered as if about to follow suit. So near and yet so far. There was nothing for it but to ditch in the stormy wintry sea. Although two of the crew were slightly injured in the ditching, the men successfully made it into their dinghy, just a few miles off Gregness near Aberdeen. As they had had no opportunity to send out any message, they were delighted and amazed shortly after 10:00 to see a Spitfire heading towards them. This aircraft was from 416 Squadron based at Peterhead. An unknown individual had picked up the aircraft on radar and put two and two together with the missing Halifax, scrambling an Anson from Kinloss, the Spitfire from Peterhead and a further two Spitfires from 603 Squadron at Dyce. Within a short time the lucky crewmen were picked up by a patrol boat, though attempts to salvage the still-floating Halifax were soon abandoned. The remaining aircraft of 76 Squadron stayed at Lossiemouth for a few more days in case the opportunity to mount another attack arose but when it did not they headed home, bringing their ground crews with them. Although ultimately unsuccessful, the raid was a bold one, bravely carried out in appalling weather.

Back at Middleton St George there was yet another VIP guest for lunch in the shape of Air Cdre HRH the Duke of Kent KG, KT, GCMC, GCVO. Gp Capt Traill assembled his crews in the locker room for an informal chat with the duke. Plt Off Michael Renaut was one of the men introduced to him, and was impressed to be asked whether he used the aircraft's brakes to counter the Halifax's notorious swing on take-off. He concluded that the charming guest was either a knowledgeable man or he had been very well briefed. The duke, who was attached to the staff of the Inspector-General of the RAF, was killed on 26 August 1942 when the Sunderland in which he was travelling to Iceland flew into a Scottish hillside in low cloud. Only Flt Sgt Andrew Jack, the 21-year-old rear gunner, survived the crash from the fifteen men on board.

At the beginning of February some long-awaited news finally arrived. The faithful but antique Whitleys of the nearby squadrons were to be phased out and 76 Squadron was to establish a conversion flight within its ranks under the command of the experienced Flt Lt C.C. 'Jock' Calder DFC. For the remainder it was to be business as usual. At least, it would have been but for the weather. Several operations were scrubbed before six aircraft finally set off towards Mannheim on the night of 11 February. It was a bitterly cold winter's night and the crews knew they were in for a long and bone-chilling night. At least the carpet of snow beneath the aircraft made navigation and target identification a little easier and eight good photographs 'provided excellent evidence that the attack was very successful'. For Michael Renaut, on his fourteenth operation but his first as captain, it was a difficult night. While on his bombing run, perhaps the most dangerous part of the operation, there were several flak bursts near his Halifax and almost immediately the port outer engine began to lose oil pressure as shrapnel severed an oil pipe. Feathering the engine, he turned for home to begin a precarious flight towards friendly territory. Flying a little above a dense cloud layer at 13,000ft and at a steady 150mph, Renaut was making slow but steady progress when his rear gunner called out that he could see a Ju88 on the starboard quarter. A nerve-tingling minute followed before it sheared off, obviously not spotting the bomber. Short of fuel, Renaut wearily eased his aircraft down on to the runway at Middleton some 7 hours and 35 minutes after he had left it.

The following day two aircraft from 76 Squadron became involved in one of the most embarrassing naval fiascos of the war. The German battlecruisers *Scharnhorst* and *Gneisenau* and the heavy cruiser *Prinz Eugen*, under the flag of Vice Admiral Ciliax, so often 76 Squadron's targets in the past, steamed out of Brest at 22:45 on 11 February and with a stray fighter, destroyer and E-boat escort sailed straight up the English Channel. It was almost 11:00 am before the Admiralty became aware that the powerful German force was just off the British coast. At 12:18 the first attack was made on them by heavy coastal batteries, but without success. At 12:45, in appalling weather conditions, six Swordfish from 825 Squadron under the command of Lt Cdr Eugene Esmonde DSO, made an extremely courageous but ultimately futile attack on the battle group. Esmonde was posthumously awarded the VC by King George VI and the remaining five survivors received between them four DSOs and a CGM. Between 14:45 and 17:00 no fewer than 242 aircraft of Bomber Command, 28 torpedo-carrying Beauforts of Coastal Command and 398 aircraft from Fighter Command scoured the seas for the ships and attacked whenever they found them. The destroyers *Campbell*, *Vivacious*, *Worcester*, *MacKay*, *Whitshead* and *Walpole* based at Harwich also made audacious attacks but no hits were obtained by any means. No. 76 Squadron's contribution was to provide search aircraft in a specified zone between 15:00 and 16:30 hours, but so murky were the conditions, with a thick cloud base at just 1200ft, that they could find no trace of the ships and returned to base.

Over a week went by before 76 Squadron was on the battle order again. Once again Bomber Command was operating in support of the Royal Navy. Fifteen aircraft, of which five were from 76 Squadron, were to bomb four airfields in Norway in order to provide a useful diversion for a Fleet Air Arm attack from the aircraft carrier *Victorious* against the *Prinz Eugen*, now sheltering in a fjord near Trondheim after sustaining damage in a torpedo attack made by HM Submarine *Trident*. The Fleet Air Arm's attack proved unsuccessful and 76 Squadron's contribution to the event was little more effective, with only two of the five aircraft making it to the wintry airfield at Lista. The crews did report hits on the airfield and the gunners had some fun shooting up the buildings. Conditions at Middleton St George had also worsened and the returning aircraft had problems spotting the snow-covered runway and judging their height accurately. Some ropey landings were made but fortunately without harm to men or aircraft. The following day 76 Squadron was withdrawn from Bomber Command's battle order to allow new equipment – early forms of GEE – to be fitted to their aircraft. A welcome ten-day period of rest and instruction followed.

On 3 March three aircraft from 76 Squadron took part in a hugely successful and even record-breaking raid. The target was in the heart of friendly territory, the massive Renault works at Billancourt, just west of the centre of Paris. By this time it was producing about 18,000 lorries a year for the German armed forces, and so was a legitimate target for a record total of 235 aircraft attacking in three waves. A large number of flares were to be dropped by the experienced crews of the first wave so that those following could clearly identify the works and bomb accurately from low level. Sqn Ldr Burdett took off from Middleton St George at 17:20 followed by Flt Sgt Lambeth and Sgt Clack. The aircraft headed south and joined up with the other aircraft due to pass over the target at an untried rate of 121 aircraft per hour. Burdett and his companions attacked on time shortly before 21:00 hours from just 3,000ft, thankful for the fact that there was no flak over the target. The official report for that night stated

the target was clearly identified and bursts and fires were observed all over the works. Bursts were seen among the buildings on the island. The gasometer and adjacent buildings were hit and a terrific blaze resulted. One 4,000lb bomb which dropped on a building to the west of the road leading from the island, caused the building to disintegrate. Photos taken at the time of the attack and by the PRU show that the attack was most successful.

Indeed it was; over 300 bombs fell on the factory, causing the destruction of 40 per cent of the buildings on the site. Production was halted for four weeks and repairs were still being

The devastation caused by the attack upon the Renault factory at Billancourt on 3/4 March 1942. *(Imperial War Museum C 4642)*

made months later. Only one aircraft was lost that night but the price paid on the ground was much greater. In all, 367 French men and women who lived in the flats around the plant were killed and a further 341 seriously injured – ironically more than twice the casualty total inflicted upon a German target on any single raid up to that time. They had chosen to ignore the air raid sirens when they went off, remaining in their homes and presumably believing it was just another false alarm caused by friendly bombers simply passing overhead.

Another very welcome respite followed although 76 Squadron continued to train whenever the winter weather allowed. This quiet period came to an abrupt end on the 27th when Wg Cdr Young led twelve aircraft and crews up to Tain; another crack at the Kriegsmarine based in Norway was clearly in the offing. Cpl Fred Healey, one of the ground crew flown to Tain, recalls landing there on an ice-covered runway, with large chunks of ice flying up and clattering against the aircraft as it rumbled and slithered to an uncertain halt. As he recalls: 'The flying ice did quite a bit of damage and I well remember having to fit a new wireless aerial to one aircraft – not an easy job. Steel wire, cold fingers and freezing wind don't mix too easily.' The hard work done out in the open by the armourers at least kept them warm.

No. 76 Squadron's role in the forthcoming attack was to drop four 500lb general purpose bombs and one 4,000lb 'dustbin' to deaden the searchlights and anti-aircraft fire from both the shore and the ship itself. Following them over the target, aircraft from 10 and 35 Squadrons were to drop 1,000lb mines as near to the *Tirpitz* as possible. The attack was timed to begin at 21:45 and Wg Cdr Young sent his Halifax rolling along the runway at 18:07 and set course for the Aas Fjord, skimming the waves at only 1,000ft, well below German radar. The navigators were able to check their route over Wick and Sumburgh Head in the Shetlands but soon after that all the aircraft became enveloped in 10/10ths low cloud that effectively put an end to any thoughts of a successful operation. The situation in the Lo Fjord, where the receding targets of the heavy cruiser *Prinz Eugen* and the pocket battleship *Admiral Scheer* lay, was no better. Although the aircraft lingered over the target area as long as possible in the hope of finding a break in the cloud, the best that could be done was to bomb unseen flak positions. Most chose to jettison their loads rather than put the lives of citizens of a friendly nation at unnecessary risk. Even then the danger was far from over. The poor weather conditions and the distance of the target from home posed dire problems for the aircraft in terms of navigation and fuel consumption. Michael Renaut described the situation: 'A quick calculation told us that we had about enough to make the coast of Scotland. I immediately throttled back and set the revs as low as I could so that we should use less fuel and we began a long haul back across the North Sea. We crossed the Scottish coast with all the petrol tanks on zero and I put down at the first aerodrome I saw – Lossiemouth.' For Flt Lt Hank Iveson the situation was the same: 'I had just told my crew to prepare for ditching when I saw the Wick beacon signalling. Landing lights on, we went straight in, cutting the inboard motors as we crossed the boundary hedge.' Almost immediately he realised with mounting panic that the brakes were not working properly and as the end of the runway came into view – with the local church and cemetery conveniently at the end of it – he swung the aircraft sharply to the right. The Halifax's notoriously weak undercarriage held for once and it bumped to a halt across the field with just 18 gallons of fuel remaining in its tanks.

One of the six aircraft lost that night was piloted by the well liked and experienced Sqn Ldr Burdett. A 'fix' was given to the W/Op by the ground tracking station at Inverness at 23:52 just as the aircraft left the Norwegian coast and a couple of hours later 14 Group reported a Halifax flying low over the cliffs at Sumburgh Head. Yet it never reached the mainland and despite the best efforts of almost twenty aircraft and two destroyers stationed nearby with the specific purpose of picking up ditched crews, no trace was ever found of the aircraft or its crew. The remainder of the aircraft remained on standby at Tain in case a better opportunity arose but they were eventually stood down and returned to Middleton St George on the 6th, having just missed a fleeting visit made by MRAF Lord Trenchard.

SHOCK AND AWE: CONCENTRATION AND MILLENNIUM

The raid on the industrial city of Essen on 10 April put 76 Squadron into the record books. Michael Renaut had taken part in the raid on Hamburg and the next morning was not too pleased to be awoken early and told to report to Gp Capt Traill immediately. More than a little apprehensive and wondering what on earth he had done, Renaut was shown into the Traill's office. There he was introduced to Air Patrick Cdre Huskinson, who had been blinded in an air raid on London earlier in the war. Huskinson explained that he had devised a new and more powerful type of explosive to be delivered to the target in a huge 8,000lb bomb

canister. Renaut was given the job of delivering the first one to Essen the following night –
or if conditions there did not permit the explosion itself to be observed, to Duisburg. As
Renaut approached his aircraft the following night, he was dismayed to see this enormous
'4 by 2' slung underneath the aircraft. It was too big to allow the bomb bay to be closed up.
Renaut did not fancy flying with so big a bomb exposed to the heavy flak he knew he would
meet over the Ruhr – that was if he ever got it as far as the Ruhr. It took the full 2,000 yards
of the runway and full emergency boost to force the lumbering Halifax into the night sky.
Once up to 1,000ft Renaut shut off the emergency boost and was alarmed to discover that
without it the Halifax headed slowly but surely earthward. It took judicious juggling of the
emergency boost and much patience to reach a paltry 8,000ft after a whole hour's flying time.
Worried about the thrashing he was giving the overworked engines and the resultant heavy
fuel consumption, Renaut plodded onwards towards the target. By the time he reached Essen
the Halifax had still only staggered up to 11,000ft, well below the normal bombing height
and well within flak range. Suddenly his aircraft was caught by about thirty searchlights and
shook violently as the flak homed in on him. All Renaut could do was lower his seat, to avoid
the glare of the lights, concentrate on his instruments and hope for the best. At 00:25 hours
the Halifax surged upwards as it was freed of its heavy load. The enormous resultant
explosion was seen to be a dull red or deep orange colour. Almost straightaway the port inner
engine burst into flames, hit by flak. The Graviner fire extinguisher did its work well and
Renaut turned for home on just three engines. The pounding from the flak continued and
one large chunk of red-hot shrapnel found its way into the leg of the mid-upper gunner,
Sgt Webb, ripping a huge gash as it went and causing him to bleed merrily. Renaut ordered
the W/Op and the bomb aimer, Plt Off 'Prof' Tim Collins, to do what they could and they
eventually bundled the stricken gunner out of his turret and attempted to render first aid, in
the form of a morphine injection. Unfortunately, in the dark confines of a bucking aircraft,
the W/Op managed to inject his own thumb with the morphine as his hands had became
hopelessly numbed by the cold as soon as he had taken off his gloves. Eventually, though,
Webb was made as comfortable as possible. Renaut could not, meanwhile, maintain height
and as he crossed the enemy batteries over Holland, his aircraft took another battering. It was
with tremendous relief that Renaut put the Halifax down at the first airfield he found,
Docking in Norfolk. The gunner was taken to hospital in Newmarket and when day dawned
Renaut and his crew counted some seventy-nine holes in their aircraft. All four engines were
so severely damaged by their ordeal that they had to be changed. After his return to
Middleton Huskinson was keen for Renaut to take another '4 by 2' but was sensible enough
to take Renaut's word for what such a load would do to the aircraft's capabilities. It was a
lucky escape for him and his crew. Flt Sgt Lambeth and his crew, however, were not so lucky,
crashing with the loss of all on board some 5km north-east of Recklinghausen.

Following a return trip to smog-shrouded Essen, the weather intervened once more,
forcing the cancellation of operations to Boulogne, St Nazaire and Dortmund. Once again,
however, something big awaited the crews of 76 Squadron. On 21 April it was announced
that a ground-crew contingent was to board a train for the long and tedious journey back to
Tain. Clearly an operation against a familiar foe – the *Tirpitz* – was on the cards. The aircrews,

again led by Wg Cdr Young, joined their colleagues on the 23rd and, after a couple of delays and postponements caused by the weather, took off and set course for the German battleship, now sheltering under the lee of the north-western bank of the Faetten Fjord, north-east of Trondheim, a target that was at the very limit of the Halifax's endurance. The aircraft of 10 and 35 Squadrons were to attack at low level – a mere 200ft – armed with mines, after ten Halifaxes of 76 and twelve Lancasters of 44 and 97 Squadrons had gone in first at 6,000ft to deliver their 4,000lb cookies and 250 or 500lb GP bombs, intended to kill and disorientate the many flak gunners known to be covering the narrow fjord. All the bombing from the first wave had to be completed by 00:30 hours, when the second wave was due to begin its low-level mine attack. It was going to be a complicated and hazardous operation, a point that seemed to be emphasised when messages were read out at the briefing from the king himself, who wished the crews 'Good luck, we will be waiting for your safe return', and from Winston Churchill, who wrote ominously, 'This mission you will be proud to tell to your grandchildren!'

Shortly after 20:00 Wg Cdr Young took off and led his squadron into the air without mishap. As it turned out, Young himself would not make it to Norway that night as two hours into the flight his starboard inner engine went U/S, forcing him to abort. His bomb-load and fuel consumption and the time restrictions of the operation made it pointless for him to continue. The rest pressed on and in decent conditions and bright moonlight it was not difficult for the navigators to map-read to the target area. Several crews reported the inspiring sight of brave and loyal Norwegians flashing V for Victory in Morse code by drawing their house curtains back and forth as the aircraft roared overhead. As the Halifaxes approached the target the sky erupted into a panorama of bright colours, blinding light and a storm of red-hot shrapnel. Already, ahead, the *Tirpitz* was disappearing beneath its protective thick and oily smokescreen. Nevertheless, the bomb-loads went down in the target area and seemed to dull the flak for a while. Flt Sgt Kenny Clack, only 19 years of age, arrived at the target slightly too late to bomb and moved on instead to attack the secondary targets *Admiral Scheer* and *Prinz Eugen*, sheltering in the nearby Lofjord. Clack's Halifax thundered over the target amid the exploding flak only to find that his 4,000lb cookie had hung up. Immediately he turned to starboard and headed round again for another run through the searchlights and exploding shells. This time the cookie dropped cleanly away and again Clack hauled the bomber hard around only to feel it shudder violently as the port inner engine was hit by flak. Worse still, the Halifax was buffeted again as it strayed into the airspace over the *Tirpitz*, providing the crew with yet more nervous moments. When the aircraft was finally out of range and things had quietened down a little, a mini conference was held, debating whether to head for neutral Sweden or Scotland, some 600 miles across the icy sea. Cheered by the thought of the destroyers stationed at intervals along the route, they opted for Scotland, with the flight engineer, Sgt Bill Lawes, anxiously scanning the fuel gauges and the temperature gauges of the three remaining engines. All the way home time seemed to stand still for the young crew. As the aircraft gradually lost height, they jettisoned anything not bolted down but ditching still looked to be the most likely outcome of the night's proceedings. Eventually a light appeared the distance. It was the airfield at Wick. However, Clack decided he could not safely land the damaged Halifax there and instead headed for

Tain, relying on there being more fuel in the tank than the gauges showed. Some 9 hours and 15 minutes after the aircraft had taken off, Clack made a successful textbook landing at Tain, only to have one engine cut out after another through lack of fuel. Closer inspection the next morning revealed over ninety holes in the Halifax. In contrast the *Tirpitz* seemed to have a charmed existence and again had escaped unscathed. Clack was awarded an immediate DFM for his courageous and skilled efforts that night. His second dickey, Ron Waite, had certainly had an interesting first operation. The official records noted that the operation was not 'completely successful': a large weight of bombs had been dropped in the target area, but smoke made it difficult to attack the primary target accurately. 'Owing to the smokescreens, it was not possible to observe the results but it is hoped that subsequent reports will disclose underwater damage that cannot be seen in daylight photographs taken after the attack.' As it happened, such hopes proved to be unfounded. A total of five aircraft fell victim to the vicious flak over the fjord. Strangely, the only aircraft loss that 76 Squadron suffered that night was more than a thousand miles to the south of Trondheim, over Dunkirk, where Sgt P.C. Morris was shot down by flak.

The weary crews were roused from their beds before noon to be greeted by the news that they were going back again that night. Full briefing was at 16:30 hours and take-off shortly after 20:00 hours. Only nine of 76 Squadron's aircraft were in a fit state to take part in the operation. The alarm sounded on the *Tirpitz* at about midnight and once again it slipped beneath its thick smokescreen, leaving the gunners on the banks of the fjord ready and waiting for the attack. Ron Waite, flying alongside Kenny Clack in the spare aircraft, believed 'the Germans must have moved in every searchlight and anti-aircraft gun in Norway to defend their prize battleship. The entire sky was swept by powerful beams, leaving no dark space of safety. The shore batteries were pumping up streams of light flak, their tracer appearing like whiplash.' Once again, however, it was acknowledged that 'the well handled smokescreen made it difficult to attack the primary target accurately though a very large weight of bombs was dropped in the target area'. From 76 Squadron only three of the crews, including Michael Renaut's, claimed to have actually seen the battleship. The *Tirpitz* seemed to have a charmed existence and once again escaped unscathed. A little ditty posted up at RAF Benson, the base from which the numerous PRU sorties to Trondheim had begun, bluntly summed up the situation in a parody of Churchill's famous words about Fighter Command: 'Re Trondheim: Never have so many gone so far for so little.' The short delay while it was decided to discontinue the attacks allowed the tired crews to relax and unwind a little in the beautiful Scottish countryside. Many remember with affection the hospitality of the local people, who often took the young airmen into their own homes for a touch of normal family life and good food. Michael Renaut, David Young, Peter Warne and New Zealander Bill Kofoed also had good food on their minds. A spot of poaching resulted in a deer being slung across the rear turret of Renaut's Halifax as it returned home on the 30th and venison was on the menu for a day or two in the mess. Perhaps this explains Wg Cdr Young's cryptic comment in the squadron's operational record book: 'All crews returned in excellent spirits having thoroughly enjoyed two successful operations and also the opportunities for sport and recreation afforded by the Scottish Highlands.'

May's account opened with an attack upon an old favourite, Hamburg, on the 3rd, conveniently the centenary of a famous large-scale fire in the city. Intending to achieve a high level of concentration and hence destruction, the crews quickly realised this was unlikely to happen as they ploughed through towering masses of dense cloud which persisted over the target area. Compelled to bomb on simple ETA calculations and guided mainly by the dull glow beneath the cloud, the crews held out little hope of success. But this time they were wrong: 113 separate fires were started and a considerable amount of the Reeperbahn and the docks area sustained severe damage. Two nights later the target was the Bosch works in Stuttgart, the first large-scale raid on this city. The aircraft headed east in good weather only to find the target completely concealed under a blanket of haze. Again the bombing was carried out largely on ETA and the sight of the glow beneath but this time it seems that a good proportion of the bombs fell on an elaborate and convincing decoy site at Lauffen, which boasted its own searchlights and anti-aircraft batteries, to the north of the city. Two nights, two different outcomes.

This busy period for Middleton St George continued on the 8th when eight aircraft were dispatched to the Heinkel works at Warnemünde. The overall plan was a complex one, with 193 aircraft due to attack in three successive waves, and it relied upon accurate time-keeping to reduce the effectiveness of the area's heavy defences. Unfortunately the timings quickly fell by the wayside and a general mêlée developed in which the large number of searchlights and flak batteries were able to put up an effective defence. The bombing accuracy was reduced by the dazzling searchlight glare and the results were only moderate. A shattering 19 aircraft, 10 per cent of the force deployed, were lost, including that of the popular Plt Off Harry Moorhouse, who died with the rest of his crew near Rostock.

The weather brought proceedings to a halt for the next ten days and a number of operations to mainly French targets were called off. One which did go ahead on 22 May to St Nazaire 'was completely foiled by poor weather conditions', according to the squadron's operational log. The 8–10/10ths cloud forced the five aircraft to jettison their loads rather than jeopardise the lives of allies in the town unnecessarily. A week later seven aircraft from 76 Squadron formed a small part of the strike force making an aerial assault on the Gnome and Rhône works and the Goodrich tyre factory and power house at Gennevilliers near Paris. The aircraft came in at just 4–5,000ft to make the most of the clear moonlit conditions and minimise civilian casualties. Reports suggested that many bursts were seen in the target areas but later PRU photos showed little actual damage. Sadly the local French population again chose to ignore the air raid sirens and 34 people were killed and 167 injured in the attack. Plt Off J.D. Anderson and his entire crew joined the casualty list when their Halifax – the only one lost that night – was hit by flak over the target and came down almost immediately. So far May, in spite of enormous efforts in terms of planning, had turned out to be a fairly typical month, with some success, some failure and some losses. It was all about to change and Bomber Command would hit the headlines around the world.

It was by now apparent to most people in Bomber Command, however tight the level of security, that ACM Sir Arthur Harris, who had been appointed AOC-in-C Bomber Command on 22 February 1942, had something special planned. On the morning of 30 May unprecedented preparations were being made all over the country for an enormous operation. Middleton St George was no exception, with all ground crews and armourers working flat out to make ready as many machines as possible. Even the aircraft of the conversion flight under Sqn Ldr Jock Calder, who was later to achieve fame with 617 Squadron as the first pilot to drop a 22,000lb Grand Slam bomb on 14 March 1945 on the Bielefeld Viaduct, were pressed into service. The briefing room was buzzing with excitement and an enormous cheer went up when the target – Cologne – and the huge numbers of bombers involved were announced. When things quietened down a little the briefing continued, closing with a message from Harris which read in part: 'The force of which you form a part tonight is at least twice the size and has more than four times the carrying capacity of the largest air force ever before concentrated on one objective. You have an opportunity, therefore, to strike a blow at the enemy which will resound not only throughout Germany but throughout the world.' No fewer than twenty-one aircraft from 76 Squadron were to take part in the biggest attack ever mounted: in all, 1,047 bombers were to take part in Operation Millennium.

Adhering to the strict timetable, and due to bomb in the third and final wave, Wg Cdr Young led his aircraft into the dark summer sky at 22:21 hours. They flew out over Spalding, Southwold and Ouddorp in the first use of the 'bomber stream' concept, where all crews followed the same route, and passed through a layer of ice-forming cloud at 10,000ft. Conditions were good, and as the third wave crossed the coast even the experienced crews

Tracer, flak and searchlights fill the skies over Cologne during the Thousand Bomber Raid of 30/31 May 1942. (Imperial War Museum C 2615)

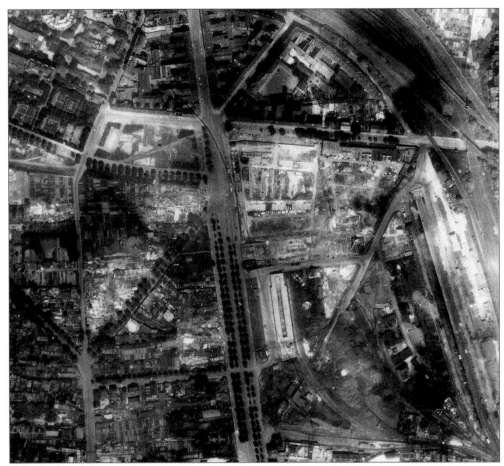

Cologne, the morning after the night before. Widespread damage is visible. *(Imperial War Museum C 2550)*

were stunned by the sight before them, as Michael Renaut later recalled: 'I simply could not believe my eyes at the Dutch coast at what I saw 100 miles ahead of us. It was a gigantic fire that an hour before had been the city of Cologne. It was on fire from end to end.' There was little need for formal navigation or precision bombing. By the time 76 Squadron's aircraft arrived over the raging inferno plumes of smoke were billowing up to 15,000ft and searchlight and flak activity had decreased markedly. Everyone on the ground and in the sky seemed thunderstruck by what was happening around them. All the aircraft returned safely to Middleton and as dawn broke the locker room resounded to the loud discussions of the night's tremendous and astounding events. Only Kenny Clack and Ron Waite's crew felt left out; the failure of their port outer engine over the North Sea had forced the disappointed crew to return to base early.

There was much back-slapping and congratulating done the next day. The local newspaper, the *Northern Echo*, headlined the 'World's biggest air raid' and all the national dailies followed suit, some edging their editions with silhouettes of bombers as they relayed the morale-boosting news that Britain *could* hit back and the RAF *could* deliver a crushing blow to the perpetrators of the Blitz. It had been a fine team effort and the squadron log offers a well merited eulogy for all concerned: 'The splendid regularity of the take-off and landings of the big number of aircraft and the courage, skill and efficiency of the aircrews concerned was equalled by the hard work, determination and enthusiasm of the ground crews who prepared the aircraft for this amazing level of serviceability.' It concluded: 'The station was privileged to take part in the biggest bomber attack on enemy targets yet made in the history of air warfare.'

The raid's effects were equally unprecedented. The pall of smoke hanging over the city was so dense that it prevented photographic reconnaissance for four days. Then the photographs revealed that some 600 acres of the city had suffered complete devastation, destroying and damaging hundreds of factories and businesses and thousands of houses. Gas, water and electricity supplies were so disrupted that the city's war output was decimated for almost two months.

Still Harris was not satisfied. Having so painstakingly assembled such an enormous force, the pugnacious and ambitious Harris was keen to make full use of it and strike again while the iron was hot. Thus on the first night of June 'Middleton St George was again privileged to take part in the second large intensity raid on enemy targets', this time the heavily defended industrial city of Essen. On this occasion the aerial armada was 956 aircraft strong, twenty-one of them provided by Middleton. Once again handsome praise was paid to the 'hard work, determination and enthusiasm of the ground staff who prepared these aircraft for the operation'. This time Wg Cdr Young, Sqn Ldr Iveson and five experienced fellow crews were to fly in the first wave to back up with incendiaries and high explosive bombs the fire-raising and flare-dropping work done by the Wellingtons of 3 Group in the newly improved 'shaker' technique. They were assigned a specific aiming point – a large shed in the middle of the Krupps works – and were due to be over the target between 00:50 and 01:05 hours. The remainder of the Middleton aircraft were to join the main force scheduled to pass over the target between 01:05 and 01:25 at 16,000ft. As the crews approached the Ruhr that night the dull red glow of the still smouldering ruins of Cologne came into view but this night was not destined to repeat the success of that raid. The ambitious plan was thwarted once again by an impenetrable layer of low cloud and industrial haze that seemed to hang permanently over the city. Many of the markers and thus most of the subsequent bombs fell to the west of the target, and as more and more crews dumped their loads faithfully on to the fires beneath, the bombing crept ever more widely throughout the Ruhr area. Damage to Essen itself was slight. Although the flak and searchlight activity was reported to be down on previous visits to this well defended target, night-fighters appeared omnipresent that night, with the Luftwaffe no doubt anticipating a follow-up to the assault on Cologne and determined to thwart it. One of the 31 bombers lost that night was from 76 Squadron. Sgt T.R.A. West, who was on his seventh operation, fell to the guns of Oberleutnant Prinz zu Sayn-Wittgenstein of III/NJG2 at 02:00 over Belgium. West and a gunner, Sgt Thompson, were killed but two of those that baled out, Sgts Wright and Norfolk, successfully evaded capture and separately made their way back to the United Kingdom via Gibraltar.

Two nights later a more typical force of 170 aircraft, including ten from 76 Squadron, made their way to Bremen. It was to prove a costly night. Sgt J.H.G. Bingham was manoeuvring his Halifax II into position for take-off at 23:03. In the dark he misaligned his aircraft with the runway and punctured his port tyre by running over a glim lamp on take-off. He made the bold decision to continue with the operation and bombed the target successfully. Upon his return at 05:00, however, he ran into difficulties and the extra drag on the port wheel caused the undercarriage to collapse. None of the crew was injured in the crash but the aircraft was severely damaged. Haze over the target once again interfered with the bombing accuracy and little damage was done to the U-boat construction yards and the Focke-Wulf factory. Nevertheless two more aircraft from Middleton were lost that night: Flt Sgt Snell's Halifax was brought down by the guns of Hauptmann Helmut Lent of XI/NJG2 over Holland, with only Sgts D. Nelson and R. Cockburn surviving, and Plt Off J.A. Philip's aircraft crashed into the North Sea just off the enemy cost leaving no survivors. It was an abrupt and depressing return to 'normality' for the crews after the excitement of the Millennium raids.

Harris was nothing if not persistent, launching two further strikes on the Krupps works in Essen. Flt Lt Renaut had an important passenger on the second attack. Standing beside his Halifax shortly before take-off at 23:07, Renaut was startled when an indistinct figure in full flying kit loomed out of the darkness and announced that he was taking the place of the second pilot for the night. It turned out to be Middleton St George's Station Commander, Gp Capt Traill, who, strictly against regulations, had decided it was time he reminded himself what things were like at the sharp end. Mindful of the status of his second pilot, Renaut took off smoothly, passed over Flamborough Head and the enemy coast at Katwijk and headed onwards to the Happy Valley. Renaut was dismayed to see ahead of him a pyrotechnic display of an intensity he had seen only rarely and he glanced across at Traill, who was surveying the scene around him with a mixture of nervousness and excitement. He was able to see at first hand the ferocity of the defences and the futility of attacking the cloud-covered city. Soon after Tim Collins had dropped the bomb-load, a Ju88 hurtled out of the searchlight glare on the starboard side, passing a matter of yards in front of the startled Renaut and Traill. It opened fire but the target was another Halifax 100 yards away to port; it quickly burst into flames and plunged earthwards in a burning tangle of metal. Neither Renaut nor Traill saw any parachutes deploy. After a tough time avoiding the seemingly never-ending searchlights and flak, Renaut politely offered Traill the opportunity to fly the aircraft home. He declined but passed Renaut a most welcome cup of his coffee from his Thermos. At the debriefing session afterwards the group captain had, perhaps, a touch more sympathy for the night Sqn Ldr Peter Warner's crew had endured. At 15,000ft over the target Warner's aircraft was illuminated by a searchlight; almost immediately others joined it, and as the aircraft twisted and turned, the flak intensified appreciably. A shell burst just under the port wing, knocking out the port outer engine and flipping the Halifax into a violent spin. For several minutes Warner heaved and strained to regain control of the heavy aeroplane. When he eventually succeeded he was at just 2,000ft. The crew quickly sorted themselves out after the hair-raising episode but the situation did not look promising. Three of the fuel tanks had been holed, one of the engines was running very roughly and all the navigator's instruments had been lost or destroyed in the spin. Best guesses and estimates were made and it was a very relieved and sorely tried crew that eventually found its way back to base and landed without further mishap.

Changes were afoot in the organisation and strength of Middleton St George. On 10 June 1942 78 Squadron, now flying Halifaxes and under the command of Wg Cdr J.B. Tait, made the short hop from Croft for a most welcome return to their former station. Croft's hastily constructed runways had become dangerously pitted by the take-offs and landings of the heavily laden aircraft and work was put in hand to repair them. The opportunity was also taken to extend the main runway from its original 1,650 yards to the more standard length of 2,000 yards. It was not to reopen until October, and in the meantime 78 Squadron would operate from Middleton. The squadron personnel were only too pleased and happily moved back into the more pleasant surroundings of an essentially peacetime-built station.

One thing that never seemed to change was the bad weather that caused the cancellation of several operations. When it did clear, as if working to a well-worn script, the target, Essen, was blanketed beneath the cloud and haze and only 16 of the 106 aircraft dispatched claimed to have identified the city. The four aircraft of 78 Squadron, like many others, turned towards the secondary target of Bonn and dropped their loads there. Three successive and inconclusive attacks on Emden followed and on the second of these Plt Off H. Norfolk of 76 Squadron failed to return, having been hit by flak over the target and then attacked by the night-fighter of Oberleutnant Prinz zur Lippe over Groningen in Holland. Norfolk immediately ordered his crew to bale out while he bravely struggled to hold the stricken aeroplane steady and level. Five men succeeded in getting out of the Halifax, with the rear gunner, Flt Sgt Salway, who had been unable to reach his parachute, holding on tightly to his friend Sgt Smith, who was well aware of the danger he was putting himself in by allowing this. Sadly the jerk of the parachute canopy opening broke the men's grip, leaving Salway to fall to his death. Smith landed safely with three other members of the crew and spent the rest of the war as a prisoner. Plt Off Norfolk's body was found within the tangled debris of the aircraft; he had bravely stayed at his post a little too long.

The next few days were to prove some of the most shattering of the whole war for many people based at Middleton St George. Most of the aircraft losses were sustained out of sight of the airfield and it was only occasionally that tragic events within view brought home the horror and dangers of the bomber campaign. Now the grim reaper was to cast a long shadow over the airfield itself. Fourteen men were to die and six more be injured in training accidents over the airfield in the space of just four days. More would be lost over enemy territory.

A little after 11:15 on the morning of 24 June, a bright but overcast summer's day, Sgt J.H.E. Bingham and his full crew were on a routine training exercise passing over the airfield at 2,000ft. Suddenly a twin-engined Airspeed Oxford from 1516 Blind Approach Training Flight, also based at Middleton, appeared out of a patch of cloud, clearly on a collision course. The pilot of the Oxford, Sgt F.R. Maron, tried to take avoiding action but there was insufficient time and the two aircraft collided and plunged to the ground near the airfield, killing all on board. Flt Sgt Stan Hauxwell recalls that morning: 'I was sitting on the top hatch of my aircraft at the time and the sight of a Halifax vertical about two fields away, that was something one could not forget. It appeared to come down so slowly and I think everyone who saw it was yelling "Pull out! Pull out!"' Sadly, there were no survivors from either aircraft. A report for the Station Commander later concluded: 'As it is necessary for training purposes for the BAT aircraft to break normal flying regulations all pilots at those aerodromes should be warned to keep a particularly sharp look-out.'

In spite of such terrible incidents, the war machine had to continue and the next day it was business as usual. In mid-afternoon Sgt R. Aston and crew took off for an air test in preparation for the night's attack on Bremen. Almost immediately things began to go wrong. One engine (or possibly both the engines) on the port side failed, causing the Halifax to wallow and stall. At only 100ft above the ground there was simply no time to do anything. The aircraft plunged to the ground and burst into flames. K.C. Haley, a radar mechanic, continues the story:

> I was with the signals van and we dashed round the perimeter track to where the crash took place. The WAAF driver and myself ran towards the burning wreck and stumbled across the body of a gunner with both legs severed. A nasty shock for both of us but the young WAAF never turned a hair. What she felt inside was another matter . . . It was not a pleasant sight and turned my stomach over.

Another man to rush to the scene was a pilot, Flt Lt Peter Dobson, who was in the watch-tower when the crash happened. He dashed down the steps into the flight van and cut straight across the grass. All the crew except for the rear gunner, Plt Off Harry Higgins DFM, were dead. He was trapped in his turret, mortally wounded, with the flames flickering ever closer towards him. Dobson immediately entered the burning aircraft and was found by the fire crews calmly and gently cradling and soothing the dying gunner.

The rest of the day proved little better. At about 20:00 that evening, while the armourers were making the final adjustments to a load destined for Bremen later that night, a cluster of incendiary bombs broke free from their rack and ignited on impact with the hardstanding. No one was seriously hurt but the Halifax was burnt out before the fire crews could bring the flames under control.

Just three days later, on the 28th, tragedy struck again in mid-afternoon. Flt Sgt S. Tackley and crew were on a training flight when one engine overheated and had to be feathered. Course was at once set for Middleton but upon arrival the aircraft lurched violently as a second engine died and it ploughed straight into the ground. All on board, including AC1 Robertson, checking some radio equipment on air test, were injured. Flt Sgt Tackley died of his wounds in Darlington Hospital the following day.

On top of all this seventeen aircraft of 78 Squadron and thirteen aircraft of 76 Squadron were part of a total force of 960 aircraft dispatched to the busy port of Bremen in the third and final Millennium raid. AVM Carr came to the station to attend the briefing and watch the take-off. Again several crews from 76 Squadron were chosen to act as markers in the first wave but one of those, Plt Off Dobson, was forced to turn off the runway as fire broke out on his aircraft. Although conditions were clear enough at high altitude for the crews to be able to see dozens of aircraft all around them, the city of Bremen was almost completely hidden beneath a layer of cloud between 3,000 and 5,000ft. Unhappy at the prospect of another wasted flight, Flt Lt Renaut pushed the nose of his Halifax steeply down and hurtled through the night sky towards the cloud at over 300mph, eventually breaking through the cloud cover at just 1,200ft. To the delight of his bomb aimer, Tim Collins, the whole of the dock area came into view, flashing beneath the speeding bomber. With his gunners blasting away frantically at the numerous searchlights and light flak positions that had now homed in on and opened up at this lone, low-level intruder, Collins released the bomb-load. Immediately Renaut hauled the stick backwards and used the aircraft's momentum to climb back up to 10,500ft and the comparative safety of the 'ordinary' flak in double-quick time. The raid as a whole was reasonably successful, causing considerable damage, but on nowhere near the scale of the Millennium raid on Cologne. A record total of 48 aircraft were lost, two of which belonged to Middleton St George. The Halifax of Sgt J.E. Meyer RCAF took off at 23:36, but no inkling as to its fate has ever been found. In addition 78 Squadron lost Flg Off J.A. Wittingham, who together with Sgt H. Dronfield died when their aircraft was shot down over the Ijsselmeer by Unteroffizier Heine Vinke of XI/NJG2 at 00:42 hours.

Two nights later eleven aircraft from 78 Squadron were scheduled to return to Bremen, only to find it shrouded in even thicker cloud than during the previous attack. The official record could only suggest that 'the crews seemed satisfied that the attack was directed against Bremen but the only results possible to observe was the reflection of fires on the clouds'. For Sgt C.G. Dennis it was long and hard night. He had taken off on time at 23:30 and came under attack from a night-fighter at 01:36 but managed to slip away virtually unscathed and continued on his way. On his homeward leg one engine began to cough and splutter and had to be feathered. The Halifax gradually began to sink earthwards and some 40 miles from the British coast Dennis ordered SOS signals to be sent. The aircraft eventually staggered over the English coast at just 200ft. As the Halifax was making its approach to Catfoss, a second engine lost power and it was with a feeling of intense relief and gratitude that Dennis finally thumped the bomber on to the tarmac at 04:35.

Two nights later Bremen was again the focus of 78 Squadron's attention. Conditions this time were a little better and considerable damage was done to the large Focke-Wulf factory, the AG Weser U-boat yard and the local gasworks. It was, however, a dreadful night for Flt Lt Woodroffe. Owing to a slight mechanical hiccup, Woodroffe took off late at 23:49 but still made it to the target on time, though outside the main bomber stream. A Ju88 picked out the lone Halifax and put in a devastating attack. The Halifax shuddered as the cannon shells hit home, but it was not all one-way traffic. The gunners managed to get in several bursts and the Ju88 was last seen diving steeply with fire streaming from its starboard engine. The euphoria of the young crew did not last long as it quickly became apparent that the Halifax had been seriously damaged in the attack. Woodroffe managed to keep the bomber in the air but found it impossible to control the landing at Docking in Norfolk. From the crash that followed only Woodroffe emerged unscathed and sadly one of the gunners, Sgt Summerfield, subsequently died of his injuries.

It had been a terrible and deadly month for the men and women at Middleton St George, and the air of exhaustion and dark gloom that hung over the airfield in the second part of the month was at complete divergence with the usual pastimes of young people and summer in times of peace. In addition, there were more great changes afoot. For some days it had been clear that something was up for 76 Squadron. Rumour and counter-rumour whirled around the station; a move was on the cards but where? When the Halifaxes were fitted with special engine filters and long-range fuel tanks, speculation rose to a crescendo. At last it was announced that the sixteen aircraft plus ground crews were to be detached from 76 Squadron and posted to Palestine for approximately sixteen days to bolster the Allied striking power in the Middle East. No. 10 Squadron based at Leeming received similar orders. Wg Cdr David Young was to lead the experienced 76 Squadron crews, leaving Sqn Ldr Jock Calder in charge of the much depleted 'home' force. Eventually all the preparations were complete and at 03:52 on 10 July Flg Off Bill Kofoed took off from Middleton St George and headed south, setting course for Gibraltar. Four days later a second group of eight aircraft led by Wg Cdr Young followed on. By 15 July the 76 Squadron detachment was operating against the enemy in North Africa, a quite different environment from anything they had experienced before. It would be mid-1943 before the members of the sixteen-day detachment returned to British shores and by then the remnants of 10 and 76 Squadrons in the Middle East had merged to become 462 (RAAF) Squadron.

In the meantime Middleton St George's contribution to the war effort would be limited mainly to 78 Squadron under Wg Cdr J.B. Tait and the inexperienced crews of 76 Squadron left behind under Sqn Ldr Calder, who immediately introduced an intensive training programme. On the 19th everything was ready for an attack on the Vulkan U-boat yards at Vegesack. One crew from 76 Squadron, that of Flt Sgt W.O. Belous RCAF, was deemed ready for operational service and was loaned to 78 Squadron for the night. Not long after take-off Belous radioed that he was returning with one engine U/S. The Halifax then came into view and crossed the airfield at 3,000ft, weaving across the sky. Soon afterwards five of the crew baled out successfully but Belous and Sgt F. Hebron died when the Halifax came down a few miles away at 01:45 near Yarm. The rest of 78 Squadron's attacking force pressed on to find the target entirely hidden beneath a blanket of cloud. Bombing was done on ETA after a Gee fix and German records state that not a single bomb landed in the town that night.

There followed three major raids against the great inland port of Duisburg on 21, 23 and 25 July. No. 78 Squadron dispatched a total of twenty-one aircraft against this target and, although the raids brought about the loss of some 31 British bombers, all of 78 Squadron's aircraft returned safely. On the 26th fifteen aircraft of 78 Squadron and three of 76 Squadron were scheduled for an attack on the well defended port of Hamburg. Flg Off Ron Waite of 76 Squadron was astonished to find his name up on the noticeboard for that night's mission with a crew he had never clapped eyes on. Perhaps it was just as well that they didn't know a lot about him: although he had several operations as second dickey under his belt, he had made just six solo landings in a Halifax and put in a grand total of 10 hours and 20 minutes night flying on all types. He did not have the best of nights.

The take-off was fortunately smooth and professional, and after an hour or so of steady flying Waite had settled down nicely and was concentrating upon the job in hand. The American

A remarkable film still showing a 4,000lb HC 'Cookie' and a 500lb bomb just after release. *(Imperial War Museum C 4525)*

drawl of his rear gunner, Plt Off Sam Glasgow, then broke into his ears informing him of the presence of an unidentified aircraft 1,000 yards astern. A few seconds later came the news that it was closing rapidly. Waite did not hesitate and threw the large bomber into a violent corkscrew manoeuvre, continuing the stomach-churning motion for several minutes before being satisfied that he had lost the mystery machine. A few minutes later flight engineer Sgt Greenwood casually mentioned that the pressure had dropped in the port inner engine, probably as a result of the corkscrew evasive action, and suggested it be feathered immediately. Waite did so at once and turned for home, realising that to press on to such a well defended target on just three engines was courting disaster. As the hydraulics were operated from the port inner engine, once the undercarriage and flaps were lowered, they could not be raised again. Having overshot on his first attempt, cursing and swearing Waite dragged the wallowing bomber round again and despite an alarming swing to port, got the aircraft down in one piece.

The remaining aircraft passed through cloud and experienced some icing but found the target area unusually clear. Considerable damage was done to several areas of the city and over 800 fires were recorded by the German authorities, 523 of them being classified as large. This successful raid cost the two squadrons based at Middleton St George one aircraft each. The Halifax of Flg Off C. Mitchener from 78 Squadron took off at 22:53 and simply vanished without trace, while that of Sgt E.J. Butt from 76 Squadron was hit by flak at 18,000ft over the target and crash-landed at Buxtehude near Hamburg, ploughing its way through a row of trees and killing three of the crew.

Two nights later orders were given for an operation to Saarbrücken. The pair from 76 Squadron and eleven of 78 Squadron's aircraft easily found the target with clear identification being possible through large gaps in the cloud. The aircraft turned for home leaving several large fires burning behind them. For Flt Sgt C.G. Dennis of 78 Squadron, his problems were about to begin. Some 80 miles from the Belgian coast his Halifax came under persistent attack from a Ju88. Cannon shells and machine-gun bullets raked the bomber from end to end and the fact that the Ju88 broke off the attack after the fourth pass with orange flames streaking from it caused only temporary good cheer. With the starboard outer and port inner engines out of action, the Halifax quickly began to lose height. Dennis struggled to keep the battered bomber in the air as long as he could in an attempt to put off the inevitable ditching for as long as possible. With great skill the pilot executed a perfect ditching and all seven of the crew were able to extricate themselves from the aircraft. After 14 long hours bobbing about in a dinghy in the English Channel, they were picked up, cold and exhausted but safe, by an Air Sea Rescue Launch. The official 4 Group report saw the operation in a very rosy light, claiming it 'provided a tonic change for the crews after a long series of well-known and heavily defended targets . . . and there is no doubt that in proportion to the numbers taking part, this is one of our best night's shows'.

A raid on Düsseldorf was scrubbed the following night but on the last day of the month the attack went ahead, with a massive 630 aircraft scheduled to take part. Eleven of these were to come from 78 Squadron and three from 76 Squadron. The attack was pressed home in excellent conditions, with the various waterways clearly visible in the moonlight. Although some of the bombing was scattered, photographs taken this time proved the crews' claims that the target area had taken a severe beating. German records confirm that it had well over 450 buildings destroyed and 15,000 more damaged, both by high explosive and by the 900 or so fires that were started. In all, 279 people were killed and a little over 1,000 injured.

Even as the crews headed for home, their job done, there was little hope of relaxation. Passing over Oudorp in Holland Ronnie Waite's Halifax came under attack from two enemy night-fighters. Several shells thumped into the cockpit and navigator's cubby hole, knocking out many of the instruments and rendering the intercom system U/S. The crew had fared little better than the hardware. Sgt Bob Pool, the navigator, had had two large channels gouged out of his wrists as a lump of shrapnel tore through the aircraft. Sgt John Miller, the bomb aimer, had been similarly wounded in the leg. No one knew what had happened in the middle and rear sections of the aircraft. Miller found the steel door across the bulkhead twisted and jammed and set about freeing it with the limited resources he had to hand. Once again the Ju88 came into attack at very close range, pulling up sharply at the last minute, thereby providing the rear gunner Plt Off Sam Glasgow with a clear shot of its underbelly. He did not squander the opportunity and poured a long burst into the aircraft, which plunged vertically out of control. By now Miller and the flight engineer Harry Greenwood had forced open the door and found the mid-upper gunner Sgt MacAuley still sitting in his turret. However, when he did not respond to sound or touch they realised something was wrong. They swiftly cut through his harness and gently lowered him to the floor, where they discovered that he was beyond all help. Half his head had been ripped off by a bullet or shrapnel. Having received first aid from the W/Op Sgt Geddie, the navigator Bob Pool insisted on doing without morphine in order to guide the stricken bomber home by the stars. Eventually the English coastline came into sight and it was decided that the best chances of survival lay in baling out. Waite held the aircraft steady while the others baled out before hurling himself out of the hatch, leaving the Halifax to crash in the Essex countryside at 03:45. Waite himself landed safely and having apologetically awoken Hannah and Edith Cox, two elderly sisters who lived in Bacon's End Cottage, was soon enjoying the inevitable cup of tea. Later that morning, as he was being driven to a railway station to begin his long journey north, Waite decided he could do with some stronger refreshment and called in to the nearby Blacksmith's Arms – only to find several members of his crew already there. The newspapers got hold of the story and the *Daily Mirror* recounted the tale in dashing terms under the headline 'Bomber Crew Bale Out – meet in the village pub'. The body of Sgt MacAuley was retrieved from the wreckage and buried in St Oswald's churchyard, Longton.

The same fate almost befell Sgt Ray Edghill, on his first operation as navigator in Sgt Tait's Halifax. On the return journey from Düsseldorf, Tait complained about the sluggish handling of his aircraft. This poor engine performance and some soggy handling characteristics forced him to make not one, not two, but three attempts at guiding the Halifax down to the runway at Middleton. As the aircraft taxied to its position at dispersal, it was greeted by the ground crew waving their arms frantically above their heads. Far from being friendly, the men were trying to warn the crew to be careful and evacuate the aircraft as soon as possible. A 4,000lb cookie had hung up and was still firmly and menacingly suspended in the bomb bay. Stan Hauxwell recalled: 'We didn't know it was there! Our flight engineer should have checked but – one of those things. The CO [of 78 Squadron] Willie Tait had done something similar earlier – I believe he got a medal. We were lucky we didn't get court-martialled!' It was an eventful end to an already eventful month.

August began with the kind of summer weather that Britain is famous for: dull, damp, unpleasant and cloudy, but Wednesday 5 August was a special day for the remaining members of 76 Squadron as Leonard Cheshire arrived at Middleton St George to take over command of the squadron. Cheshire, who was promoted to the rank of wing commander within a couple of days, already had an impressive track record and an enviable reputation. Much has been written about this remarkable man but what follows is the impression he made upon a young pilot on the airfield at the time, Plt Off Ron Waite:

His arrival stimulated our enthusiasm like a breath of fresh air. Without impairing his position as CO and avoiding any cliques, he had the ability to be friendly with those under his command. It would have been a mistake to assume, because of his youth and camaraderie, that he lacked resolution. He was a fair and firm disciplinarian, always looking for the highest standards of efficiency.

Cheshire was, in fact, to have several days to settle in before his first operation with the squadron on the 11th.

Bad weather thwarted the first two planned attacks upon Osnabruck but the third attempt, on 9 August, proved successful. Of the seven aircraft of 78 Squadron bombed-up and ready that night, only four made it into the air. The remaining three were held up by an unusual and dangerous mistake. Sgt Roy Goode, an ex-Halton Apprentice who had remustered as a flight engineer, recalls:

> One evening we went out to fly operations and as the electrician connected the batteries, the bombs started to fall off our aircraft. He realised what was happening and pulled the battery lead off so that only the wing bombs fell. These were incendiary bombs and started to burn and set fire to the tyres and bomb doors. The brakes were released and the aircraft pushed on to the grass away from the burning bombs. The fires on the tyres and bomb doors were put out and the bombs on the hardstanding covered in foam and left to burn out. We were lucky as there were several 1,000lb bombs in the bomb bay and the flames were all around them.

It could have been much worse but the delay caused was sufficient to prevent the bombers waiting to take off from being able to catch up the rest of the aircraft and their part in the operation was scrubbed. Conditions over the target were reasonable but for the first time the German radar operators succeeded in partially jamming GEE, thereby causing a considerable amount of unexpected confusion. The bombing proved to be scattered though some damage was caused to the busy dock area. It was to be the last operation for Sgt W.A. Wilson and his crew, who took off from Middleton St George shortly after midnight and failed to return. Three bodies, those of Sgts Ironmonger, Howard and Poter, were washed up along the Danish and Dutch coasts but of the others there was no trace.

The next raid, on 11 August, proved to be one of the most costly that Middleton St George would ever experience when 78 Squadron lost four of the seven aircraft that took off. Leonard Cheshire, the new CO of 76 Squadron, was the sole representative of his squadron. The target was the chemical works in Mainz and conditions were clear and ideal for bombing. Sgt Tait, with Ray Edghill and Stan Hauxwell among his crew, took off at 22:06 and were still over the UK when the fun began. A lone Luftwaffe intruder pounced on the unsuspecting Halifax and raked it with cannon and machine-gun fire. Sgt Butler in the rear turret reacted immediately, got off a quick burst and shouted for his pilot to break to port and begin the stomach-churning corkscrew evasion technique. For 20 heart-stopping minutes the deadly game of cat and mouse continued until, frustrated, the German pilot gave up the chase and went off in search of easier prey. By this time the battle-scarred Halifax was considerably off course. Stan Hauxwell takes up the story: 'We lost an engine over the French coast and its companion on the starboard side decided it was quitting too. Unable to maintain height we turned back.' The shaken crew jettisoned their bomb-load and headed north, landing back at Middleton St George about midnight.

The remainder pressed on to find the target almost clear and a concentrated attack in progress. The squadron log recorded that 'the impression was formed that, including the 1000-bomber raid on Cologne, this was the most concentrated attack yet carried out'. For once the impression was supported by considerable photographic evidence of the damage caused, much of which was collected by Leonard Cheshire himself, who coolly orbited the target for much of the raid taking photographs at periodic intervals. While his aircraft emerged from the flak barrage unscathed, others were not so fortunate. Flg Off D. Kingston's damaged aircraft eventually came down near Mean in Belgium, killing all but two of the crew, and all of Flt Sgt J. Fleetwood-May's crew perished when their Halifax crashed into the North Sea. Only one of the bodies, that of Plt Off J.F. Myrick, was ever recovered. The crew of Sgt E.G.S. Monk fared better, with all but two, Sgts J. Peart and J.A. Mitchell RCAF, surviving to become POWs. Two of them, Sgts Monk and Kimber, showed great determination and imagination in their attempts to escape. Knowing that RAF personnel were treated as high-risk and valuable prisoners, and were therefore generally subject to even tighter supervision than usual, they swapped identities with two sappers by the names of Simmons and Maynard. It took until January 1945 for the airmen to make a successful break from their camp in Poland. After several days spent tramping eastwards through the bleak Polish winter landscape, often finding shelter in barns and sheds, the intrepid airmen eventually met up with the vanguard of the advancing Soviet army. Having convinced the Russian soldiers of their identities, they were passed on to the British Embassy in Moscow and on 31 March 1945 Monk and Kimber set foot on British soil again, some two and a half years after leaving it.

There was to be another evader among a crew lost that night. Flt Sgt A.E. Fay was a W/Op in WOII W.E. Lunan's (RCAF) crew. The Halifax had already turned for home when three heavy shells burst simultaneously under the aircraft, causing the port inner engine to catch fire and the outer to stop. The bomb aimer, Sgt Hower, suffered several wounds to his leg. The stricken aircraft plunged earthwards, barely under control, and as the crew attempted to bale out to safety a night-fighter, attacking from the front, delivered a brief but devastating attack, raking the bomber with cannon and machine-gun fire. Finding that the intercom was out of service, Lunan, an experienced pilot on his 26th operation, ordered Fay to pass the order to bale out to the other crew members while he fought to keep the Halifax under some sort of control. This brave and courageous act was to cost the young pilot his life. Having passed on the order, Fay launched himself into the darkness barely 1,000ft above the Belgian countryside. Although he twisted his ankle on landing, he quickly buried his parachute and headed away from the crashed aircraft, now burning fiercely a couple of miles away, in an attempt to avoid the search that he knew would follow. His luck was in and, after only a couple of hours of painful hobbling, he came into contact with some brave and friendly locals, who passed him on to the local Resistance unit. A few days later he was taken to Brussels and spent an interesting week there watching and logging the aircraft using Evere airfield, information that he duly passed on to RAF Intelligence upon his return. He was quickly passed along one of the escape lines through France and successfully crossed the Pyrenees into Spain, where he was interned for a while in the squalid holding camp at Miranda. Released from there by the efforts of the British Embassy, he returned to Britain via Gibraltar in the autumn of 1942. Following his successful evasion he returned to his native Canada, where he took a pilot's course and gained his wings in October 1943 – a double notable achievement. The raid on Mainz, though successful, had been very costly. Of the 56 men who left Middleton St George that night, 16 were killed. Of those shot down, only one evaded capture. Eleven others were captured, although two subsequently escaped. The mood on the airfield was subdued the next morning as the scale of the losses became apparent. Stan

Hauxwell recalls the sense of shock and despair that pervaded the atmosphere as the bad news spread: 'Being back so early we stayed in the mess. We were awakened by a flight sergeant bursting into the room crying "They are all gone, Sir, they are not coming back. Mr Kingston, Mr Fleetwood-May, they're all gone."' A signal arrived from Bomber Command HQ at High Wycombe at noon the following day giving all members of 78 Squadron, aircrew and ground crew alike, a week's leave.

Middleton St George suffered a loss of a different kind on the 13th when the Station Commander, Gp Capt Traill, relinquished command and was posted as an adviser to the Director of Air Bombardment USAAF. Shortly afterwards he was posted again, this time to a small air staff under the command of Air Cdre Lawson attached to HQ V Army Corps in Tunisia. Traill had been a popular commander, who had skilfully guided the airfield though its difficult birth pangs and early days on operations. His farewell eulogy in the station log is much more than merely formulaic pleasantries:

> The departure of Gp Capt Traill was the occasion of a display of affection and esteem from all ranks who felt that, not only had the station lost a brilliant commander, but the personnel throughout had lost a trusted friend. Gp Capt Traill's interest in the welfare of the station and his close association with the personnel in their games, recreation and leisure hours, had endeared him to everyone and he left with the warmest wishes of the station for his success in his new job.

Traill had begun his career as a naval cadet, seeing action for the first time off the Dardanelles in 1915, before transferring to 20 Squadron, Royal Flying Corps, with which he served throughout the Somme offensive and beyond. Subsequently he went on to become an air vice-marshal. He was succeeded at Middleton by Wg Cdr (later Gp Capt) W.N. McKechnie GC.

Middleton St George's war resumed on the 20th with three aircraft being dispatched to Dijon and Lyons on a Nickel raid. Ron Waite, flying on his first operation since his eventful trip on 31 July, set off to Dijon with a crew he had never flown with before. It was a long trip, some 1,300 miles in total, and was to serve as a 'live' air test to establish the accuracy of Gee over long distances. Not very reassuringly, the Squadron Navigation Officer advised his crew to maintain normal navigational techniques and procedures in case the high-tech equipment broke down! Only a couple of searchlights waving vaguely in their direction marked the aircraft's passage into enemy territory and Waite maintained his course serenely, patiently waiting for new instructions from the navigator and the new wonder box. He flew on deeper and deeper into enemy territory, growing more anxious by the minute. His patience eventually wore thin when the snow-capped peaks of the Alps came into view, shining in the faint moonlight. The navigator responded with commendable swiftness, turning the aircraft around and successfully navigating his way to the target – without the dubious aid of the new technology. Even so dawn was breaking as the Halifax thundered over the slumbering port of Le Havre and nearby Dieppe where the Canadians had fought so valiantly just a couple of days earlier. Short of fuel, Waite touched down at 10 OTU's base, Stanton Harcourt in Oxfordshire, only just managing to stop before crashing through the boundary fence on the short

1,000-yard runway. With the return journey to Middleton St George added on, the flying time for the operation was a mammoth 9 hours and 20 minutes. To make matters worse for the tired and frustrated pilot, an interview shortly after landing with 76 Squadron's CO Cheshire left him in no doubt that it was the captain's responsibility to ensure that any operation went smoothly, whatever the circumstances. Whether because of this operation or not, it was to be Waite's last from Middleton St George, as he was posted a couple of days later to 1658 HCU, Riccall. The move did him no harm in any case, as he later rose to the rank of squadron leader and enjoyed a successful career in Bomber Command.

Although only a few people knew it at the beginning of the month, September 1942 was to prove a major turning-point for Middleton St George. The predominantly British 76 and 78 Squadrons were to leave and the last day of the month would see the arrival of 419 Squadron RCAF to begin a new era for Middleton St George as a base for Canadian airmen. Nevertheless the month began as many had before it, with an operation against the marshalling yards in Saarbrücken. The crews reported that they had been able to identify the yards visually and an 'exceptionally close concentration of bombing' during the raid caused numerous enormous explosions and vast fires that were still visible for 100 miles of the return journey. As they landed that night the weary crews at least had the consolation of a job well done. They would have been very surprised and dismayed to find out that not a single bomb had fallen on the target of Saarbrücken. The Pathfinders had erroneously identified as the target the small town of Saarlouis, 13 miles to the north-west and situated on a similar river bend. The Main Force then bombed the markers, devastating the unsuspecting town. Casualties, though heavy, were limited by the fact that many people had been able to take shelter in the strong concrete bunkers of the Siegfried Line which skirted the town. For Plt Off H.G. Sherwood this error was immaterial. He died as his Halifax fell to the guns of Hauptmann Wilhelm Herget I/NJG4 at 03:30 hours over the de Blankaart nature reserve in Belgium. Fortunately the remainder of his crew survived to be taken prisoner.

The following night ten aircraft from 76 and 78 Squadrons were in action as part of a 200-strong force that carried out a highly successful attack upon Karlsruhe. This time the newly formed Pathfinders made no mistake, illuminating the target accurately, and a huge conflagration was seen spreading in all directions with frightening speed through the dock area along the Rhine and across the rest of the town.

Of course, there was no such thing as a routine raid. On 6 September a total of eight aircraft – five from 78 Squadron and three from 76 Squadron – took off and set course for the major inland port of Duisburg. Once again there was a thick blanket of haze over the city, which the crews felt prevented accurate bombing. Nevertheless, German records show that they considered it the heaviest raid upon the city so far, with 114 buildings destroyed, 316 severely damaged and a fatal casualty list with 86 names on it. Although none of the eight aircraft lost came from Middleton St George, the night was not without its problems for the aircraft based there. Sgt Al Moir picked a bad night to have problems in closing his bomb doors. The resultant increase in drag made his Halifax hard to control, with the port wing constantly trying to drop, requiring several long hours on the return journey of constant effort on the part of himself and his second pilot to hold it steady. His second pilot that night was none other than Gp Capt McKechnie, Middleton's new Station Commander. Likewise, Sgt Bill Richardson had an interesting first operation as captain. While approaching the Ruhr his aircraft came under determined attack from a night-fighter which managed to score several hits before losing contact with the vigorously corkscrewing bomber. Having checked that everything was working just about all right, Richardson gamely resumed his course only to find his aircraft illuminated by several searchlights soon afterwards. Unable to shake them off, despite twisting and turning through the night sky, Richardson and his crew braced themselves for the barrage of flak that they knew would soon follow. It buffeted the Halifax severely, causing further damage, before the aircraft eventually managed to claw its way out of the flak and slip back into the welcoming embrace of the dark night sky once again. The crew pressed on to Duisburg to complete their mission and brought the battered Halifax safely back to RAF Wattisham after a very determined and trying night's work. The crew was commended for remembering 'what they were told and in spite of all temptation to the contrary, they did not lose height. It was a fine show on the part of a new crew.'

> An unintentionally successful night resulted from a raid upon Frankfurt on the 8/9 when, owing to a mistaken identification of the target by the early flare-droppers, a very heavy concentration was achieved over the Russelheim area where a very large Opel works are situated. This was a target well worth destroying as they were probably big producers of tanks and other MT.

So 4 Group records described the missing of Frankfurt by some 15 miles. Nevertheless it proved a costly attack for the men from Middleton St George. Sgt J.E. Nicholson of 76 Squadron, flying with his regular and highly experienced crew, was still over Yorkshire when the photoflash prematurely ignited in the bomb bay, causing a serious fire to break out. Nicholson quickly realised he had no alternative but to make an immediate forced-landing wherever he could. The Halifax did not make it. A few seconds before the pilot could get the aircraft down on to the ground, it erupted in an enormous explosion, hurling debris over a wide area around Haltby, a few miles east of York. All the crew were killed instantaneously and what was left of their remains was collected for burial. The only positive thing to come out of this unfortunate fatal accident was the recommendation made to the Court of Enquiry that photoflashes should no longer be stored within the bomb bay. The rest of the crews passing overhead probably saw the funeral pyre below, a chilling reminder for one and all of what might lie ahead for them that night.

It was to be quite some time before some of the crew flying with Flt Lt P.H. Tippetts-Aylmer DFC were to stand on British soil again. W7782 EY-C was the first aircraft to take off from Middleton St George that evening. Although it had just been fully overhauled, there had been no time to carry out a full air test before the operation proper and while it was still over England the voice of the rear gunner, Plt Off E.W.T. Gibbs, crackled over the intercom to inform his captain that one of his guns was U/S. Tippetts-Aylmer, an experienced operational pilot, decided that this was insufficient reason to abort the mission and pressed on. As the aircraft crossed the enemy coast at 15,000ft between Ostend and Dunkirk the

Canadian mid-upper gunner announced that his turret would no longer revolve properly, thereby raising the spectre of potentially lethal blind spots in his observation and vision. Again Tippetts-Aylmer accepted the calculated risk and pressed on. At 22:40, when flying at 18,000ft over Namur, Plt Off Gibbs suddenly shouted 'Turn to port' over the intercom but cannon and machine-gun fire was already raking the bomber, destroying the intercom system and causing the incendiary bombs to ignite in the bomb bay. The night-fighter put in three more successful attacks before Tippetts-Aylmer gave the inevitable order to bale out. Pausing only to clear the escape hatch, Sgt J.A. Winterbottom, the bomb aimer, quickly hurled himself out of the aircraft and into the eerily quiet blackness, swiftly followed by the W/Op, Sgt R. Brown, whose last act in the stricken Halifax was to hand the pilot his parachute. Another Canadian, navigator Sgt Branden, had calmly cleared his table and packed away his maps before becoming wedged in the escape hatch. In normal circumstances the spectacle he presented might well have been a humorous one but these were far from normal conditions. It was only with the greatest difficulty that he managed to extricate himself and fall clear. The flight engineer, Sgt Hodge, swiftly followed but, unfortunately, he was to be the last to escape from the doomed bomber. As the four men gently drifted through the chilly night air, they watched their aircraft hit the ground and burst into flames as the bombs exploded. Each hoped desperately that no one was left inside it.

Sgts Winterbottom and Brown landed close to one another about 4 miles south of the village of Andenne in Belgium. Quickly burying their parachutes, the pair set off at a brisk pace away from the general area of the crash site, keeping a sharp look-out for both Germans and their comrades. Not long afterwards it grew light and the pair cautiously approached a man who was walking through the fields. He quickly worked out who the bedraggled strangers were and was already well enough informed to tell them that one of their crew was in hospital with a broken leg, another, like themselves, was still at large but the bodies of the three others had been found among the wreckage. It soon became apparent that the man was not simply wandering around the countryside at dawn by chance; he was a member of a local Resistance unit out searching for the downed airmen. Events moved rapidly and the pair found themselves moved efficiently as 'parcels' along the well organised Comète escape line. By 4 September they had crossed the Pyrenees into Spain, where they were detained before being transferred to Gibraltar. On 19 October Winterbottom and Brown safely made it back to the UK where, after a thorough debriefing, they enjoyed a well earned period of leave.

Once again the personnel at Middleton St George had little time to grieve over their losses. Orders came through from Bomber Command HQ that seven aircraft from 78 Squadron and five from 76 Squadron were to take part in a large raid on Düsseldorf. The crews were delighted to find the Pathfinder's new markers, a converted form of a 4,000lb bomb nicknamed 'Pink Pansies', clearly visible through the persistent industrial haze. All parts of the city were heavily hit, as was the neighbouring town of Neuss. Much damage was caused to industrial, commercial, public and residential properties and production was significantly reduced. In all 132 people were killed and a further 116 still counted as missing two days later. The price paid by Bomber Command for this success was, however, heavy. A total of 33 aircraft – or 7.1 per cent of the attacking force – were shot down. One of them, flown by Plt Off C.J. Stevenson, came from Middleton St George. It crashed somewhere over the target area, leaving no survivors. It was to be the last aircraft from 78 Squadron lost while operating from Middleton St George.

Although it was hardly thought of as anything special on the day itself, 16 September proved to be a red-letter day in the history of Middleton St George as it marked the final operational sortie made by a British squadron from the airfield in the Second World War. Fittingly, the target chosen by Bomber Command for that night was an old favourite, the industrial city of Essen. Shortly after 20:30 the stillness over the airfield was shattered by the throaty roar of the thirty-six engines powering the nine aircraft, five from 78 Squadron and four from 76 Squadron, that were destined to take to the hostile skies that night. In two of the aircraft mechanical problems were discovered that were sufficiently serious to prevent them from taking off. The rest made their way around the perimeter track and patiently waited one behind the other, at the end of the main runway, awaiting the green light to take off. One by one the heavily laden aircraft began to trundle down the runway before gathering sufficient momentum to lumber into the darkening night sky, anxiously watched by a sizeable audience of ground crew and WAAFs until they were out of sight.

As usual, Essen was buried beneath a thick blanket of smog and haze and, in spite of the best efforts of both the Pathfinders and the Main Force crews, the bombing became scattered, with explosions rocking adjacent towns like Bochum and Wuppertal. However, a considerable weight of bombs did fall upon the target causing far more damage to Essen than most previous raids. The vast Krupps works was hit by a number of high explosive bombs and an impressive total of 33 large and 80 medium fires were left blazing throughout the city as the bombers turned for home. The German defences were even more effective than usual, taking a fearsome toll. Some 39 aircraft, a massive 10.6 per cent of the attacking force, were shot down that night either by flak or by the increasingly effective night-fighters. Among them was Australian Plt Off Campbell and his crew who had had a very dicey do over Bremen just three days earlier, enduring a long-running duel with a very persistent night-fighter. This time there was no escape and on the return leg over northern France the Halifax was attacked and shot down by Oberleutnant Hubert Rauh of XI/NJG4. There were no survivors.

Back on the airfield everyone was busily packing up, preparing to move the aircraft, servicing equipment and personal possessions. It was a mammoth task. Lorries were loaded up with spares and machinery, creating large amounts of bumf and an enormous headache for the over-worked Adjutant and the administrative officers and staff. Everything, in true service tradition, had to be accounted for or its absence, for whatever reason, adequately explained. Friendships were broken and hundreds of people uprooted from their familiar surroundings and many a pint was sunk in remembrance and tribute. The destination for both squadrons was the comfortable and well established pre-war station at RAF Linton-on-Ouse, some 40 miles further south in Yorkshire. The 76 Squadron Conversion Flight, having just returned to Middleton St George after a spell at nearby Dalton, was posted to Riccall in Yorkshire, where on 7 October 1942 it merged with 10, 102 and its old friend 78 Squadron Conversion Flights to become 1658 Heavy Conversion Unit. Middleton St George's new owners were to be Canadians, who were destined to make a great impact on both the war and the local area.

The station log for 18 September 1942 recorded the tumultuous change in prosaic yet proud terms:

> In fulfilment of the policy of creating an all-Canadian Group manned by all-Canadian Squadrons, the departure of 76 and 78 Squadrons from Middleton St George to Linton-on-Ouse took place today. Thus was broken a long record of achievement in which this station felt justly proud. 78 Squadron opened operations from here in April 1941 and from both Middleton St George and Croft put up some very fine operations. 76 Squadron was born on the Station and was the first Halifax Squadron to operate from Middleton St George. Under successive squadron commanders, this squadron maintained a grand efficiency and both from home base and advance bases, created for themselves a splendid reputation. The departure of these squadrons took place in an atmosphere of sadness and regret, marking, as it did, the end of a phase in the life of the station; the end of an effort into which had been crowded so much enthusiasm, energy, courage and "guts". So we look forward to the arrival of new squadrons and a new phase, fortified by the memories of the departed giants of 76 and 78 Squadrons.

It was a fitting summary and a moving tribute to two squadrons that had courageously fought their way through the long and dangerous early days of the Strategic Air Offensive with considerable distinction. Their aircraft had ranged far and wide over enemy territory and Occupied Europe, doing their best to hinder and hamper the Nazi war machine. Night after night Middleton St George had dispatched men to face the increasingly formidable defences over targets like Bremen, Kiel, Essen, Mannheim, Wilhelmshaven and Cologne in Germany, St Nazaire, Brest, Le Havre and Dunkirk in France and the *Tirpitz* up in frozen Norway. Nor were the night-fighters and flak the only threats and dangers to the young men aboard the aircraft; often the natural elements – cloud, wind, electrical storms, fog and even the darkness itself – conspired to make life difficult, sometimes impossible, for the crews in their attempt to return safely to the airfield they called home. Almost a hundred aircraft that had taken off from Middleton St George had been lost. The overwhelming majority of the 550 or so young men in those aircraft had been killed, each one representing a shattering personal tragedy for the friends and families involved. Only a lucky few survived to spend the war as prisoners, spending many months in increasingly unpleasant conditions behind barbed wire. Indeed, it is all the more remarkable that in the face of such losses – and Middleton St George had its fair share of bad nights – those young men, many of them still in their teens, and each in his own way fighting his own personal battle, found the courage to carry on night after night and do what they perceived as their duty for their family, friends and country. It was, perhaps, patriotism in its purest form and it is surely worthy of the highest praise and admiration of those of us in successive generations who, fortunately, have not been called upon to serve in the same way. It is not surprising, therefore, that among the aircrew and ground crews, who, although not faced directly with danger each night, worked extremely long hours in often difficult conditions in support of Middleton St George, there was a bold, vivacious spirit and a strong feeling of *carpe diem*. For who could tell when it all might come to an abrupt end?

CHAPTER 3

Life on the Airfield

Middleton St George was to be home for several hundred men and women at any one time during 1941–2. For some their stay was all too brief, either because of the unfathomable vagaries of the posting system or because of violent death or injury. But others were able to stay a little longer and put down roots, at least those of a service kind, and like hundreds of thousands of other servicemen and women they settled down to make the best of it. As far as an operational airfield went, Middleton St George was a comfortable and well equipped one, having been built to basic pre-war designs and specifications. However, the day-to-day running and working of the airfield offers a snapshot of life on a Bomber Command station that will be instantly recognisable to those who served on other similar stations. It therefore provides a fascinating vignette and portrait in miniature of service society at a crucial time in Britain's history.

It would be unreasonable to suggest that there was no friction or tension from time to time among the inhabitants of a fairly closed world, thrown together by random chance and fortune. Petty theft, brawls and minor infractions of the law were common. Nevertheless, the relationships between those who lived and worked at Middleton St George were remarkably harmonious, with most people linked by a common purpose and united in their desire to do their bit. Many friendships forged there – mostly over only a brief period – have endured for decades and reflect the passionate and extraordinary nature of life on an operational RAF station during the war. The tumultuous events through which those men and women lived have left an indelible print upon their minds and characters ever since and form a strong and common bond between them. Yet such is human nature that however unusual or extraordinary the occurrences and experiences, they are usually normalised and made to seem ordinary and routine, part of everyday life – at least to those who were there.

Men and women arrived at Middleton St George from training schools all over the United Kingdom. For most it was their first operational posting and they often arrived with the usual heady mixture of apprehension, bewilderment and excitement. In the days before widespread and almost instantaneous travel, few probably had a clear idea of where Middleton St George – or even County Durham – actually was, let alone what it might be like. At the time the north-east of England was, in many ways, misrepresented and had little going for it in terms of reputation. It was cold, windy and full of coal mines, pit heaps and heavy industry. Most young men and women upon arrival were pleasantly surprised by the green and relatively rural surroundings.

The main point of assembly and arrival was the Victorian splendour of Darlington railway station. From here, new arrivals were often driven the 5 or 6 miles to Middleton St George itself in one of the station's 3-ton trucks, clutching the sides of the vehicle and their bulky kit with equal tenacity. For others, their first sight was less salubrious, arriving at the tiny Dinsdale Halt branch line station with its single windswept platform. At least it was closer and offered the opportunity for a pre-arrival inspection of the airfield as the railway line ran along the perimeter fence. Many eyes no doubt eagerly scanned the unfamiliar surroundings that were to become their home for an indefinite period, as the young men and women of all social classes, ranks and trades made their way along the narrow roads through the typical south Durham villages of Middleton St George and Middleton One Row, eventually arriving at the airfield known locally as Goosepool.

What happened next was largely dictated by the rank the new arrival held. Plt Off Ron Waite's arrival on 2 January 1942 is quite representative of the treatment afforded to officers. He arrived at Dinsdale shortly before midnight following a gruelling journey from Inverness that had taken almost 24 hours. Groping around in the near pitch black, he managed to stumble across a telephone box just outside the station and called the Guard Room to arrange transport to the airfield, being uncertain as to how to get there. A few minutes later a perky WAAF pulled up in a small van and whisked him swiftly along the unlit lanes to the airfield. The first point of call was the aforementioned Guard Room, where no one had any record of his imminent arrival or, indeed, his very existence. Once all the paper work had been duly completed, the same WAAF then safely guided the van through the stygian darkness to the officers' mess:

> The entrance was the most imposing I had seen since I left Cranwell, with its pillars and lofty, mahogany-framed doors. The centrally heated warmth inside was as welcome as it was unexpected. The whole place seemed deep in slumber. The row upon row of black, enamelled coat-hooks in the cloakroom were mostly empty, apart from a service coat here and there. After hanging up my own coat, I wandered into the ante-room. The large hide armchairs were unoccupied and popular magazines lay on the sturdy square tables. One or two RAF-crested bone china coffee cups and saucers were left on a side table.

Having found his way to his room and noted that his room-mate was absent, Waite fell asleep. He was awoken at about 07:00 by the sound of crockery clattering in the dining hall. The two main corridors of the building converged in this well decorated, large and airy room where there were a number of neatly laid-out trestle tables and benches. Breakfast itself was taken from a serving hatch along one wall.

The 21-year-old navigator Plt Off Geoffrey Whitten and his newly graduated crew arrived a little earlier in the day in early September 1942 but they were equally impressed with their new surroundings:

In spite of the new entrance, the elegant style of the original officers' mess is easily recognisable today. (C.J. Archer)

It was a daunting prospect to step from the relative safety of training into the thick of the bomber war. For the moment, we were taken up with the joy of at last finding ourselves on a pre-war station after trekking from one hutted camp to another during our various training courses. This looked, indeed, a very civilised place from which to go to war. The three commissioned crew members, pilot, bomb aimer and myself, were even more impressed when shown their quarters in an officers' mess that bore some resemblance to a four-star hotel (my only acquaintance with which hitherto had been the commandeered establishment I'd briefly guested at during initial training at Torquay and Bournemouth). There were spacious and peaceful ante-rooms, with comfortable armchairs and a supply of newspapers and magazines, as well as a couple of bars where one could be politely served with beers or spirits, 'during hours' of course. Above all, there was a dining room whose splendour was only excelled by the food served therein. Its rather splendid fittings included a named pigeon-hole for each officer's napkin (some of us had to learn not to call it a serviette!).

We were, remember, already three years into the war and rationing was widespread and becoming severe. Yet the standard lunchtime buffet, spread out the full length of one wall, could hardly have been surpassed at the Savoy in peacetime. Tactful enquiries among the older residents as to how this could be were met with winks, nose-tappings and mystifying hints about the connections and activities of the Mess Committee.

This 'palace on the Tees' was to be the best billet Whitten had during his five and a half years in the service, a fact emphasised by his next posting to Riccall near Selby. 'We arrived at a rural slum, with living quarters all too recently risen from the alluvial mud and runway concrete that looked as if it needed another week or two to set. Thirty minutes' flying time from Middleton St George but it could have been a light year away.' Of course, some did their best to soften the blow when it became known just how bad conditions at Riccall were. H.D. 'Roger' Coverley, a Halifax pilot with 78 Squadron, arrived at Middleton St George a couple of weeks before their departure for Riccall in September 1942. He recollects 'some wild parties prior to our leaving Middleton, in which items of furniture, such as easy chairs and so forth, were removed from a hotel in Darlington and flown down to Riccall (where I completed my training) to embellish the Nissen-hut mess. I recall sitting in the back of a Halifax – piloted, I believe, by "Bunny" Bunclarke – and holding on to a potted palm "acquired" during the previous night's carousing.'

As Middleton St George expanded operationally, the number of personnel increased considerably. The number of officers, for example, exceeded that which the mess could accommodate and quite a few were passed across to a requisitioned house called Dinsdale Hall. Originally built for the Thompson ship-building family in 1895, it was now owned by D. Denis Williams, the managing director of Henry Williams Ltd, a local engineering firm. He was a keen supporter of the RAF, having already donated the money required to buy a Spitfire. A large and pleasant Tudor-style house, it was set in its own landscaped grounds and situated midway between Middleton St George and its satellite airfield Croft. In turn, this too became full and Stan Hauxwell remembers that in 1942 some of 78 Squadron were obliged to 'live out' at Dinsdale Hall: 'I was in a hut on the front lawn; the atmosphere was generally damp and sleep was not easy to come by.' But being several miles from the airfield, the billet did have an air of tranquillity and relaxation about it. Surrounded by its own gardens, which bordered the scenic River Tees and unspoilt pastureland, it was a place where the aircrews could get away from the rigours of their nocturnal operational duties. But for those who enjoyed the less reflective and contemplative lifestyle commonly found among young men under extreme pressure, Dinsdale Hall was not the most suitable nor the most idyllic spot. As Stan Hauxwell continues: 'The major problem for us, of course, was that Dinsdale Hall was rather remote and the transport very infrequent. When the prospects for survival are not good, the belief that it would always be someone else who bought it was a great comfort. For most, as their time might be too short, what they wanted was to play some more stupid games, have another drink and forget about it. That was the general attitude.' Many aircrew returning from a night out found that they had missed the transport back to the Hall and were faced with a tiresome walk in the dark. The route from the station, via the lanes and roads, was less hazardous but appreciably longer than the short-cut which led over the stepping-stones in the Tees and then across country. The effects of weak beer and youthful exuberance often combined to ensure that many airmen staggered into the grand Hall soaked through and muddy. John Driffield, who arrived at Middleton St George in 1941 and served with both 76 and 78 Squadrons, noted cryptically: 'For my time, all 76 Squadron aircrew were billeted in Dinsdale Hall. I had a really good time. As a result we became quite friendly with some of the local farmers and less so with others!'

For the early other ranks arrivals at Middleton St George living conditions were also more than tolerable and certainly much better than in many of the hastily constructed wartime 'utility' airfields. Cyril Tuckwell, then an AC2 Fitter IIE, was posted to 76 Squadron in June 1941, after training at Cosford, Cardington and Gloucester. He was very pleasantly surprised and found that Middleton St George was

> an extremely nice camp with brick-built two-storey sleeping accommodation. It was centrally heated during the winter months with radiators in all the sleeping quarters. As in all these types of camps, alongside the roadways were paths of concrete slabs, under which were the water pipes, lagged heating pipes, electrical cables and telephone cables. There was a central boiler house, which supplied all the hot water to every building in the camp. There was also a water tower in which the water was pumped to give the necessary pressure to supply the whole camp. It proved to be a very workable system. In fact, the camp was almost like a little town.

Later arrivals, however, did not always enjoy such luxurious surroundings. The ubiquitous Nissen hut, into which large numbers of airmen and women were unceremoniously dumped, began to make an appearance, though to a far lesser extent than on many other airfields. Essentially a corrugated steel structure of a semi-circular section bolted directly to a concrete base, Nissen huts were cheap to make and easy to assemble. However, they were notoriously lousy to live in. A slug-shaped oven in summer, the hut became an uninsulated ice-box in winter, totally dependent for heat upon a coal-burning stove that was notoriously hard to light and keep going and produced very little heat except in its immediate vicinity. Fuel shortages did little to help the situation, often drastically reducing the times when a fire could be lit. Dampness and condensation, even leaks, were common problems, while a rain shower could make the inhabitants feel as though they were sitting inside a tin can being pelted by stones. No matter how hard the residents tried, Nissen huts and their variants were very difficult to make comfortable and homely.

On occasion, though, even the huts were a longed-for luxury. LAC J.D. Shepherd, an airframe fitter, recalls a time

> at the beginning of the conversion of the whole Group to four-engined aircraft and during the ensuing months, Middleton St George played an important part in this process. As I recall it, aircrews were trained at specialised Conversion Units but ground crews in the various trades were dealt with in two ways. Some were seconded from existing Whitley squadrons, spending several weeks with us for experience, while others joined the squadron virtually as supernumeraries until they were competent to join other newly re-equipped squadrons. The effect on the station was most marked and for a time the overcrowding was such that some personnel, including myself, were accommodated in tents on the field lying between the Oak Tree and the railway bridge on the Dinsdale Road.

The WAAF living quarters, a motley collection of hastily erected buildings known as the Waafery, were off the airfield site, a little way down the Middleton Low Road, not far from the railway bridge and a radio station. Ken Haley, a radar mechanic, recalls: 'the WAAF site was a little distance from the main camp on the road to Middleton One Row. Though, as I recall, there was a well used short-cut across the fields!' It was, of course, strictly out of bounds to all male personnel. However, the administrative staff always tried to keep some spaces for visitors of the legitimate kind. One such visitor caused a considerable stir among the male population. Stan Hauxwell takes up the story:

We were sitting in the sunshine outside the Flight Office one afternoon in July or August [1942] when we saw an interesting sight. A 76 Squadron aircraft was just touching down at one end of the runway and at the other a nice new Halifax was also touching down. At the last moment they swerved and passed each other without mishap. We went over to the new aircraft when it halted to give some forceful comments to its captain. The hatch opened and out jumped a small figure in white overalls, pulling off a helmet to reveal a mass of blond curls. "Oh ——," she said, "I nearly bent the ——ing thing that time!" I think gobsmacked is the appropriate modern expression. We were just so shattered that a tiny blonde could handle a heavy Halifax entirely on her own that we forgot about the landing!

Others preferred to get away from it all entirely. Michael Renaut teamed up with his friend Geoff Thomas and took two unfurnished rooms in Darlington. 'This was strictly against regulations but who was to know that we weren't among the hundreds in the mess? I did all the cooking while Geoff attended to the bedmaking and keeping the flat clean. It was great fun.' Their major concern was to be on site in time for briefing and, as a result, much of their time was spent on the airfield, especially as a recall even after a stand-down was not unheard of.

Married men could sometimes obtain permission to live out officially, as Cyril Tuckwell did.

After a while I obtained permission to live out so I brought my wife and son from Somerset to rooms at a farm halfway between Darlington and Middleton St George. I remember at one time with an air force friend of mine going into a field behind the farm and picking pounds of mushrooms. Anyway, a little later on we managed to find rooms in Middleton St George near the station. It meant that I didn't have quite so far to cycle to the aerodrome. I'm afraid we didn't get on too well with our new landlady. Coming back from one leave we found that some other airman had been sleeping in our bed, even though we had paid up our rent for the period. So we moved rooms and went to live at Yarm, a few miles to the east of the aerodrome. The house was owned by a mother and her daughter. Yarm was a little village consisting of a long central street. It was a delightful little village. My impression of it was that in that street every third building was a pub. Of course, not really. But that was the impression I got at the time.

The other buildings on the airfield were of a diverse nature, scattered in an apparently haphazard fashion across the airfield, but each one containing another vital component in the smooth running of the airfields. The Met. Office and Flying Offices, for example, were both buildings of the Nissen type, furnished for functionality rather than comfort. Ron Waite remembered his first visit to see 76 Squadron's B Flight Commander, Sqn Ldr Packe, in his office in January 1942:

> B Flight's Office was typical; a room about 12ft square with brick walls covered in peeling paint. The one concession to comfort was a strip of threadbare carpet, which, in its heyday, had borne an oriental design. There was an assortment of chairs and two trestle tables, one of which performed the function of office desk. On its well worn top stood a bottle of red ink, a ruler and the Flight Authorisation Book. The red ink was used to enter night-flying hours in the aircrew's log books. Two cocoa tin lids, encrusted in grey cigarette ash, served as ashtrays on the other table. On the wall behind him was a board which contained a chart of names.

Most of the technical workshops and offices were grouped around the permanent hangars or the dispersal points. There were workshops for instruments, wirelesses, fitters, armourers, motor transport sections, electricians, radar and a whole host of other trades and administrative support that were involved in maintaining the increasingly complex and sophisticated aircraft and equipment. There was a Maintenance Flight where major repairs and servicing were undertaken and sub-sections for A and B Flights where ground crews carried out the day-to-day routine maintenance and were in regular contact with the aircrews. Much of the work on the aircraft had to be done outside in all weathers on account of a great shortage of covered work areas. Struggling to repair or service an engine or bombing-up a Halifax in the open in January was hard and demanding work. The hours were long, and rewards and praise in short supply. Nor did the work fit neatly into formal duties or shift patterns and often when there was a 'flap on' or when an aircraft needed extra fuel or rebombing after a last-minute change of target, crews worked double-shifts to get the job done. Cpl Fred Healey, a wireless mechanic, recalls the events of Christmas Day 1941. 'I was about to enjoy my Christmas dinner, served as was traditional by the officers, when the tannoy interrupted with an announcement: "Will Corporal Healey go to M for Mother – there is a howl on the intercom!" Fortunately, an electrician friend had a vehicle at hand for such emergencies and we were not delayed long.'

Radar Mechanic Ken Haley mentions another occasion in July 1942, which illustrated the frustrations of service life:

> One evening a tannoy message ordered all radar mechanics to report back to the section. There we were met by a signals officer who told us to take out of all the aircraft the Gee equipment, including the leads and aerials. He said he would arrange for the airmen's mess to give us a meal when we finished. So at 4.00 a.m. we went along to the mess for a bite to eat but the NCO in charge when we eventually found him told us where to go and what to do when we got there! I think he thought we had just come back off leave and wanted something to eat. However, when we threatened to call out the Duty Officer he relented

Handley Page Halifax B Mk I L9530 of 76 Squadron undergoing maintenance in the summer of 1941. Ground crews usually worked outdoors – lovely in the summer, but a feat of endurance in the harsh north-eastern winters. *(Imperial War Museum CH 3393)*

and came up with an excellent early breakfast. As it turned out there was no need to work all night as the planes had to be fitted with long-range fuel tanks before flying out to the Middle East. We could have done the work quite leisurely over the next 10 days!

However, there were some lighter moments and a few perks. For Ken Haley, the delicate and unreliable nature of the Gee equipment, and the resultant complaints from the irate crews who depended on it, meant that he often got to fly on local test flights to test the box of navigational magic in the air. Cyril Tuckwell, who was chosen (on account of his ability to type faster with one finger than his fellow fitters) to run the Technical Records Office, which supplied the latest technical information on all subjects to the various trades, became airborne unexpectedly one evening:

One other little job we had to do was to wheel the Station Commander's light aircraft from one end of the hangars to the other end up by Flying Control. One of my mates suggested that as I was a qualified engine fitter the easiest way was for me to get in the cockpit and taxi it. So into the cockpit I got and everything was going lovely until there was a sudden gust of wind down between the hangars and the next thing I knew was that the ground was 6 feet below me. In other words I was flying. I could see myself on all sorts of charges as I gently eased the joystick forward and cut the engine as soon as the wheels touched the ground. But of course, we didn't have far to push it then and my mates quickly caught up with me, as I climbed out of the cockpit. Needless to say we finished that job in record time.

Like tradesmen the world over, the ground crews were quick to spot any opportunity to establish profitable sidelines. Cyril Tuckwell again remembers clearly the wide ranges of artefacts made to make life easier or more comfortable; some were sold on to others or presented to many a grateful and duly impressed girlfriend or wife.

> There was a corporal who made his own cigarette lighter out of a common shell case and when he lit it, it was like a munitions flame-thrower. Another thing we did, we used to hammer a sixpenny piece flat and thin, bend it in the middle, put it in a vice, squeeze it together, bend the two sides outwards and file it into the shape of a Spitfire aircraft, soldering a small safety pin underneath in the fold to make quite a presentable brooch. Another thing we got a craze for, we used to get a scrap piece of clear plastic, file it into an oval and polish it. Then from an air force tunic button, we'd file away the surrounding metal from the crown and albatross and with the help of a hot soldering iron press them into the Perspex, then again with the soldering iron put a small safety pin on the back. The result was another very presentable brooch. These two items became quite a craze among the fitters. Another craze was making antimacassars or chair backs. We made up a square wooden frame with nails all round the edges of the frame. Then we used several different reels of Sylko and the end result, after criss-crossing and knotting the Sylko where the strands crossed and eventually cutting the work off the frame, was a very artistic chair headrest back.

Nevertheless for the most part the routine was one of fairly monotonous hard work, enlivened only by infrequent periods of leave (six days every six weeks for aircrew, if they survived that long, and every three months or so for the remainder) and a busy social life.

Not that every night was a party night. The majority of men and women, after working long hours on duty with little opportunity for rest and relaxation, usually felt shattered and with another shift to come, often felt inclined to stay in and read, write letters, play cards or make do and mend. Often the aircrew lived a more vivacious lifestyle, seeking solace and respite from the nagging fear of flak, searchlights and night-fighters, the incessant noise and vibration of the engines, the freezing temperatures endured inside the uninsulated Whitleys and Halifaxes, the long hours huddled in a cramped gun turret and the distressing spectre of watching friends being wounded, maimed or killed. Ron Waite vividly remembers the shock of finding his Canadian room-mate had been killed: 'I liked him but had only had a short time to get to know him; within a week or so the Padre and another officer were sorting out his clothes, papers, photographs and personal letters.' Returning to his room barely a couple of hours later, he discovered the next occupant had already moved in.

One of Michael Renaut's most unenviable tasks was to meet and look after the parents of an airman killed in a training crash. He nervously greeted the parents and the young man's fiancée at Darlington station and escorted them to the airfield. The young girl was carrying a bulky parcel that contained the wedding dress she had recently bought. She insisted that she wanted to place this personally by her fiancée's side in the coffin. 'It was a harrowing sight – this girl sobbing her heart out – I felt quite helpless and on the verge of tears myself. I knew that there were only sandbags as makeweight and charred flesh in the coffin and I simply didn't know how to dissuade her.' Eventually she was persuaded by Renaut and the Padre that it was better for her to remember her fiancée as he had been and she agreed to allow them to place the wedding dress in the coffin instead. After lunch and a tour of the airfield, Renaut escorted the grieving trio back to Darlington station and was deeply moved when the father grasped his hand and said with great dignity and manifest gratitude, 'Thank you for your kindness; if the circumstances were not so tragic, we could almost have enjoyed ourselves.' It is small wonder that young men faced with such circumstances and living in the topsy-turvy world of normality by day and extreme abnormality by night, felt the need to follow the Roman writer Horace's dictum: 'Inter spem curamque, timores inter et iras, omnem crede diem tibi diluxisse supremum' (Horace, *Epistles* 1:4, 12–13 – 'amidst your hopes and cares, fears and troubles, treat each day that dawns as if your last'.)

For many the most frequent venue for entertainment and social relaxation was the mess, either the officers', the sergeants' or the airmen's depending on rank. Here the men (and in their own mess, women) could relax, have a drink, enjoy a sing-song around the piano, play cards, have a game of snooker or a quiet chat, mulling over the events of the day and the prospects for the future. Operational requirements made the wild party nights far less frequent than films might suggest. They tended to occur for a particular purpose, such as the celebration of a decoration awarded to a member of the squadron, distinguished visitors (as for example the brief stay of the Russian officers) or even, as Jack Moorfoot found out on the night of his arrival in July 1941, to cheer people up after a period of heavy operational losses.

Formal dances were regularly held in each of the messes and here servicemen and women could legitimately fraternise with one another on station. Although romance, however short- or long-lived, did blossom from time to time for some, for most it was simply an opportunity to be young, free from worries and have simple uncomplicated fun. In common with most young people the world over since time immemorial, sex was very much on the agenda. However, such encounters tended to be furtive and brief, partly as a result of the moral opprobrium which was still firmly attached to sex outside marriage and partly for want of a suitable private place. The Station Medical Officer, who from May 1942 was Flt Lt W.P. Griffin, kept records on pregnancies and instances of venereal diseases in his monthly report and the figures for both remain surprisingly constant yet low, given the large number of young people from all walks of life who were thrown together in one confined space. Many women appear to have considered it their compassionate duty to at least spend time with some of the young aircrew whose futures were so uncertain.

One rather obvious ingredient necessary for a good dance was a band and Middleton St George was especially lucky in this respect. From among those serving on the airfield there could always be found those who in civilian life had been professional or semi-professional musicians. One such was John Shepherd:

At Middleton St George [there was] a station dance band of ten or so members, of which I was one, playing double bass. Frequent dances were held on the station in the building

containing the Naafi canteen and the airmen's mess, which could be made into one large
room by removing the dividing partition. This arrangement was also used for shows by
visiting ENSA and local artistes as well as by the station's own concert party. The band was
in demand for outside engagements and played regularly for dancing at Darlington Baths
Ballroom. During the war cinemas did not show films on Sundays but there was a good
demand for entertainment and Sunday concerts were very popular. These were usually held
in cinemas and we appeared a number of times on such stages in Darlington.

On a good night the hot, sweaty and smoky atmosphere was thick enough to cut with a knife
and many men and women returned on such nights worn out but happy – with some, no
doubt, paying the penalty the following morning. The dances did, however, do wonders for
morale and the spirit of comradeship.

Touring ENSA companies also called in to the airfield from time to time. These were
considered red-letter events, as such shows provided a high standard of entertainment with
many well-known actors, actresses, singers and dancers doing their bit for the men and
women in uniform. Ron Waite describes one such show in spring of 1942.

At the top of the bill was Renee Houston and the comedian duo Jewell and Warriss. The
camp cinema was packed with airmen of all ranks. The audience was warmed up from the
start, when Jewell and Warriss made a lively entrance from the back of the theatre. The
lowest ranks were in the back seats, the AC 'plonks', who were greeted by Warriss with
'Ullow mates . . . ow are yuh?' As he approached the NCOs his voice became more
deferential: 'Good evening, Flight Sergeant,' and, addressing the Station Warrant Officer,
'Nice of you to come, Sir.' Upon reaching the front row, where Group Captain Traill was
sitting, both comedians fell to their knees in homage. 'Your slaves . . . O Mighty One,'
quoth Warriss, which brought the house down.

A little later, following a performance by an attractive and greatly appreciated chorus line,

the house lights went down, the orchestra began to play and as the curtains parted, Renee
Houston, appearing like a dream, stepped into the spotlight. Her lively personality came
over the footlights before she had said a word and her renowned lovely figure, clothed in a
gown of gold and scarlet diagonal stripes, drew gasps and cheers from an appreciative
audience. After her first number about two dozen airmen eased themselves from their seats
and quietly left. This was not lost on Renee who, realising they were about to leave on a
mission, waved to them and wished them luck.

The next day Waite and Sqn Ldr Jock Calder took to the skies to return a teddy bear that
belonged to one of the girls in the show. The bear had a log book with all the airfields it had
visited and once it had been duly endorsed, Calder had promised to return it to its pretty
owner, who was now staying in a country house near Bridlington. It was a somewhat
unorthodox mission that both men enjoyed and the bear baled out bang over the target.

A few lucky men even succeeded in striking up relationships with the beautiful actresses and dancers. One such man was Michael Renaut, who fell hook, line and sinker for Hazel, 'a terribly attractive girl with an hourglass figure'. The pair enjoyed several days out while she was in the area and the pilot never missed a show. After staying to watch the end of one show in Northallerton, Renaut discovered that he had missed the last bus back to Darlington, leaving him facing a 20-mile walk back to the airfield. Luckily the friendly station master took an interest in his story and found some transport for him, otherwise Renaut would never have made it back to the airfield before the midnight deadline. Once the delicious Hazel's tour moved out of the area, both of them moved on to pastures new. This was a fine example of the kind of relationships that flourished briefly and then withered in wartime Britain.

Transport was always a problem for those seeking entertainment beyond the Naafi or the Salvation Army Canteen where a solid and substantial wad, usually of corned beef, and tea could be cheaply bought to supplement the canteen food, which though adequate was rarely sufficient to satisfy the voracious appetites of hard-working young men and women. Airfields by their very nature and location were usually fairly remote places, far from any major town or cities. On this front, Middleton St George fared better than most, being only a few miles from Darlington, Stockton and Middlesbrough.

Some of the officers were able to buy old cars locally as few civilians had any use for them, given the petrol shortage. However, maintaining and fuelling them was difficult and most of the cars acquired were notoriously unreliable. Equally difficult was driving itself. The blackout made finding one's way a significant challenge and many were the occasions when an Austin 7 or something similar, laden with revellers well beyond the manufacturer's specification, gently slid off the road into a ditch while returning home from a night out at hostelries like the Croft Spa Hotel and the George at Piercebridge, both picturesquely situated on the banks of the Tees.

Others acquired motorbikes, bicycles or used the transport provided, service or civilian. Most evenings at about 18:00 hours a bus left the airfield bound for Darlington, taking those fortunate enough to be off duty out for the night in the many pubs in the town. Though fads quickly came and went, the Fleece remained a favourite throughout the war years. For those not wishing to walk back, the bus made the return journey at 22:00 hours. Some came to Darlington from further afield and thoughtfully brought their own transport with them. John Duffield, a pilot with both 76 and 78 Squadrons, comments: 'I think Darlington must have earned quite a reputation as we frequently had three Fairey Swordfish aircraft of the Fleet Air Arm visit us at the airfield. They would arrive with their bicycles tied under the aircraft and then go off for the night.'

Others headed off towards Stockton and Middlesbrough to sample the night-life there. The easiest way of getting to these towns was to take the train, which passed through Dinsdale station. As Derek Beasley, who as an AC2 in 1941 worked for the Station Engineer Officer, Flt Lt Lane, recalls: 'The line used to pass along the edge of the camp and a favourite trick for personnel returning from the Stockton area was to jump off the train when it slowed down in the vicinity of the camp. This was a lot easier than walking back from Dinsdale station.' A popular form of entertainment in Stockton was greyhound racing at the dog track.

Many people enjoyed a modest flutter on the races but few did as well as Michael Renaut. One afternoon he backed all six winners and took away the princely sum of £18.

Closer at hand and well within walking distance were the Oak Tree and Devonport public houses, which really became extensions of the airfield itself and were popular venues for locals and servicemen and women alike. Indeed, places like these were among the few places that service personnel could meet local people. Pressures of time, duties and lack of mobility prevented widespread travel around the area. Some did make the effort to visit the beautiful and historic cities of Durham to the north and York to the south. In the summer trips to coastal resorts like Redcar, Saltburn and Whitby were popular. Sometimes their duties allowed the servicemen to see something of the local area, possibly while delivering or collecting equipment or spares from other stations scattered around North Yorkshire or recovering downed aircraft like the Wellington which crashed on 21 May 1942 near the mining town of Crook in County Durham, some 25 miles from Middleton St George, killing all five men on board.

But, as so often in life, it is the simple things that stick in the memory. One of Cyril Tuckwell's most vivid memories is of 'one summer evening while cycling back from Darlington at the end of my day off. I was sitting on a field gate at the side of the road and eating a bag of chips I had purchased at a fish and chip shop in Darlington before riding back to the camp. Those chips tasted delicious and I'm afraid I sat on that gate, looking at the glorious countryside around me thinking "what a lovely war".'

Often, the saying goes, a change is as good as a rest and from time to time events occurred to break up the general run and routine of things. Visits by dignitaries and high-ranking officers were viewed as both a blessing and a curse, providing a welcome change but also a corresponding increase in formality and bull. More popular was one of Gp Capt Traill's schemes to foster inter-service cooperation by arranging visits to Royal Navy establishments and ships on the Tyne or at the Royal Navy submarine training base at Lythe, near Whitby. Plt Off Christopher Cheshire, for example, was among a party enjoying a pink gin in the wardroom of a submarine when it was announced that the greatly feared German battleship *Bismarck* had been sunk. Similar visits were arranged to watch exercises carried out by the army on the North Yorkshire Moors and in Northumberland. Few airmen volunteered to take a direct part, though many looked forward to the 'battles' that took place in the mock attacks made by army and Home Guard units on the defences of the airfield. Equally popular, and with an even more practical application, were the mock evasion exercises undertaken by aircrew to give them some experience of landing in unknown territory and having to avoid searching hostile forces. Transported blindfold in a lorry and dropped off at an unknown location some distance from the camp, it was the aircrew's job to return to base by whatever means possible, without being apprehended by the army and Home Guard units. Many and ingenious were the means employed in getting back to the airfield.

Many people, locals and service personnel alike, recall the fascinating entertainment inadvertently provided by the movement of a badly damaged Halifax. It was due to be taken from the airfield by road to a Maintenance Unit for what amounted to a rebuild. The wings had been removed and neatly stowed beside the fuselage, which was loaded on to a massive

Queen Mary transport vehicle. Everything went smoothly until it reached the railway bridge between the airfield and Middleton St George. The Halifax became wedged solid as it rather belatedly became clear that the load was too high to pass beneath the bridge. Word of what had happened quickly spread around the airfield and the local area and a sizeable crowd soon gathered to watch the embarrassed airmen struggle vainly with the problem. Little advice was asked for but much was given as the crowd settled down to watch the proceedings. After all else had failed, it was decided to deflate all the tyres on the Queen Mary, and this proved just enough to allow the load through, scoring the brickwork as it went, to great applause and cheers. The weary airmen now had the long and laborious task of reinflating all the tyres. All told, the mishap provided almost a full day's free entertainment for all but the Queen Mary's crew.

For those not taken with the more studious and sedentary pastimes offered by the library and education service with its courses and lectures or with treading the boards in one of the many theatrical productions, there was always a healthy and thriving programme of sport. Football dominated the scene and there were regular inter-squadron, inter-flight and inter-section fixtures, both within the station and with other stations and local towns and villages. Middleton St George was blessed with good outdoor sports facilities and under the guidance of Flg Off Dace and a physical training corporal by the name of Warburton, himself a former right-half for Middlesbrough, they were used as often as operational commitments allowed. In the summer the station fielded a couple of strong cricket teams and regularly played against local teams – usually understrength on account of the war – from Darlington, Redcar, Stockton and Durham, as well as from within the services. Whatever the sport – football, cricket, snooker, even table tennis – the matches were usually hard-fought, with a considerable amount of section, squadron or station pride being at stake. From time to time less mainstream sporting activities were arranged, such as boxing bouts, swimming competitions in Darlington or Stockton Baths (already well known to many aircrew as the venues of their regular dinghy drill), and even, on occasion, for the officers at least, clay pigeon shoots or hunting in the local countryside.

Like any village or town society, there was always plenty to do at Middleton St George for those who looked for it. But, inevitably, what was on offer did not suit everybody. In many ways the experience of being on an operational airfield was similar to being at a university or college – though obviously the latter lacks the utter seriousness of purpose of the former. Nevertheless at a time when few young men and women could afford to have the opportunity of benefiting from a university education, the lifestyle and range of experiences encountered on an airfield served much the same purpose, turning often naïve young people into mature and more worldly-wise adults. Many complain about the pressures placed on young people today in terms of education and employment, and they are indeed great in the highly competitive modern world. However, they pale into insignificance beside the pressures and responsibilities faced by the wartime generations. Mistakes or miscalculations then might well have led to the death not only of the perpetrator but to those of many others as well. The vast fighting machine that was Middleton St George relied upon every tiny cog doing its job properly and to the best of its ability. Any team is only as strong as its weakest link.

Middleton St George achieved the happy knack of being both an efficient and a happy airfield: no mean feat when its purpose and the consequences of that purpose are taken into account. With that in mind, who can complain about the light-hearted excesses that were occasionally indulged in by young men and women placed under considerable and unrelenting strain? Rather, it is perhaps more surprising just how few examples there were of excess or failure to cope adequately. Perhaps the young men and women expected less and were satisfied with less in the war years; they knew their place and what was expected of them in a more well defined social structure than their counterparts today; and it is certainly true that for many the war opened up whole new vistas of opportunity and experience. But for others it closed them abruptly and finally. It is an interesting academic question – and one that I hope will not be answered in practice – as to whether the British people would react any differently today and be less willing to make sacrifices, less compliant and less satisfied with their lot, if placed in a similar set of circumstances. I like to think that they would not.

CHAPTER 4

A Long Way from Home

For many young Canadian men, military service was seen not only as their patriotic duty but as their passport to the wider world. In the days before international travel was commonplace, there was little opportunity for the average man to venture beyond his local area, let alone his national border. Canada, although vast and prosperous in spite of the upheavals of the depression, was a relatively new country and its ties with Britain, for the vast majority of Canadians the mother country, remained strong. Having dispatched tens of thousands of soldiers overseas to help Britain's titanic struggle against a continental foe in the First World War, it seemed entirely natural for the English-speaking Canadians to do so once again in the Second. Here was a chance to fight for King, Country and Empire against an evil regime; here was a chance to maintain the traditions and high martial standards set by their fathers; here was a chance to break free from the humdrum existence of ordinary life and see something of the world. For those selected as aircrew, the glamour boys of the armed services, the world, both literally and metaphorically, seemed to be at their feet.

Most of the young men had never been abroad before and, coming as they did from a country untouched and unscarred by the physical assault of war, they had a lot to learn about life in wartime Britain. For many, after months spent training in British Commonwealth Air Training Plan bases such as Brandon in Manitoba or Moncton in New Brunswick, embarking on one of the large liners used to shuttle human cargoes across the Atlantic was the beginning of an exciting adventure, spiced up by the very real dangers involved. German U-boats were unceasingly scouring the seas and had even been spotted operating as close inshore as the mighty St Lawrence River. For the excited RCAF men, the voyage across the hostile Atlantic was the culmination of a great deal of hard work and waiting.

David Lambroughton's experience was typical of many:

Our ship, the SS *Andes*, carried a few thousand RCAF aircrew and ground crew and five thousand Canadian Army soldiers. It was originally scheduled to sail from Halifax in November 1943, but someone decided to delay our voyage until April. Better, I suppose, to feed us in Canada than use up valuable shipping space in the hostile North Atlantic. We were packed in, twelve to a cabin. We slept in our own day clothes. I recall the shortest airmen slept in the bath tub. I was fortunate. I had a porthole at eye level. The army boys were put in the decks below us. I woke up on Easter Sunday morning 1944 to the sound of a million seagulls in Liverpool harbour. We scrambled topside to see the harbour and we caused the ship to cant seriously and we were ordered to spread our numbers to even things out. I clearly recall the sight of sunken ships in the harbour, some resting on their keels, superstructure above the water, and one of the Liver towers broken, like an elbow.

Such sobering sights as these, and the long train journey south through the bomb-scarred towns, did far more than anything else to bring home to the enthusiastic and fresh Canadians the harsh realities of wartime Britain.

Not that the authorities in Canada had omitted to give the men due guidance. The RCAF Public Relations department had published numerous pamphlets and laid on compulsory lectures outlining the essential dos and don'ts of daily life in Britain. Airmen billeted on a family, for example, were advised to take their ration cards with them and to expect small portions and a limited range of foodstuffs and meals. They were warned that winters would be quite cold but above all damp, causing discomfort beyond the capacity of most houses to stave off. Far from being hailed as avenging saviours, the young Canadians could expect to be confronted by a cool, British reserve, exacerbated in military circles by their higher rates of pay. There was also a class system that was far more rigid and well developed than the men were used to back home, and breaches of the unspoken code were taken seriously. Above all else, they were told, they should not poke fun at what they might consider quaint and old-fashioned customs and, in particular, at the wide variation in regional accents and dialects. The Canadians in 6 Group fared especially badly in this latter respect, being faced with the often impenetrable Yorkshire and Durham dialects. Britain, they were reminded, had been at the sharp end for some considerable time and life there should not be expected to be one long round of fun. There was, after all, a war on.

Much depended on where the airmen were posted. Many of the airfields in 6 Group were hastily constructed during the war, and were veritable paragons of functional austerity. They were often remote and windswept, and unnecessary frills and creature comforts for those serving there were few and far between. Those stationed at places like Linton, Leeming and Middleton St George fared much better as they were pre-war built or designed permanent bases. Plt Off Ian Duncan, who flew with 419 Squadron in 1943, lived in the purpose-built mess. He recalls: 'The officer accommodation was very good; two or three to a room with a sink, the bathroom being down the hall. We had a batman to make the beds and keep the rooms tidy.' Plt Off David Lambroughton, another 419 Squadron pilot, was equally lucky in the early months of 1945. 'I was fortunate to be assigned a bed upstairs above the kitchen. Our mess had 12 bedrooms, intended to be single rooms but they had "become" twin rooms. We were the envy of the Nissen dwellers.'

Nissenville, as it was unofficially known, was the overflow accommodation site, an unappealing collection of corrugated steel huts resembling shiny metal slugs. Situated just off the station, the huts were like ovens in summer and freezers in winter, and often their inhabitants had to plough through considerable quantities of mud to get there or to visit the communal ablution blocks. Ian Duncan sampled life in the huts for a while and did not like it one bit, finding them

as cold as the proverbial witch's tit. I never could get warm in them. The hut in which I was billeted had six beds, one in each corner and two in the middle, next to the sole means of heat, a small cast-iron stove whose pipe ran straight up to the roof, so when the stove was on at night I roasted until it went out, then froze. One method of getting warm was to schedule your turn at the bath-house for an evening bath, put on your flannel PJs under your battle dress, cycle like mad to the bath house, run the water as hot as you could possibly stand, jump in, soak up all the heat, dry off, dress as quickly as possible, dash back to the hut, undress and then jump into bed without any loss of motion.

The servicewomen stationed at Middleton St George belonged to the WAAF, although towards the end of the war they were augmented by a small number of personnel from the Canadian Women's Division, first formed on 2 July 1941. Segregation of living quarters was absolute and strictly enforced, with the WAAF compound being a little outside the station boundary. Conditions there were no more luxurious than on the main Nissenville site. Margaret Fairless, a WAAF who worked in the maintenance section ordering and cataloguing spare parts, recalls: 'We lived in huts with a stove in the centre and had to keep them spotlessly clean, no easy job when they were often surrounded by mud. The "ablution" bathrooms and toilets were ten minutes' walk away, so we had to be pretty tough in winter.'

There could also be other, more unexpected inconveniences to living in basic conditions off site. On 10 October 1943, for example, the Waafery came under attack from a large and stubborn force of cows. Having broken out of a neighbouring field, the cows ambled over the WAAF site from 19:30 hours to 07:00 hours, skilfully rebuffing all attempts by would-be cowboys to drive them off. It was officially, if humorously, logged that 'their heavy breathing is reported to have disturbed several people's slumbers'. Such incursions were obviously the exception but the women clearly had difficulty in living the night down. A month or so later the ungentlemanly teasing was still rife, as the entry in the station log for 17 November notes: 'Assistant Accountant Officer Flt Lt Stroud reported that he ran down a cow outside the Waafery and knocked it into a ditch. Considerable relief was felt throughout the station when it transpired the cow was a four-legged one.'

In spite of this vast expansion of cheap, basic and easily constructed accommodation, it was still not enough. The total number of personnel stationed at the airfield continued to grow, peaking at almost 2,000 in late 1944. Consequently a number of large local houses, notably the lovely Dinsdale Hall on the southern side of the River Tees, had to be requisitioned, and other airmen found themselves billeted with civilians in the local area. For many of the Canadians, the conditions they found in wartime Britain came as an unpleasant surprise and many took some time to adjust. Many of the houses in nearby villages were terraced and small and generally fairly spartan. Toilets were almost invariably situated at the bottom of the back yard, baths were of the tin variety and generally placed in front of the fire when in use, and internal heating was non-existent apart from the household fire, itself often less than roaring on account of the fuel restrictions and shortages. To those with high expectations of life in the mother country, the living conditions and lack of education of the locals came as quite a shock. On Boxing Day 1943 Flt Lt Maxwell had a meeting with Mr F. Swales, a chimney sweep from Darlington, to discuss a possible contract, and wrote in the station log: 'This man can neither read nor write, although born in England; hardly expected to find such cases over here.'

Nor were the local people, themselves often overworked and barely keeping body and soul together, universally welcoming to the young Canadians. With their rates of pay substantially ahead of those of their British counterparts and their initially brash and open manner seeming very alien to the bluff and reserved northern folk, quite a number of Canadians did not find a home away from home as expected. Misunderstandings were commonplace as each side struggled to learn the other's expectations, customs and even language. Although in most cases a pleasant enough modus vivendi was reached, the initial encounters did much to sap the morale of the young men who, as they saw it, had come so far to help.

Indeed, the morale of 6 Group remained poor and somewhat brittle for much of the first year of its existence, something which concerned Brookes, its commander, greatly. In a memo sent to all stations in March 1943 Brookes commented upon 'a marked deterioration in general smartness and turnout of all ranks'; he was particularly scathing about his officers, whom he thought 'walked in a slovenly manner with their hands in pockets'. With the Group itself suffering badly from growing pains and working its way up a steep learning curve, and the largely inexperienced crews living in a wartime environment far removed from their own and suffering serious casualties, it is not surprising that mistakes were made, problems occurred and morale dipped in some areas. That said, in the majority of cases it was open house for the Canadians right from the start and whatever the locals had was theirs for the duration, and very much appreciated it was too. As Flg Off J.A. Westland of 419 Squadron in mid-1943 put it: 'We all got along magnificently and we Canadians thought England and the English had fantastic spunk and we were really proud to be there.' David Lambroughton, serving with 419 Squadron a year later adds: 'I loved the English countryside, good roads and light traffic. I did have two bicycles stolen, probably by Canadians replacing stolen ones. I got caught in a London air raid once and was impressed by the discipline of the people in the underground shelters. I found them all happy and optimistic.' Time and increased familiarity did much to break down any barriers and build up strong bonds which, in some cases, have lasted more than sixty years.

Indeed, the fostering of good relations between the servicemen and women and the locals was an official and accepted part of a station commander's job. The men and women under his command would obviously be far more contented and efficient if they were able to enjoy an active social life both within and beyond the confines of the station. With this in mind there was a busy programme of official as well as unofficial events, while local communities were often just as keen to support 'the lads and lasses' in the front line. On 29 May 1943, for example, the station personnel took part in a large march-past through Darlington as part of the Wings for Victory campaign. Alongside detachments from the Army, the Royal Navy, the National Fire Service and the Land Army marched those from the RAF and RCAF. The spearhead was formed by the RAF Service Police, the centre by a detachment of WAAFs and the rear by an RCAF section headed by a Cameronian Pipe Band. The section comprised 24 NCOs, 19 officers and 3 ground flights, all under the command of Sqn Ldr G.N. Goff. With the pipers marching at 100 paces a minute 'an excellent display was put up by all'. The men and women from Middleton also displayed for the crowds of interested locals some of their hardware, including an 8,000lb bomb and two 4,000lb bombs, 'labelled accordingly' and mounted on bomb trolleys, and a complete gun turret. The importance attached to such public relations exercises can be seen from the list of dignitaries taking the formal salute on this occasion: AOC 6 Group AVM Brookes; Brig Gen G.M. Gilmore of Northern Command; Gp Capt A.D. Ross; Mayoress Mrs Jackson; Deputy Mayor Dr Sinclair; and the Town Clerk, Mr H. Hopkins. The Mayoress hosted a formal reception after the parade.

There were several other showcase occasions, such as Battle of Britain day. On 26 September 1943, for example, to mark the enormous and inspiring achievement of 'The Few', fifty airmen and fifty airwomen under the command of Flt Lt R. Bowron paraded through the streets of Darlington prior to attending the church service. The salute on this occasion was taken by Gp Capt A.D. Ross. (He was subsequently promoted to the rank of air commodore and in June 1944 won the George Cross for his efforts to free a crew trapped in a blazing Halifax at Tholthorpe; his selfless bravery cost him his right hand.) Often the station received invitations from local communities who were keen to meet some of the boys in the front line, for whom, indirectly, they might have worked many hours. On 8 January 1944, for example, Flt Lt Westland of 419 Squadron travelled the few miles to the pretty Yorkshire village of Stokesley to present a plaque in recognition of its inhabitants' outstanding contribution to the 1943 Wings for Victory campaign. Some of the young men, unused to such public relations work, found these formal occasions difficult, but most understood the value of such events and acknowledged the very genuine need to say thank-you to the hundreds of communities that were labouring flat out on their behalf.

Other links with the local community were far less formal. Sport, particularly football, has always been a passion in the north-east and the mixed RAF/RCAF teams were happy to take on the locals. In March 1943, for example, a team from Middleton St George took on one from Middlesbrough Police away, winning by a convincing margin. The team and its large gathering of voracious attendants were guests of the police after the match before moving on to the Steel Works Social Club and finally to the Fire Station for a dance with music provided by the Fire Service band and later the Boys' Band. There was even a short star turn provided by the BBC radio star Beryl Orde. A raffle raised £5 for the RAF Benevolent Fund, a useful by-product of a most enjoyable day. The Chief Constable, Mr A. Edwards, later wrote to the station to praise the contingent's 'exemplary behaviour'.

British summer sports provided the Canadians with a new challenge: mastering the intricacies of cricket. In 1943, in their first entry to the prestigious local tournament for the Harrison Shield, the team from Middleton St George put in a highly credible performance, reaching, to their surprise and delight, the semi-final. The team's gloom at their defeat was short-lived and quickly dispelled by an excellent 'post match do' at the Dinsdale Golf and County Club, a couple of miles from the station, where all personnel were considered honorary members. After a few pints of the local brew, thoughts turned to the future and plans were eagerly made for next year's assault on the trophy., Now that the Canadians, the station records state, 'have become interested in the game of cricket and many inter-station matches take place with colossal scores and many a laugh, it is rumoured that possibly next year we will begin to understand the game better and put up a better show against the people who call us foreigners'. Indeed, the 'foreigners' quickly became proficient at the game and competed in the local Northern League with some distinction for the remainder of the war.

It was only natural, however, that the Canadians would bring their own sports with them and in turn introduce them to the locals. The one that made the greatest impact was ice-hockey. There were few ice-rinks in Britain at the time but the young men stationed at Middleton St George were better off than most. Some 20 miles to the north of the station lay the small but beautiful city of Durham. Famous for its magnificent castle and cathedral, dominating the city from high above the River Wear, which almost encircles them, Durham was also home to an ice-rink of sorts. An odd edifice consisting of a large and somewhat dilapidated big-top marquee, supported by stout wooden posts driven through the ice and into the ground, it was none the less an ice-rink and it proved a mecca to the Canadians throughout 6 Group. Vince Elmer, who served with 419 Squadron, commented: 'For Canadians this was paradise. Even with the tent over it and the poles down the middle of the ice we all flocked there in the winter.' Teams came from throughout 6 Group and beyond to play, more often than not coming off second best to the men from Middleton. In March 1944, for example, the Middleton St George team battled its way through to the RCAF Overseas Hockey Final in Liverpool, eventually beating Wellesbourne 9–5 in an exciting and hard-fought match. As well as the well supported inter-station matches, with the teams often boosted by the presence of seasoned pre-war professionals, such as 419 Squadron's Sqn Ldr J.K. Goldie, there were other benefits. Where better for a Canadian to show off his skills and impress the fairer sex? As Vince Elmer remarked, 'we taught a good number of Waafs to skate there'. The rink and the city with its old streets and many pubs became a favourite venue for a day out when off duty.

Many locals remember the skilful players and boisterous antics of the airmen. Robert Hutchinson, who served at Middleton St George after the war, recalled spending many of his teenage hours at the rink, having travelled out from Sunderland:

I used to spend quite a lot of time and pocket money learning to figure-skate at the ice-rink in Durham. It was underneath a large marquee but it was quite unique and very popular. It was also very popular with a large group of Canadian airmen who came to skate and play ice hockey, about which they were very enthusiastic. I remember them as a noisy but good-natured bunch and I don't recall any nastiness.

They certainly sparked off an interest among the local lads that would continue to flourish for the next fifty years, during which the Durham Wasps ice hockey team became one of the most successful teams in the country – even playing in a slightly more modern and orthodox building! The link between Middleton St George and the Durham Wasps goes right back to the start. When the Wasps played their first competitive match against the Kirkaldy Flyers on 18 October 1947, the line-up contained three Canadians who had served at Middleton St George, Earl Carlson, Gordon Belmore and Billy Britt, all of whom had stayed on in the area at the end of the war. The ice-rink at Durham was to remain the home base for the Wasps until the late 1990s, when the team moved to more modern facilities in Sunderland.

Sport also played an integral and crucial part in the social and community life within the station itself. Various sports were played, some competitively and some recreationally, the idea being to involve as many of the men and women as possible. Swimming parties regularly visited the public baths a few miles away in Thornaby, and boxing and PT classes were held in the station gym, while inter-section and inter-station competitions in football, softball and athletics proved popular distractions from the harsh business of war. In July 1944, for example, Middleton's softball team beat local rivals Linton 11–8, and a five-event Track and Field day was held for the women on the station. Cpl Philips from 419 Squadron won first prize in four of the events, clearing no less than 5ft 1in in the high jump. ACW Cheesemend won the fifth event, the ball-throwing competition, with an impressive distance of 138ft. The previous summer a team of ten athletes had taken part in the YMCA Auxiliary Service competition held in Ripon, coming in a respectable fifth.

Even for the less actively minded there was a great deal to do and to get involved with on the station, particularly for the non-flying personnel who tended to stay put for a longer period of time. Although the station had a thriving amateur dramatics society, it was official organisations such as ENSA ('Every Night Something Awful', as the unkind critics dubbed it) and the YMCA that provided most of the theatrical entertainment. It was possible to see several professionally produced and performed plays a month at the station, if one could get a ticket. Such touring parties worked hard, putting on several shows a day in order to fit in with as many shift patterns as possible. On 6 September 1943, for example, the YMCA-sponsored 'Theodora goes wild' received a rapturous response from the airmen and women in the NAAFI at the 18:00 hours show and an equally warm welcome at the 21:00 hours show in the officers' mess. A fortnight later the cast performing 'Babes on Broadway' followed a similar pattern.

Occasionally something out of the ordinary would be attempted. On 22 November 1944, for example, the station log notes: 'ENSA presented a ballet in the NAAFI which, unfortunately, did not appeal to the rank and file of the station, although it was very well presented.' Four weeks later, however, an equally cerebral and highbrow presentation met with great popular acclaim. The same log records that on 18 December 1944 'a recital by the celebrated pianist Shulamith Shaf, probably the most outstanding musical programme ever presented on the station, was given in the NAAFI and was a great success'. At the other end of the scale, upwards of 300 people were attending Bingo nights in the winter of 1944 and at one point earlier that year a Bridge craze swept the station.

For those who liked to be doing, there were several practical activities and pastimes on offer. In the spring of 1943, for example, the Air Ministry arranged an Arts and Handicrafts Exhibition in London, intending to showcase the many different skills to be found around the empire. Fifteen pieces were sent to the capital from Middleton St George and it was considered that 'an excellent standard of work was achieved, of which a tapestry picture by Corporal Boundy was quite outstanding'. Such was the success of the event that 6 Group continued to organise such shows and competitions for the remainder of its time in the UK. Arrangements were even made for special shipments of cotton, wool, felt and other materials to be brought from Canada as such items were in short supply in strictly rationed wartime Britain.

Although the RCAF on the whole tended to recruit from the better educated members of Canadian society, some men and women took the opportunity to broaden their education further and acquire new skills and qualifications by making full use of the educational programmes available. Middleton was a typical large station and boasted a well stocked library, offering a range of both fiction and non-fiction books, a news room displaying the latest maps and information about the war around the globe as well as detailed news about events back home in Canada, and a large lecture room. Many talented and knowledgeable speakers were found from among those serving on the station but the majority were teachers from the Continuing Education Department in Leeds. Some of the lectures were intended only for interest, but many were formal regular classes in support of academic or trade qualifications. As time went on, the thoughts of many began to turn towards life after the war. Although it was expected that there would be opportunities for employment after the war, it was clear that there would be intense competition for the best jobs among the thousands of young men and women whose only experience of employment and adult life was war work of one form or another. Those with an eye to the future decided to make good use of their time and signed up for whatever they felt would be most useful. The RCAF recognised the need to provide both advice and training and in January 1944 began to train its first group of Education Counsellors at RCAF Rockcliffe. One of these graduates was Flg Off Bill Farmer, an ex-armaments officer, who took up residence in the Education Office at Middleton St George. Several hundred personnel passed through his team's hands, gaining hope for a future after the war and the means to achieve it.

For many of the men and women based on the station the war simply heightened the natural feelings among the young to seize the day and let tomorrow worry about itself. Social life on the station could be hectic for those who liked it that way and it often seemed that only the slightest excuse was necessary to arrange a party or dance. Female company was at a premium and it was often said that the best dances were held in the Waafery. In October 1943, for example, it staged two major social occasions. On the 5th it held a dance, but with a twist: admission was only available on production of 1lb of rosehips per person. These were taken to a collection centre in Darlington and all proceeds from their sale went to the RAF Benevolent Fund. The station's contribution was a whopping 266lb, with the Armaments Section alone collecting no less than 31½lb; the sum raised seems paltry by comparison at £2 4s 6d, but as the dance itself was a great success it was a most useful by-product. Three weeks later, alongside a doubles tennis tournament sponsored by the YMCA, the Waafery staged a Halloween Fancy Dress Ball. Wartime shortages on cloth and material simply added a greater challenge to produce a suitable costume. 'A hilarious time was had by all' the station log records, and certainly it was an enjoyable night made all the better by the chance happening that neither of the station's squadrons was on operations that night.

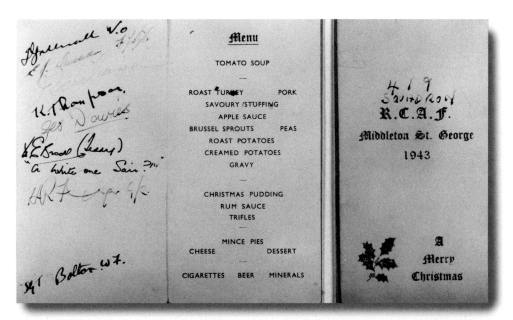

A 1943 Christmas menu from RCAF Middleton St George. *(Author via Mrs Penny Smith)*

Middleton St George, like most stations, boasted its own resident dance band, known as 'All Clear'. Normally a 12-piece band, it could on occasions split up in order to meet its heavy commitments, as it did on 2 December 1943 when it was booked to play a station dance in the NAAFI and another in the officers' mess at neighbouring Croft. The RCAF Concert Band 'The Blackouts' were also regular performers at Middleton St George dances and shows. If commitments, war-based or otherwise, prevented such a semi-professional turn-out, then second best was a pile of records, a gramophone and some amplifying kit, all generously donated by the YMCA. Other local charities also made generous donations to make the RCAF's spartan conditions more homely and pleasant. In May 1944, for example, Flg Off Martin had several meetings with Mrs Barnham of the County Welfare Office in Durham; the result was a truck-load of games, tables and chairs, along with curtain material and pictures to brighten up the station sick quarters and the airwomen's rest rooms.

Links with the local Durham community were very much a two-way process. In December 1943 it was decided to hold a Christmas party on the WAAF site for a group of local children. The idea grew and grew until the number of attending children reached 110, at which point it was decided that enough was enough. Jellies, trifles and cakes were produced in the mess by the WAAFs, while a veritable army of volunteers decorated the whole mess and extension room in festive fashion. Station personnel also turned their hands to entertainment, providing a magician, a ventriloquist and the requisite Father Christmas distributing small (often home-made) gifts. They also arranged a film and cartoon show. The event was such a success that an even more elaborate bash was arranged for Christmas 1944.

On this occasion seventy-five underprivileged children aged between 6 and 10 were collected from York by Flg Off Martin and Flg Off Tome with the help of the MT section and brought to the airfield by 15:00 hours on 23 December. There they joined a further 230 children from the local area in the WAAF site. Airmen and women joined in playing party games until tea, prepared once again by the WAAFs, was served at 16:00 hours. Two 'Rocky Mountain Singers' were found to deliver the entertainment during the meal, which was supplemented and enlivened by items sent direct from Canada. Father Christmas, ably played by WO E.A. Huestis, turned up to give each child a toy, an orange and some sweets, all rare commodities in the wartime north-east. After more games, the party was brought to a reluctant close at 17:30 hours and the children, 'tired and happy after the afternoon's activities', were taken home, leaving a mountain of clearing up behind them. Within a few hours many of the airmen and women who had arranged this wonderful suspension of reality were preparing to launch a major attack on Lohausen, an airfield just outside Düsseldorf.

Christmas, of course, does not happen every day and most of the personnel spent their time lounging around on the station, in the various messes or in the pubs in the local area. Plt Off Ian Duncan recalls how he spent much of his free time.

The large lounge was the place where we spent a great deal of time reading, drinking and talking. Reading, in the main, was the selection of daily newspapers, *Aeroplane* and *Flight* magazines and any other material which had been brought into the mess; shove ha'penny boards occupied many an hour with pints of beer and the same could be said for the dartboard. I spent many a night writing letters to my folks and to my girlfriend back home. Sometimes, on my nights off or early in the evening, we would go into Darlington for afternoon tea at the Imperial and then go to a movie and return by bus to Middleton St George.

Sgt D. Richards remembers how living off the station at Dinsdale Hall posed particular problems:

The bus back to our billet was about 6.30 p.m. and there was also the problem of changing into our 'best blue' for going out. As there were only three 25-seater buses for two squadrons there were never enough seats. If we wanted to get into town, the train was best and we cycled to the station and left our bikes locked up in a room there. This meant catching the last train back about 11.00 p.m. and it was pretty hopeless trying to get one's bike out of the large number jammed into the room! In any time off I used to get away into Darlington or, mostly, Stockton. There I could get a 5-shilling dinner at, I think, the Black Lion, now sadly demolished. I usually frequented a dance hall, for 1 shilling weekdays, 1/6 on Saturdays. It had no licence but I was never a drinker. I do remember calling in once on a mess dance with some girls bussed in but I was not impressed and preferred going out.

Everyone had their own particular favourite haunt and, as Dave Roberts succinctly put it, 'a trip to Darlington or Stockton for a dance or the pictures and for a few jars was, for most of us, the order of the day on stand-down nights'. The Fighting Cocks in Darlington, the Vane

Arms, the Unicorn and the Black Lion in Stockton all received their share of visits from the young men and women based at Middleton St George, as did the Royal and Palais de Dance. David Lambroughton in 1944 found 'Stockton to be a live city with 64 pubs. We often chose the Vane Arms as our first stop on a Friday evening.' On the whole the local people took this friendly invasion of their pubs, dance halls and cinemas in good heart and many took these newcomers under their wing. Ron Cassels of 428 Squadron has fond memories of the nearest pub to the airfield, the Oak Tree, which was run by husband and wife team Red and Mary and handily situated just outside the station's gate:

> We had to pass it to get to the mess or to Nissenville. It became a favourite stopping place. The law required them to close at 11.00 p.m. and Mary would go around calling, 'Come now, all you lads and lasses, have you no homes to go to?' This evoked a loud chorus of 'No!' After we became known to them we went out the front door at 11.00, hopped over the fence and re-entered through the kitchen to continue our drinking and darts-playing for another hour or two.

The Oak Tree enjoyed the significant advantage of not requiring any transport to reach it. Many lovely hostelries such as the Spa Hotel in Croft or the George at Piercebridge were simply too difficult for most of the airmen and women to get to and they became prized havens of exclusivity for those with a means of transport. Ron Cassels bought an old Norton 500 for £28 but as 'I couldn't get a licence, insurance or petrol legally, I did without the first two. The petrol was no problem as we used 100-octane aviation fuel and mixed oil with it so that the valves would not burn out.' A fellow crew member bought a share in an old car so they could visit the Davenport, an off-the-beaten-track pub with marvellous views over the River Tees:

> It was a narrow winding road to the Davenport and we would race to see who could get there first and when it was time to return we would race back to Nissenville. It was quite a ride without headlights. For some reason or other we never had an accident on the Davenport road in spite of giving ourselves a lot of opportunities. Both Wimp and I survived without a serious bike accident but the car didn't, as Mac and his bomb aimer pals wrote it off one night.

The fate of this car was shared by many others but provided nobody else was involved, or seriously hurt, the officers of the law generally turned a blind eye.

Perhaps the best-known of all the illegal motorcyclists at Middleton St George was Father Lardie, the station's Catholic priest. He was following in the tyre-marks of his predecessor Father Giroux, who broke his arm on his motorcycle and later raffled the machine in August 1943 for the benefit of the CO's Benevolent Fund. Lardie purchased a motorcycle in order to be able to visit the crews at each aircraft shortly before and after operations. However, his application for an official permit and fuel ration was turned down, forcing him to join the ranks of illegal motorists. Ron Cassels recalls that Lardie felt guilty about his bike but he practised for a few days until he was ready to use it for an operational take-off. The ground crew who looked after his bike had it ready for him and he started off to visit aircrews. He came down the perimeter track with the bike belching great clouds of smoke. Everybody had fun teasing him about his fuel or asking if he was trying to lay down a smokescreen. The ground crew had put in extra oil and had a real laugh at Lardie, who really didn't want to advertise that he had a bike.

It wasn't only Father Lardie who benefited from his new mode of transport. Chas Huff recalls an incident from the summer of 1944:

We were on ops one night and I had arrived late at the flight shack to change into my flying suit. By the time I had got everything on and got to the door, the last truck had left for the dispersal. Just then, Father Lardie, the RC padre, came along on his motorcycle and stopped and asked if I needed a ride. I climbed on behind him with my electrically heated inner flying suit, bulky outer flying suit, mae west, parachute harness and boots. With one hand holding my parachute, we took off like a scared rabbit down the road around the hangars and out on to the perimeter track in the pitch black. Our Lancaster KB745 V for Vickie was not too far round but by the time we got to the dispersal I was thoroughly shaken. From then on flying on ops did not seem to be as bad! This was only one of Father Lardie's numerous helpful deeds. Many nights he would go into Darlington, Stockton, Middlesbrough or Thornaby on his motorcycle to bring air force lads back to Middleton St George.

For all his bonhomie and willingness to share the dangers of those men and women in his care, Father Lardie did not neglect his priestly pastoral role. In one of his many sermons he observed, 'it is true that our morality or lack of it is no worse than on many other stations and, perhaps, a great deal better than some, but it is also true that there are a number of you here who would gladly give their right arm were they able to return to their wives, their families or their girlfriends as clean and unsullied as they left. And it is also true that there are a number of men who have lost that sense of decency and, in some cases, their sense of shame.' The urgency and excitement of total war, the uncertainty and transitory nature of life in a Britain still under direct attack, and the simple mix of young men and women in unusual and extraordinary circumstances undoubtedly led to a breakdown of pre-war sexual morals and the broadening of sexual licence and acceptability. Husbands and wives, never knowing when or if they would meet again, young men and women far from home and parental restraint, the experienced and the inexperienced, often felt the need to love and be loved with an intensity they had never come across before. It was a heady mix but one that was, perhaps, not unexpected in time of war. However, as in any group of people, there were great variations in views and behaviour and there was certainly no mass movement towards a sexual free-for-all, especially as the authorities worked hard to prevent one. Airwomen frequently attended lectures on social hygiene and the more discreetly named mothercraft, both on the station and at the Memorial Hospital in Darlington. Men were urged by a variety of films, slide shows and posters to 'keep it in their pants'. Stomach-churning films graphically depicting the effects of venereal diseases were regularly shown and specially trained officers toured the stations delivering lectures packed with dire warnings and gory illustrations. Physical FFI (Freedom From Infection) inspections were an unwelcome and intrusive but regular feature of service life.

Sqn Ldr Kyle, Middleton St George's long-standing Medical Officer, recorded VD cases as part of his monthly report and they tend to bear out Father Lardie's view. The Canadians, far from home and, perhaps, a little more 'exotic' to many British girls (and airmen to boot), do seem to have lived it up a little more than some. Infection rates among the British Army averaged at between 9 and 12 cases per thousand throughout the war years; in 1943 6 Group's infection rate was running at 33 cases per thousand, a figure that was more in line with US Army figures. Middleton's sick quarters treated and recorded around 10 or 12 cases per month, putting it well below the 6 Group average. Nationally and probably locally, the number of illegitimate births doubled in wartime Britain to around 9 per thousand.

Many of the liaisons formed outlasted the war and some, of course, endured for lifetimes thereafter. Certainly by February 1946 some 7,197 war brides had left Britain for Canada with their RCAF husbands, taking with them no fewer than 2,466 children. The way of life many of them would encounter in Canada could be very different and, as might be expected, some marriages would make it and some would not. One article published in Middleton's station newsletter *Flarepath* in 1945 put it a little more humorously:

Ah were a hearin' thuther day that another one o' our flatlanders is planning on a tie'ng thet thar matrimonial knot. Wal these hyar English wimmen may be OK but ah don't reckon they would be a pullin' a plow or choppin' a coupla cord o' wood afore breakfast like our own gals back in the hills. Ah aint a wantin' no arnyment fur ma wife. When yuh gets hitched yuh gotta thet thar preacher feller $2 an I'm a wantin' sumthin' useful fer al thet money.

Either way many men did find it comparatively easy to meet both servicewomen and civilians and to strike up friendships and relationships. Indeed, then, like now, such relationships played a crucial role in the lives of the young men and women and tended to dominate their letters and conversations and to guide their general social life. Yet, even with the understandable spirit of carpe diem prevailing, as it had done in intense war situations since time immemorial, the younger men and women stationed at Middleton St George appear to have had a clear and acute awareness of just why they were there in the first place. For all the very necessary and pleasurable distractions, their primary aim was to prosecute a war as firmly and efficiently as possible. As aircrew member Dave Roberts, who met his wife when she was serving as a WAAF at Middleton St George, put it: 'Social activity was limited and purely secondary, operational flying was what we were there for.'

There was, of course, a great deal more to it than just operational flying, although that was the absolute *raison d'être* of the station. A bomber airfield at war was a bustling and exhausting place where the relentless and frenetic pace of occupational life seldom slackened. Close on two thousand men and women laboured long and hard to mount hundreds of sorties

A typically busy scene. A considerable number of men, skilled in many different trades, were involved in keeping a single bomber in the sky. *(Author)*

a month, each playing their part in the gigantic machine which was dealing such mighty blows to the Third Reich. However, besides this direct application of effort, there was, as in any community, a myriad of different tasks and occurrences that together formed working life on the station. The station sick quarters, under the command of Sqn Ldr Kyle for much of this period, was always busy treating the usual illnesses that tend to afflict the general population, as well as those more specific to aircrew. One of the SSQ's more unpleasant tasks was to deal with the aftermath of aircraft crashes. In May 1944, for example, a Stirling bomber from 1654 HCU on a training flight came down 3 miles west of Aycliffe in County Durham. When the news of this was received, an ambulance and a medical officer were dispatched to the scene as quickly as possible. Unfortunately all of the crew on board were dead as a result of multiple injuries and burns, but it still fell to the ambulance crew to bring the charred remains back to the station morgue to await arrangements for burial. Officers and men could also have the unenviable task of forming burial parties for deceased aircrew, many of whom were buried in West Cemetery in Darlington.

Other accidents happened on the airfield, bringing home to everyone the costs involved in waging total war. On 11 June 1943, for example, a 428 Squadron Halifax crashed immediately on take-off, setting off the enormous 4,000lb cookie and hurling flames, smoke and debris high into the sky. Amazingly the pilot, Sgt W. Lachman, was found injured but alive, still strapped into his seat which had been blown some 30 yards from the blazing wreckage. Of the rest of the crew there was little trace. Sqn Ldr Kyle treated and stabilised Lachman in the SSQ before arranging for his transfer to Northallerton Hospital. Several other airmen and women were treated for minor cuts caused by flying glass as the massive explosion smashed windows all around the airfield.

The results of motor crashes involving lorries, cars, motorcycles and even ordinary bicycles also kept the SSQ busy. Such accidents were usually caused by the inexperience or youthful exuberance of the driver and the obvious difficulties of driving at night within the wartime restrictions. Sadly, there were many injuries. On 26 February 1944, for example, LAC McCarthy, an MT driver, ploughed his light van into the back of an unlit parked vehicle. He was detained in the SSQ suffering from cuts and fractures to his left knee-cap and right ankle. Two months later another MT driver, LACW E.R.M. Wherry, was treated for shock and minor injuries after the right front wheel of the small Morris ambulance she was driving simply fell off as she was approaching the Croft Spa Hotel en route home from Northallerton Hospital. She was officially 'commended for her skill in handling a three-wheel vehicle, keeping it on the road and avoiding injury to the Nursing Sister and patients on board'. Four days later LAC Middaugh received serious injuries as a result of being hit in the dark by an unknown truck as he crossed the road near the Oak Tree pub and Main Gate. Even unexpected encounters with two-wheeled transport could cause injury. In September 1943, for example, Sqn Ldr Kyle treated an unnamed WAAF who had been knocked down by a bicycle in the black-out and left lying injured for some time; a few days later a tactfully unnamed airman was treated for minor injuries received after riding full tilt one night into a 'stray cow'.

Given that many people on the station were working with explosives, fuel and machinery, incidents and injuries were inevitable and Middleton St George suffered its fair share of mishaps. Familiarity with any situation tends to breed contempt but the consequences in such dangerous circumstances could be very serious. In May 1944, for example, two airmen received serious burns in separate incidents involving petrol. On the 6th LAC Balten suffered severe burns to his hands and left leg after fire broke out as he was filling the tank of a running motor from an ordinary bucket. A fortnight later LAC Kennedy ended up in SSQ with second-degree burns to his legs and right arm as a result of a fire at No. 1 Dispersal, probably caused by a lighted cigarette. The station authorities took a dim view of such lapses and came down hard upon the perpetrators of such carelessness which threatened the efficiency of the airfield. So, when there was an avoidable accident at No. 2 Petrol Installation Aviation in November 1944 which put both A and B delivery pipes and hoses out of action, the matter was reported to the Station Adjutant and the petrol-issuing clerk, LAC Jones, was placed under open arrest pending further investigations.

The maintenance of peak efficiency and discipline is always a difficult and contentious issue; court-martial records, for example, still remain classified today, more than sixty years after the end of the war. Most minor breaches, such as exceeding the duration of passes or leaves, drunkenness, mild insubordination or general misdemeanours, were usually dealt with at section, squadron or station levels. With transport at a premium, cars, motorcycles and even bicycles became popular targets to 'borrow'. One night in April 1944 the SSQ's new Ford van was borrowed from outside the sick quarters by a person or persons unknown. He was clearly too lazy or too late to walk to the Armaments Section, where service police found the van the next day. It had collided with a bomb-trolley, which fortunately was empty at the time. The culprit was not found. However,

AC2 Prefontaine was caught for 'being in improper possession of another airman's bicycle' and was awarded 28 days' detention by the Station Commander. The record notes that this was not an isolated incident. 'This is the airman's second offence of a similar nature in the past four months. He is a nuisance to the service and now has both sides of two conduct sheets filled'.

Other offences could be a little less obvious and take some time to uncover. In November 1943, for example, an investigation was held into delays in dealing with matters in the Accounts Section. It was found that AC2 Dione, a French-Canadian, had not bothered to deal with some of the postal invoices and had merely hidden the letters in drawers and cupboards. Upon being questioned he helpfully pointed out, 'Dey're only little ones. I send all the big ones away firs'.' Indeed, as the men and women at Middleton St George were so far from home, all mail was very precious and any tampering with it was considered very bad taste. Hence on 6 January 1944 a formal court-martial was convened under the Presidency of Sqn Ldr M.B. Sinclair, RCAF Overseas Headquarters, to hear the charges against LAC M.E. Girling, who stood accused of no fewer than 95 offences, 89 of which were of theft from the station post office – 'a record, though an unenviable one' for a total of charges made against an RCAF man. He was found guilty of embezzlement, theft and being AWOL while on a charge and was sentenced to two years in detention.

Others took a much more patriotic view and were eager to help the war effort in any way. One way of doing this was by giving blood, a simple but effective way of saving lives. The mobile transfusion service, based in Leeds, was a frequent visitor at all 6 Group airfields but found those at Middleton St George particularly keen. Responding to the demands of inter-station rivalry in March 1944, some 472 station personnel donated 59 gallons of blood, beating the record held by RAF Acklington in Northumberland. Five months later in August the station set another new record for any unit in the Canadian armed forces, when 657 donors provided a massive 82 gallons of blood. The donors were encouraged by the recent landings in Normandy and the knowledge that Canadian soldiers were in the thick of it. The blood was transferred to the Army Blood Supply Depot in Bristol before being flown out direct to Normandy.

A great deal of money was raised for the war effort, a much less specific but still very important cause. Inter-station competitions were arranged as part of the national Victory Loan campaigns, with token prizes for the station that raised the most cash. A 'Moose Stampede', for example, was arranged to raise funds for the sixth Victory Loan campaign in April 1944. As the station newsletter put it: 'Flt Lt Art Crawford, our adjutant, was the spearhead for the attack on the wallet. Crawford can talk you into buying a bond while you're still paying for the last one.' The seventh Campaign that October was the most successful, with the station raising a massive $178,050, over $100,000 more than its original target, which was matched on day one of the campaign. Much of the money had been raised by a Victory Dance held in No. 2 hangar on the 12th, supported by a gigantic raffle.

There were also a few other formal occasions to break up the more usual humdrum wartime existence. A succession of distinguished visitors, such as Lord Trenchard and AM H.I. 'Hughie' Edwards, made their way to the airfield to make inspections, hold discussions or simply fly the flag. AOC 6 Group, AVM G.E. Brookes, was a fairly regular visitor to interview candidates for commissions, even though many aircrew were automatically made officers in the RCAF. Other officers formed Trade Boards to assess the skills and capabilities of those working in the many different air force trades, and they were not always happy with what they found. One Trade Board, led by Flg Off S. Foye in August 1943, reported: 'After long discussions, it was found that Canadian personnel were not qualifying for various trades as was expected and it seems in Canadianising the station, the personnel are not fully qualified to take over responsible positions, therefore the situation is not a happy one.' For those involved, each interview or visit could have been an important date in the calendar and it is essential to bear in mind that many of the stresses and preoccupations regarding each job on the ground were much the same as in civilian life and would have loomed large in an individual's life.

Wg Cdr Maxwell, the station's Senior Engineering Officer, had a torrid time in the spring and summer of 1944. Spare parts were the bane of his life, especially as the policy of Canadianisation and the development of the Lancaster X dictated the use of Canadian versions whenever possible. The sheer scale of the logistics involved in supplying a full Bomber Group from Canada provided a difficult challenge. So he must have been all the more galled at the end of April to find that two carefully boxed artificial horizons, cajoled from another 6 Group station, had been stolen from the LNER Passenger Baggage room at

The famous Avro Lancaster 'Ruhr Express' landing at RAF Northolt on its arrival in the UK. KB700 was the first of the 300 Canadian-built Lancaster Xs manufactured by Victory Aircraft in Malton, Ontario. *(Imperial War Museum CH 11041)*

Dinsdale station. It had evidently been an opportunistic theft as they were later found dumped in a field between Dinsdale and Darlington, the thief obviously disappointed to find his haul of no use to him. However, time was precious and a fortnight later Maxwell was still visiting the police station in Darlington to chase up the investigation, since it was a non-military crime and therefore out of the jurisdiction of the service police.

Even the supply of basic maintenance essentials often failed. June 1944, for example, one of the busiest months of the entire war for the station, saw Maxwell making several trips to Darlington in order to buy tools and order certain items to be made by local manufacturers. The arrival in August of a dozen radiators, long on order, was a sufficiently noteworthy cause for celebration that it features heavily in the station log. However, the dozen turned out to be Middleton St George's entire allocation and by mid-September Maxwell was forced to make his own arrangements. The policy of Canadianisation came a distant second to necessity and Maxwell paid a personal visit to A.V. Roe in Manchester to make contingency arrangements to supply spare parts from British sources. Within two days another twenty radiators and many other parts necessary to keep the Lancasters in the air came through the gates of Middleton St George. This brief snapshot of the difficulties endured on a day-to-day basis by a 'penguin' officer provides an illuminating counter to both the stresses of operational flying and the gaiety of some aspects of the social scene.

Any visit by a high-ranking officer or VIP resulted in a high level of spit and polish, or bull. At Middleton St George two such visits stand out, both in 1944. The first was that of His Eminence Cardinal Jean Marie Rodrique Villeneuve, the Archbishop of Quebec, who arrived on 28 October, accompanied by Air Cdre the Rt Revd Monsignor J. Charent, Principal Chaplain Air Force Headquarters, Ottawa, and a whole host of aides. A formal reception was laid on for them, as was a special dinner in the officers' mess that evening. The following day at 10:45 Mass was celebrated in French and English in the station chapel for a congregation so large that it spilled outside. The less charitable were quick to surmise that not all were willing celebrants, given the consistently poorly attended weekly services. Either way, it was a significant and moving visit made all the more poignant by its renewal of the distant yet emotive links with home far away.

The second was the royal visit on 11 August 1944, an event which involved everyone on the station in one way or another. Careful yet discreet preparations had been made for the arrival of King George VI, Queen Elizabeth and Princesses Elizabeth and Margaret as part of their whistle-stop tour of 6 Group. The royal party arrived at 16:15 hours precisely and straightaway embarked on a tour of the airfield and its aircraft. By 16:40 the King was chatting to a selected group of ground and aircrew before fitting in a quick cup of tea with the senior officers on the station. The highlight was a formal parade during which there was an investiture of twenty-one airmen, awarded the DFC, DFM or DSO. This was followed by a formal presentation of 419 Squadron's crest by the King to Wg Cdr Pleasance. Princess Elizabeth, it was noted, was particularly intrigued by its motto, 'Moosa Aswayita', written in the Cree language and taken in honour of 'Moose' Fulton, the squadron's revered first commander. By 17:45 it was all over and the royal party swept on to further engagements. However, the effect of this visit on the morale of

The beautiful young Princess Elizabeth proved a huge hit with all ranks during her visit to Middleton St George in August 1944. She is seen here with AVM C.M. 'Black Mike' McEwen, AOC 6 Group, and Air Cdre R. McBurney, OC 64 Base, RCAF (Middleton St George). *(Department of National Defence PL 32652)*

those serving at Middleton St George should not be underestimated or discounted. The station record simply stated: 'It was in all aspects a case of they came, they saw and they conquered.' Photographs of the visit, particularly the investiture, appeared in the local and national press and over the Atlantic in Canada; it was a powerful reminder of the strong ties binding the two nations together and a symbol of the genuine appreciation felt in Britain for Canada's unstinting and effective support in prosecuting a long and bloody war. The following day AM L.S. Breadner, AOC RCAF Overseas, received an official letter. 'Their Majesties wish me to thank you and those associated with you for the admirable arrangements made for their visit yesterday to the Canadian Bomber Group. The King and Queen thoroughly enjoyed their day and were much impressed by all you had to show them.'

By the time the Lancasters were lined up on the runway shortly after the end of the war in Europe, ready to head back across the Atlantic, their crews and support staff had made many friends, not only in the local area but in Britain and throughout the Empire. One WAAF, who served as a batwoman on the station, wrote many years later:

I often like to recall the happiest story I know. Their task was completed and they had helped us do a grand job. All the Lancasters were lined up on the runway, waiting for the crews to fly back to Canada. They were given a grand send-off, saying a last farewell by dropping flares as they made for home. We were so proud of them and the famous Lancaster which had done so much to shorten the war. Our thoughts went out to the mothers and fathers, wives and sweethearts who would never see their boys again.

Many of the men lost had no known grave and those that did lay thousands of miles from home, making it impossible in most cases for the family to visit. In addition to those scattered throughout northern Europe, almost 850 young Canadian airmen are buried in cemeteries around North Yorkshire and County Durham.

Sometimes local people took it upon themselves to visit and tend these graves. Mrs Betty Elnridge, whose husband was serving in the RAF overseas, recalls that her mother-in-law lived near West Cemetery in Darlington and that one day at a friend's house they met two Canadian airmen from Middleton, who told them

about one plane that had returned from a raid with three of the crew being killed. My mother-in-law said could we write to their families as we often used to walk in the cemetery where these people were buried. We wrote three letters and my mother-in-law heard from the mother of one and I heard from the mother of another one. The wife did not write back to us. I wrote to mine all during the war and we used to visit the graves, at first just a mound of earth with a cross and finally with a headstone. I sent his mother a photo of his grave. He was Sgt Jette and his family farmed just near Quebec. We wrote till the end of the war and then we stopped. My mother-in-law and I thought by visiting the graves and putting flowers there sometimes, it would help their families. [It was] just a little gesture as they were so far from home.

These simple sentiments, revealed well over half a century later in a letter to the author, speak volumes about the unity of spirit and purpose prevalent during the war. Indeed, that spirit of caring remembrance has remained very much alive throughout the postwar years and into the twenty-first century on both sides of the Atlantic. On 9 February 1943 Kamloops City Council passed a motion officially adopting 419 Squadron. Fifteen months later, on 29 May 1944, the small airfield outside Kamloops was renamed Fulton Field at a ceremony attended by the Governor-General of Canada, the Earl of Athlone. The ties between squadron and city remained strong throughout the war and the squadron owed many of its comforts to the generosity of the townsfolk thousands of miles away. In spite of several periods of disbandment, the link survived and on 9 February 1993 the City Council reaffirmed it. In a well attended ceremony Mayor Cuff Blanchflower granted the squadron the freedom of the city and unveiled a plaque to the squadron at the airfield. In return the squadron, under the command of Lt Col Erlandson, presented the town with a pedestal-mounted CF-5 fighter.

Nor had the Canadians of 419, 420 and 428 Squadrons been forgotten in the United Kingdom. Eddie Scott-Jones, himself a pilot with the best part of thirty trips under his belt, and stationed at Middleton St George, explained in a letter to the author how the memorial at the airfield came about:

I think I can lay claim to originating the memorial. At the time I was dismayed that there was nothing at Middleton St George to pay tribute to the Canadians (and RAF) who failed to return. So after a lot of doodling and rough sketches, I produced a design and colour drawing of it in situ, in front of the hotel (once the officers' mess). Next step was to contact a sculptor and here I was fortunate to have one on my doorstep, one James McLaughlin, an artist of top rank. He was able to give me a breakdown of costs so the next thing was fundraising both here and in Canada. The form of the memorial I wanted was a smooth piece of Welsh slate for the lettering and squadron crests, enamelled, and mounted on a rough-hewn block of Parbold granite. With the cooperation of the quarry manager we were able to buy a piece of rock just as it came off the face after blasting. One side had to be sawn smooth to take the slate. I was helped at this stage by Harry Prendergast, ex-428 Squadron, who lived near me [in Knotty Ash, Liverpool]. The slate complete with all lettering and crests was secured to the rock with phosphor bronze bolts.

The memorial was formally placed in front of the entrance to the hotel at the airport and dedicated before a large gathering of veterans, dignitaries and well-wishers on 15 June 1985. There to help carry out the proceedings was Father J. P. Lardie, who gave a moving address:

We Canadians are not warlike people. Twice, however, in this century it was thrust upon our nation to stand against aggression and join with our allies in a war that was not of our making. It was our turn, in that second conflict, to take our stand, if necessary, even to the death, in a struggle against the tyrant who had set his legions loose upon the earth to conquer the world and crush beneath their marching feet even our belief in God who made us.

Then after those bitter years of war, when we went back to our own land to take up normal life once more, we did not all go back. There were many of our brothers who did not make that journey home, whose broken bodies are buried in a half a dozen countries across the Channel or here in England in places such as Harrogate and Runnymede. For most of them it meant the kind of separation from their families that death does not normally impose. And our hearts go out to the families of those good men, many of them just boys, whose loved ones have never even had the privilege of visiting their graves.

So it is with mixed emotions that we have come back to the Royal Canadian Air Force Base that was known to us as Middleton St George. We have come back to the place where we gave so much of ourselves in the struggle to save our kind from the tyranny of a madman whose purpose it was to enslave us all. And having given all that we were asked to give for our country and for human kind, we can now take pride in the memory of what was accomplished on and from this RCAF base from 1942 to 6 May 1945.

In those three years our company here was made up of transport drivers and bomb-dump personnel, of pilots and PT officers, of administration clerks and wireless operators, of bowser drivers and de-briefing clerks, of engine mechanics and bomb aimers, of mid-upper gunners and cooks, of central record clerks and navigators, of flight engineers, of rear gunners, and chaplains – yes chaplains, Protestant, Catholic and Jewish, whose duty it was to provide the facilities of spiritual life to all who shared their faith, and to keep before the minds of all that the only killing that could be done by civilised men was done in self-defence.

One day, when the history of the twentieth century is finally written, it will be recorded that when human society stood at the crossroads and civilisation itself was under siege, the Royal Canadian Air Force was there to fill the breach and help give humanity the victory. And all those who had a part in it will have left to posterity a legacy of honour, of courage, of valour that time can never despoil. It is for this that we have come so far to pay our thanks to God, for, in the final analysis, the victory was His, not ours, and for that may His Holy Name be for ever praised.

Three thousand miles across a hunted ocean they came, wearing on the shoulder of their tunics the treasured name 'Canada', telling the world their origin. Young men and women they were, some still in their teens, fashioned by their Maker to love, not to kill, but proud and earnest in their mission to stand, and if it had to be, to die for their country and for freedom. They gave what they had, all of them, and so this monument stands in mute tribute to their valour. It stands on soil that once was part of England but now, for as long as this island shall last, it can rightly be called 'A Tiny Piece of Canada'.

In the early summer of 2004 the role of the Canadians at Middleton St George again came to the fore in the north-east of England. It had long been felt by local politicians that the name Teesside Airport did not give the correct impression – after all, it is in County Durham and some miles from Teesside. After much wrangling, it was decided to rename it Durham Tees Valley Airport, hardly a mellifluous title, but it kept most of the councillors happy. However, one of the suggestions had been to name it after Andrew Mynarski, who won the Victoria Cross while based at Middleton St George. The suggestion struck a chord in the minds of the local population and, backed by the *Northern Echo*, an appeal was launched to create a memorial to this courageous Canadian airman. The 'Forgotten Hero' campaign set itself a target of £40,000, but such was its widespread public appeal that, including a grant from the Heritage Lottery Fund, it reached the astonishing total of £76,000.

North-east sculptor Keith Maddison, himself an aviation enthusiast and RAF Reservist, was commissioned to produce the 8ft 6in bronze statue of Mynarski in full flying kit, saluting with his parachute ready, just as he was in June 1944. The statue, cast at the Black Isle bronze foundry in Nairn, near Inverness, was to be unveiled at a ceremony held at the airport on Saturday 4 June by Colleen Bacon and Sherry Sullivan, the daughters of Pat Brophy, the rear gunner that Mynarski had battled so bravely to rescue. Shirley Friday, widow of bomb aimer Jack Friday, flew in from Thunder Bay in Ontario and Ellen Vigars made the shorter journey from Guildford in Surrey to attend. Quite a number of veterans, not so young as they once were, assembled from all over Britain, Europe and Canada, to take part in the proceedings and the proud march-past.

Colleen Bacon, the daughter of Pat Brophy, unveils the statue of Andrew Mynarski VC on 4 June 2005. (*Northern Echo*)

Prime Minister Tony Blair, whose Sedgefield constituency included the Durham Tees Valley Airport, could not attend, but was quoted by the *Northern Echo* as saying, 'I think it is a fantastic commemoration. By celebrating Mynarski's bravery, the statue will remind everyone who passes through the airport of all those who sacrificed and risked so much. It reminds us of how we struggled for freedom and democracy in this country and what a great deal we owe to my father's generation.'

If the ghosts of the young British and Canadian airmen were watching on the morning of 4 June 2005, one thing would have made them smile. The weather was atrocious but the heavy rain showers failed to dampen the spirit of the occasion. The ceremony began at 11 o'clock sharp, and the magnificent statue was duly unveiled and dedicated. At 11:30, the air began to carry the distant but unmistakable roar of four Merlin engines. All in the large crowd, young and old alike, raised their eyes and scanned the leaden sky for the first sight of the Lancaster of the Battle of Britain Memorial Flight. The 60-year-old bomber flew low and slow overhead, everyone's heads turning to follow its graceful progress. The local Middleton St George Primary School children then led the renditions of the Canadian and British national anthems before the final march-past, which included both veterans and contingents of the Air Training Corps from Canada and the local area. The salute was taken by Canadian Col Dan Edgar, representing the Canadian High Commissioner.

Sherry Sullivan summed up her feelings on that day to waiting journalists from both Britain and Canada: 'I felt proud to be a part of all this and the heritage that goes with it. It has been an experience beyond words.' Her sister, Colleen Bacon, added: 'It has been a phenomenal day. To have that kind of recognition given in England and to know it was initiated by the English I think was an incredible honour.'

Sixty years on the overwhelming majority of people in Britain have not forgotten the war, nor the many thousands of men and women from around the world who helped them to win it. That is how it should be, and long may it be so.

CHAPTER 5

The Dawn of a New Era

For the best part of a month there was no operational flying at Middleton St George, allowing a great deal of essential maintenance work to be carried out. It was not until 15 October 1942 that the skies over Middleton St George once more throbbed with the roar of powerful aero engines. The Wellington IIIs of 420 Squadron, under the command of Wg Cdr D.A.R. Bradshaw, appeared as dots on the horizon, then grew larger and finally, after circling their new airfield like moths around a lamp, came gently to rest on the tarmac runway. The crews jumped out of their aircraft, keen to explore the new surroundings that were to be their home for the weeks ahead. After the spartan wartime station at Skipton, where 420 Squadron had been the first residents a couple of months earlier in August 1942, the crews were delighted to find themselves at what was effectively a peacetime-designed airfield. Even with its fair share of huts and sheds, the quality of the surroundings at Middleton St George was considerably better for the crews and airmen. Alan Helmsley, a Canadian navigator, arrived at Middleton on 15 October and, in the chill of autumn, was immediately impressed by two features notably absent at Skipton: excellent food and central heating.

Helmsley had little time to enjoy his comparatively luxurious surroundings, for that night 420 Squadron contributed seven aircraft to a posse of 289 bound for that old chestnut, Cologne. The raid proved unsuccessful on account of the effect of different winds from those forecast and a thick belt of cloud over the target. For Helmsley and his crew the night was an eventful and tense one as their aircraft sustained damage over the target and

> on the return the port tanks were leaking petrol and at the Dutch coast both engines were leaking oil. With Vollum [W/Op Bob Vollum RAF] pumping oil and the port fuel gauges reading zero, we just managed to reach the English coast and land at an airfield near the Thames estuary. The port engine died on the approach at about 400ft but Wilson [Doyle Wilson RCAF] managed a good landing. The tail wheel was smashed, however, and we returned to Middleton St George by train the next day.

The Wellington III of 420 Squadron crewed by Flt Sgt L. White, Flt Sgt G. Bing, Flt Sgt J. Joynt, Sgt D. Smyth and Plt Off F. Buck, all of the RCAF, was not so lucky, with nothing being heard of it after take-off from Middleton at 18:52 hours.

For 420 Squadron this night was nothing out of the ordinary; it had endured many similar ones since its first operations on 21 April 1942. It had been 'been brought into being on 19th December 1941,' the official diary recorded, although 'it was then of course no more than a name. It is hoped in time that this squadron will be composed entirely of Canadian personnel. The object of 420 RCAF Squadron is to become an operational squadron in the shortest possible time and the effects of all personnel will be bent to this aim.' The enthusiasm and determination were maintained as the long-awaited day came. 'Red letter day. We were okayed for operations. Everyone was as keen as mustard to start the real job of bombing the enemy.' Since that day in April 420 Squadron had attacked most of the big targets in Germany and was now ready to carry the war to the enemy from a new home base.

The early winter weather, however, did not prove helpful in this respect, forcing the cancellation of several scheduled attacks upon Emden, Krefeld and Norden. It was not until the last day of the month that an attack was actually carried out. The target for just eight Wellingtons, three of which were provided by 420 Squadron, was Emden, not that any of the crews could in fact see it. The town was blanketed by 10/10ths cloud and the best that the crews could do was bomb on ETA and dead reckoning, scant reward for all the nervous tension and poor flying conditions they had endured. A new squadron but the same old problems.

A further raid to Duisburg on 4 November also fell victim to the weather but on the 6th 420 Squadron sent three aircraft on a daylight raid to Wilhelmshaven, intending to take advantage of the cloudy conditions the Met. officers had predicted. In the event the cloud proved far more of a dangerous hindrance than anything else. Plt Off J. Hudson could not find a break in the cloud over the target and made the bold decision to drop down beneath the cloud, crossing the inland port at just 800ft, seemingly the sole target for every anti-aircraft gun in the area. Hit by the wall of flak being hurled into the sky, Hudson turned away and headed towards the clouds once more, letting his bomb-load go as he passed over a 4,000-ton barge. No results of this action, which took place at 13:46, were seen. Plt Off J.B. Burt failed to locate the target area in the murk but instead bombed an unidentified coastal inlet in which three 100ft-long barges were moored; again no results were visible. The third crew, piloted by Sgt R.E. Taylor, also failed to locate the target but attacked what he believed to be the main built-up area of Norden at 14:20 hours from just 50ft. Dust, debris and extremely low altitude combined to thwart any assessment of the damage caused. All three crews were more than happy to make it home, the last at 17:20 hours. Bombing by day was not any easier than bombing by night.

Even so-called milk-run Gardening sorties were far from easy and sometimes dangerous, as events two days later showed. Ten aircraft from 420 Squadron were dispatched to lay mines off Necturn in the early evening of 8 November. Three were unable to locate the correct drop-zone in the appalling weather conditions and returned with their mines onboard. Six did carry out the operation as planned, but another, that of Sgt Lawson, strayed off course and into the strong defences of Borkum. Dropping like a stone from a vulnerable 3,000ft to just 50ft, he banked hard and flew out to sea with his flaps shot to pieces, his intercom system U/S and his W/Op badly wounded in the leg.

Except for a scattered and ineffective attack on Hamburg and two successful mining operations on 10 and 16 November, 420 Squadron did not have a chance to carry out operations as the capricious weather once more clamped down. There was, however, much to do, especially as the station's second unit, 419 Squadron, had taken up residence between 9 and 11 November. It would be several weeks, however, before 419 Squadron joined the Order of Battle properly as it was deep in the throes of conversion to the four-engined Halifax II.

In fact 419 Squadron had been one of the first Canadian bomber squadrons formed, coming into being at Mildenhall in Suffolk on 15 December 1941 under the command of Wg Cdr John Fulton DFC. Fulton, a native of Kamloops in British Columbia, was one of the many Canadians who crossed the Atlantic in search of a pre-war career with the RAF but transferred to the RCAF when the opportunity arose during the war. Known throughout his career as 'Moose', it is his nickname that has lived on in 419 Squadron in its various guises ever since. It was he who led the squadron on its first operation, an attack on Brest on 11 January 1942, and his professional yet aggressive approach did much to foster the strong squadron spirit that characterised 419 Squadron's outlook on the war. Awarded the DSO for his leadership and flying skills in a raid on Kiel in April 1942, Wg Cdr Fulton failed to return from a raid on Hamburg in the early hours of 29 July 1942. The last message from his aircraft was brief, stating simply: 'Fighters, wounded, 500ft'; the QDM bearings placed it 10 miles west of the Frisian Islands. No trace of the experienced crew was found. Nevertheless, 419 (Moose) Squadron remained, in many ways, Fulton's and it was a battle-hardened set of crews who made the short flight from Croft on the other side of the River Tees to Middleton St George on 11 November 1942.

The lengthy conversion process became even more drawn out owing to a shortage of aircraft on which the pilots, aircrew and ground crews could work. This slow build-up of aircraft and stores was not helped by Flt Sgt Frederick, who misjudged his landing on the airfield on the morning of 30 November, wrecking the undercarriage and damaging the propellers and engines. Though in some ways it was a welcome break for them, it was also frustrating for the members of 419 Squadron to watch 420's aircraft operating full steam ahead.

The weather cheered sufficiently on 20 November to warrant launching a major raid on the Italian industrial city of Turin. Seven of the nine aircraft scheduled to take part flew that morning to the advance base of Harwell in Oxfordshire in preparation for the night's long journey. A total of 232 aircraft ploughed on through 10/10ths cloud but, as predicted by the Met. Office staff, the clouds melted away as they crossed the Alps, and Turin was easily located and identified in bright moonlight. Flt Lt L.S. Anderson described the sortie as 'very successful from the operational and navigational point of view. The whole trip was over 10/10ths cloud with the exception of the target . . . we identified the target by the PFF flares and the sight of the Rip and Po rivers.' One column of smoke from the north-west section of the city was reported to reach over 4,000ft up into the night sky and Turin certainly suffered a heavy blow as 117 residents lost their lives that night with a similar number wounded.

Two nights later Wg Cdr D.A.R. Bradshaw led eight of his crews on a trip to Stuttgart, again taking off from Harwell. Once again the bombers had to plough through heavy cloud, though this did thin sufficiently to allow glimpses of the ground in the target area. This was all the Pathfinders needed and their dazzling markers burned brightly, a beacon for those following behind. Bradshaw wrote in his report:

> PFF flares illuminated on time and very accurately. Many aircraft appear to have arrived on target before time. When green and red marker flares were dropped, a large number of aircraft bombed in the first five minutes. Bombs appeared to fall in the built-up area. Target could be easily identified visually, streets, houses and rivers, showing up clearly in the moonlight. Fires grew as the attack progressed and were still visible 150 miles from target.

The raid was indeed successful and town records from Stuttgart show that the railway station suffered severe damage that night, possibly caused in particular by two unidentified and very low flying bombers.

Low flying was obviously the order of the day, as Plt Off J.B. Burt recounts:

> The second pilot was flying us home when we ran over Paris. I took over and descended to 50 feet to get out of the searchlights and light flak and received a direct hit on the aircraft, smashing the hydraulics and causing the wheels to come down. A direct hit behind the instrument panel made all flying instruments and engine instruments U/S, except the port rev counter. The starboard engine was hit which caused rough running and loss of engine oil. The rear gunner put out several searchlights and stopped guns by fire from his turret. Sqn Ldr Williams, the second pilot, was hit slightly in the leg by flak. Crash-landed at Hunsdon.

On 23, 25 and 26 November 420 Squadron was again involved in general Gardening operations. The murky winter conditions made accurate positioning of the mines very difficult and several aircraft were forced to bring their 'vegetables' back to base. The report of Flt Lt L.S. Anderson, who took off at 16:48 on the 26th, gives a flavour of such a sortie:

> Very unsuccessful trip. Brought vegetable back. We flew in and out of 8/10 cloud over England. The trip out in the Channel was below 10/10 cloud and we were unable to see the sea. I flew for another hour and due to the lack of fixes I assumed we would be unable to pinpoint the islands in such conditions. Thus knowing we could not drop our mines on DR I turned and headed for Predonack.

Flying in such tricky and hostile conditions was very wearing on the crews and the sense of failure which often went with them did little to raise their enthusiasm for such mining trips. This was, as it turned out, the last operation of the month as the murky winter weather put paid to those sorties planned.

The pattern continued in December, with raids on Hannover, Cologne and Duisburg all being planned and then called off on account of the weather. There was, however, plenty of action at Middleton St George, where a succession of high-ranking visitors kept the station on its toes and ensured that there was a healthy amount of bull. The visits by AVM Carr,

AOC 4 Group, and AVM Brookes RCAF lasted for two days, and they were followed a couple of days later by AVM Curtis RCAF, Deputy AOC Overseas, all paving the way for the official handover of Middleton St George to the Canadians at the end of the month. Curtis, a veteran of the RNAS in the First World War, did at least get to see an operation take place as on 6 December 420 Squadron contributed ten aircraft to a large raid on Mannheim. Three of the crews were forced to return early with mechanical trouble but the remainder pressed on in atrocious conditions only to find the target area completely smothered by a thick and impenetrable layer of cloud, offering no chance of an accurate and concentrated attack.

Two more night mining operations were undertaken before the crews swapped theatres of war and set course for the Italian industrial city of Turin on 9 December. This was to be the first of three raids on the city in rapid succession, designed to bring home to the Italians the cost of their involvement in the war. Eight aircraft left Middleton St George that morning, making the short trip to Harwell in Oxfordshire in not much more than an hour. In good conditions the Pathfinders easily located the target and dropped well-placed markers which resulted in accurate and concentrated bombing, damaging both residential and industrial areas of the city. In all 212 people were recorded as losing their lives with another 111 seriously injured that night; as the squadron record puts it: 'the attack was considered highly satisfactory'. Indeed, the fires were still burning the next night when a force of over 200 bombers attacked the city again.

The following day saw a significant change take place on the station with Gp Capt W.M. McKechnie GC being posted to Whitchurch Heath. His successor as Station Commander was Gp Capt Dwight Ross, whose main task it was to oversee the smooth handover of the base to the RCAF and its expansion to two fully operational squadrons. The next ten days were frustrating for the young crews, with mining operations being slated for each day before the fickle winter weather clamped down either in England or over the target area.

GARDENING AND THE BATTLE OF THE ATLANTIC

On 22 December 420 Squadron provided the full attacking force for a daylight cloud-cover raid on Emden. Bomber Command had flirted with this kind of daylight raid on and off for two years, never quite achieving the success such a raid promised yet never quite failing badly enough to put an end to such a highly dangerous mode of attack. On this occasion not only did the cloud cover stretch right across the North Sea, offering the six Wellingtons welcome protection, but also right over the target area, preventing them from any semblance of an accurate assault. It was not for want of trying on the part of the crews; Alan Helmsley recalls what he describes as a nuisance raid: 'We were a lone Wellington in cloud all the way and let down to 450 feet before the target became only slightly visible. Crowther (the bomb aimer known as Buss) let the bombs go but could not be certain of what was achieved.' Only three other crews bombed the Emden area, with one frustrated crew unable to release its load over the target owing to technical problems and another unable to locate the target area and releasing their bombs over a town identified as Pilsum. All crews, at least, managed to find their way back to base safely.

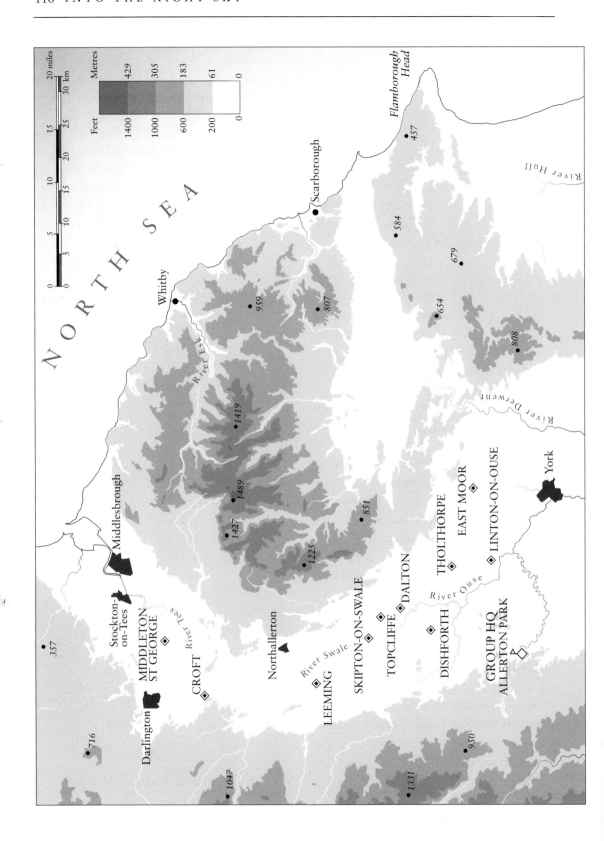

The station diary notes: 'The Christmas period was marked by incessant low cloud which made ops impossible. Consequently the station was given over to seasonal revelry and a good time was had by all. The weather did not provide a white Christmas but the Canadian personnel enjoyed themselves thoroughly.' Indeed, the Canadians had a double reason for a celebration at the end of the month; not only was it New Year, but it was also the date of the official handover of RAF Middleton St George to the RCAF. The station diary added:

At 0001 hours Middleton St George and Croft were transferred from 4 Group RAF to 6 Group RCAF. A new era started today and the official birth of 6 Group RCAF was registered. All concerned realised that there was only one goal ahead and that was to do everything possible to ensure that under its new control, the station and its satellite should maintain its grand record of service and efficiency.

AVM G.E. Brookes was the AOC of 6 (RCAF) Group from its creation on 1 January 1943 until late February 1944. *(Department of National Defence PL 142657)*

For everyone at the station, once the festivities were over it was very much back to business.

Although the weather continued to take a heavy toll of scheduled operations, the general routine went on regardless. On 4 January Sqn Ldr Hewitt and AVM Brookes interviewed NCO candidates for commissions. That afternoon Brookes played host to the Inspector-General of the RAF, the former AOC Bomber Command, ACM Sir Edgar Ludlow-Hewitt KCB, CMG, DSO, MC, on his flying tour of airfields in the new group. Routine flying practice was carried out whenever conditions allowed; there were two matters of interest in this month.

Many others before him and after him might well have found themselves in a similar situation following a bout of youthful exuberance but Sgt Clary was sufficiently unlucky to make a slight misjudgement and get caught. On the 5th Clary found himself facing charges of flying negligently in such a manner as to cause his aircraft to clip a tree, causing damage to the aircraft, and of endangering the lives of his crew by flying recklessly at less than 70ft. These were serious charges, especially at a time when both crews and aircraft were at a premium. He was found guilty as charged, but such was the pressing nature of the circumstances that he was given only a severe reprimand and a reduction in his seniority, thereby delaying his promotion to higher rank.

The second incident had more tragic results. At 12:26 a Wellington from 427 Squadron based at Croft attempted to land at Middleton St George in poor visibility. Drifting too far down the runway, the aircraft overshot and came to rest just inside the boundary fence with one wing sticking out over the adjacent railway line. Within two minutes a goods train from Eaglescliff came thundering along the line. Unable to stop in time, the train ripped the wing from the fuselage. The petrol in the wing tanks ignited and engulfed the goods train in flames. The stoker, in an attempt to escape from the raging inferno that had engulfed his cab, jumped from the moving train and was killed. Fortunately, the crew of the aircraft, which also caught fire, managed to escape unhurt. The pall of smoke was visible for some miles. Such were the dangers of flying at the marginal limits of safety, even without the interference of the enemy.

The crews on the station, who passionately disliked being able to actually watch the loss of aircraft, had another nerve-jangling experience later that day. Ten of 420 Squadron's aircraft were scheduled for a mine-laying operation, and were actually airborne and passing over the coast when the signal to cancel reached them. Alan Helmsley was in one of those crews, and wrote in his diary: 'weather has been bad lately, with snow, rain and cold, cold wind. Hell of a country in winter.'

The following night proved to be a red letter one, with the first operations undertaken by 419 Squadron since their conversion to Halifaxes and their arrival at Middleton St George. Indeed, it was a busy day for the ground crews, preparing six of 419 Squadron's Halifaxes for a mine-laying operation and nine of 420 Squadron's for a similar mission off Terschelling. Of the latter, one aircraft returned early with a dead starboard engine and another brought back its vegetable after failing to locate the checkpoint, leaving the remaining seven aircraft to carry out their orders successfully. In contrast, 419 Squadron's night was more exciting. One of the Halifaxes failed even to make the starting line as a result of a sudden attack of the gremlins. Ian Duncan, the bomb aimer in Sqn Ldr Clark RNZAF's crew, was in 'the first aircraft off at 4.30 p.m. The duration of the flight was 5 hours and 30 minutes in which we dropped two 1500lb mines off Simonsland. On this occasion I note that the navigator brought us right on the pinpoint but that I as the bomb aimer did not identify it right away so we went out to sea, came down lower and dropped the mines to my satisfaction and returned home without further incident.'

There were, however, incidents a-plenty for Flg Off Pat Porter and his crew that night. All of the crew were actively engaged in scanning the skies and seas as the Halifax bumped its way through a solid blanket of thick cloud, dropping down to less than 1,000ft. Lying in the vulnerable bomb-aimer's position in the nose, George Sweanor recalls that he suddenly saw a dark shape loom out of the murk directly in front of him but before he had time to shout any warning the aircraft 'filled with cordite fumes as two streams of tracers joined just above us. In this new light I could see German flak ships firing at us: two were to port, one to starboard.' Sweanor first shouted for his pilot to dive in order to get beneath the line of fire but quickly changed his tune as the white-capped sea rushed up to meet him. Skimming just above the stormy sea and weaving madly the Halifax succeeded in avoiding both the unwelcome attentions of the flak ships and a watery grave. The crew then put themselves back on track and dropped their vegetable in the correct patch without further interruption. On the return leg the crew reported seeing a sudden flash lighting up the night sky, and this may well have been caused by Sgt F.H. Barker's Halifax exploding. Certainly, no trace of the aircraft was ever found, although six weeks later the body of Sgt D.A. Watson, the bomb aimer, was found washed up on the coast of Sweden. He lies in Grebbtad, Sweden, after being laid to rest with full military honours. This loss, as the first for some time, was taken especially hard.

On the night of the 15th four Wellingtons of 420 Squadron and six Halifaxes of 419 Squadron were dispatched to attack Lorient, an important French port that was then being used as a crucial U-boat base. This was 6 Group's first bombing mission and all the crews were anxious to show what they could do. The PFF did an excellent job of marking that night and their dazzling colours captivated Ian Duncan: 'I was so engrossed in watching the TIs going down that I forgot to release the bombs and so we had to go round a second time, much to the disgust of the rest of the crew. Fortunately, there were few searchlights and even less flak; as a matter of fact, there was more activity on crossing the coast.' As it turned out, the marking was far more accurate than the bombing which had wandered towards the town centre where over a hundred buildings were destroyed or damaged and a dozen people killed.

The winter weather clamped down once more and it was not until the 21st that the aircraft based at Middleton St George could take to the skies operationally, gardening in the 'Nectarines' area off the Frisian Islands. Three nights later three aircraft of 420 Squadron were put down for one of the most dangerous and nerve-wracking types of operation, a cloud-cover daylight raid on Essen. As it happened, the cloud cover was too good, hampering visibility and target identification. One aircraft bombed, from low level, a railway station believed to be Dornum, also shooting up a train to good effect east of the station (an attack confirmed as successful by a crew from 425 Squadron), while the second bombed what was identified as Tettiens and the other hit either Werdu or Stedesdorf. This was once again hardly a ringing endorsement of the effectiveness of this kind of raid, but at least all three aircraft made it home safely.

No. 419 Squadron was busy that night, making its contribution to the Battle of the Atlantic with an attack on Lorient as part of a series of raids intended to disrupt U-boat activities. The weather was atrocious during this period and the crews regularly met with severe icing, torrential rain, electrical storms and dense cloud stretching from virtually ground level to 22,000ft. Several crews decided to jettison their loads, turn round and head for home through the murk. Alan Helmsley's crew had a different and unusual reason for turning back:

All went well until we crossed the French coast at 18,000ft when Wilson [Douglas Wilson RCAF, pilot] passed out. Just as Vollum [Bob Vollum RAF, W/Op] got the cabin door open and could see Wilson, he regained consciousness, planted both feet on the instrument panel and hauled back on the control column. We lost about 3,000ft. The G-force from the pull-out flung us on to the floor but the wings stayed on. The compass was rendered U/S and Wilson decided to turn back. We made it to the English coast after dropping the 4,000lb bomb in the Channel and landed at Turweston, a satellite of Chipping Warden. Owing to bad weather, we did not return to base until 1 February. Although medical examinations could not account for Wilson's collapse, he was grounded and finally returned to Canada. This broke up the crew which was beginning to work well together.

Other procedures were revealed as not working so well that night. Sgt D. Sanderson's crew from 420 Squadron had turned around on account of the dreadful conditions but had difficulties in jettisoning their bomb-load over the Channel. Sanderson decided to put down at the first airfield he could find and managed to locate Exeter. Unfortunately the aircraft crashed on landing just after 23:00 hours, killing Flt Sgt Daunton, the navigator, Sgt Bittner, a gunner, Flt Sgt Sealy, the bomb aimer, and Sanderson himself. Three of them were buried at Exeter but Sealy, though Canadian like the others, was buried in Bridgwater at his family's request. However, the sad arrangements for this did not go as smoothly as they should, as the squadron's log records:

> The usual procedure of casualty signals and circumstantial reports got under way with considerable difficulty. Due to the Canadianisation policy, the squadron orderly room has been stripped of nearly all its experienced personnel. Drastic postings have made it difficult or almost impossible to get a man trained on one job, with the result that a smooth working system is lacking. It is strongly recommended that a policy is adopted whereby, where postings are necessary, they can be carried out in a more practical manner.

It was a small yet poignant reminder of the practical and human implications of political policy. No news was ever received about the fate of another of 420 Squadron's aircraft lost that night, that of Plt Off E.J. Stanton. It was, perhaps, the unfortunate victim of the predicted heavy flak reported over the target area. It was a sad note on which to end what had been a frustrating month in both operational and human terms, especially after the high hopes and spirits at the Group's inauguration.

Two social events did, however, go down a bomb, coincidentally yet neatly one for each squadron. For 419 Squadron it was the party held after receiving the news that the town of Kamloops in British Columbia wished to adopt 419 Squadron in commemoration of its first CO, the late Wg Cdr 'Moose' Fulton, who was a native of the town. For 420 Squadron, it was an enormous bash held at the Bath Hall in Darlington, complete with a 12-piece band, to commemorate the anniversary of the squadron's formation.

However, on 2 February it was back to business and 419 Squadron's Halifaxes were dispatched to the Kattegat to lay mines. Owing to driving rain and snow and 10/10ths cloud, five of the crews were unable to locate their target area and headed for home. Only three were confident enough of their position to risk dropping their mines, though two of these were on ETA. The 3rd saw Middleton St George make its greatest effort for some time, providing a nominal total of twenty-three aircraft for an attack on the dockyards of Hamburg. As it turned out, only four of these aircraft actually bombed the city, the rest being forced to return early as a result of harsh weather and severe icing. The heavy cloud conditions resulted in both marking and bombing being scattered, though several large fires were started, two of them in major oil depots. A total of 55 people were killed and 40 injured on the ground and 16 bombers, some 6.1 per cent of the attacking force, were lost in the air, brought down either by flak or by night-fighters – a neat balance in numerical terms only. One of those lost that night came from 419 Squadron. Sgt J.D. MacKenzie's Halifax had been a few minutes late crossing the French coast and was hurrying to make up time when the intercom system packed up. Although this was a legitimate reason for turning back, especially in such lousy conditions, MacKenzie decided to press on. Flying at 21,000ft and still some 25 minutes from the target, the Halifax was unexpectedly raked by machine-gun and cannon fire from an aircraft identified by the gunner as either an Fw190 or an Me110. Whichever it was, the incoming fire killed the pilot and set fire to the incendiaries in the bomb bay. In spite of the best efforts of the flight engineer, Sgt W. Duthie, the fire began to spread and it became clear that the Halifax was doomed. The defunct intercom system did not help matters, nor did another attack from the night-fighter that sent the burning bomber spiralling earthwards. Only three men, Sgt Garnett, Sgt Marquand and Flt Sgt Milton, managed to scramble out to spend the remainder of the war as POWs. The other four crew members were buried in Sleen cemetery, close to where the Halifax crashed.

There was little time for sorrow as the next night 419 Squadron provided six of the 188 bombers dispatched to wreak havoc upon Turin. The trip was not too unpleasant, as Ian Duncan recalls: '4th February to Turin was our one and only Italian trip; we broke out of the clouds in time to see the mountains and as we were at 16,000ft, it was quite a sight; operationally, it was an early trip but it was long at 9 hours and 35 minutes.' The PFF flares were reported as being on target, though they were scarcely necessary given the good visibility. Wg Cdr Fleming noted seeing separate major fires and postwar records confirmed that considerable damage had been done to the city. All the pilots reported that the flak was plentiful but very inaccurate and uncoordinated, thereby allowing the crews unaccustomed freedom for manoeuvre. Only three aircraft were lost on the raid, none from 419 Squadron.

Also busy that night was 420 Squadron, sending twelve bombers to Lorient in order to keep up the pressure on the U-boat pens. Unusually their loads were made up entirely of incendiaries and clear conditions allowed the crews to drop them on a clearly identified target area. Large concentrated areas of flames were visible for some distance on the homeward journey. After another mining trip involving both 419 and 420 Squadrons on the 6th, a total of twenty-two aircraft from the squadrons headed for Lorient again on the 7th. The attack was designed to take place in two stages, the first aircraft with incendiary loads aiming for the PFF markers and then another wave carrying high explosive loads. Although thick cloud was encountered en route, the target area was quite clear, at least until the smoke from the raging fires restricted the view. The raid was judged as 'exceptionally successful' by the crews, an opinion confirmed by PRU sorties. After a few days off on account of duff weather, it was off to Lorient once more on the 13th. The two squadrons contributed an impressive twenty-eight aircraft as part of a massive force of 466 aircraft whose intention was to blast the port out of operational business. Once again, the attack was in two waves, making the most of the clear conditions over the target. As Alan Helmsley of 420 Squadron put it: 'visibility was good. The fires, exploding bombs, bursting flak and streams of tracer along with searchlights provided quite a show.' That night, it was definitely better to watch the show from above rather than below as massive damage was done to what remained of the town, barracks, docks and technical facilities at a cost of just seven aircraft. One of these, flown by Plt Off L.G. Gibson, came from 420 Squadron. The other crews could still see the fires burning when they were some 80 miles away from the port, though as conditions worsened further north many were advised to put down at the first available airfield.

The following night saw the squadrons make a return to a well visited German target, Cologne, but only as a brief interlude. On 16 February Bomber Command made its final hit for some time at Lorient. In response to orders from the Air Ministry, acting in support of the Royal and Merchant Navies, 1,675 aircraft had dropped almost 4,000 tons of bombs on the French town, which had been all but ruined and abandoned. The campaign cost 24 aircraft, or 1.3 per cent of the attacking force, but it did seriously hamper the servicing and resupply of the U-boats based there. On this night the skies were once again clear over the port and the PFF was able to identify and mark the target accurately. All the crews reported enormous explosions and fires in the target area. Perhaps the most notable aspect of the raid, according to the station log, was the smooth efficiency with which the aircraft had taken off from Middleton St George; it took the ten aircraft from 420 Squadron just 6 minutes to get airborne, and 14 minutes for the thirteen Halifaxes of 419 Squadron. It was noted as 'a feat of which both squadrons and station may be justly proud'.

The focus now switched to the port of Wilhelmshaven, which was, unusually, found to be bathed in bright moonlight but still managed to avoid severe damage, with most of the ordnance falling in open country. Within 24 hours the crews were back again, this time failing to find the port beneath the thick cloud. Most of the bombs fell well to the north of the target. German records stated that only three people were injured that night. As it turned out, following the cancellation of several operations on account of the weather, Wilhelmshaven was again the name on the operations board for 24 February. Once again the port escaped serious damage as heavy cloud forced the PFF to rely on sky marking and the resultant bombing was scattered widely. Although the flak was sardonically reported as being 'below par', a number of fighters were operating over the target, one of which made an unseen pass at Sgt Bell's Halifax, punching two gaping holes in the fuselage. There was, however, something to cheer the weary crews in the mess on the morning of the 26th. An article in the *Daily Mail* read:

> Nearly all the Bomber Squadrons in Wednesday night's attack on the naval base and submarine building yards at Wilhelmshaven were from the Canadian bomber group formed in January, stated the Air Ministry News Service. Other objectives in N.W. Germany were also attacked. As in the case of the recent heavy raid on Bremen, not one of our aircraft is missing. The attack was concentrated into a little over 20 minutes and by the time the raid was over, fires had taken hold and were glowing through the clouds. The defences seem to have been strengthened since the last attack but searchlights were hampered by the weather and one pilot reported that when he was approaching the target he found a cone of six sticking up motionless through a cloud.

The article was clearly based on the crews' debriefing reports and represents a fair interpretation of what was considered as accurate at the time. Specific claims for destruction are notably absent.

The night of 25 February was not one of Middleton's finest. Three Halifaxes were scheduled for the usual run to mine the waters off the Frisian Islands. One failed to start with a serious electrical fault, one returned early when the rear turret went U/S and the third, flown by Sgt P.S. Harrison, clipped a tree at the end of the runway. The collision damaged the port wing's leading edge and the port outer engine's propeller tips and cowling, causing it to cut out. Harrison managed to keep control of the lumbering bomber and coax it around the circuit before making a difficult but safe landing.

The following night witnessed Cologne's heaviest raid since the Millennium raid the previous May. For 419 Squadron the night gave cause for celebration. The port outer engine on Plt Off Sherk's Halifax packed up when he was still some 75 miles short of the target area. Though losing both speed and height, eventually bottoming out at just 9,000ft, and mindful of the increased risk he and his crew were facing, Sherk decided to press on and held his course for Cologne. Having bombed the target, Sherk landed safely at Middleton St George; for his courage and determination he was awarded an immediate DFC.

The penultimate day of February saw Middleton St George return to its familiar role of gardening, once again off the Frisian Islands – not that there was anything routine or humdrum about the constant dangers such regular sorties often encountered. Before Sgt McIntosh's Halifax could drop its mine, the aircraft was hit by an accurate burst of fire from one of the several flak ships in the area. This was swiftly followed up by a series of damaging bursts from the cannon of a prowling night-fighter, which set the fuselage on fire. This unexpected carnage resulted in the deaths of the flight engineer, Sgt A.D. Grogan, and the rear gunner, Sgt G.I. Dunbar, and the wounding of the navigator, Sgt A. Mellin, who took a bullet in the leg that shattered his fibula and tibia bones. In spite of this, while the rest of the crew battled with the flames, Sgt Mellin took over the duties of the flight engineer on top of those of navigator in order to assist McIntosh in coaxing the battered bomber back to Britain. The Halifax, with its three mines still on board, eventually clawed its way back to Coltishall, where McIntosh successfully crash-landed it. For his outstanding efforts that night, Mellin was awarded a CGM.

A second aircraft, that flown by Sgt M.F. Gray, also got into difficulties that night. The Halifax had suffered several near-misses from flak en route to the target off Simonsland and had successfully dropped one of its mines when severe engine trouble caused an immediate loss of height and hydraulic power. It was clearly unable to manoeuvre or stay in the air, so Gray warned his crew to prepare for a crash-landing – a desperate venture by night. He managed to put the large aircraft down far more gently than expected and all the crew managed to get out and scramble into the dinghy before the bomber sank.

Fortunately a brief Mayday had been picked up and at first light three aircraft of 419 Squadron and two of 420 Squadron set out to search for the downed crew. It was not until the late afternoon that the CO of 419 Squadron, Wg Cdr Fleming, spotted the little dot bobbing around on the wintry North Sea and set in motion the final stages of rescue. For one member of the crew the ordeal had been especially tough; it was Flt Sgt R. Harling's second ditching with 419 Squadron. It was rare to survive and be rescued from one ditching, and almost unheard of to make it through two.

The final operation of the month was to St Nazaire, another important Atlantic coast base for U-boats. The importance of the attack can be judged from the size of the force dispatched, some 437 aircraft, of which a dozen were from 419 Squadron and one from 420 Squadron. In excellent clear conditions the vast majority of the bombs landed in the dock area and surrounding streets, destroying 60 per cent of the mostly evacuated built-up area. The burning cauldron that was St Nazaire was visible from the English Channel. There was, however, considerable flak and night-fighter activity over the target, punching several large holes in the starboard wing of Sgt Jackson's aircraft and causing two aircraft to crash-land, one at Exeter and the other in southern Ireland. The defences did not have it their own way that night; the mid-upper gunner (Plt Off R.J. Wagner) and rear gunner (Sgt J.A. Weeks) of Plt Off J.D. Dickson's crew accounted for no fewer than two night-fighters, one a Ju88, the other an Me110, both of which were observed exploding on impact with the ground. This success was mentioned later in their citations for the DFC.

CHAPTER 6

The Main Offensive

THE BATTLE OF THE RUHR

March got off to a dreadful start. On the afternoon of the 1st Flt Sgt Townsend and his crew took off on a routine air test ahead of the night's operation to Berlin. Witnesses noted that the aircraft was flying straight and level at about 1500ft when one of the wings seemed to tear from the trailing edge and shear off. The aircraft simply plunged to the ground in open country at Yafforth near Northallerton in North Yorkshire, only 15 miles from Middleton St George. All on board were killed; three of the Anglo-Canadian crew were laid to rest in West Cemetery, Darlington, on 5 March. The station log's description of the events includes the sentence, 'perhaps no crew has been missed more than this one and the tragedy of it was that most of them were near completing their tour of ops'. It was with heavy hearts that a dozen crews of 419 Squadron set out for the German capital just a few hours later. For once the weather was clear and the 300-strong force left 'a carpet of fires' that was still visible one and a half hours after leaving the target. Indeed, bombing photographs revealed that the attack had spread out over almost 100 square miles but caused particular damage in the south-west of the city. However, Bomber Command did not have it all its own way and seventeen aircraft were lost that night, some 5.6 per cent of the attacking force. One of them was that of Plt Off A.J. Herriott DFM of 419 Squadron, an old campaigner in the RAF who had won his medal in December 1940. Only two bodies have ever been found and the rest of the crew are remembered on the beautiful memorial overlooking Runnymede in Surrey. All in all, the first day of the new month was not a good one.

By contrast, 5 March proved to be one of Bomber Command's best nights of the war so far, the target being the industrial city of Essen, home of the massive Krupps works. Ian Duncan recalls the importance of the raid being stressed at the crew briefing and that the attack had to be pressed home in spite of the heavy defences. Over 400 aircraft set out for the Happy Valley, though a whopping 13 per cent of them turned back on account of mechanical problems. Once again Bomber Command turned to technology in order to improve the accuracy of its bombing and on this occasion the Pathfinders, led by high-flying Oboe

Mosquitoes, did an excellent job. The Main Force attacked in three waves over a 40-minute period, with 419 Squadron's Halifaxes in the first wave and 420 Squadron's Wellingtons in the second. All the crews were confident of the success of the raid. 'Krupps has had it. The reflection of the fires looked like a sunset 150 miles away' was the opinion of Sgt P. Cozens, while WO G.H.T. Tubman of 420 Squadron, who was over target at 21:27 hours in his Wellington, claimed the raid was 'the finest precision bombing I have ever seen. PFF did an excellent job. The centre of the target was like a seething pot, boiling over with fire.' When the reconnaissance photographs were studied, they revealed over 160 acres of devastation in Essen, with 53 separate buildings within the Krupps works itself damaged or destroyed. In addition, over 5,000 homes were classified as destroyed or seriously damaged and German records reveal that 482 inhabitants were killed, the largest number in any raid over Germany to that point. No wonder 'Bomber' Harris sent out a message to each station congratulating the crews on their efforts. Fourteen aircraft, or 3.2 per cent of the attacking force, were lost. One of those, that of Sgt L. Bakewell, belonged to 419 Squadron and another to 420 Squadron, that of Plt Off R. Graham.

Little is known of the loss of Plt Off Graham's crew, but six men survived from Bakewell's crew and the story of Sgt A. Turner, the flight engineer, is a remarkable one. The night went wrong early when Turner reported problems with one of the Halifax's engines. When the pilot, Sgt Bakewell RAF, found that he could just about maintain his speed and height, he decided to press on to the target as he had been encouraged to do at the special briefing. By the time the Halifax reached Essen it was down to 11,000ft and on the final run-in it descended further as the starboard inner engine finally gave up the ghost. Alone so low in the sky, it was soon picked up by the searchlights and given a rough time by the flak gunners only a few thousand feet below. Struggling on and buffeted by the explosions, the Halifax managed to clear the target area and fly into most welcome darkness. As it passed over the Zuyder Zee no fewer than three Ju88s were spotted by the rear gunner, Flt Sgt J.R. Couper, coming in to attack; worse still, Couper discovered his turret had been rendered immobile by flak damage. Bakewell immediately threw his aircraft into a desperate lumbering corkscrew manoeuvre but it was not enough to shake off all three hunters. Very soon the bomber became a mobile furnace and the order to bale out was given. Only Couper, perhaps wounded or killed in the attacks, failed to get out of the aircraft. The others were captured almost immediately upon landing, except for Turner. Having passed out as he scrambled clear of the blazing bomber, he came to only a couple of hundred feet above the Dutch countryside at Buiksloot, north of Amsterdam. After a safe landing, he tore off a piece of his parachute to staunch the flow of blood coursing from a gash above his eye. Then he checked his compass and set off to the south. As he went he vaguely remembered the evader drill taught back in England and duly ripped off his flight engineer's badge but, still dazed, he left his Canada badge, his sergeant's chevrons and even his flying helmet still firmly in place. He quickly arrived at the banks of the Noordzee Canal from where he could see Amsterdam. Walking along the canal, Turner came across three German E-boats on which the crews were enjoying a lively party. Alongside was a small rowing boat. Taking advantage of the revelry going on a few feet away, Turner jumped in, cast off and quietly rowed to the other side. Quietly picking his way past the houses on the outskirts of the city under the cover of darkness, he had reached Diemeroug by morning where he hid in a wood and treated himself to a Horlicks tablet, his sole sustenance for the day. Having consulted his escape map, when darkness fell he set off towards Hilversum by the simple method of following the railway line. He had to lie low while several German patrols went past on routine duty but he kept on walking until dawn when he found a haystack, in which he hid, slept and enjoyed another Horlicks tablet.

When night came, he set off once more but soon ran into a large group of around 200 German soldiers at an important railway crossing. One of the sentries challenged him and briefly flashed a torch over him. Turner uttered something indistinct that he hoped sounded like 'nein' and generally German and was dismayed when the sentry began walking alongside him, still jabbering away in German. More German-like noises were made by Turner, who was delighted and amazed in turn to find that the sentry had escorted him through the group of soldiers milling around before indicating that he could continue along the track by himself. Concluding that the sentry must have only glimpsed his RCAF uniform, and probably mistaken it for something else, Turner, once he was out of sight, turned off the track and ran like hell for an hour before taking shelter in another haystack and devouring the inevitable Horlicks tablet.

At dusk he set out once again but soon came to a canal. He undressed and, holding his boots and as many of his clothes as he could manage above his head, swam across and continued his epic hike. Cold and now very hungry, Turner decided to break in to a henhouse he had come across, and in the pitch darkness managed to locate a few eggs which he threw down his throat with delight. A little later he saw some empty railway freight cars and decided to get into one and await developments. Amazingly they were soon hooked up to an engine and set off. Tired and still in some discomfort from his rough escape from the aircraft, Turner was delighted with the progress he was making until he noticed a sign at a station: Aachen. Jumping out as soon as he could, he resumed his walk. Realising that he could not go on like this indefinitely, he resolved to ask for help at the next farmhouse he came to. When he had finally built up the courage to take this dangerous step, he was turned away at once by the farmer. At the second farmhouse he tried, he was more fortunate and was taken inside. His brave and kind hosts provided some food for him and offered him a mirror. It was only then that he realised he was still wearing his flying helmet. He was badly bruised and had blood matted in his rapidly developing beard – all in all, he was not a pretty sight.

When the farmer went out of the house Turner was wary of being betrayed but the man soon returned with another who could speak English. He proceeded to question Turner thoroughly as to his actions and his time in England before leading him to another house where he was give a bath, tidied up and provided with civilian clothes. Unfortunately it was reported that the Gestapo had arrived unexpectedly in the village and, fearing the consequences of discovery, the Dutchman led Turner out to yet another haystack for the day. He bravely returned that night to take him to the Dutch–Belgian border where he was given instructions on how to reach Liege, where it was thought he might be able to find help. Well supplied with food and water, Turner set off again, walking for seven hours beside a power line before creeping into another haystack just before dawn. He was awoken a few hours later by a pitchfork wielded by a large and uncooperative Belgian farmer. On his way once again, this time in daylight, Turner saw two women and asked them, in very bad French, the best way of getting to Liege. He was duly directed to a tramcar in the village of Barchon. On arrival, he walked around the city for some time with little in mind, before deciding to head out towards Mons. On his way he came across a small café which still had in place a pre-war sign reading 'English spoken here'. Turner simply went inside, sat down and asked for a cup of tea. The waiter took the hint and fetched from out the back the English speaker. By fortunate chance Turner had located a member of the Resistance and from then onwards he was passed along an organised escape line, finally returning to England, via Gibraltar, before the end of June.

For all the careful planning and regimented organisation within Bomber Command, there was no accounting for human error. A. Simpson, an RAF veteran of 419 Squadron, takes up the humorous story:

On 8th March 1943 we had been briefed for operations on Munich. There were three early returns of the squadron. The reasons were varied but one of them was to be the subject of this story. The pilot of this particular aircraft had taken off for the operation without his wireless operator (Sgt B.E.C. Chambers), who had forgotten his flight documents and had dashed away to the Flight Offices to collect them. His absence was not discovered by the rest until they were well and truly airborne. Because of his absence they were obliged to return to base and landed, after burning off some of the fuel load and jettisoning the bomb-load, to face the wrath of the CO. They were not very popular in that quarter.

Anyway, the upshot of the whole affair came with the next operational briefing, when, before the whole squadron, replicas of the Irremovable Digit (the station log gave it its full title 'The Most Highly Derogatory Order of the Irremovable Finger') signs manufactured in the engineering workshops were presented along with a citation and all the trimmings to the pilot and his W/Op by the CO. Then when the hilarity had died down the serious business of the briefing for the night's work began. But the point had been made and I remember that my own skipper intensified his already strict rollcall before taking off on any flight, be it operational or otherwise. I feel that I should also tell you that, sadly, both of these men were later killed in action.

For the rest of 419 Squadron the raid on Munich was regarded as spectacularly successful. Sqn Ldr Clark noted that 'the whole town along the river bank appeared to be well alight' and German records show that great damage was caused to the city that night, most notably putting the BMW aero-engine plant out of commission for six weeks. The same records note that in excess of 14,000 anti-aircraft rounds of mixed calibre were hurled into the night sky but only one bomber was brought down by the barrage over the city.

Two nights later on 11 March the target was Stuttgart. Taking off from 19:00 hours, one of the 419 Squadron crews had a bizarre encounter en route to the target. Pushing on through the clear sky and enjoying the decent visibility, Sqn Ldr Clark 'had an encounter with a Wellington which was obviously being used by the enemy, but, unfortunately for the enemy, on a night when no Wellingtons were in the attack. This aircraft was hit and claimed as a probable.' Though such aircraft are known to have been used by the Luftwaffe to infiltrate the bomber streams, it is likely that the rear gunner, Flt Sgt J.A.L. Brunet, misidentified an Me110; either way, no harm was done to the Halifax and the suspect twin-engined aircraft was last seen heading earthward in flames. The raid itself was not a great success, with the first wave, of which the 419 Squadron aircraft were part, arriving well after the PFF markers had gone down. It also seems likely that dummy target indicators, recorded as being deployed for the first time, also decoyed many of the bombers. Either way, Stuttgart escaped serious damage. Essen, the following night, did not.

It was not, however, all one-way traffic and there was a reminder of the risk of a German attack on the 14th when the coastal towns to the north and east of the station were hit by a significant bomber force, causing considerable damage and numerous casualties.

A much-postponed and ultimately devastating raid on St Nazaire finally took place on 22 March before bad weather once again disrupted Bomber Command's plans, forcing the cancellation of attacks on the great ports of Kiel and Hamburg. The next attack took place on the night of 26 March when 419 and 420 Squadrons contributed twelve and eleven aircraft respectively to a total force of 455 aircraft bound for Duisburg. As there was 10/10ths cloud over the city, the crews were almost totally reliant on the presence of accurate TIs but the first few aircraft over the target found none and were forced to orbit the area for some time while under fire from below. Unfortunately no fewer than five of the Oboe-equipped Mosquitoes had been forced to abort on account of technical problems and a sixth became the first Oboe-equipped Mosquito to be lost in action. When some sky markers were eventually put down they were widely scattered and the bombing followed suit. As Sgt L.M. Morahan, who was over the target later on in the raid at 21:35, put it, 'nothing was seen on the way in or out but one or two sky markers. Reflections of some bomb bursts on the way back.' One consolation for the crews was that the heavy cloud hampered the use of the searchlights. This raid attracted considerable attention in Canada as a reporter made a broadcast for the Canadian Broadcasting Company describing the raid itself and the events before and after at Middleton St George.

The following night eleven Halifaxes of 419 Squadron and fifteen Wellingtons of 420 Squadron were slated to attack Berlin, although late in the day the Wellingtons were stood down, giving the crews a welcome night off. It was almost a night off for the residents of Berlin too as the markers came down well short of the capital, and to judge by the Main Force's bombing photographs showing ground detail no bombs fell within 5 miles of the target. Indeed, most of the bombs fell between 7 and 17 miles short of the city and German records show that they thought the target was intended to be Teltow, some 11 miles to the south-west, where a large Luftwaffe technical store was destroyed. To make matters worse, the crews had to endure heavy flak throughout the long run in and out of the area as Flg Off C.E. Porter and his crew in Halifax DT634 found out. Theirs was to be a difficult night. Several miles to the south of Bremen the Halifax unexpectedly ran into brief but heavy flak and a few minutes later Porter was forced to feather the starboard outer engine. The matter was put to a vote and it was decided to press on to Berlin, but when this proved impractical Porter put in a one-aircraft attack on Magdeburg instead.

Some 45 minutes later, ploughing on steadily homeward, the bomber was set alight by a burst of cannon fire from an unseen night-fighter. The crew set about the blaze but it was soon clear that there was little that could be done to save the aircraft. Porter, wounded in the attack, gave the order to bale out, only to be told that the escape hatches had buckled in the heat and could not be opened. The crew battered away at them with axes and eventually prised one open and jumped out into the inky darkness, at a height of only 1500ft. Flg Off George Sweanor handed Porter his parachute and helped him to put it on, telling him 'to get himself out as we didn't have much hope' before baling out at just 600ft, believing his friend Porter was just behind him. Instead, Porter, unwilling or perhaps unable on account of his injuries, to leave, continued his battle to keep the aircraft in the air. Porter's selfless actions saved the lives of his crew, all of whom were taken prisoner, but only at the cost of his own life. He lies in Ohlsdorf war cemetery near Hamburg.

The giant machine that was Bomber Command ground on regardless. The following night saw everyone at Middleton St George making another large effort, putting up eight Halifaxes and fifteen Wellingtons as part of a 323-strong force attacking St Nazaire. The conditions were excellent for bombing and the visibility was sufficiently good to render the well placed TIs superfluous. The dockyard area received a severe battering and the glow of the fires was still visible as the aircraft flew back over the Channel Islands. The attack, in which the Station Commander himself, Gp Capt A.D. Ross, took part, was not without its hitches and misfortunes. Alan Helmsley recalls his part in the raid: 'On March 28th it was St Nazaire but the engines were cutting out and spluttering. We had to turn back. Our load of bombs and incendiaries was dropped on a hilly part of the country near Busby Hall, causing great fires.' Sgt G.K. Smallwood's aircraft did reach the target but appears to have gone into an inverted spin as a result of a near-miss. Unable to regain control, Smallwood gave the order to bale out and the bomb aimer, Sgt R.C. Douglas, who was handily placed to bale out, promptly did so. The rest of the crew were hurrying to follow suit, struggling to make their way to the hatch, when Smallwood regained control of the bomber at 7,000ft and immediately countermanded his order. The Halifax and its six remaining crew members returned safely to base. Douglas was not so lucky. Having endured a little over two years as a POW he was killed, along with twenty-eight others, on 19 April 1945 when four RAF Typhoons inadvertently attacked a column of POWs on the march near Grasse. Such is the random nature of life and death in war. Sadly, 419 Squadron also suffered another loss that night, when the aircraft of Sgt R.F. Becket was shot down near Nantes with the loss of the entire crew.

April 1943 began as March had ended, with an official stand-down, but on the 2nd 420 Squadron sent three Wellingtons to join a small force attacking St Nazaire. This was to be the last in a long sequence of raids on the port and a couple of days later 'Bomber' Harris was released from his obligation to harass the French ports as part of the Battle of the Atlantic. Once again the weather was clear and the defences moderately light, enabling an accurate attack to be made.

The following night saw 419 Squadron open its account for the month with another attack on Essen in the heart of the Happy Valley. In spite of an intense and prolonged flak barrage, working in conjunction with the most extensive and dazzling array of searchlights yet

A German 88mm flak battery in action. Huge numbers of these formidable weapons were deployed across the Third Reich to counter the Allies' Strategic Air Offensive. *(Imperial War Museum MH 13407)*

encountered, the city centre and western districts of the city took a severe beating. Sgt P.S. Johnson experienced the other main source of danger, in the shape of a devastating attack by an Me110. Although Johnson took immediate evasive action and managed to shake off his attacker, the brief pass had reduced the rear turret and tail section of his aircraft to a shambles, wounding three of his crew in the process. He managed to coax his aircraft back over the North Sea and put down at the first available airfield, RAF Coltishall in Norfolk. Plt Off R.D. Boyd and his inexperienced crew were not so lucky, being shot down by Hauptmann Herbert Lutte of III/NJG1 near Essen. There were no survivors.

The next morning six crews from 420 Squadron were posted to 1659 Heavy Conversion Unit at Topcliffe as the first group from the squadron to convert to the Halifax. For the remainder it was business as usual and on the 8th Middleton St George went back to war, contributing thirteen aircraft to the raid on Duisburg. This night provided 419 Squadron with a proud milestone, the squadron's thousandth sortie. It was not, however, to be either a happy or a successful night.

Heavy icing en route caused problems while 10/10ths cloud rising to 21,000ft effectively negated the efforts of the PFF. Intense predicted flak and heavy night-fighter activity added to the woes of the crews and resulted in the loss of two of Middleton's crews. Plt Off W. Walkinshaw and his crew of 420 Squadron were killed near Essen, and only one member of Sgt J.M. Morris's crew, Sgt L.E. Turner, the flight engineer, survived when his aircraft came down near Bochum. Turner recalled the Halifax taking evasive action in the target area, but did not 'remember anything more of what happened in the aircraft. I became conscious on my way down for a very short time. After hitting the ground I remember no more until waking up in a bed in a police station or some place quite similar. A German told me all the crew were dead, that I was now a POW and that for me the war was over.'

The crews were not in action again until the night of 10 April, when twenty-seven aircraft from 419 and 420 Squadrons formed part of a massive 500-plus formation attacking Frankfurt. Once again, it was not a good night. The thick belt of cloud over the target prevented any observation of the ground and the sky markers tended to get swallowed up in the vast swathes of murk. The bombing was widely scattered, though not through any fault of the crews. Flg Off Boyce of 419 Squadron reported orbiting the target area for 20 minutes in the hope of locating a decent group of markers and only at the end of that perilous time did he resort to bombing the glow beneath him. All the aircraft from Middleton St George left the target area safely but one, a Wellington piloted by Plt Off C.W. Jackson, did not make it home. For some reason the crew lost their way and, having run very short of fuel, decided to set the automatic pilot and bale out. As it happened, they were over Tenby in Pembrokeshire and all landed safely apart from Jackson. As the last man out, he fell into the sea and drowned. His body was later recovered and he now lies in St Mary's churchyard in remote and beautiful Carew.

On the 16th it was revealed that the two squadrons would operate that night over separate targets: 419 Squadron was off to Pilsen, the home of the massive Skoda works, while 420 Squadron was on a large-scale diversionary raid to Mannheim. The Pilsen raid involved one of the longest penetrations into enemy-held territory of all, with a round trip of some 1,800 miles. The raid took place in good conditions with excellent visibility under the silvery glow of a full moon. Buildings on the ground were clearly identified and the marking and bombing, carried out without great interference from the ground defences, was concentrated. Unfortunately the crews had found the wrong buildings. Their bombs fell accurately not on the Skoda works, which received no hits at all, but on a large asylum some 7 miles away. Worse still, a depressing 36 aircraft, some 11 per cent of the attacking force, were lost, mainly to night-fighters. Luckily 419 Squadron was spared any losses that night but many of the tired crews considered themselves fortunate to make it home; as Ian Duncan, a bomb aimer, put it, 'Our longest trip was on the 16th to Pilsen, a duration of 10 hours and 20 minutes. On the way home we got a bit off track and took a few hits on the starboard outer engine, which provided power for the nav. aids so we were reduced to using radio aids and map reading as it was broad daylight by the time we landed at base at 7 a.m.'

The Wellingtons of 420 Squadron were far more successful over Mannheim, in spite of a particularly vicious flak barrage. The conditions were good and the PFF and Main Force dropped their loads accurately on the town, causing widespread damage. The crews returning from Pilsen reported seeing 'a seething mass of flames in the city', a veritable cauldron of fire. However, the cost was again worryingly high at eighteen aircraft. In fact the aggregate total was the highest of the war to date at some 54 aircraft, or 8.6 per cent of the force committed. One of this number came from Middleton St George, an aircraft from 420 Squadron flown by

Sgt L.M. Horahan. It was shot down over Luxembourg, leaving Sgt K.T.P. Allen as the sole survivor of the crew.

A two-day stand-down for Middleton St George followed Bomber Command's worst night of the war. However, 17 April was not without its interest, as the ORB of 420 Squadron records:

Much excitement prevailed on the news that the Squadron was selected to go to North West Africa. Each section is busy picking the best men and fitting them into their position in the establishment. As we are not taking RAF personnel in our ground crew, the task therefore before us is to have the vacancies filled as quickly as possible from other squadrons. Equipment has to be sorted and crated and labelled with our unit number and colours. Personnel have to be kitted with tropical kit, receive medical and dental attention, to be issued with fire arms, etc. This looks like big doings for the squadron and we are 100% for it.

This final departure was still some way into the future and in the meantime both normal operations and conversion to the Halifax remained very much the order of the day. The following night saw 420 Squadron stood down and 419 Squadron scheduled for an attack on Stettin, the principal port for supplying the German troops in northern Russia. Twelve of the fourteen aircraft made it to the target though the route was a little unusual, as Ian Duncan points out: 'On the 20th we flew to Stettin, what was interesting was that we flew fairly low over the North Sea and then dropped down to 800ft across Denmark, then climbed up to 10,000ft to bomb in good visibility and returned home much the same way as we had come. It was later found that this had been the best raid to date.' Indeed, the marking had been spot on and over 100 acres of the town centre was destroyed; more than twenty separate fires were still burning some 36 hours later when a photo reconnaissance aircraft flew over the shattered port. As ever, there was price to pay and one of the aircraft lost came from 419 Squadron. Plt Off T.E. Jackson's mixed RAF/RCAF crew was shot down by a night-fighter about 30 miles north-west of Stettin and all survived bar Flt Sgt D.A. Watkins RAF, a veteran of almost sixty bombing sorties. He had just been recommended for the DFM and his medal was gazetted posthumously on 20 June 1944.

On 23 April it was announced that all but eight of 420 Squadron's aircraft would be stood down and transferred to 427 Squadron, based at Middleton St George's satellite station on the other side of the River Tees at Croft. The eight remaining operational aircraft, it was decided, would also fly out of Croft, meaning that 420 Squadron's part in Middleton St George's war effort was over.

After a most welcome and almost unheard-of six-day break it was back to business on 26 April, when 419 Squadron put up thirteen aircraft in a raid on Duisburg. The important German inland port provided as hostile a reception as usual, with a massive array of searchlights and a dense flak barrage supplemented by an active and numerous night-fighter force. In spite of this, the city was soon a dense mass of flames, with many of the fires merging together to create an uncontrollable ball of flame. Although photo-reconnaissance revealed that a considerable quantity of the bombs had fallen to the north-east of the target, such was the tonnage of bombs dropped that night – almost the same as on the Millennium raid on Cologne not far short of a year earlier but delivered by a little over half the number of aircraft – that the city still suffered massive damage. All 419 Squadron's aircraft returned safely from the raid, but the fire and rescue crews at Middleton St George still had a busy night. Wellington F for Freddie of 420 Squadron, battle-damaged and heading for Croft, did not make it and crashed between the two airfields, killing the second pilot, Sgt I.C. Alder. It had been a bad night for 420 Squadron as all of Sgt E.L. Newburg's crew lost their lives when they were shot down by a night-fighter near Breda in Holland en route home. These were the last casualties 420 Squadron suffered prior to their departure to 311 Wing in 205 Group in North Africa at the end of May.

The final attack of the month was made on the 30th in 10/10ths cloud and severe icing conditions. Nothing could be seen of the target area and the bombing was considered very scattered and ineffective; however, German records reveal that the raid did in fact cause new areas of damage in the city and in the gigantic Krupps works. The crews' dissatisfaction with the raid is well illustrated by the B Flight Commander, Sqn Ldr Pattison:

I briefed the squadron at 18:00 hours after the take-off time had been changed several times and Command had refused to decide whether it would be sky or ground marking technique by PFF. After briefing, the group captain read us a message from Joe Stalin thanking us for hitting the great German industrial centre. The Met. wallahs were a little unsure of themselves tonight, forecasting a westerly wind for take-off, a great front over the North Sea, and solid cloud over Europe from the ground up to 15,000ft. Then, from out of nowhere, those same weather merchants dug up some new winds and a new position for the frontal system over the North Sea, all of which necessitated a change in our tactics and also a much easier take-off.

There followed bags of panic as harassed navigators sweated to prepare their new flight plans and worried-looking skippers scuttled about rounding up crew members who had temporarily 'bogged off'. Then, to complicate matters further, the local wind changed. All aircraft had therefore to taxi in the dark from one end of the aerodrome to the other, a feat that was somehow performed without a single plane becoming stuck in the mud. As I was taxiing my aircraft to the marshalling point, flying control sent out a man to tell me that the Met. people had changed their minds and that there would be a west wind for take-off after all. So we marshalled at the east end of the drome, which proved to be the right end. This caused considerable confusion, as all the aircraft were taxiing out by this time, and positioning themselves at the other end of the field. But the mess finally straightened itself out.

W for Willy, myself and crew got airborne on time and climbed over base, setting course at 17,000ft. Almost at once we ran into the front and were flying in this cloud with solid stuff below us. This gave us good protection from fighters but made it impossible to use astro-navigation as only the stars directly above us were visible.

We reached the Dutch coast at 22,000ft and met little opposition. At the turning point in Germany, just north of the target, we were 15 minutes late because of faulty winds. From then on, despite our relatively great height, we were subjected to rather intense and accurate flak. When our ETA over target was up, there were no target markers to be seen and I was getting a little worried, especially since we were being buffeted around by flak, and the Ruhr is no place to lose one's bearings. Just then a white flare burst behind us, followed by a red which shot out green stars. We swung round to do an orbit and got back on the heading for a bombing run. I don't think there was another aircraft around at the time because we got quite a pasting on that bombing run. We could hear the crumps of bursting shells and the tinkling of splinters on our wings and fuselage. We had an uneventful trip home, except that the gunners (Sgts G. Clarke and J. Miller) were very cold. The temperature up there was minus 40°C.

At least all of 419 Squadron's crews returned home safely.

The weather in Britain is notoriously fickle and provided a constant source of both amusement and frustration for the Canadians, who were used to more settled weather patterns. The first three nights of May saw 419 Squadron slated to go to Duisburg but on each occasion the operation was scrubbed late in the day on account of bad weather. The next night witnessed the first major attack on Dortmund, carried out by 596 aircraft, the largest 'non-thousand' raid of the war to date. It was 419 Squadron's largest effort of the war to date too, putting up eighteen aircraft. The PFF marking was good and the conditions quite clear and, although decoy fires did attract some bombing, over half the Main Force hit within 3 miles of the target area, wreaking havoc on this previously untouched city. Then on the 9th orders were received for yet another raid upon Duisburg and the whole station began the well-drilled process of putting everything in place for that night's raid. However, it was to be a wasted effort for at 22:30, less than an hour before take-off, the raid was scrubbed. The Command stand-down continued on the 10th, which was just as well given that a snowstorm raged over Middleton St George all morning in spite of it being May. The break gave the ground crews time to catch up on their work and they were able to field eighteen aircraft for operations on the 11th. Initially the target was Bochum but at 18:00 this was altered to Duisburg, necessitating a change of fuel and bomb-loads. The fitters and armourers immediately set to and prepared the aircraft, only to have the operation scrubbed at 22:00 hours, just minutes before take-off. Such changes and cancellations were very unpopular with all concerned, wasting effort and creating tension.

The following night, the 12th, was set to be Duisburg once again, but no one was too convinced that the attack would take place after the recent false starts. This suspicion was strengthened when the original demand for a squadron maximum effort was reduced to a call for just eleven aircraft. However, the raid went ahead in spite of the poor weather forecast. As it turned out, the clouds cleared over the target and only a thin layer of industrial haze was left to disguise the city. Such was the damage wrought that night that Duisburg did not need to feature on the Command's target list for quite some time. The defences, however, put up an equally strong showing, bringing down some 34 aircraft, two of which were from 419 Squadron. Flt Sgt J. Palmer and his crew were killed when a night-fighter shot their Halifax out of the sky on the return journey over Holland in the early hours, while WO1 G.A. McMillan's aircraft was a victim of the intense flak over the target.

McMillan's crew had successfully bombed Duisburg in spite of being coned by searchlights, but as the bomb doors were closing it was discovered that a fair proportion of the incendiaries had hung up. McMillan decided to try to drop them over the greater Duisburg area and flew straight and level to help the crew in their efforts to release the remainder of the load. The Halifax was badly shaken as a shell burst just to the starboard side of the cockpit, damaging it and the inner area of the wing. With the Perspex shattered, McMillan was forced to wear his goggles to protect his face from the freezing 200mph slipstream. For some minutes it looked as if the crew had got away with it, as the bomber continued to plough on steadily, but the situation gradually deteriorated as the holes in the wing began to open further and allow fuel to seep out. This quickly ignited and the order was given to bale out before the already serious situation worsened any further. All of the crew made it out of the aircraft except McMillan, yet another brave pilot who battled on just a little too long to keep the aircraft in the sky to allow his crew to escape. Sgt W.H.D. Alison RAF, the W/Op, was found seriously injured and was pronounced dead on arrival in hospital.

Nor was that all for the night. Plt Off Dickson had successfully bombed Duisburg and made it back to Middleton St George. Although warned by the control tower, Dickson, no doubt worn out and simply relieved to be home, did not make sufficient allowance for the new wind direction and the fact that he was to land on the short runway. As a result, his Halifax went straight off the end of the runway at speed with the brakes squealing in protest. The bomber hit a tree stump and spectacularly split in two, the last 20ft of the main fuselage, complete with one bemused rear gunner, being left behind as the rest ploughed on. Luckily there were no casualties and when the aircraft did eventually come to a halt, it was well clear of the runway and the landing procedure continued without delay.

There were no delays or doubts with the next operation. The target for the following night was Bochum. There was, as forecast, no cloud over the target and even the ubiquitous and semi-permanent industrial haze seemed less concealing than usual. However, the fires 'were not as conspicuous or extensive as might have been expected'. One thing all of the crews did agree on was that the defences over the Ruhr were as immense and vicious as ever. Once again, it was a black night for 419 Squadron. Of the ten aircraft that took to the skies that night, two returned early, another dropped its load on a defended area near Bonn, having drifted off course and failed to locate Bochum, and two were lost. The first, that of Sgt G. Adams RAF, crashed near Mönchengladbach, leaving no survivors; the second, that of Sgt W.H.S. Buckwell, was shot down by Hauptmann Herbert Lutje of III/NJG1 at 03:30 hours near Dalen in Holland.

The squadron's third double loss in three operations hit hard back at Middleton St George. Over forty trained aircrew had vanished from the local scene and everyone at the station knew that there would be no let-up in the offensive and that even more losses would be only just around the corner. But that corner turned out to be a little further away than expected. For the next week the squadron was stood down and its activities restricted to training on night-time cross-country flights or local Bullseye exercises in which the aircraft tested and provided practice for the national defence system. However, on 23 May sixteen aircraft were scheduled for an attack on Dortmund as part of a force which numbered 826 bombers, the largest non-

Millennium raid of the war so far. The massive force flew through good weather and reached the target, which was cloud-free, in good order. The Main Force pounded the northern and eastern areas of the city, devastating some 150 acres, smashing over 2,000 buildings, including many industrial premises, and killing or injuring not far short of 2,000 people. It was a devastating raid and its success was readily apparent to the crews involved. It was not all good news, however, and 38 aircraft were lost to the ever-vigilant German defences. One of these belonged to 419 Squadron.

Sgt F.A. Dunn, the flight engineer, was the sole survivor of the crew. He recalled the port inner engine suddenly bursting into flames while still en route to the target, though he could not specify whether it was caused by the attentions of flak or a night-fighter. With the fire burning out of control, the Halifax was then coned by several searchlights and buffeted by flak. The pilot, Sgt A.S. Green, a man with thirteen operations to his credit, then shouted: 'I guess we've had it boys. Better get out, any of you that can.' Dunn takes up the tale:

As I picked up a fire extinguisher and approached the flare chute where a small fire was burning, an explosion knocked me out. I have a blurred recollection of trying to get up but gravity and weakness prevented me. Regained consciousness in the [aircraft] wreckage and crawled out of a hole. The nose was missing and the fuselage was red-hot forward and in flames from tip to tip, ammo was popping, rear gunner not in smashed turret. Aircraft was headed north, house 20 yards to port, trees 50 yards behind, hedge in front. I left the area, Germans later told me that six bodies were found. My watch had stopped at 01:40.

The men and women back at Middleton St George could only guess at all this but they had a grandstand view of the demise of Flg Off Weedon's Halifax L, which crash-landed in Dinsdale on its return as two engines unexpectedly cut out on the final approach to the airfield. On this occasion the crew managed to scramble out of the wreckage without any serious injury. This was considered a minor miracle by all who witnessed the crash on the grounds of the severity of the impact, which tore off a wing. It really was miraculous, for subsequent investigation of the wreckage showed that the fuel lines had been damaged by falling incendiaries over the target but had somehow held together long enough to reach home – almost home, anyway.

The weather, which had led to the cancellation of attacks on Düsseldorf and Cologne, was still marginal on the 27th when 419 Squadron prepared for another attack on Essen in the heart of the Ruhr. The low cloud and general industrial murk over the city necessitated the use of sky markers and the resultant bombing was widely scattered, a fact noted by many crews taking part. The formidable defences once again took their toll, with 23 aircraft, 4.4 per cent of the attacking force, being lost. Another had a very lucky escape. Flg Off McIntosh from 419 Squadron had both his inner engines knocked out by flak, along with the rear turret and W/T receiver. There was further damage to the port wing. Although the prospects didn't look too rosy, McIntosh gradually coaxed his battered aircraft first over a good stretch of enemy territory and then over the hostile North Sea, slowly losing height as he went. Passing low over the coast, bang on track, McIntosh located the airfield and put his aircraft down on the tarmac without undue drama or problems. Sqn Ldr Pattison described this superb feat of airmanship as 'one of the most remarkable shows I have ever seen – without parallel on the squadron'. It was also recognised more formally by the award of a DFC, gazetted that September.

Next came Wuppertal. The raid itself proved to be enormously successful. Over 700 aircraft accurately pounded the Elberfeld and Barmen districts of Wuppertal in excellent weather and good visibility. All of 419 Squadron's successful crews reported very concentrated marking and bombing and extensive fires spreading rapidly thousands of feet below them. The fires amalgamated into a mini-firestorm that raged out of control, eventually devastating 1,000 acres of Barmen's built-up area, including five major industrial plants, over 200 general industrial premises and 4,000 houses, and damaging many more. It is estimated that well over 3,000 people lost their lives that night, making it by far the most destructive raid on Germany in the war to that point.

Once again the bombers did not have it all their own way and 33 aircraft were shot down, two of them from 419 Squadron. This was the squadron's fourth double loss in six operations. Sgt P.S. Johnson and his mixed RAF/RCAF crew were shot down by a night-fighter flown by Oberleutnant Rudolph Altendorf of I/NJG4 south-east of Mons, leaving no survivors. Among the dead was Briton Sgt C.P. Baker, at just 18 years of age the youngest man in Bomber Command to die in 1943. From the other crew there were three survivors. Sgt F.E. Winegarden's crew had suffered from gremlins in their intercom system during the pre-sortie air test and upon landing the system was repaired. However, it failed again after the crew had successfully bombed the target and its failure could well have contributed to the aircraft's loss. The POW interrogation reports noted a surprise attack by a fighter and 'the engineer said that the whole port wing was on fire. The aircraft started rushing, losing height. Pilot gave orders to bale out. Navigator went first, bomb aimer second, then the W/AG. What happened after we left, I don't know; we are the only three saved.' Plt Off Bell and his crew had a difficult night too, having lost the port inner engine to flak over Liege. The blast also damaged the hydraulics used to control the bomb doors, which opened, causing heavy drag and a loss of height and manoeuvrability. Prompt action with an axe by the flight engineer, Sgt W.B. Taylor, solved the problem, as he severed the pressure lines completely to allow the doors to be closed manually by a hand pump. The aircraft landed safely at Swanton Morley after initially being considered the third aircraft lost by the sombre men and women left waiting and hoping at Middleton St George.

There things were about to change, settling into a happy format that was to remain unchanged for the rest of the war as 428 Squadron took its place alongside 419 Squadron.

The ninth Canadian bomber squadron to be created, 428 Squadron was formed at Dalton as part of 4 Group on 7 November 1942. The first member of the squadron was the Medical Officer, Flt Lt E.J.A. Lindsay, who arrived at Dalton on 1 November, the day before the squadron's CO, Wg Cdr A. Earle RAF. Flying Wellingtons, the squadron notched up its first operational sortie on the night of 26 January 1943, when it took part in an attack on the U-boat base at Lorient. Since then, 428 Squadron had had a busy schedule and showed every sign of living up to its motto, *usque ad finem* – right up to the end. Upon arrival at

Middleton St George, the squadron began to retire its trusty Wellingtons and convert to the four-engined Halifax.

As it turned out June began with a ten-day stretch of stand-downs and cancelled operations. It was not until 11 June that an operation to Düsseldorf went ahead. Although some of the marking and bombing went astray, the majority of the tonnage dropped landed in Düsseldorf, devastating over 130 acres of the city and destroying hundreds of industrial premises and private dwellings. Almost 1,300 people lost their lives in what proved to be the most effective raid of the war on this city. Although successful for the Command as a whole, it was another bad night for the men and women stationed at Middleton St George. The night's work got off to a horrific start when J of 428 Squadron crashed on take-off, setting off its 4,000lb bomb. The resultant explosion and fireball caused considerable blast damage to the station's buildings and was heard and seen for several miles around. The stunned station personnel were more than amazed to find that the captain of the aircraft, Sgt W. Lachman, who was found some

The official crest of 428 Squadron with its Latin motto, *usque ad finem* – to the very end. *(Author)*

30 yards from the aircraft, still strapped in his seat, had, as the station log put it, 'miraculously escaped with a few broken bones and some concussion'. He was taken to Northallerton Hospital. The rest of his crew were not so fortunate. The take-off continued, and each of the young crews as they passed overhead must have said a little prayer and thought, 'there but for the Grace of God, go I'. Things did not get much better as the crews flew into not one but two very active weather fronts, causing severe icing and a number of electrical problems with turrets and intercoms. No fewer than five of 419 Squadron's aircraft were forced to return early. Several more were damaged by flak, and for Flg Off W.J. Boyce one hit was enough to send his aircraft with its mixed British and Canadian crew crashing to the ground. The Halifax had successfully bombed the target and was some 10 miles out of Düsseldorf when it was fully illuminated by one of the blue master searchlights. For a while nothing else happened and then up to fifteen separate searchlights locked on to the aircraft and held it fast, in spite of the best efforts of the pilot. Then a single shell, thought to have been the first one fired, burst directly below the Halifax, wounding three of the crew and throwing the aircraft into an uncontrollable spin. Boyce immediately gave the order to bale out and struggled to gain some sort of control in order to enable the crew to do so. He partially succeeded but only at the cost of his own life, leaving his own escape too late.

According to Flg Off D.J. Black, the navigator, Boyce 'fully realised the danger but he would not leave the aircraft until the crew were safe'. His courage and tenacity bought enough time for five of the crew to bale out safely.

Operations were on again the following night when just over 500 aircraft headed for Bochum. The target proved to be cloud-covered but accurate Oboe-directed sky marking enabled the Main Force to smash around 130 acres of the city, far more than the initial crew reports, describing scattered bombing, had suggested. Once again 419 Squadron featured on the list of losses. The moon on this night was both very bright and low in the sky, a combination that created a glare on the gunners' Perspex shields and severely hampered their view. Sgt D.L. Gray, the rear gunner in Sgt B.D. Kirkham's crew, had alerted his skipper to this problem on several occasions but given the course for home and the position of the moon there was little that could be done beyond being extra vigilant. Shortly after 02:00 hours an Me110 made full use of the moonlight to attack from below and astern, making an unseen diagonal pass. The first the crew knew of it was when the cannon shells ripped their way through the starboard wing, turning the inner engine into a blazing mass. It was immediately apparent that the Halifax was doomed and Kirkham gave the order to bale out. All seven of the mixed RCAF/RAF crew got out successfully, to spend the rest of the war as prisoners.

There were, however, some celebrations back at Middleton St George when it became known that the night-fighters had not had it all their own way. Over Steenwijk in Holland Plt Off R. Harling, the rear gunner in Flt Sgt M. Gray's crew, sighted two Ju88s shadowing his aircraft. As one of them approached to about 500 yards, Harling gave the order for evasive action and at the same time put in a four-second burst that tore into his German assailant. The fighter caught fire and was seen plunging earthwards, out of control. The other fighter broke off in search of easier prey. This action was later mentioned in Harling's citation for his DFC. Nor was this the only success of the night. Another rear gunner, Sgt W.M. Barnes in Sgt C.M. Coutlee's crew, had a long-running battle on the return leg of the journey with a very persistent Ju88. The night-fighter made several attacks but came off worse in the end, eventually bursting into flames and crashing into the sea. One success against a night-fighter was comparatively rare but two in a single night for one squadron was almost unheard of and a feat worthy of note and celebration.

The squadrons now enjoyed a lull in operations, as several were planned and then cancelled · on account of poor weather conditions either at home or over the target area. By this time 428 Squadron's conversion to the Halifax V was coming on apace and four of the squadron's crews were loaned to 419 Squadron for the next operation to attack the Schneider armaments works at Le Creusot, 170 miles south-east of Paris, on 19 June. The weather turned out to be ideal for the attack and the defences proved far lighter than expected. Unusually the Pathfinders were ordered to drop only flares to illuminate the target in order to help the crews identify the factory complex visually. The 6 Group squadrons came in at between 5,000 and 9,000ft, fully aware that accuracy over this target, which was surrounded by Allied workers and housing, was essential. Many of the crews found the target smothered in heavy, greyish white smoke caused by earlier bombs and Sqn Ldr Pattison of 419 Squadron was not alone in making several runs before turning for home with his bomb-load still on board, having failed to identify the target clearly. Others were luckier. Flg Off MacIntosh was credited with bringing back one of the finest target photographs ever seen on the squadron. Such photographs confirmed that all the aircraft had bombed within 3 miles of the target, but only 20 per cent had hit the factories themselves. Nevertheless severe damage and disruption had been caused and, as 6 Group records noted, there were 'clear indications that the target had been successfully attacked. The German High Command also admitted that colossal damage had been done and heavy casualties suffered,' although it should be remembered that such an admission was in German interests within Vichy France at this time.

The night of 24 June 1943 was to be one of the worst in Middleton St George's wartime history. No fewer than three aircraft, two from 419 Squadron and one on loan from 428 Squadron, failed to return from a raid on the Elberfeld area of Wuppertal. The raid itself delivered another massive blow to the industrial sprawl of the Ruhr, with around 90 per cent of the target area being completely destroyed and approximately 3,500 people being killed or injured. Any thoughts of a job well done were forgotten as the news of the losses spread around the stunned airfield. One of the crews, among the most experienced on the squadron, was led by Flt Lt B.N. Jost DFC, on his second tour of operations. His aircraft, C for Charlie, was approaching the turning point when the gunners reported a shadowy but suspicious shape looming out of the gloom, slightly below and to starboard. Although Jost immediately began to corkscrew, the cannon shells from the fighter were already ripping into the fuselage and port wing. All the crew then set to trying to bring the raging fires under control but it soon became apparent that they would not be able to do so. Four of this crew, comprising members of the RCAF, RAF and RNZAF, successfully baled out and were reunited in Stalag Luft 3 several weeks later.

By comparison, another crew lost that night, that of Sgt G.V. Neale, was very inexperienced, the pilot having done the most operations, with his total being just five. About 01:00 Neale was orbiting south of Cologne to waste time when three Fw190s made almost simultaneous attacks from behind and astern. Both starboard engines were put out of action and serious damage was caused to the fuselage. Incredibly Neale managed to keep the savaged Halifax in the air, hoping to ditch as far across the North Sea as possible. When it became clear that this was not going to happen, Neale put on his landing lights and pulled off a superb night-time crash-landing at Wageningen, not far from Arnhem, in a field full of startled cows. The crew's luck held and they were all able to scramble out more or less unhurt. They made off in two groups in different directions, but soon their luck ran out and they were quickly captured. The third aircraft lost, that of Sgt R. Whitfield of 428 Squadron, was shot down by Hauptmann Hans-Dieter Frank of I/NJG1 over Eindhoven, with the loss of all on board.

Less than 24 hours later, and in spite of the heavy losses, Middleton St George mounted another large operation, putting thirteen of 419 Squadron's Halifaxes into the air bound for cloud-shrouded Gelsenkirchen. Bombing conditions over this 'oil target' were abysmal and what the raid had achieved was anybody's guess as the weather did not allow any accurate assessment. Equally cloud-shrouded was Cologne on the 28th and hopes were not high for success once the reports went into Group HQs around the country. In fact, the raid was the worst experienced by this oft-bombed city during the war. Over 6,000 buildings were destroyed and a further 15,000 damaged, and 230,000 people were forced to abandon their damaged homes. Some 4,377 people lost their lives that night and industrial production was shattered for some time to come. Bomber Command's losses were down a little, at 4.1 per cent of the attacking force, but one of the aircraft lost belonged to 419 Squadron, shot down by Major Gunter Radusch of I/NJG1 near Eindhoven. The aircraft's captain was Plt Off H.W. Fowler, who had been on the squadron just eighteen days but was already on his eighth operation. Among the crew was Flt Lt A.C. Raine, the Squadron Signals Leader, who was well on the way to completing his second tour, having been one of the early Moosemen serving in 1942. His loss was keenly felt and put a further dampener on what had been an operationally successful but costly month.

July began with a Dominion Day service in Ripon Cathedral, but there was little time for relaxation or thanksgiving. On the 3rd the men and women based at Middleton St George had a very busy day, preparing no fewer than thirteen aircraft from 419 Squadron and ten aircraft from 428 Squadron for an attack on the battered city of Cologne. The attack was an undoubted success and the fires and vast explosions were still visible to the crews over 100 miles away. Sadly 419 Squadron lost Y for Yoke that night and with it probably the most experienced crew in the squadron, each man having twenty-five or more operations to his credit. Unusually the Halifax was shot down by a standard single-engine day fighter as part of the trials, codenamed Wilde Sau, organised by Major Hajo Herrman to use them to boost night-fighter numbers.

It was approaching 01:00 hours when, over Belgium, a single searchlight tracked Plt Off R.A.M. Bell and his crew; fighter flares suddenly lit up the night sky and the Halifax's aircraft approach early warning system, known as Monica, began to beep out its grim warning. Flt Sgt G.F. Aitken, the rear gunner, called for evasive action just as an Me109 tore in from the port quarter below with all guns blazing. It came round for a second pass and set the port inner engine ablaze and wounded the second pilot, Sgt J.A. Anderson, and the flight engineer, Sgt W.B. Taylor. Unfortunately, at this crucial moment Aitken's guns stubbornly refused to fire and the fighter returned for a third pass before being joined by another, drawn by the light of the blazing bomber. This time the starboard tank was set alight and Bell gave the order 'bale out as fast as you can'. Five of the crew successfully did so, landing near Louvain in Belgium, but Bell and the two wounded men did not.

Two of the crew, Bob 'Willy' Williston, the bomb aimer, and Doug Arseneau, the W/Op, fell into the care of local Resistance leader François Daman, who knew that a bomber had been shot down in his area and was scouring the woods for the crew. Doug was found by a young man and a woman who brought civilian clothes and shoes and quickly buried his parachute and uniform. The pair led him to two bicycles and, with the young man as his guide, Doug found himself pedalling his bicycle, with a pretty girl perched on the handlebars, through lanes and villages busy with locals and German soldiers enjoying a Sunday stroll. After three nerve-wracking and bone-shattering hours, they arrived at a house inside the walls of Louvin, not far from a large Philips factory, which was heavily guarded by the Germans. Willy was also picked up and taken to another house where he was questioned by François Daman. A few days later, after their identities had been confirmed by sources in London, the two men were moved separately to one house after dark, slipping through the shadows to avoid the German curfew patrols. At one point Doug, following his guide Hortense Daman, François's teenage sister, came within sight of the Kommandantur and the sentries appeared to hear the couple creeping along. Hortense swiftly grabbed him and indiscreetly pulled him into a doorway and engaged in a somewhat passionate embrace with the stunned airman. The sentries lost interest and the pair resumed their journey. The two Canadians were delighted to meet one another in the tiny terraced house of Joan and Philemon de Witt. The pair found their confinement in the tiny house very frustrating but arrangements for papers, clothes and travel took a considerable amount of effort and time – especially as the penalties for being caught were extreme. Their days were brightened by the visits of the highly attractive Hortense, who brought whatever food she could gather up from various sources. After a while the pair were moved on and eventually arrived in Brussels, where Doug endured a tram ride surrounded by curious and talkative German soldiers. The pair stayed in several houses in Brussels, being moved every couple of days before joining up with an American airman, John Anderson. Finally they were told to get ready for the journey towards the French border. The airmen were heading out of the city in a car driven by their guide, known as Marcel, when they were flagged down by a single German soldier. As soon as the car came to a halt several more armed German soldiers appeared, pointing their rifles and machine-pistols at the stunned occupants. After a few words and an exchange of papers 'Marcel' was allowed to go his own way but for the three airmen it was the end of the road. The men were barely questioned at St Gilles prison before being passed on to a POW camp in Germany, confirming their suspicions that the escape line had been infiltrated at some point by German agents. They were more fortunate than several of their brave helpers, although François and Hortense Daman did survive the war, in spite of several very close shaves.

On 13 July orders were received for an attack on Aachen, the final sortie of the Battle of the Ruhr. As the city was not a regular target, it was expected to be a reasonably easy operation. Unpredicted strong tail-winds meant that much of the Main Force arrived at about the same time as the PFF but conditions were clear enough to proceed without the markers in the early stages and the city suffered a concentrated and punishingly effective attack, described by local German officials as a *Terrorangriff* or terror attack. The ground defences were every bit as light as hoped but the night-fighters were out in force, blasting twenty aircraft out of the sky. By a dreadful twist of fate, no fewer than four of these were from Middleton St George.

Flt Lt D.S. Morgan was flying steadily at 16,000ft, oblivious of any danger, when 'a Luftwaffe fighter took us completely by surprise'. The first pass was devastating, raking the entire fuselage, wrecking the intercom system and smashing the elevator controls. The aircraft shuddered and Morgan only prevented the Halifax from stalling by 'kicking hard on the rudder'. The order was given to bale out, both verbally and via the call light, and the aircraft came down near Waalwijk. Two of the gunners, Sgts T.N. Pritchard and M. Edwards, lost their lives. A similar fate befell another Halifax from 428 Squadron, that of Flt Lt W.G. Weeks, who was shot down near Namur with the loss of all on board. A third 428 Squadron aircraft, piloted by Plt Off W.D.F. Ross, also came down near Namur in the early hours of the morning, having been badly damaged by flak over the target area. The crew fared much better on this occasion, with all members surviving. Two of them, Sgt D.J. Webb and Sgt E.A. Bridge, were lucky enough to make contact with the local Resistance and were eventually returned to Britain via the highly successful Comète escape line.

The fourth aircraft lost from Middleton St George that night belonged to 419 Squadron. N for Nan, flown by 2/Lt B.J. Furey USAAF, had suffered badly from gremlins since take-off, first with an intercom failure, which was eventually patched up by the W/Op, Sgt J. Gilchrist, and then with the rear guns failing to fire during the routine test firing over the North Sea. Although this too was cleared up by the gunner, Flt Sgt W.C. Batkin RAF, both problems would have been legitimate reasons to turn for home. Nevertheless, Furey pressed on and it was not long after crossing the enemy coast that Sgt K. La Salle shouted the warning that there was a Ju88 approaching from the starboard quarter. Unfortunately, no one spotted another coming in from the port quarter and the first anyone knew of it was when its cannon shells ripped through the aircraft, setting it on fire and leaving a large hole where Batkin's rear turret used to be. Although Furey took immediate evasive action, he could not avoid the second pass which caused further damage and sealed the fate of the bomber. Everyone except Batkin, a veteran of some twenty-seven operations, managed to bale out to spend the rest of the war as prisoners.

THE BATTLE OF HAMBURG

Hamburg was one of Germany's great cities and its leading maritime centre, both militarily and commercially. Although it had been targeted a number of times in the past, it was decided to deal it a series of heavy blows in an operation codenamed Gomorrah. To help achieve this with the minimum of casualties among the bombing force, the use of Window, black slips of paper exactly 27cm long and 2cm wide, with a thin layer of aluminium foil stuck to one side of the paper, was authorised for the first time. Experiments had shown that large numbers of such strips dropped in an area would confuse the German radar system that controlled both the ground and airborne defences, rendering it effectively blind. Window had been available for over a year but had been withheld for fear that the Luftwaffe would acquire and then copy it for their own use over Britain. Although still very much present, it was felt that by the summer of 1943 the threat posed by the Luftwaffe was greatly reduced and that the protection afforded by Window was now worth the risk. For a few months, it was felt, Window might turn the hard-fought battle in the night skies over Occupied Europe Bomber Command's way.

Indeed it did. On 24/25 July, in clear conditions, 728 aircraft dropped 2,284 tons of bombs on to the hapless city in just 50 minutes, wreaking immense havoc. Only 12 aircraft were lost, just 1.5 per cent of the attacking force. As 6 Group's war diary noted: 'This was an excellent attack, with a high degree of concentration. The target area was left a mass of fire with dense black smoke rising to 19,000ft. Many heavy explosions were observed. The defences, which were strong in the initial stages of the attack, became very wild towards the end.' The crew reports noted, 'thirty or forty beams would build up to a cone – on nothing' as the defenders groped blindly around the night sky. Indeed, Wg Cdr M.M. Fleming, the CO of 419 Squadron, felt that 'the greatest danger was the risk of collision with other aircraft over the target' – he had had four near-misses in his brief time over the city. Best of all for the night, all of the Middleton St George aircraft returned safely.

Aiming to make hay while the sun shone, Harris ordered another 700-plus raid the next night. The target was an old favourite, Essen, in the heart of the Happy Valley. With good visibility over the target, marred only by patchy cloud, the bombers delivered the heaviest blow that Essen had yet received. Such was the scale of the damage to the vital Krüpps works that it is reported that upon seeing it, Dr Gustav Krupp suffered a serious stroke from which he never fully recovered. The smoke billowed up to 20,000ft and the dull red glow of the widespread fires was still visible to the crews as far west as the Dutch coast. Once again, losses were relatively light at 3.7 per cent of the attacking force, but on this occasion one aircraft failed to return to Middleton St George. The crew's only survivor, WO L. Chapman, the pilot, described what happened:

After dropping our bombs . . . we flew into a thunderhead and . . . something collided with the tail of the aircraft. The controls were knocked out of my hands and jammed into the forward right-hand position. The aircraft rolled into an inverted dive from which I was

The port of Hamburg after the devastating fire raids in July 1943. The Battle of Hamburg showed what Bomber Command could achieve when its resources were deployed in concentrated fashion. *(Imperial War Museum C3672)*

unable to recover. The crew, not having their chutes fastened on, were not able to escape in time. I had a seat pack and made my way through the escape hatch above – actually below, as the aircraft was inverted, my head. I baled out at very low level, swung over on my parachute, then touched the ground in a suburb of Essen.

By a quirk of fate, Chapman's second pilot on this attack, aiming to gain operational experience, was Flg Off Handforth, who had been Chapman's instructor back in Canada.

At least 419 Squadron managed to square the tables a little when Sgt L. Northcliffe managed to shoot down an Fw190 that had attacked his Halifax near the French coast. On this occasion there was little doubt as to the veracity of the claim, as Northcliffe fired over 500 rounds at the fighter, which exploded in mid-air in an enormous fireball visible for miles around.

On the 26th 6 Group was stood down, ahead of gearing up for one of the most destructive raids of the entire war the following night. It had been another hot and dry summer's day in Hamburg and the population, still recovering from the raid just a couple of nights earlier, did not expect another attack so soon. When the sirens wailed, the people hurriedly headed for the shelters, unaware of what was to come. It was awesome: 729 aircraft dropped 2,326 tons of bombs in a very concentrated pattern, starting massive fires. As the fires began to spread, they formed a growing expanse of flame, drawing in vast amounts of oxygen and creating winds of up to 150mph. This effect, known as a firestorm, resulted in tremendously high temperatures, destruction on a massive scale and the deaths of perhaps 40,000 people, many of whom died and were cremated in the large air raid shelters. To Flg Off D.O. Laidlaw of 419 Squadron the sight from above resembled 'a volcano, belching fire and smoke, with sparks scattered around the base'. On the ground Polizeipräsident Kehrl, the Police Chief and Air Protection Leader of Hamburg, described the hellish scene:

> before half an hour had passed, the districts upon which the weight of the attack fell . . . were transformed into a lake of fire covering an area of 22 square kilometres. The effect of this was to heat the air to a temperature which at times was estimated to reach 1,000°C. A vast suction was in this way created so that the air stormed through the streets with immense force, bearing upon it sparks, timber and roof beams and thus spreading the fire still further and further till it became a typhoon such as had never before been witnessed and against which all human resistance was powerless.

Immediately after this raid, 1,200,000 people, two-thirds of Hamburg's entire population, fled from the city, fearful of another catastrophe. For those back in the north-east of England the perception was very different – it was simply another good night's work.

On 28 July the whole command was on stand-down before operations were declared for the following night. To the crews' surprise the target was again Hamburg. They were aware that the USAAF had also attacked the city twice by day on the 25th and 26th, and it was clear that nothing less than the total annihilation of the city was being attempted. It was a maximum effort for the ground crews at Middleton St George, making ready no fewer than sixteen Halifaxes from 419 Squadron and seventeen from 428 Squadron. The bombers found the target covered by a mixture of haze and smoke from the still-smouldering fires but they dropped another 2,318 tons of bombs on to the city and, as the Group record put it 'once again, the crews returned enthusiastic over the result'. Massive damage was caused to areas of the city not yet touched by the raids and fires once again raged out of control as the exhausted and depleted fire units had little to fight the fires with. The only fly in the ointment from the bomber crew's point of view was the gradual increase in the toll the German defences were exacting – now up to 3.6 per cent of the attacking force. One of the bombers lost belonged to 428 Squadron. Sgt D.H. Bates's aircraft was shot down by a night-fighter and exploded in the vicinity of Luneburg, leaving only one survivor, Sgt P. Demcoe.

The final night of the month was due to see another major attack on Hamburg but this was called off on account of poor weather conditions but not until 22:32, too late for the crews to do anything useful with the night. However, the port was still very much on Harris's list and it was chalked up as the target for 2 August. The crews had considerable misgivings about this attack as the Met. officers at the briefings informed them that they were almost certain to run into major electrical storms. The 'gen' proved 'pukka' and the bombers were confronted with an almost impenetrable wall of cumulonimbus cloud towering up to 25,000ft. The battering dished out by the storms as they ploughed through the murk was enough to convince a quarter of the attacking force to turn around and head for home; indeed, for 6 Group, a little further north, the figure was 57 per cent.

Those that did carry on displayed considerable courage and determination but their task was far from easy, especially as the dire conditions prevented any marking of the target at all, resulting in the widespread scattering of the bomb-loads all over northern Germany. Sgt J.S. Sobin from 419 Squadron ran into heavy icing and made the decision to jettison his load and turn for home. Almost instantaneously there was a blinding flash and all four engines fell silent and the entire electrical system packed up. The W/Op later reported, 'I am quite confident that it was lightning that struck us.' Whatever it was, the aircraft turned on to its back and headed earthwards; only three of the crew managed to bale out. Two aircraft from 428 Squadron were also lost that night. They were commanded by Plt Off V.T. Sylvester and Sgt M. Chepil, who had been awarded an immediate DFM for his courage and determination on the Le Creusot raid in June. No trace was ever found of Chepil's aircraft or crew, and of Sylvester's crew only two bodies were recovered from the North Sea. One of these was that of Flg Off Harvey Funkhouses, who had only recently joined 428 Squadron, along with his best friend, Flg Off Len Rogers. The pair had been friends in their home town of Port Colborne, Ontario, and had joined up together and trained together before being shipped to England together and posted together. Now they died together on their first night on operations, flying as second pilots to Chepil and Sylvester respectively. The night had been a very bad one for the men and women stationed at Middleton St George: three aircraft lost, several others damaged and all for very little harm done to the enemy. Gone were another twenty-three young men, who took off full of hopes and fears. This was the human side of the harsh statistics of war.

Those statistics were, however, very favourable to Bomber Command. In spite of the final raid's failure, the largest port in Europe and Germany's second city lay in ruins. Some 45,000 people had lost their lives, with over 1,000,000 more made homeless; the shipyards were badly damaged, with some 180,000 tons of shipping sunk in the harbour; and thousands of commercial and industrial premises were destroyed or damaged. Albert Speer, Hitler's armaments minister, believed another half a dozen attacks on this scale would bring Germany to her knees; she would be unable to continue to fight. Goebbels wrote that the firestorm and destruction 'staggered the imagination', and Erhard Milch, the Luftwaffe General at the Air Ministry, cautioned, 'if we get just five or six more attacks like these on Hamburg, the German people will just lay down their tools, however great their willpower. . . . What the home front is suffering now cannot be suffered much longer.' This would all have been music to Harris's ears and he certainly had every intention of delivering much more of the same.

THE GERMAN HEARTLAND

As it turned out, there was a break in the momentum for the men and women at Middleton St George. However, the senior officers on the station had other matters to occupy their minds, notably the continued high incidence of early returns caused by mechanical and technical failures. This came to a head when an RCAF Trade Board, conducted by Flg Off S. Foye, visited the station on 6–7 August and concluded 'after long discussions it was found that Canadian personnel were not qualifying for various trades as was expected and it seems in "Canadianising" the station, the personnel are not fully qualified to take over responsible positions which they will be required to do in the near future. The situation is not a very happy one.' There would be much discussion and hard work to do if the station was to take its place in the first division in terms of operational serviceability, as both military and political necessities demanded. This telling vignette provides a sharp insight into the crucial and ceaseless battles waged on the ground to improve the efficiency of the war effort.

Politics occasionally played a significant role in the choice of target. Although the weather forced the cancellation of an attack on Turin, the crews did make the long and penetrating flight to Milan, a new target for them. The raid, which was part of a series intended to bring home to a wavering Italian leadership and population the dire effects of continuing with the war on the Axis side, was a heavy one and caused severe damage to this important industrial city. To the crew's delight there was virtually no opposition and only three bombers failed to return out of a force over 500-strong. All the Middleton crews made the long journey home to land safely.

There was a brief lull in operations before preparations began for an unusual and important attack on the night of 17 August. When the target, Peenemünde, was announced at the briefing, very few had ever heard of the tiny place on the Baltic coast. The true purpose of the raid – to destroy the German V1 and V2 research programmes – was deliberately withheld by the intelligence services so as to avoid rumours of super-weapons slipping out and spreading panic among the general public. Nevertheless, the crews were told that the target was a scientific and technical one of extreme importance. As D.J. Richards, a navigator with 428 Squadron, recalls: 'We were simply told that, if not successful, we would go back the following night, but that the defences were light.' The last part at least went some way to

The top-secret German rocket research centre at Peenemünde after the raid of 18 August 1943 in which 419 and 428 Squadrons took part. *(Imperial War Museum C 4783)*

cheering up the sceptical crews, who were already somewhat concerned at the idea of attacking from comparatively low levels on a clear night, bathed in bright moonlight.

Thirty-one Halifaxes took off from Middleton St George bound for Peenemünde. The outbound flight was smooth and for once the moonlight was sufficiently bright to allow crews to actually see several of the bombers around them. The Canadians of 6 Group were in the third wave to attack the research site. Sgt J. McIntosh of 419 Squadron describes the scene that greeted him as he approached the target:

Our first sight of the target was like coming around a corner to face the lights of a Xmas tree. . . . Keary, my bomb aimer, was up on the flight deck, and was also a witty fellow, but our total crew reaction was 'Jesus Christ! Whose surprise party is this one?' The sky in front of us was full of activity. There was not another word said, except by the bomb aimer after he had gone back to his position and by the navigator. We made our run in total fright, except for 'right, right, left, left, steady, bomb doors open, steady, bombs away, steady, bomb doors closed, steady, flash camera, run over, off target'. It took for ever to make that run and the whole crew was tense, over the target it was like daylight. It was the only time I ever saw at least 10 other bombers almost like we were in formation. It was also the only time I ever saw German fighters in the air. They were dodging around with several good targets in the moonlight. I saw at least 5 bombers going down; one blew up in the air within a thousand yards of us.

McIntosh eventually made his way back to the USAAF airbase at Bassingbourn and, exhausted, landed at 05:53 hours after a mammoth 8 hours and 40 minutes in the air.

Flg Off J.A. Westland of 419 Squadron recalls his time over the target as 'really a very stunning affair. Everyone did a fantastic job. I and my crew were carrying incendiaries only and they caused the target to look like a 24th May sparkler [Canada's Fireworks Day]. Actually, I don't think anyone except the first crews over the target really saw the ground as the area quickly became an obscured mass of great billows of smoke and flames. Those damned fires must still be burning!'

The fires did indeed burn for some time. The raid, controlled successfully by the Master Bomber, Gp Capt John Searby of 83 Squadron, was a great success, dropping 1,800 tons of bombs into the relatively small target area with considerable accuracy. By most estimates the attack put the German rocket programme back by about two months – a vital delay when one considers that the first V1s landed in Britain in the critical month of June 1944 and the number of casualties they, and the later V2s, caused in a short time. The cost, however, was high in human terms but in military terms it was a good deal for the objectives achieved. In conditions ideal for night-fighters, some 40 aircraft, or 6.7 per cent of the attacking force, were lost. However, the bombers in the last wave suffered most heavily as more and more fighters were directed to the area, with 6 Group at the top of the loss table with 12 out of 57 – some 19.7 per cent – of the aircraft dispatched. Half of these aircraft had taken off from Middleton St George, with 419 and 428 Squadrons sharing the losses equally: from 419 Squadron the crews of Flg Off S.M. Heard, Sgt J.M. Batterton and Flt Sgt S.T. Pekin; from 428 Squadron the crews of Flt Lt G.W.N. Fanson, Sgt W.W. Blackmore and Sgt J.F. Sheridan. In all, thirty-eight men were killed and five taken prisoner.

Losses on this scale had a profound effect on all personnel at Middleton St George, particularly among those serving on the squadrons, but there was little to be done except carry on. By chance, there was a short break in operations and it was not until the 22nd that some thirty aircraft were scheduled to attack the industrial town of Leverkusen, well-known for its IG Farben chemical plant. The day's preparations did not begin well as, on a routine air test, W for William had problems with its undercarriage, forcing Sgt R.K. Metherall to carry out a wheels-up crash-landing. Fortunately none of the crew was injured in the incident. For flight engineer Sgt Bob Packer it would be his first operational sortie:

We took off at 8.20 p.m. rather nervous about our load and the length of the runway. Anyway, we got off OK climbing into the sunset looking longingly at Darlington and Stockton as they passed beneath our wings, setting course at 8,000ft for Germany. Reaching the English coast, we set our final course for the German coast. Searchlights waved, with a few occasional bursts of flak greeting us. We had been routed over two heavily defended areas. Luckily for us, aircraft in front of us bunched over these areas, causing the searchlights and guns to open up, enabling us to slip in unmolested. Just before reaching the target my oxygen tube came adrift. By the time I had corrected this, I was nearly out. I found out what lack of oxygen for a few minutes can do to the human body when at a height of 20,000ft. It gave me a tremendous headache. So bad was my head, in fact, it interested me a lot more than the target. In any case, the target was a quiet one; a few searchlights and a bit of flak, not half as bad as the coast. We let our 2,000lb HC go, with the accompanying incendiaries, and got away. On the whole trip (which took 6 hours and 30 minutes), we sighted just one German fighter, an Me109. He did not see us, for which we were truly thankful. We got back to base to find none of our squadron aircraft missing. We got to bed at about 5.00 a.m., to be awakened next morning at 11.30 to be told to report to sections. Getting to sections, we found we were on again.

The target this time was Berlin. It was to be a maximum effort with sixteen aircraft from each of 419 and 428 Squadrons scheduled to take part. As on the previous night, when six aircraft either failed to take off or returned early with bona fide mechanical faults, the attacking force was reduced to twenty-eight. For once, the weather was kind to the bombers and the raid, though scattered, succeeded in causing severe damage to the massive city. The station log recorded it as 'key for the largest and most successful ever to be launched against the capital' and the enormous fires were recorded as still being visible from the air 108 miles away. Nevertheless, the city's defences still managed an awesome display. As Sgt Packer recalls:

Getting near the target we could see a tremendous area of searchlights over Berlin, like nothing I had ever imagined. There was plenty of flak going up, which, fortunately, fell in intensity as we approached. Suddenly, a tremendously intense flare burst above us, followed by four or five more. These were fighter flares making the sky as light as day. Anyway, there was a large explosion in the sky behind us. This was an aircraft going down. It seemed an eternity before we were in a position to drop our bombs.

The explosion Packer saw was just one of the 56 aircraft shot down that night, a massive 7.9 per cent of the attacking force and the highest total lost in a single operation so far in the war. One among that number belonged to 428 Squadron. Flt Sgt H.A. Read's Halifax was badly shot up by a night-fighter and four of the crew baled out to become prisoners. However, the bomber managed to stay in the air and Read headed in what he thought was a homeward direction, determined to get as far as he could. When the Halifax finally gave up the ghost, Read gave the order to bale out. Unfortunately Sgt C. Crampton failed to do so, becoming trapped in the forward escape hatch, but Read and Flg Off J.J. McQuade did and floated down to earth safely. To their surprise, they found themselves in neutral Sweden and were interned.

Four nights later the power of Bomber Command was turned upon Nuremburg, the 'Nazis' Holy City' as the station log put it. Yet again, headaches were caused for the technical officers at Middleton as four of the thirty-two aircraft returned early with mechanical problems. Although conditions were clear, the attack was not a success. There were, however, some bright spots: Sgt W.H. Barnes, the rear gunner of 419 Squadron's X for X-ray, was credited with shooting down his second aircraft, a highly unusual achievement, and Flg Off H.T. Brown, flying on his fourth operation with 419 Squadron, was awarded an immediate DFC for his courage and determination in pressing on to Nuremburg and bombing from just 9,000ft, having lost an engine en route.

The penultimate day of the month witnessed a highly successful raid on Mönchengladbach, just a few miles from the Belgian border. It was to be a very busy night for some of the twenty-eight crews from Middleton St George. For the second operation in succession 419 Squadron's X for X-ray came under sustained night-fighter attack. Sgt M. Potter, the rear gunner, succeeded in blasting the Fw190 out of the night sky but not before it had caused considerable damage to the Halifax, some of which only became apparent after Sgt M. Bullis had pulled off a difficult landing back at base. The second aerial victory of the night belonged to another rear gunner, T/Sgt B. Blount USAAF, won while flying at 19,000ft over the target area. Once again a night-fighter attack caused severe damage to his aircraft and set it on fire. The British flight engineer Sgt J.N.S. Ashton reacted at once, emptying the contents of first one extinguisher and then another on the blaze as he moved along the burning aircraft, skilfully bringing the flames under control and finally putting them out altogether. For his prompt and courageous action in saving the aircraft and his fellow crew members, Ashton was awarded an immediate DFM.

Bob Packer, and the rest of Sgt Marjoram's inexperienced crew, had a hard night. They scanned the darkness anxiously as they watched night-fighter flares creeping towards them, clearly following the vapour trails cutting through the night sky. Several explosions and streaks of fire lit up the darkness as bomber after bomber fell victim to the roving fighters. As the Halifax approached the target

the rear gunner broke through on the intercom, saying his turret had jammed out on the beam and he could not shift it. Before anyone could go to the rear gunner's aid, he yelled directions to avoid a German fighter coming in to attack. We corkscrewed out of the way and dropped our bombs. The corkscrew was so violent that it upset the Elsan. We soaked the mid-under gunner and his intercom plug and lead. Suddenly the intercom spluttered and went dead. Now we were in a hell of a fix. We could see five fighters engaging aircraft in front of us and we did not think much of our chances without any intercom.

There was little time to try to effect any repairs so the crew had to rely on the system of call lights for communication, with a series of dots representing corkscrew port and dashes starboard. 'Suddenly these light flashed a series of dots and the pilot threw the aircraft into a violent corkscrew. Things continued in this way for a solid half hour, during which time we were attacked and got away from five separate German fighter aircraft. We crossed the coast at a speed of 240mph [at an] indicated 7,000ft, so that meant we had lost 13,000ft in avoiding the fighter attacks.' This skilful piece of flying and the superb teamwork were mentioned in Marjoram's later award of the DFC and in rear gunner Rocky Sullivan's award of the DFM.

August 1943 certainly had a sting in the tail as far as the crews of 419 and 428 Squadrons were concerned. The target for the last night of the month was Berlin. The raid was intended to be the most concentrated of the war, with well over 600 aircraft passing over the target area in a little under 30 minutes but, as with the best-laid plans, it was not to be. Although the flak seemed a little lighter than usual, cloud and unforeseen problems with the H2S used by the PFF led to poor marking and somewhat scattered bombing. The attack demonstrates how differently the crews could view the night's operation. One of 419 Squadron's crews reported 'such an uneventful trip that one of the pigeons laid an egg on landing', yet 47 of the bombers were lost, mostly to night-fighters who were now perfecting their technique of illuminating the bombers with flares to create an 'aerial flight path'. No fewer than five aircraft which took off from Middleton St George failed to return.

Sgt B.R. Harrison of 428 Squadron and all his crew were lost in the target area, coming down near Holzdorf. There were three casualties in Sgt J.D.A. Este's crew when their Halifax crashed and exploded spectacularly near Oberhaching, having been hit by flak. A freak accident cost Sgt W.D.L. Cameron and three of his crew their lives that night. Their Halifax had carried out a successful bombing run when a single-engined fighter smashed head on into the port wing. The aircraft seemed to stop in mid-air and shuddered violently, before putting its nose down and lurching earthwards. K for King of 419 Squadron was flying steadily over Hannover when suddenly fighter flares fell on either side of the bomber and almost instantaneously a Ju88 closed in to rake the Halifax from end to end with cannon fire, setting it well alight. The order was given to bale out as the pilot, Flt Lt D.J. Corcoran, struggled to keep the blazing aircraft level. After that, Corcoran remembered no more, regaining consciousness as he floated serenely earthwards beneath his parachute, having been thrown free as the aircraft exploded. His rear gunner, Flg Off D.E. Larlee, was also lucky to survive, having endured some terrifying seconds as he bounced around in the slipstream, still attached to the doomed bomber by his left foot, which was wedged tight in the turret. Eventually gravity did its job and, leaving his boot behind, Larlee came safely to earth to be greeted by some irate German farmers waving shotguns at him. Two other crewmen survived, WO A. MacKenzie, who was wounded in both legs, and Sgt W.E. Greensides, who knew little of his escape from the aircraft and only came to when roughly roused by his German captors. The third of 419 Squadron's losses that night was the bomber flown by Flg Off R. Stewart and his crew. They too fell victim to an unseen night-fighter in the Black Forest area, all but three of the crew managing to bale out. It had been a dreadful night for the squadrons based at Middleton St George but, as the station log noted, with 'operations gaining momentum' such nights were to became far more frequent and, if ever they could be, routine. In return for the heavy losses sustained in August, 419 and 428 Squadrons had dropped no less than 1,223,060lbs of high explosives, incendiaries and mines on Axis targets.

The next target was the city of Mannheim, which, in clear conditions, suffered an exceptionally heavy and accurate attack, described in the city records as a 'catastrophe'. Once again many night-fighter flares were noted and a night-fighter was probably responsible for bringing down the Halifax flown by Flg Off J.A. Studer of 419 Squadron, which crashed near Wiesbaden, killing all on board. Flak accounted for 419 Squadron's other casualty, Sgt F.B. Allan's Halifax, which disintegrated over the target, leaving only one survivor, Plt Off J.R. Harris. While these losses could not be avoided, others could. Again one aircraft from each squadron returned early and two others collided while taxiing, putting both bombers out of commission for the night.

There was little time for recriminations or rest as orders were received for an attack on Munich the next night. Unpopular with the crews on account of its considerable distance and

Most maintenance work on aircraft was undertaken outside. It was hard, tiring and particularly unglamorous work. *(Author)*

redoubtable defences, Munich got away lightly that night, blanketed as it was by thick cloud. By good fortune all of 419 and 428 Squadrons' aircraft emerged unscathed. However, there were yet more Gremlins afoot; no fewer than five other aircraft either failed to take off or returned early on account of mechanical problems. The politically driven policy of Canadianisation at all costs was undermining the efficiency of the squadrons in the line.

There was a welcome break from operations, punctuated by an outbreak of spit and polish in preparation for a visit by AOC-in-C Bomber Command, 'Butch' Harris, on the 14th. For unknown reasons the visit was cancelled at the last minute after Harris had visited Linton and Tholthorpe, but AVM Brookes, AOC 6 Group, flew in anyway and enjoyed the excellent lunch laid on for his boss. The following night, 15 September, Middleton St George went back to war. The target was a special one: the Dunlop rubber factory at Montlucon in central France. Having been briefed to take particular care to avoid the neighbouring residential area, the crews were relieved to find the defences as negligible as predicted, enabling them to come in at just 4,000ft and see the accurately laid PFF markers clearly. Every building in the factory complex was either destroyed or damaged, without significant collateral damage. Only three of the 369 aircraft involved in the attack were lost; one of them, however, belonged to Wg Cdr D.W.M. Smith, 428 Squadron's CO, who was leading a scratch crew of experienced and semi-screened personnel put together on the day of the raid. Hit by falling incendiaries over the target, the Halifax came down near Cerilly, just 35km north of Montlucon. For navigator Flt Lt E.B. Mason it was his second experience of baling out:

I knew the drill well, having practised it many times. First you folded your seat up, then disconnected the intercom and folded your light and table up. You removed the escape hatch in the floor and passed it to the W/Op, who stored it in his cubicle; then you snapped on your parachute, stowed beneath your seat, and sat at the escape hatch opening waiting for the signal from either the W/Op or the bomb aimer who were still on the intercom. I received the signal to go, so left the aircraft. I remember seeing no fire and the flying attitude of the Halifax seemed normal. The thought crossed my mind that the rest might fly back to the base without me. That thought soon left as the ground was coming up fast. I guided my chute towards the middle of a small field and landed in what I suspect was a potato field.

No one would ever have guessed what the next twelve months had in store for him. Having walked for two nights without making significant progress, Mason approached Monsieur Raynaud, a man he judged old enough to have fought against the Germans in the previous war, and told him who he was. Taken back to the family home, he was well looked after, before being moved on and given documents to make him Rene Legrand of Montlucon, born 15 December 1908. He was eventually taken to Clermont-Ferrand where he spent a while helping to bring in the local grape harvest before being taken out to a small Maquis camp under the command of a man known as 'Duranton'. Over the next few days he was joined there by three of his crew mates and a couple of other evaders. Within a week or two, it was decided that there was room for six airmen to squeeze into a Lysander that would be landing near Bordeaux in the October full moon period. Mason was not to be included in this half dozen, who, after several false starts, eventually made it back to Britain in mid-November.

By this time the Germans had penetrated the escape organisations and raided many of the safe houses, capturing or killing many of their workers. It was a difficult time. One of the airmen in Mason's group was killed by the Germans on 9 December at a road-block near Martres-de-Veyne. Constantly moving around remote and isolated areas, in January 1944 Mason received orders from London to stay put and assist the teams of SOE agents who would soon be parachuted into France in preparation for the invasion. It was March before Mason's group linked up with a three-man SOE team in the Mont Mouchet area. This became a major centre for the Maquis, which eventually grew to be several thousand strong. Mason and several other airmen assisted with weapons training and the interrogation of young men brought in claiming to be Allied airmen. One or two who were not what they said met with summary justice.

Early in June 1944 the Germans attacked the Maquis centre and Mason and the other airmen found themselves fighting in a full-scale running battle, which the lightly armed guerrillas could not win. As the Germans closed in a couple of days later, Mason was part of a small group who broke through the enemy cordon and made it to another SOE group run by the redoubtable Nancy Wake. The Germans attacked this group within a few days and Mason, in the company of Denis Rake, the group's radio operator, made his getaway. At one point, with bloodhounds and their handlers in sight, Mason carried both the exhausted Rake and his radio across a river on his back and into the woods beyond. They made their way north-west, carefully avoiding the Milice and German patrols, and eventually joined up with another Maquis group near Farges. For another month, working alongside another SOE team, the group received and distributed arms and explosives as well as harassing the local German forces who were by this time more or less confined to a handful of towns. By the end of August the fighting in that part of France was over, so Mason and four other airmen made their way to an Allied airfield at Toulouse. From there, they were flown to Algiers and onwards to Britain via Gibraltar. Mason landed in England on 22 September 1944, a little over a year after he had taken off from Middleton St George.

'In order to help the Allied armies in Italy, Bomber Command attacked the railway marshalling yards and switching station at the entrance to the Mons Cenis tunnel at Modane.' This tunnel, as the station log recorded, was a main link between France and Italy and, once again, was only lightly defended. Though considered successful at the time, the raid caused only minor disruption, with many of the bombs falling outside the confines of the steep valley. The route over the Alps posed unusual problems for some of the crews. John Turnbull of Govan, Saskatchewan, whose elder brother also became a highly decorated bomber pilot, recalls:

We had been flying through wispy cloud which appeared harmless but found ice was building up. Gradually we lost lift. With bright halos around the tips of the propellers we just sank lower and lower into the Alps. It was an eerie feeling. Soon we were in a great valley with towering mountains on each side and I wondered if we would ever get out. I made the gentlest possible 180° turn. Slowly the ice began to melt and eventually we were able to arrest the sink and climb.

Only three aircraft were lost but, once again, one of them was based at Middleton St George. Flt Lt A.N. Quaile and his experienced crew were attacked by a night-fighter on the homeward leg of the mission. Machine-gun and cannon fire ripped through the port wing, setting both engines alight and leaving no room for doubt that baling out was the only option. At once navigator Plt Off L. Aspinall went to open the escape hatch, only to find that it was jammed shut. Even the urgent assistance of the W/Op, Flt Sgt T.J. Bright, failed to shift the cover, the opportunity to bale out disappearing with each passing second. The bomb aimer, Plt Off G.T. Graham, was a heavily built gentleman and he cleared the others out of the way and simply jumped up and down on the hatch. This quickly proceeded to give way, launching both it and the bomb aimer into the night air, wrenching Graham's neck in the process as he had forgotten to disconnect his intercom plug. Although the others followed on in the regulation manner, the pilot Quaile almost did not make it. As he made his way out of the cramped cockpit of the Halifax, he snagged the release ring of his parachute on the throttle quadrant, causing it to open partially. Frantically gathering up the billowing silk in his arms, he made his way to the open hatch and unceremoniously leapt out into the slipstream, landing not far from Lisieux. No fewer than four members of this crew were able to evade the Germans and make their way back to Britain – a feat almost unheard of.

Graham, after walking for several days, asked for help at a remote farmhouse. He chose well, and was swiftly passed along an escape line. He made it back home by the end of October. Flight engineer Sgt L.F. Martin landed in thick forest and began his escape dangling under his parachute some 30ft off the ground. It took an hour of vigorous swinging and bouncing to get free, and then he crashed to the ground, knocking himself out in the process. As he made his way out of the forest and into more open countryside, he was spotted by a woman who was waving her husband off to work. This chance meeting also proved a fortuitous one and Martin too joined an escape route, returning to safety via Gibraltar. Gunner Flg Off Smith was just as lucky. Having met up with a teenager who promised to help, Smith was given food and overnight lodgings in several houses, each time being asked to move on the next morning. He ended up in Lisieux, a town crowded with Germans, many of whom were looking for him and his fellow crew members. Tired, hungry and thirsty, Smith simply picked out a cabinet-maker's shop at random, went in and said who he was. It proved to be an inspired choice. After a little while a lady who spoke English was brought to the shop and set in motion the long and dangerous process by which Smith was returned to Britain in December. No details are available of Flt Sgt Bright's evasion.

Two hard-hitting but routine attacks followed, if such extraordinary events can be so labelled, against Hannover and Mannheim, each of them costing two more crews. There was even worse to come. After a few night's rest sixteen aircraft from 419 Squadron and one fewer from 428 Squadron were sent back to Hannover in an attempt to destroy the centre of the city. As it happened, unexpected wind conditions meant that the PFF marking veered towards the north of the city, which suffered badly in the initial stages of the raid, starting large fires still visible 150 miles away, before the bombing strayed out into open country.

It had not been an easy night from the start, with no fewer than six of Middleton's aircraft being forced to return early as a result of heavy icing. Although 419 Squadron remained casualty-free, for 428 Squadron, fast becoming a real 'Ghost' squadron, it was another story. Sgt D.A.J. Griffin was the only survivor in Sgt J. Farmer's crew when it was hit by flak over the target and crashed in Holland shortly after midnight. Flg Off M.G. Whalley's Halifax came off the worse in an encounter with a night-fighter over the target, leaving only Flg Off W.B.L. Higgins and Whalley himself as survivors. Almost certainly the same fate befell the crew of Flg Off R.M. Sherback, all of whom were killed when their Halifax crashed. Plt Off M. Kogan, an experienced campaigner, was captain of one of the bombers forced to turn back after encountering heavy icing. Having made it back to the English coast near Hull, the port inner engine packed up, swiftly followed by its starboard counterpart and the ASI. Kogan gave the order to bale out but before he could follow his crew out of the escape hatch he caught sight of the flarepath of RAF Ludford Magna and decided to try to land his valuable aircraft there. However, it very soon became apparent that, with two engines dead, he had little room for manoeuvre and he decided to simply put the aircraft down, making a successful wheels-up crash-landing. O for Orange was written off but, more importantly, all of the crew survived unharmed. U for Uncle, under the command of Sgt R. Wilson, was less fortunate. Four of the crew lost their lives when the battle-damaged Halifax crashed near Parham in Suffolk while heading for Framlingham airfield to make an emergency landing. It was 428 Squadron's worst night of the war to date and, coming on top of the heavy losses already sustained in August and September, it was hard to bear. Indeed, such losses were beginning to undermine the level of operational experience within the squadron as a whole and, in turn, its operational efficiency.

The balance sheet for September was about even. On the plus side, 419 and 428 Squadrons had delivered 999,472lb of bombs on German and French targets in September, causing considerable damage and destruction. On the negative side, 419 Squadron had lost six aircraft and 428 Squadron no fewer than eleven, including one flown by their CO, Wg Cdr D.W.N. Smith; in addition, the return early rate stubbornly remained unacceptably high, in spite of the best efforts of all concerned. With the onset of winter and longer nights everyone knew there would be hard times ahead.

The first day of October was a bit of a farce in operational terms. Initially fifteen aircraft from 419 Squadron and thirteen from 428 Squadron were scheduled to take part in an attack on Stuttgart. The well-oiled wheels of the station machine swung into action, preparing maps and parachutes, fuelling, bombing-up, making engine and technical checks and doing a thousand and one other jobs, great and small. The operation was called off at 14:00 on account of inclement weather. The crews happily dispersed to make the most of an unexpected afternoon and evening off, while the ground crews began to undo much of their work. At 14:52 operations were officially back on and the police in Darlington were alerted to round up the crews and ferry them back to the station as soon as possible. By 16:00 the briefing was under way and the ground crews back to working flat out once more. At 16:18 orders were received scrubbing the operation once and for all.

Two nights later the target announced was the Hessian city of Kassel, an attack which claimed another three aircraft from 428 Squadron, continuing its grim run of ill-fortune. The following night ops were on again, the target being Frankfurt. Three of 428 Squadron's aircraft fell victim to gremlins before take-off but the rest pressed on and contributed their loads to the most devastating attack the city had suffered in the war to date, with the eastern districts and inland docks being particularly hard hit. Although only ten aircraft were lost from the 406-strong force, three of them had taken off from Middleton St George. No. 428 Squadron lost the brand-new Halifax flown by Flt Sgt J. Harkins. The navigator, Sgt D. Richards, picks up the story:

The fighter raked our starboard wing with bullets and, no doubt, cannon, setting the two engines on fire, plus the petrol tanks. My first realisation of trouble was the appearance of a small curl of smoke and two small holes in the port skin of the aircraft. I then noticed a small graze on the ball of my left thumb. At the same time the rear gunner was calling for a turn and, almost immediately, came the order from the pilot to abandon the aircraft. The drill was for the navigator to fold up his table and then the seat, lift up and drop out of the hatch in the floor. However, the seat would not lift, even after attacking it with an axe, and presumably was damaged by the firing. Accordingly, I told the crew to use the rear hatch which they did. I clipped on my parachute and then that of the pilot and exited from the rear, dropping peacefully in freefall to clear other planes, opened my parachute and dropped unfortunately into the arms of some Hitler Youth. Later I learned that the pilot had rolled around the plane as it went into a spin and, luckily out of the hatch.

Harkins and a gunner, Sgt N.W. Lee, managed to evade capture and return to the UK, while the flight engineer, Sgt A. Scott, who had sustained severe arm injuries, was repatriated in February 1945. For Richards and the rest of the crew it was to be a long spell behind the wire.

The other two aircraft lost were from 419 Squadron. Flg Off W.H. Hamilton's experienced crew fell victim to a night-fighter some 40–50 miles east of Mannheim. Once it was hit fire broke out and took hold rapidly, forcing Hamilton to shout, 'Prepare to bale out. I can't hold the controls much longer.' Unfortunately the bomber went out of control almost immediately thereafter and the pilot and three of the crew did not have time to get out before the aircraft hit the ground. Of the second crew lost to a night-fighter en route home, that of Sgt A.R. Fare, there was only one survivor, Sgt W.L. Renner, who later managed to hook up with a Belgian escape line and successfully evade capture. He was eventually moved to a house in Fairoul where he remained hidden for over eight months before being liberated by American forces early in August 1944.

On 7 October there was a change in command. Wg Cdr Fleming, 419 Squadron's CO, was deemed to have finished his second tour and was posted to Allerton Park as 6 Group's Senior Operations Officer. He had played a crucial role in bringing 419 Squadron through a busy period of the war and had become a popular and respected commander. The party to bid him farewell and celebrate the award of his DSO was a boisterous and happy occasion. The day of Fleming's departure, 8 October 1943, was to provide a significant milestone for the station – its 250th operational night. The target was Hannover and the damage done was immense. A few nights later it was Kassel's turn. The destruction caused by this accurate and concentrated raid, which fuelled a mini-firestorm, was colossal, destroying over 60 per cent of the city's housing and over 150 industrial premises, including the three Henschel aircraft works which were producing parts for the V1. Over 5,500 bodies had been recovered from the debris by the end of November.

Sadly, 419 Squadron's only casualty of the night was the newly appointed CO, Wg Cdr C.A. McMurdy. Bob Packer, a flight engineer in 419 Squadron, describes the evening:

We were ordered to attack Kassel. At briefing we had our new Wg Cdr, a young Canadian of about 22 years of age. Our old CO had finished his tour. This boy was pretty good and had been under the old Wg Cdr's wing for approximately three months. His last words at briefing were, 'Well fellows, it's a lot of fun'. Anyway not many of us looked at it in quite the same light. Those were his last official words he was to say as we lost only one aircraft that night but he was the pilot. We heard later that the pilot and engineer, a boy from Wales, were killed, the rest of the crew got away with their lives and were taken prisoner.

In fact, Packer's information is not quite right as five of the crew perished as a result of an attack by no fewer than three fighters working together, leaving the port engines and wing ablaze.

McMurdy's replacement was Wg Cdr W.P. Pleasance, formerly a flight commander with 431 Squadron. As it turned out 428 Squadron received a new CO, Wg Cdr D.T. French, at about the same time, following Wg Cdr Suggitt's posting to 5 Group.

There was a Group stand-down for the next few days and this was prolonged by a spell of foggy winter weather, restricting operations to just a single attack on Düsseldorf. On

This photograph of a single Lancaster X bomb load, taken at Middleton St George, gives some idea of the scale of the aerial bombardment carried out primarily upon Germany during the Strategic Air Offensive. Pictured here in April 1944 are Wg Cdr W.P. Pleasance, commanding 419 Squadron from October 1943 to August 1944, and Flt Lt J. Stewart. *(Department of National Defence PL 29078)*

Armistice Day a special operation was laid on, requiring five of the best crews from each of 419 and 428 Squadrons. One of these crews included Bob Packer in 419 Squadron.

We were detailed for a very unusual trip, our crew being the only NCO crew detailed. The rumours going around during the day were terrifying, as the bombs were all 1,000lb HE. Each aircraft carried one overload tank, 11 x 1,000-pounders and no incendiaries. First rumours said we were going to make an attack on Berlin, then Berchtesgarten, then Kiel, next Norway, until we were on edge. We were at briefing well before time, and crowded into the room with our eyes searching the route map on the wall. There was a red ribbon stretching from our base over France and over the Alps and stopping at Cannes on the Riviera coast. The moon was full that night so we did not think much of our chances. We had our own aircraft and took off later in the afternoon. As we headed over the coast, land could be seen in dark contrast to the glittering sea which was under the full reflection of the moon. Down below us, an aircraft suddenly flicked across the sky, shown up in the moonlight, followed by two more. These aircraft looked like Ju88 fighters, so we began to feel very uncomfortable.

After about an hour's flying we ran out of the clear sky into thick cloud, which relieved us greatly. We stopped in cloud until we reached the Alps, which we could see standing out like jagged teeth in the moonlight. We climbed to 15,000ft and started crossing the mountains. It was the most amazing sight I have seen before or since. Occasionally, in the white wastes below, we could see the light from a lonely mountain village, usually on the side of some huge river, which we could see as a dark trail of ink spilled on a snowy white tablecloth. Getting nearer the coast of the Riviera, we found we were 50 or so miles off course, which we had to make up before reaching Cannes. Suddenly we saw an expanse of level whiteness in front, behind which the sea sprawled and an occasional jagged peak broke the levelness [sic] of the mist, which looked like islands in a sea of snow. In the distance, off to our right, we could see the photoflashes exploding as the attack on Cannes commenced. We were afraid we would be too late but diving at speed to 10,000ft we arrived over the target, defending which an occasional shell burst futilely. We dropped our bombs, reaching base after an uneventful journey back over the Alps and France. We found all our aircraft had returned safely. We later received a target token for the trip. It was not until later that we realised how hopeless it would have been to be shot down in the mountains as even if we had baled out we had no chance of survival. The trip took us 10 hours exactly. We could hardly walk when we left the aircraft.

The target in this seaside resort that was so favoured by the rich and famous before the war had been the large railway yards but these were not hit during the raid. Unfortunately, most of the high explosive, in spite of the great care taken by the experienced crews, landed on residential areas. Thirty-nine people lost their lives. The local German-controlled newspapers were trenchant in their condemnation of the barbaric behaviour of the Allied bombers, keen to make best use of this propaganda windfall.

In the next few days there was little opportunity for flying, but on the 16th and 17th several hours were spent scouring the North Sea for a dinghy containing airmen from a

Flying Fortress that had ditched on the way back from Norway. There was a large element of 'it could be me' among the crews on such sorties and it was with great joy that a member of Flt Sgt Metheral's crew spotted a dinghy bobbing around in the wintry seas. As the Halifax turned to confirm the sighting, the 419 Squadron crew lost visual contact and there were several anxious minutes before it could be located.

The radio operator at once reported the position and the Halifax stood guard over the dinghy waiting for help to arrive. Unfortunately, darkness intervened and Metheral headed for home. The next day, at first light and in heavy sleet, three aircraft took off from Middleton St George to search for the dinghy, but could find no trace of it in the choppy seas. It was a heartbreaking and tragic end to the operation.

The following day saw a return to the main business of Bomber Command, with an attack on the heavily defended city of Mannheim. It was a tough night for the crews, with harsh weather conditions almost matching the danger of the active defence mounted by the Germans. The temperature at 20,000ft that night was −40°C and there were several cases of frostbite among the Middleton St George crews. It was not only the exposed gunners who suffered; two of the navigators became frostbitten in the draught from the camera hatch. The young crews faced other serious problems and mishaps too. For example, 428 Squadron's N suffered a complete intercom failure en route to the target, leaving the bomber in a very vulnerable state. Sgt Haynes, working at 20,000ft without the aid of oxygen, methodically checked the system and finally located the root of the breakdown by the rear turret. He managed to cobble together an effective repair before passing out through lack of oxygen for the best part of an hour. The aircraft bombed the target and returned home safely, thanks largely to Haynes's outstanding efforts. Another 428 Squadron crewman that night acted beyond the call of duty. Flg Off F.B. Watkins' Halifax was damaged by a night-fighter over Ostend. Rear gunner Sgt Perehinski, although wounded in the head, continued to return fire and give precise instructions on evasion to his pilot, enabling him to lose the fighter and carry out a landing at the emergency Woodbridge airfield.

Bob Packer in 419 Squadron also had a hard night.

We started off by being off track, dodging flak and fighters with the accompanying searchlights. Eventually we found the target which we found we had overshot by about 50 miles. We had to race back and, scared to death, get through the fighters patrolling the area with nothing to distract them from our kite. We decided to attack, although the raid was officially over by 12 minutes. We drove over the target, among hundreds of searchlights. This became one of my worst experiences as, coned by nearly all the lights and with flak being thrown up at us, we were apparently the only plane in the area, and as such an insult to the defences. We got our load away and started climbing and corkscrewing out of the target area. Suddenly the searchlights left us and concentrated on another aircraft to our right and just behind, which appeared to be in the same fix. He got away as we did. I never want to attack late again. We had more trouble coming off the target, ending up 50 miles off track, between Calais and Cap Gris Nez. We had a devil of a job getting over the coast, tons of flak being thrown up at us. We thought we had been hit once when the kite lurched and dropped like a stone but we pulled out OK.

Two other 419 Squadron crews were not so fortunate.

If the raid on Mannheim had not been a conspicuous success, the one on Leverkusen the following night was an unmitigated disaster. City records note that only a single bomb fell on the urban area, in spite of an attacking force of 266 aircraft. The weather was so bad that only a handful of German aircraft managed to take off but still 428 Squadron lost two Halifaxes. Flt Sgt M.C. Shepherd and his crew all made it out of their badly mauled Halifax as it limped over the Dutch border. Three of them, Flt Sgt D.K. MacGillivray, Sgt N.M. Michie and Sgt S. Munns, managed to evade, but the others were captured soon after landing. Sgt K. Hawthorne and his crew got a little further, just making the Kent coast. The aircraft had been badly buffeted by flak over the target and this had reduced the navigator to a state of numbed shock, obliging the bomb aimer to plot the course for home. He did his job well and was on track when, a few miles short of the English coast, the port outer engine gave up the ghost and caught fire. The order to bale out was given. The mid-upper gunner, Sgt J.A. McEwan, went out first and landed in the sea. He was never seen again. The rest came down on the coast itself and survived, though the W/Op refused to fly again and was returned to Canada. The aircraft eventually came down in a cemetery near Canterbury, causing a considerable and most unpleasant mess.

THE BATTLE OF BERLIN

On 22 November AVM Brookes, AOC 6 Group, watched the largest force yet to take to the skies from Middleton St George – thirty-four Halifaxes, seventeen from each squadron based there. Their target was the German capital, Berlin, which was shrouded by dense cloud but was still hit as hard as at any time during the war; perhaps 175,000 people were bombed out that night and 2,000 killed as vast swathes of the city were laid waste by the deluge of high explosive. Smoke was seen rising to 20,000ft, the result of mini-firestorms creating a raging inferno on the ground. The defences were vicious and both 419 and 428 Squadrons lost a crew. Luck, as ever, played a big part in this life and death struggle. Gunner Flt Sgt J. Lesage had notched up no fewer than 25 trips in his nine months with 419 Squadron and was drafted into a novice crew, with an average age of just 20, as a last-minute replacement. The flight engineer, Sgt W.B. Jones, had just turned 18 years of age. On only his second operation, he was one of the youngest members of the RAF to be killed in 1943.

On 25 November thirty-two heavily laden aircraft took off from Middleton St George bound for Frankfurt. Predictably for the time of year, thick cloud was encountered throughout the journey but it cleared sufficiently to make life easy for the German night-fighters. Sqn Ldr J.R. Beggs of 428 Squadron was badly mauled by a night-fighter over the target itself and left with both starboard engines blazing furiously and one of his crew, Sgt P.J. Barske, mortally wounded. There was no option but to bale out and six of the crew did so to become POWs. WO J.R. Morrison in E for Easy of 419 Squadron got the prize for the greatest escape of the night, shaking off no fewer than four separate night-fighter attacks with barely a scratch to show for the encounters. His colleague Sgt G.M. Scade was in Y for Yoke, which suffered its first attack at 01:45 as it entered the target area; the first the crew knew of it was when tracer arced towards the bomber. Scade threw the Halifax all over the night sky, losing 10,000ft in the process of shaking off his assailant. Then course was resumed and all was calm until well into the journey home. A more persistent and wily attacker simply held back and followed the bomber as it executed the normal corkscrew evasive procedure, emitting accurate bursts of fire as the opportunity arose. The damage caused was considerable, especially in the nose area where gaping holes allowed a 200mph gale to whistle through the entire aircraft, making severe frostbite almost inevitable. The slipstream sucked all of Sgt W.R. Dickinson's navigational charts clean out of the Halifax and wrecked much of the interior equipment. The night-fighter eventually broke off the attack only 30 miles short of the enemy coast, leaving Scade and Dickinson working in freezing conditions to find their way home in an aircraft that was barely able to remain airborne. But they did exactly that, thereby saving both themselves and their fellow crewmen; both men were awarded the DFC for their skill and courage.

Keen to keep up the pressure on the Nazi hierarchy, the next night Bomber Command ordered attacks to be made on both Berlin and, as a diversion, Stuttgart. Middleton's aircraft were scheduled to take part in the diversionary attack, though once again three aircraft succumbed to mechanical problems. The rest pressed on in difficult conditions to find the city blanketed by cloud, and as a result much of the bombing became scattered. Once again 419 Squadron featured on the casualty list. Sgt S.E. Clarke and his entire RAF/RCAF crew, on only their second operation, perished when their bomber was brought down near Sankt Ingbert. While any loss had a considerable impact upon all the men and women based at Middleton St George, that impact was multiplied several times over when the loss was actually seen by those serving at the airfield. Ten Lancasters from 1 Group had been diverted to Middleton St George and, perhaps unfamiliar with the approach patterns and certainly exhausted, one of the pilots collided with Flt Sgt R.M. Buck's 428 Squadron Halifax which was making a regular approach to the runway. All of Buck's predominantly British crew and all of the Lancaster's crew bar the mid-upper gunner, who received serious injuries and burns, perished just a half a mile from the runway. The resulting explosion and fireball was clearly visible to all around and rammed home to everyone the dangers involved and the thin dividing line between life and death in carrying out the strategic air offensive. An inquiry found that the Lancaster from 103 Squadron had attempted to land without permission and had ploughed into the unsuspecting Halifax at a little over 500ft. It was a tragic end to the operational month. The gloom was lightened by one long-awaited event, the delivery to 419 Squadron on the 29th of KB700, the first Canadian-built Lancaster X, christened the 'Ruhr Express'. Although this was a significant political milestone, it was to be some time before the gremlins would be fully wiped out, particularly with regard to spare parts and servicing, and the whole squadron equipped with the new aircraft.

By this time, after a considerable period of intensive operations, the main runway at Middleton St George was in desperate need of attention and it was hoped that the 'wonders and blunders boys' could carry out the extensive repairs in December, when there would be fewer nights suitable for operations. As it turned out, the weather was obligingly awful. Indeed, there were only three nights when ops were on in December. The first saw the bombers bound for Leipzig, a major industrial centre noted for its enormous Junkers aircraft factory. Three of 419 Squadron's aircraft returned early with mechanical problems in spite of thorough ground checks, but the rest ploughed on through thick cloud, heading towards Berlin before breaking off to Leipzig as a small Mosquito force carried on to the German capital as a diversion. In spite of the cloud, it proved to be the most successful raid of the war on the city, laying waste a good number of residential areas and industrial premises, including the Junkers works. Only Plt Off R.K. Metheral of 419 Squadron and his crew had had a difficult time, having lost the starboard inner engine while still 75 miles from the target. Losing height slowly but surely, Metheral pressed on to Leipzig where his was the last aircraft to drop its bombs that night. His Halifax trundled home over an hour after the rest of the bombers from Middleton, much to the relief of all those in the air and on the ground. For this and other sorties on which he set 'a fine example of skill, courage and devotion to duty', Metheral was awarded a DFC.

The second trip was on the 20th, when fourteen aircraft from each of 419 and 428 Squadrons were scheduled to attack Frankfurt. The Germans picked up the force on their radar almost as soon as it formed up and tracked it all the way to the target. It was a torrid night for Bob Packer and his crew, flying a brand-new Halifax:

> We took off OK but then found that the kite was a very poor climber and we nearly pulled the engines off their mountings trying to gain height. Eventually we managed to reach 19,500ft near the target. We had planned to lay a false fighter flare 30 miles north of the target but these were dropped in the target area by mistake, added to which the Germans started to send down their own flares, so altogether the night was not night but day. Kites were going down all over the place but we tore over the target, dropped our load and dived out, weaving all the way. We saw several fighters, who apparently did not see us, which was a good thing. We reached home to find 419 Squadron had all their kites back but 428 Squadron lost two aircraft. In one of them was a crew on their last trip. It is very disturbing to a bomber station when a thing like that happens. Trip took 7 hours and 15 minutes.

The 428 Squadron crew that almost made it was that of Plt Off W.J. Armour DFC, with all the men being lost bar one. The other crew was that of Flt Sgt J.L. Keighan, the sole survivor when the aircraft crashed near Mendig.

Christmas Day dawned without further offensive operations being carried out. Imagine the furore when at 09:50 hours orders for a 'total effect' attack on Berlin winged their way to Middleton St George from Command HQ. The Christmas feeling was forgotten and preparations for the operation commenced immediately – but the Christmas feeling returned with great strength when the operation was cancelled just 10 minutes later. Perhaps the order was someone's idea of a joke. In fact, it was not until the 29th that 419 and 428 Squadrons made their third positive contribution to the war effort in December.

The human cost of the offensive. Berlin, December 1943. German civilian casualties are laid out in a makeshift mortuary. *(Imperial War Museum HU 12143)*

Almost inevitably, the red line on the map at the briefing stretched to distant Berlin, which, with equal inevitability, was buried deep beneath the wintry murk. After the long lay-off from operations 419 Squadron was able to muster seventeen aircraft and 428 sixteen, though even then two were non-starters on account of brake and engine trouble. Over Berlin columns of smoke were reported as billowing up to 20,000ft and the dull red glow of burning fires was visible to the crews up to 100 miles away. Several diversionary raids succeeded in keeping losses to a minimum, with only 20 aircraft being lost. Flt Sgt R.L. Thompson's Halifax was over Berlin when the port outer engine spluttered to a halt before catching fire. The blaze quickly took hold, fanned by the massive airflow, and the crew immediately abandoned the Halifax, thereby gaining the unwanted honour of being Middleton St George's final operational loss of 1943.

For 6 Group, the raid had been a significant milestone: at the end of its first year it had launched its largest ever strike force – 135 aircraft – against the capital of Hitler's Third Reich. As AM L.S. Breadner, the new AOC-in-C RCAF Overseas, put it in a message to mark the Group's anniversary, 'the splendid record of your Group which reached a peak on Wednesday night reflects a fine esprit de corps which I know will be maintained and enhanced in the New Year'. Middleton St George had played a significant role in most of 6 Group's operations and had witnessed many changes. Gp Capt Ross, the Station Commander, summed it up as follows:

This ends the first year of Middleton St George as an RCAF station. There have been many changes in personnel and organisation in the past year and by the end of the year there were only four officers left on station who were here a year ago. This year has been a successful one from all points of view. The operational effort can be considered a credit to Bomber Command and the RCAF. No. 419 Squadron in particular has maintained a high standard of efficiency as an operational unit and is being closely challenged by 428 Squadron which came to this station about the middle of the year. The squadrons have had their periods of good and bad luck as regards casualties and the spirit of all ranks on the station remains at a high level. Aside from the WAAF, the personnel on the station here gradually changed from RAF to RCAF, this being a gradual process during the year. At the beginning of the year the percentage of Canadian personnel on the station including the squadrons was 24 per cent and at the end of the year it had risen to 67 per cent. These figures take into account personnel of the RAF Regiment and the Airfield Construction Flight. All ranks on the station look forward to the New Year with hope and are confident that it will be a successful one for the station. All are determined to do their bit to try to end the European War this coming year.

The high hopes for the New Year were quickly smothered beneath the leaden skies of winter in north-east England. Only a few sorties to garden the waters off the French coast were possible before it was back to the war with a bump on 20 January. The target was Berlin.

The lay-off allowed sixteen Halifaxes from each squadron to be made ready but once again the gremlins came to life, forcing three aircraft to either fail to take off or return early on account of mechanical problems. As expected, there was a complete layer of cloud blanketing the German capital and, though the markers appeared to be accurate and concentrated, none of the crews could offer concrete evidence as to the raid's effectiveness beyond reporting a large red glow. The capital's defences were at full throttle that night, bringing down 35 bombers, 22 of which were Halifaxes. Three of them were from Middleton St George. Plt Off M.L. Bullis and his crew had had a difficult flight from the onset, plagued by a series of intercom failures. The crew made the bold decision to continue and all was well until, just 20 minutes away from the target, the Halifax was raked from end to end by an Me109 which came out of nowhere. Three of the crew, including Bullis, were wounded and the flight engineer, Flt Sgt D.B. Ferguson, was killed in the devastating attack. The rear gunner, Sgt M. Potter, managed to get in a quick burst, and the Me109 was seen to dive away trailing smoke, heading down to an uncertain fate. Bullis managed to regain control of the Halifax at 6,000ft and even gradually coaxed it back up to 18,000ft as he headed west. Unfortunately, their course took them near Hamburg and predicted heavy flak soon smashed both port engines, compelling Bullis to order an immediate bale-out. Bullis intended to stay at the controls and try to land the aircraft because one of the wounded men, Sgt F. Sanderson, was unable to move. However, when the blazing port wing sheered off, it became clear that to stay in the bomber was pointless suicide, and Bullis followed his crew members out of the hatch.

The other 419 Squadron crew lost that night had also suffered badly from technical failure. Flt Sgt I.V. Hopkins could not get M for Mike to climb no matter what he and flight engineer John Chambers tried. After 50 minutes the Halifax had still only reached 5,000ft in spite of all the instruments on the panel reading normal. In desperation Chambers checked everything he could think of and eventually discovered that the undercarriage had not fully retracted. Several more ups and downs succeeded in coaxing the recalcitrant undercarriage into a near-normal position but it was still necessary to jettison the incendiary load in order to climb to a safe height around 20,000ft. No more trouble was experienced until a night-fighter was spotted closing in near Leipzig. As Hopkins began corkscrewing, the starboard outer engine suddenly burst into flames without a shot being fired. No sooner had the propeller been feathered when a Ju88 put in a series of attacks which caused severe damage and set the plane alight. The inevitable order followed and everyone made it out of the blazing bomber. Jon Chambers recalled what happened to him.

> I baled out at about 13,000ft and landed in trees on the perimeter of an anti-aircraft battery somewhere on the outskirts of the city. I was captured before I had time to unbuckle my chute and was taken to a hut inside the battery. Perhaps I was fortunate that my hosts were members of the Volkssturm and fairly elderly; and they treated me more with curiosity than hostility. Their hospitality did not last long – I was handed over to the local police who turned out to be a right shower, inclined to knock you about a bit if you didn't stand up all the time or refused to answer pointed questions. I had collected a few pieces of cannon shell in my rear end during our evasive action and they reluctantly had to take me to the nearest medical outfit for attention. This turned out to be the local aerodrome, where the station MO extracted the bits with tweezers – without anaesthetic of course – applied antiseptic and pronounced me fit for the cooler.

Chambers was to remain a POW until St George's Day 1945, when he was 'freed by the glorious Cossacks and you have never seen such an evil, filthy looking lot in your life. They marched us back into Russian territory where in fact we were treated worse by the Russians than the Germans.' Even so, he fared better than his fellow crew member, WO2 W.E. MacKenzie, who was among those killed on 19 April 1945 when several Typhoons strafed a POW column, having mistaken it for a Wehrmacht unit.

In the same attack on Berlin 428 Squadron lost one aircraft. Unusually, six of the seven crewmen managed to evade – a massively unusual achievement at this stage of the war. Fred Reain was the pilot of the Halifax when it was hit by flak, forcing him to give the order to bale out. As he fell through the air, Reain passed through a heavy snow shower before landing to find it a wet and miserable night at ground level:

> The first obstacle I had to cross was a river. I never learned to swim so this was a bit of a problem. I grabbed a bit of a log or something, made sure my mae west was secure and paddled across. I still don't know where the hell it was but I think it was near Metz in France. I holed up right away as soon as I got rid of my chute. My favourite hiding places were barns because I was a farmer and I knew what to expect in them. Invariably there was straw or hay and grain. The big thing was to find a way into them.

Reain stayed in several barns and eventually was directed to a 'man who could speak perfect English. This man suggested that I should put back on my RAF uniform and go into Charlon-sur-Marne and give myself up to the Germans. I left his house. My helpers told me later that he got in touch with the Gestapo immediately.' That same night the wary and ravenous Reain was staying in another ramshackle barn when a 15-year-old boy brought him food, a large lump of pickled pork. 'He gave me quite a bit so I saved some for the next day. When I looked at it in daylight it was crawling with maggots but it didn't bother me all that much. I scraped them off and ate all the meat.' He eventually made it to the Pyrenees and with a small group of evaders 'walked endlessly up into the hills. We never slept in a place with heat and our food was always cold. When we were ready to move, we drove sheep up the mountain to hide the scent that we would leave and in that way fooled the German guards with their tracking dogs. But there was snow up there and it was getting colder. I had wooden shoes at the time and you have to travel a long way to get anywhere going up a hill.' The party eventually made it into Spain where they were promptly arrested and interned. After a while a Spanish guard came up to Reain and a couple of friends and said brusquely, 'You, you and you. Be at the side door of the building tomorrow morning at seven o' clock.' Suspicious but curious, the trio appeared as directed to be met by the same Spanish guard. 'Then someone opened the door from outside and this handlebar moustache and long face appeared and said in a distinctly English voice, "All right chaps, come along with me".' They did and a few days later were in Gibraltar.

For those who had returned from Berlin safely, there was precious little time to relax. The following night orders were received to carry out an attack on Magdeburg. It was to be a black night for those stationed at Middleton St George. Although the initial stages of the outbound flight took place in 10/10ths cloud, this gradually cleared over Occupied Europe and the German fighters tore into the bomber stream for much of the journey, wreaking havoc as they went. Fighters and flak accounted for no fewer than 57 aircraft, or 8.8 per cent of the attacking force, with the Halifax component of the force suffering most at 15.6 per cent losses and 6 Group losses the highest at 12.2 per cent. Sid Philip, a navigator with 419 Squadron, was on his very first operation and was lucky to see a second. His aircraft arrived late over the target and was buffeted by heavy flak. They returned safely and in the morning light were astonished to see eighty-five separate holes in the battered bomber.

Bob Packer remembered this night as one of the worst of his tour:

We saw at briefing that we were routed over the Heligoland Bight. This seemed to be suicide hour, and it turned out to be a correct deduction in the wide sense. As soon as we touched the area of the Bight, we were under fire from the most heavy and accurate flak in Germany. Kites were going down all over the place and we were weaving all over the sky, trying to keep ourselves all in one piece. Eventually, we reached the target and dropped our bombs and started back for home. Then we found that the Met. winds were out and we were miles off track; eventually we reached what we thought was the coast, only to find we were again off the Bight but we were by no means alone as we could see, judging by the amount of flak around us. The whole area was a mass of fire. Getting over that coast was one of the worst memories of my ops; it seemed to take hours, dodging flak and fighters. When we got away at last, we were all limp with the strain. The trip took 7 hours and 39 minutes.

Several others would gladly have swapped places as three of Middleton's aircraft failed to return. The 6 Group summary of the night included none of the personal drama, noting dryly that 'due to weather conditions being favourable to both enemy fighters and flak, casualties were somewhat heavier than usual'. Little accurate assessment of the night's attack could be made, though the station records optimistically stated, 'There appears to be no doubt that the attack was very successful'.

All flying was temporarily suspended at 15:30 on 22 January when the ever-present construction flight accidentally cut through the power cables to the Watch Office, cutting off all ground to air communications. While other checks on the cabling were being carried out, several cables were found to be in a parlous state on account of rats gnawing their way through the lead outer casing. On the same day a Mosquito from RAF Dyce on a routine flight crashed near the airfield; both men on board were found dead by the emergency crews dispatched from Middleton.

The final raid of the month took place on 29 January when fourteen aircraft from each squadron were scheduled to take part in the thirteenth major raid on Berlin in the recent campaign. It wasn't all plain sailing. Three aircraft from 428 Squadron were forced to return

A sea mine being dropped off the mouth of the River Elbe on 22/23 March 1945. Nos 419 and 428 Squadrons became specialists in this unglamorous but effective form of aerial warfare, known as 'gardening'. *(Department of National Defence RE 41882)*

early on account of mechanical problems, and Flt Sgt F.M. Palmer, an experienced pilot halfway through his tour, and his entire 419 Squadron crew were lost when their bomber came down over Germany. Otherwise, the raid proved to be almost trouble free for the Middleton crews. The flak over the capital seemed muted and the crews from 419 and 428 Squadrons reported seeing only a single night-fighter. They were far more expansive than usual about the raging inferno they had seen far below, heaving with mighty, multicoloured explosions. However, it had become very clear that the bombers were having a hard time in the hostile skies over Berlin, especially the Halifaxes, which were sustaining higher casualties than the Lancasters.

As a result, the Halifaxes were all but withdrawn from the battle and redirected to other worthy but less headline-grabbing targets and sorties. Both 419 and 428 Squadrons came to specialise in gardening, eventually acting as pathfinders for other squadrons on large-scale mining operations. Although this was considered a mundane task, sea mines, of which 22,000 were dropped in 1944 alone, were an immensely effective weapon, not only sinking merchant vessels, interfering with U-boat trials in the Baltic and undermining the morale of German sailors and those who traded with Germany, but also occupying some 40 per cent of the entire German navy's operational resources. These sorties were undoubtedly less risky than those over Berlin or the Ruhr but they were not without their dangers, as quite a number of men based at Middleton St George were to find out to their cost. Many simply vanished without trace, swallowed up the inhospitable North Sea or English Channel.

FROM GARDENING TO OVERLORD

February began in frustrating fashion as half of the airfield lighting 'disappeared' as a result of 'careless handling of drag lines by contractors working on the extension of the perimeter track in front of the hangars'. It was all repaired by the next day when a total of nineteen aircraft were scheduled to lay mines in the waters off Kiel, the first of many such runs. Several crews encountered a little flak over Heligoland and Kiel but otherwise it proved to be a quiet and relatively successful operation. The next night half a dozen Halifaxes from both squadrons were sent to plant their vegetables off La Rochelle. Two of 419 Squadron's aircraft were forced to turn back when their H2S – vital in pinpointing the correct dropping zone – packed up but the rest were able to find the target, even taking bearings from the coast through breaks in the cloud. However, the timing of the operation left something to be desired as some crews were still in hostile air space when day dawned, leaving the lumbering bombers hideously exposed. Flg Off L.T. Lucas, flying in H for How, had an unpleasant encounter with a roving Fw190 on an early morning patrol. The fighter was spotted by Sgt R. Johnson, the rear gunner, and it broke off after a brief exchange of fire that caused no apparent damage to either aircraft. Bruce Betcher, an American serving in the RCAF, vividly recalls that nerve-wracking return flight as dawn broke, having already been buffeted by flak over the target.

The return leg took us over eight German fighter airfields. The navigator said we were an hour from the French coast. We thought we could formate on other aircraft but when

daylight came we were all alone. We knew we were goners . . . however, we never saw
another aircraft until we were over England. The wind was 110mph making our ground
speed about 130mph!

It must have seemed a very long journey home.

The target on the 5th was the Oslo coastline, codenamed Onions, and on the 10th it was
Beeches off St Nazaire. The following night it was Jellyfish off Brest, where the crews were
less than happy with the flak that hurtled up towards them from an estimated 40–50 flak
guns, aided by a dozen or so searchlights based around the port. Fortunately the flak, like the
light variety which streamed towards the bombers from Pointe St Mathieu, proved ineffective
and caused no damage. Next up was Borkum and Nectarines II. It was to be a lonely and
eerily quiet night for the crews, who were met by a thick blanket of cloud rising to 6,000ft
and a complete absence of opposition. Wg Cdr Pleasance had a frustrating night when his
H2S set failed over the target area. In spite of the dangers involved, he circled the area for
20 minutes in the hope that it could be coaxed back into life but, as is the way, it remained
stone dead until the disgruntled squadron commander had recrossed the English coast. What
6 Group dubbed 'a totally uneventful operation' nevertheless caused the loss of seven young
lives. Flt Lt D.D. Laidlaw, an experienced pilot over halfway through his tour, failed to return
and simply vanished without trace, causing considerable sadness and puzzlement in the
squadron. When reports came in towards dawn of an aircraft having crashed in the North
Pennines, six aircraft immediately took to the skies to help in the search. When they were
forced to return on account of thick, low cloud, a party of ground crew was quickly mustered
and dispatched to the area by road. In spite of a thorough search in dreadful winter weather,
no wreckage was ever found and the search was called off.

'We had dreamt, in our innocence, that Berlin was finished, but here we were again,
detailed to attack the worst of all targets.' So wrote Bob Packer, expressing sentiments that
were no doubt shared by many at Middleton St George. It was scheduled to be a massive
attack, with 891 aircraft, including over 300 Halifaxes, setting out to pulverise the German
capital. The raid took place in 10/10ths cloud but proved very effective, the record total of
2,642 tons causing grievous damage to the centre and south-western parts of the city. The
beefed-up defences, however, continued to be very vigorous and exacted a heavy toll. In all,
43 aircraft failed to return, including one from 419 Squadron, that of Plt Off J.A. Parker,
which came down in the Baltic; only four bodies were later washed ashore.

Unfortunately conditions in the north-east had deteriorated and several crews received
unwelcome news, as Bob Packer recounts. 'Suddenly, just as we were feeling happy and ready
for bed, the W/Op called up to say we were diverted to Bury St Edmunds, an American
drome. After landing, we were given a meal and put to sleep in a huge Nissen hut used as a
cinema. The Yanks were extremely good to us and very interested in our obsolete kites. The
Yanks treated us better than any RAF station I have been diverted to. We were there three
days and had a very good time.'

The time taken to sort out all the aircraft which had landed away from home and the
persistent inclement weather meant that Bomber Command put on no further operations

until 19 February, when there was to be a deep penetration raid to Leipzig. This blind attack, carried out in thick cloud and in the teeth of strong winds and stormy conditions, proved to be one of the worst nights of the war for the Command. A terrifying 78 aircraft – some 9.5 per cent of the massive force – failed to return; worse, some 14.9 per cent of the Halifaxes which made it to the target did not make it back to British shores and, as a direct result, the Halifax squadrons were withdrawn from operations to Germany. Part of the deadly confusion, described here by Bob Packer, stemmed from incorrect Met. forecasts:

> We began to come up against trouble due to the Met. winds being wrong. After tacking about the sky, endeavouring to keep on course, we arrived at the target area half an hour before time. This is one of the worst things that could happen as it gives the German fighter controller time to bring his fighters up. We started to orbit and then kites started going down. I have never seen anything like it. We saw at least 30 kites go down in 15 minutes. A yell from the rear gunner made the pilot dive and swerve. As he did so, a Ju88 dived past our tail going down in an uncontrolled dive, with one engine aflame. We were dodging fighters all that trip and when not fighters, our own bombers.

In total, three of Middleton's aircraft failed to return and several more had close shaves. In 428 Squadron all of Flg Off A.W. Woolverton's crew perished when their aircraft came down over Holland. Flg Off Blake's crew had an amazing streak of luck, their Halifax returning home safely despite being damaged by flak and sustaining serious damage from no fewer than eleven separate fighter attacks. The chief architect of their miraculous survival was the rear gunner, WO Houston, who, although wounded in the shoulder and afflicted by a faulty intercom, both fended off several attacks with his accurate shooting and alerted his pilot to the danger of attack by making use of the call light system. Both men were recommended for gallantry awards as a result of this protracted action. In 419 Squadron Flt Sgt D.K. MacLeod and his entire crew perished and were lost without trace. Flg Off L.T. Lucas was dog-legging to waste time en route to the target when his bomber was bathed in the light of several fighter flares. Almost immediately thereafter cannon shells ripped through the port wing, setting the fuel tanks alight; another burst killed two gunners, Sgts J.F.C.R. Dehoux and P. Newbery, and set the fuselage ablaze into the bargain. There was no option but to take to the silk, something which four members of the crew managed to do successfully. Flg Off A.J. Byford's Halifax was also raked by cannon fire en route to the target. In spite of sustaining considerable damage, he elected to press on and bombed on time. On the homeward journey the Halifax was attacked again and the rear turret was shattered and put out of action. However, the gunner, Sgt N.C. Fraser, stayed at his post and gave a steady stream of instructions to Byford to help his pilot evade repeated attacks. Eventually Byford shook off his assailant and managed to fly his battered bomber home. In recognition of their courage and skill, Byford was awarded a DFC and Fraser a DFM.

On the 24th the new mining specialists carried out a new style of operation. Eleven aircraft from 428 Squadron set out to an area north of Kiel, supported by six aircraft from 419 Squadron. The latter aircraft went ahead and dropped marker flares to pinpoint the start of the timed run to the drop zone. They then carried on to lay their 1500lb mines, followed by the aircraft from 428 Squadron, which based their calculations on the markers dropped by 419 Squadron. In order to mislead the German defences, which were very much alert to such mining operations, a further four 419 Squadron bombers set off a little before the main group and headed for Heligoland Bay before simply turning for home at 5500N; 0600E. It was hard to judge how successful these elaborate plans actually were as none of the photographs taken showed anything but 10/10ths cloud. Apart from a small amount of flak from Kiel, the bombers met with no opposition and returned safely.

An equally complicated sortie was carried out the following night. The scale of these gardening operations can be easily seen from the total of 131 bombers engaged in mine-laying in the Kiel area alone that night. Such a number would have been a decent total effort for Bomber Command in the early days of the war. Aircraft from both 419 and 428 Squadrons acted as markers for 3 Group and the rest of 6 Group, and the sky-marking technique was deemed to be useful and successful by all concerned, especially as on this occasion gaps in the cloud increased the level of accuracy achieved. Once again there was little flak or night-fighter activity reported, although presumably one or the other accounted for Flg Off A.L. Warren and his 419 Squadron crew, all of whom were lost without trace on this sortie, a sharp reminder that there was no such thing as an easy operation.

The beginning of the new month saw a change in command at 6 Group. Brookes had been in command since the outset and was now in poor health, weary and worn out by the strain of the day-to-day grind of running such a large and complex organisation. In his farewell message to all 6 Group personnel, Brookes wrote:

> In leaving the Group I do so with a feeling of deep regret for I have experienced the greatest personal satisfaction in playing my part in its formation and expansion. Our task has not been an easy one but because of the outstanding cooperation of all ranks comprising the Group, it can safely be said that we have succeeded in forming a group well worthy of its place in Bomber Command.

It had not been an easy or smooth path but the Group's operational efficiency was steadily improving and many of the original kinks had now been ironed out. Brookes's successor, AVM C.M. 'Black Mike' McEwen MC, DFC, was known from his service in the First World War, in which he notched up twenty-eight confirmed kills, and from his stint as Station Commander at Linton to be a stickler for both discipline and high standards of airmanship, backed by rigorous training. Don Lamont of 428 Squadron recalls one visit made by McEwen to Middleton St George. It was a quiet lunchtime and the men on the squadron were in the mess chatting or lounging around, buried in their newspapers and magazines. Everyone failed to note McEwen come in alone and unannounced, and they were immediately blasted by 'a rather severe lecture on deportment and protocol' for not standing up and greeting him properly. He was none the less popular and widely respected as it was known that he had been on, and continued to go on, a number of operations, despite direct orders to the contrary. Significantly he was also the favourite choice of Harris, who remained concerned about the fluctuating level of early returns and non-starters within the Group. McEwen immediately initiated a more hands-on approach which quickly bore fruit, helped significantly by a lengthy period of stability, something his predecessor had never enjoyed. This was brought about by the switch of targets and the lower loss rate thereby incurred. Indeed 428 Squadron did not lose any aircraft until the middle of April, and this did much to boost morale after the heavy losses previously sustained. The interval also offered the crews the opportunity to gain the experience necessary to increase their chance of survival.

'A small and difficult target' was the station log's way of describing the SNCA du Nord aircraft factory, formerly owned by Potez, which was the destination for the first raid of March. As was the case with all targets over France, the crews were exhorted to be as accurate as possible with their loads in order to avoid unnecessary casualties among the population. However, over the next few months thousands of Frenchmen and women were killed and injured by Allied bombing raids, leading to considerable anti-Allied feeling, which was effectively and skilfully exploited by the Vichy and German regimes.

On this occasion the raid was both accurate and successful. Coming in through scattered cloud at just 6,000ft, the first crews were dismayed to find no markers and were forced to go round again. Six long minutes were to pass before the red TIs lit up the centre of the factory. Had such a delay occurred over Germany, it would almost certainly have resulted in heavy casualties. Meeting with almost no opposition, the Halifaxes roared over the target again and crews reported watching the bombs 'bouncing off the V-shaped roofs'. Severe damage was done to the factory and the crews' claims of accuracy were confirmed by some spectacular target photos. This raid set the pattern for several more to follow.

The next night some twenty bombers left Middleton St George to lay mines off the River Garonne near Bordeaux. It was a perfect night and the crews had no problems in locating the target area and delivering their load accurately, 'with practically no incidents of any kind', as the station log put it. Less than 24 hours later ten aircraft were over the heavily defended inner harbour at Brest, planting yet more vegetables. The new and greatly preferable pattern of operations seemed set.

The repertoire was extended with the next attack, directed against the marshalling yards at Trappes, a suburb of Paris, and the first made as part of the Transportation Plan drawn up to paralyse the French railway system in preparation for the invasion. It was a hard day for the ground crews preparing the aircraft in bitterly cold weather, especially the armourers who had to bomb-up twenty-five aircraft with a record total of 12,000lbs of high explosives each. All the aircraft took off and reached the target on time. Apart from a slight ground haze visibility in the bright moonlight over the yards was excellent and the crews had no difficulty in visually identifying the railway lines by the light of both flares and accurately positioned target indicators. The crews were very pleased with the attack and they had every reason to be so as no rolling stock was able to pass through Trappes for almost a month.

The next morning orders were received for a similar attack on the marshalling yards at Le Mans. This order caused considerable consternation as a good number of aircraft had not yet returned from their diversion the previous night, when Middleton had been shut on account of the lousy weather conditions. The squadron log takes up the story: 'As each aircraft arrived

TARGET TOKEN

TARGET   TRAPPES

DATE   6/7 3 44

CREW

S/L DYER
F/O MACKENZIE
F/O SWENERTON
F/S BROOKS
SGT DUNCAN
SGT BRITTAIN
SGT BOLTON

AIR VICE MARSHAL
AIR OFFICER COMMANDING
No 6 (RCAF.) GROUP

Target token for the Trappes raid of 6 March 1944.The photographs taken over the target area were carefully scrutinised to judge the success of the attack. Crews whose photographs revealed the target area were awarded a target token as recognition of a job well done. They were highly prized by the crews. *(Author via Mrs Penny Smith)*

back, the minute the kite reached dispersal, the ground crew made their inspection, the armourers bombed-up and it was rushed to the marshalling point and the number available rose steadily from four to nine in slightly over 2 hours, which is a very good show on the part of the ground crews and armourers.' Their efforts to get the aircraft ready were officially recognised by the CO, Wg Cdr French, at an impromptu party held in their honour. As it happened, their work went more smoothly than the attack itself. The Pathfinders were very late, obliging many aircraft to orbit the target area for the best part of quarter of an hour. When the ground markers did eventually go down, most were simply swallowed up beneath the prevalent thick cloud, giving the by now fraught crews little, if anything, to aim at. Several of Middleton's crews did not feel confident about hitting the target and, in accordance with orders, did not release their bombs. Although the crews could not have known it at the time, the attack turned out to be very successful, with over 300 bombs falling on to the railway yards and causing considerable havoc. Unfortunately, about 30 bombs fell wide of the mark and claimed the lives of 31 French civilians. None of the 304 aircraft taking part was lost: it was a stark reminder of the difference between operations over France and Germany at this time.

Working under the misapprehension that the previous raid had been less than successful, a total of twenty-eight crews from 419 and 428 Squadrons were ordered back to the marshalling yards at Le Mans. With each aircraft carrying 5 tons of high explosive, the Halifaxes needed all the runway to get airborne. There were no doubts this time. All the crews managed to bring back a photograph showing the aiming point and the station log happily recorded 'generally the attack appears to have been a great success'. Indeed, it was, destroying 15 locomotives and 800 wagons as well as severing the tracks at several points and damaging the nearby Renault works. Unfortunately, almost 50 civilians were killed and a similar number wounded by stray bombs.

The Germans, however, were quick to respond and a couple of nights later, on the 15th, the crews met with a plethora of searchlight batteries, as the station log put it, 'in a solid mass over an area 25–35 sq. miles, north and slightly east of Amiens'. Bob Packer of 419 Squadron remembered the lights well:

We took off, setting course for France at 12,000ft. As we began crossing the French coast, a huge nest of searchlights opened up, trying to ensnare us. At the height we were flying at, it was simple for the searchlights to get and hold us. All I can say about this effort is if the Germans had a few light and heavy guns there we would have lost half the force, but apparently they had no guns there but just relied on their fighters which we ran into outside the searchlight belt waiting for our bombers to be coned. We got through eventually, after one of the worst searchlight experiences I have had.

This was a telling remark from a man who had seen both Berlin and the Ruhr on several occasions.

Target token for the Le Mans raid of 13 March 1944. *(Author via Mrs Penny Smith)*

The powers that be obviously agreed with the crews' pessimistic verdict on their nocturnal work and promptly gave orders for them to attack Amiens again the following night. This time, a little wiser, many of the crews managed to skirt around the worst of the searchlights and reach the target more or less unhindered in a deadly game of cat and mouse.

Both 419 and 428 Squadrons also continued with their role as head gardeners, acting as pathfinders for by-now often substantial forces of well over a hundred aircraft. On 22 March, for example, while an 800-strong force headed for Frankfurt, 128 Halifaxes and 18 Stirlings made their way to Kiel Bay. For most crews it was a quiet night's work but for Plt Off G.R.M. Peck of 419 Squadron and his crew it was far more eventful.

While crossing the Danish coast en route to the target, W for William's port engine unexpectedly burst into flames. As the Graviner system quickly doused the flames, Peck decided to carry on, losing only a little in terms of height and speed. For a while, it seemed to have been both a courageous and a correct decision as the Halifax made it to the target area, dropped its mines and headed for home. Then, midway over the North Sea between England and Denmark, the port inner engine burst into flames. Again it was successfully extinguished and feathered, but with both port engines out of commission it was clear that ditching into the wintry seas was the only possible end to the operation. Peck managed to coax the Halifax to fly a little longer, covering precious miles towards the British coast and giving the W/Op plenty of time to send out position reports and SOS signals. The ditching when it came, still 50 miles from the friendly coastline, was a textbook one and, unhurt, the crew quickly scrambled into the dinghy. A mercifully short time later an Air Sea Rescue Warwick from Thornaby came into earshot, having seen the Verey cartridge fired from the dinghy. It dropped a number of flare floats and sent out an updated position report. Much to the crew's unbounded relief and joy, an armed trawler located them a couple of hours later and heaved them on board to warmth and safety. To everyone's surprise, W for William was found nearby, still bobbing up and down amid the waves, over 3 hours after it had come down into the sea. A few well-placed shells sent the reluctant bomber to the bottom. It had been a smooth ditching and rescue operation but it had also been a harrowing experience none the less, all the more so as it was the very first operation for Peck and his crew. In recognition of his 'inspiring leadership, great determination and devotion to duty', Peck was awarded an immediate DFC, while three of the crew had this episode highlighted when they were put up for non-immediate decorations later on.

The Transportation Plan continued to gather momentum. On 25 March fourteen Halifaxes from 419 Squadron and sixteen from 428 Squadron struggled into the night sky bound for another marshalling yards' target, this time at Aulnoyne, 45 miles due east of Cambrai. Many crews brought back excellent photographs, revealing concentrated and accurate bombing of the markers, which, as the station record pithily noted, 'were not over the aiming point'. Only one aircraft was lost that night but it belonged to 419 Squadron. Plt Off H.C. Eyjolfson and his equally balanced RCAF/RAF crew had the misfortune to suffer a double engine failure on the outbound leg of the journey. Eyjolfson immediately turned for home and jettisoned the bomb-load into the English Channel. Although still heavily laden with fuel, which he had no opportunity to use up, Eyjolfson decided to attempt a landing at RAF Ford in Sussex. Unfamiliar with the surroundings and with the Halifax wallowing all over the sky, Eyjolfson misjudged the landing, overshot the runway and ground to a halt in the adjacent ploughed field. The bomber, which had had its mainplanes torn off by the impact, the engines ripped from their nacelles and the fuselage holed and twisted, caught fire and quickly became a raging inferno, far beyond any means of control. Incredibly, there had been just enough time for the crew to scramble clear with just a few cuts, bruises and broken bones.

Railway marshalling yards were again the target on 26 March when almost thirty aircraft from Middleton St George formed a third of the force dispatched to attack Courtrai in Belgium. A slight low-level haze prevented clear observation of the target and this was, as usual, made far worse by the billowing balls of smoke and debris thrown up by the bomb bursts. Later photo reconnaissance produced a figure of 100 bombs falling within the yards out of a possible total of around 1500. The remainder landed in residential areas, killing over 250 Belgian civilians. Nevertheless, the bombs that did fall there caused considerable havoc in the yards and the Germans were compelled to draft in over 1600 unemployed civilians and local inhabitants to clear the debris and repair the tracks; the first train passed through just three days later. The price of Overlord was already a high one.

On the night that the Germans and Belgians succeeded in reopening Courtrai, 419 and 428 Squadrons helped to close the railway yards at Vaires near Paris. In clear skies and bright moonlight, the 76-strong force delivered an accurate and concentrated attack that totally devastated the target area, which measured just 300 by 150 yards, and caused very little collateral damage. Two ammunition trains were caught in the attack and the resultant explosions were probably those which Flt Lt T.D. Virtue of 419 Squadron described as 'volcanic eruptions'. German records state that 1,270 German soldiers were killed in the brief whirlwind of high explosive. Only one aircraft was lost but it belonged to 419 Squadron. WO2 J.A. Greenage and his crew took off at 18:19 and were never seen or heard of again.

An unusual event took place on the 29th which demonstrates the dangers involved in even routine flights. Bob Packer recalled that this was the day that he and his crew first flew a Lancaster X:

We did our first circuits and landings in the famed 'Ruhr Express'. This aircraft was not up to much and did not have a good reputation with flying men. After half an hour flying, we had an uncomfortable five minutes due to running into a flock of seagulls, one of which smashed through the bomb aimer's position panel in the nose of the kite, with a noise like a shell bursting as it hit the Perspex. It hit my leg (I was in the second pilot's seat) and then flew down the fuselage in several pieces. I had my best blue on as we were supposed to be going on leave. This was all messed up with pulped flesh and blood. The bomb aimer was very lucky having just left the nose of the kite before the bird hit us or he would have been injured.

Packer's supposedly routine flight was mirrored by many others as the crews gradually converted to the Lancaster. Unfortunately, political expediency once again got in the way of operational efficiency as the Lancasters, built in Canada exclusively for the Canadian Group, suffered numerous teething troubles and as the main source of spare parts was several thousand miles away, shortages and delays became all too common. Engineer and supply officers were often forced to become adept at temporarily cannibalising aircraft, adapting and scrounging parts from whatever sources they could find; it was a crying shame given the enormous efforts made to maintain the maximum firepower possible.

As the station record put it, 'to celebrate the commencement of Double Summer Time, it was cold and dull with very low cloud. Rain began before dawn and continued, with only short breaks, until after midnight.' However, when conditions allowed, the squadrons were out gardening, usually seeing no results from their nocturnal efforts but trusting that they would follow in due course. Otherwise, the crews headed for transportation targets in France such as the Lille-Délivrance railway yards in Lille and the Merelbeke-Melle yards in Ghent. After the former, the crews returned home full of reports of massive multicoloured explosions, raging fires and smoke billowing up to 12,000ft; they were confident that the yards had been all but obliterated. Although they could not have known it, the force of almost 300 bombers had succeeded in dropping just 49 bombs on to the yards, destroying some track and over 2,000 badly needed trucks and wagons. The remainder of the high explosive bombs landed in the residential area of Lomme, killing 456 Frenchmen and women and destroying or damaging some 5,000 houses. Anti-British feelings ran high because of events such as these and Marshal Pétain, leader of the Vichy regime, capitalised on this during his tour of northern French towns. The people turned out in their thousands to greet him.

The raid on Ghent provided a milestone for the RCAF. All of the 122 aircraft taking part, of which twenty-four belonged to 419 and 428 Squadrons, came from 6 Group, making it the first all-Canadian assault of the war. The crews taking part were less than enthusiastic about the efficacy of the attack, reporting only small explosions and fires, but as it turned out the raid did cause considerable damage to the yards, severing the main line to Brussels – but only at a cost. In all, 428 Belgians died and 300 or so more were injured. Although strenuous efforts were made by both planners and crews to keep casualties to a minimum, they had always been an accepted part of the execution of the Transportation Plan, upon which the success of the invasion itself might well have depended.

Not that everything went smoothly even on the station. For example, 428 Squadron's log tells a typical story:

One of those days today. Sixteen aircraft were detailed for ops which were scrubbed by 10:10 hours. Arrangements then made for fighter affiliation but these were scrubbed as all available aircraft were detailed for a raid which was also scrubbed within ten minutes. However, sixteen were then detailed, this time for a bull's-eye which was also scrubbed by 17:30 owing to weather. A regular shambles all day; bags of flap and panic resulted in several section leaders endeavouring to drown their sorrows in the evening. Has anyone an aspirin?

On the 18th a dozen aircraft from 419 Squadron and sixteen from 428 Squadron took to the night skies, this time to do a little gardening both south of Copenhagen and off Rostock respectively. All but one located and mined the target and made it home safely. Initially it

B711

Lancaster Xs ready for take off at Middleton St George in the late spring of 1944. KB711 in the foreground failed to return from the attack upon the railway yards at St Ghislain on 1/2 May 1944, the first Lancaster X lost on operations. *(Department of National Defence PL 29474)*

was thought that Plt Off J.D. Quinn's bomber had come down in the North Sea and a Lancaster X was sent off to carry out a search, at the same time hoping to locate the crew of a downed American aircraft. This was the first fully operational use of a Lancaster X but it was nevertheless unsuccessful as no trace of either aircraft was found. The bodies of Quinn and Sgt M.J. Petrina were eventually washed up in August on the shores of Denmark; the other five young men have no known grave.

The Germans were getting wise to the type of targets being hit and had increased their defences substantially wherever possible; flak units were redeployed and night-fighters were also increasingly on the prowl. Both forms of defence contributed to the demise of the 428 Squadron crew led by Flt Lt C.G. Ford during a raid on the railway yards at Lens. The aircraft was badly damaged, and Ford ordered the crew to bale out. Three did so but the rest elected to remain with the aircraft for as long as possible. Willing the bomber to keep flying a little longer, Ford and the three remaining members of the crew were delighted to see the British coast come into view. Ford found the nearest airfield he could (a USAAF base at Attlebridge in Norfolk) and crash-landed there at 01:20 hours. All four men on board were injured and one rear gunner, Plt Off A. Shaw, died as a result of a fractured skull sustained in the crash. Ford was awarded an immediate DFC for his efforts in trying to ensure the safety of his crew.

The marshalling yards at Laon were the next major target. A particularly large number of flares were dropped over the target and Plt Off Judlesch of 428 Squadron was typical in noting that 'midnight was as light as day', even at 7,000ft. Some of the flares were way off target but the Master Bomber, Wg Cdr A.G.S. Cousens of 635 Squadron, quickly spotted this and redirected the Main Force, leading to a concentrated attack on the yards. Cousens was subsequently shot down and killed. The beefed-up defences, however, took their toll and nine aircraft, some 5 per cent of the total attacking force, failed to return. One of these was flown by an American serving with the RCAF, Lt Chuck Thomas of 419 Squadron. Bomb aimer Flg Off John Neal describes what happened:

Our Halifax bomber was shot down by an Me110. We were hit just as I was ready to drop my bomb-load. There was a tremendous flash. I jumped out of my prone bombardier's position to see what had happened. The pilot shouted, 'Get the hell out of here. Bale out!' 'Wait,' I said, 'I've still got my bombs on board. Let me get rid of them.' I went forward as everyone sat tight and the doomed Halifax roared earthwards, dumped the load and we all baled out.

Only Sgt V.A. Knox, the rear gunner, did not make it, but he may well have been killed in the initial attack. Unusually, four of the crew succeeded in linking up with the Resistance or friendly locals and managed to evade capture.

Neal himself hid. He slept in woods by day and marched by night, living on a not very satisfying diet of Horlicks tablets. By the third night he was desperate and decided to knock on the door of a small cottage and announce 'Je suis Canadien'. He had chosen well, as the cottage was occupied by several Polish women refugees and their children who, though poor, were delighted to provide him with a meal there and food to take away with him. He walked throughout the damp and chilly night before coming across two farmhouses, each with a haystack, about dawn. For no good reason he picked one rather than the other and, having climbed in to the hay, fell fast asleep. He was woken by the farmer who announced that he could help as he had friends in the Resistance. He added, 'You made the right choice. If you had chosen my neighbour's haystack, you would have been in the hands of the Gestapo now. That man is a collaborator. He has turned in Allied men in the past.' Neal stayed for over two weeks on that farm near Suzy before being moved to Bithancourt Marizelle, where, to his delight, he was reunited with his navigator, Bob Lindsay. Neal was moved twice more as part of a plan to get him to Plouha, where he and his small group would be picked up by submarine. Unfortunately D-Day intervened and the scheme was called off. It was not until 10:00 hours on 1 September that American soldiers arrived to liberate the pretty little village of Bethancourt-en-Vaux where he had spent much of the summer. 'The celebrations', he wrote, 'lasted for three days, the highlight for us being the gathering of thirty-three evading and escaped Allied airmen from the surrounding area.' Ironically, Neal's route back to Britain took him through Laon, the place where his European odyssey had begun five months earlier.

Back at Middleton St George 419 and 428 Squadrons continued their hectic whirl of mining and attacking railway targets, often achieving widely different results but generally

Sqn Ldr H.R.F. Dyer DFC and crew photographed on completion of their tour in April 1944. From left to right: Flt Sgt E.J. Duncan, rear gunner; Sgt G. Britain, mid-under gunner; Flt Sgt W.E. Brookes, W/Op air gunner; Flg Off R.A. Mackenzie, navigator; Sqn Ldr H.R.F. Dyer DFC, skipper; Flg Off Swenerton DFC, bomb aimer; Flt Sgt W.F. Bolton, flight engineer. *(Author via Mrs Penny Smith)*

taking a steady trickle of casualties. The waters off St Malo, Cherbourg, Le Havre, St Nazaire and Morlaix all received several visits, often in the face of heavy flak. An operation against the marshalling yards in the station's near-namesake, Villeneuve St Georges, south-east of Paris, in spite of clear conditions went sufficiently badly that Plt Off Marjoram, an experienced campaigner, suggested that some markers had even fallen on the wrong side of the River Seine and that 'the T/A looked as though it had hardly been bombed'. The situation was exacerbated by the fact that the Master Bomber was all but inaudible on account of successful German attempts at jamming. Although many crews did the best they could in difficult circumstances, and indeed some damage was done to the southern end of the yards, some pilots, like 419 Squadron's Flg Off Barclay, chose not to release their bombs and brought them back home. The next attack was on the marshalling yards at Aulnoye. This time the crews steamed in at just 4,500ft, thankful that opposition was mercifully light, but were prevented from exactly pinpointing the railway yards by a ground haze. However, the PFF marking was bang on target and the Master Bomber was both clearly audible and very switched on, maintaining full control of the direction of the operation. The bombing was highly concentrated and caused massive damage and dislocation to the railway network in the region.

For 419 Squadron it was a special night, as it saw the first offensive operation carried out by a Canadian-built Lancaster. Thirteen of the squadron's bombers, including eight of the new Lancasters, were scheduled to attack the airfield and railway yards at Montzen on

Scaffolding towers and ladders were just a few of the necessary pieces of equipment necessary for servicing aircraft. Occasionally, aircraft collided with them when landing or taxying, sometimes with spectacular and tragic results. *(Author)*

27 April. The Middleton aircraft were in the first wave to bomb and saw little in the way of the results of their efforts, although it was felt that the raid, under the watchful eye of the Master Bomber, was going according to plan. Night-fighters, however, were very active, clawing over 10 per cent of the bombers taking part out of the sky. One of these belonged to 419 Squadron's Plt Off R.A. McIvor, who was lost, along with his entire crew, when his bomber came down near Maastricht. It was the last of 419 Squadron's Halifax losses but no better for that. Flt Lt J.D. Virtue's Lancaster returned early in unusual circumstances. Soon after crossing the English coast Sgt L.G. Turner, the mid-upper gunner, fell seriously ill, being scarcely able to breathe. Virtue immediately brought the bomber down to 12,000ft but Turner did not improve and it was decided to turn for home. They were met by an ambulance on landing and Turner was whisked off to hospital, where it was discovered that his right lung had collapsed. It was to be 419 Squadron's last operation of the month and this proved to be a stroke of luck as 30 April was the day set aside for a special squadron bash. No expense was spared nor detail overlooked in the decoration of the tables and rooms nor the after-dinner entertainment. The culinary highlight was moose meat and venison – some 200lbs of it shipped across by the generous Civilian Auxiliary in the squadron's adopted town of Kamloops.

On May Day 419 Squadron was back in action, sending nine Lancasters to attack the marshalling yards at St Ghislain. Apart from a slight ground haze, visibility in the bright moonlight was excellent and the PFF markers were easily located by the crews who, with the guidance of the Master Bomber (whose instructions seemed to be accompanied by music supplied by the German counter-measures units), delivered a devastating and destructive attack. The benefits of the Lancaster were immediately apparent as Flt Lt J.G. Stewart managed to haul some 14,000lbs of high explosive into the night sky, a total far beyond the capabilities of the Halifax. Bob Packer and his crew were greatly impressed: 'This trip was a milestone in our career in bombers, as we flew in a Lancaster X (V for Victory). We found this kite to be a lot better than the old Halifax in manoeuvrability and speed. The trip itself was quiet, as also was the target.' However, even the Lancaster was not immune to losses. Plt Off J.C. McNary's C for Charlie had the dubious honour of being the first Lancaster X lost in operations. McNary had been forced to make several orbits around the target area to waste time before carrying out a successful bombing run. Flt Sgt R.C.D. Long, the bomb aimer, who survived along with four other members of the crew, made this report: 'After leaving the target, we climbed for height to cross the coast when a fighter was sighted far below us against the cloud. Lost sight of him and were then raked by cannon fire from below before we had located him. Fighter was in blind spot below us. Fire broke out almost immediately in the cabin and the pilot gave orders to bale out.' McNary, like so many other pilots, never made it out and Long guessed that he had waited to help the W/Op, WO T.L.E. Chartrand, who had been badly wounded in the stomach. In any event their bodies were found in the wreckage of the Lancaster which came down in a gasworks in Ghent. One of the gunners, Sgt D.S.M. Sangster, was so badly wounded in the arm and head that he was repatriated by the end of the summer.

Mining operations continued but on 9 May 419 Squadron was assigned a new type of target, with which it would soon become familiar. The destruction of the gun emplacements at St Valery-en-Caux, 15 miles south-west of Dieppe, was another step in the softening-up process prior to invasion. These were small targets and ones which, initially, both Harris and established wisdom thought beyond the capabilities of his bombers. In general, this was proved not to be the case but on this night it was. On a mostly clear night the eight PFF Mosquitoes arrived a couple of minutes late and then scattered their red markers over a half a mile of cliff-top coastline. The 56 Halifaxes, all from 6 Group, did the best they could to pick out the robust concrete structures 6,000ft below them but failed to achieve more than harmless near-misses.

Operations were soon on again, with a trip to the marshalling yards in Louvain in Belgium. Only two Lancasters were lost on this sortie but both came from 419 Squadron. W for William and its experienced crew, led by Plt Off H.I. Smith, fell victim to a roving night-fighter and crashed a few kilometres from Brussels, killing all on board. Plt Off B.F. Edwards and his crew were far less experienced but X for X-ray suffered exactly the same fate as W for William, coming down to earth near Diksmuide in north-western Belgium. The raid itself was highly successful and repairs were still having to be carried out in Louvain some six months later. The cost was distressingly high, though, with 160 Belgians in the town being killed and over 200 more injured. This was the worst casualty list and destruction suffered by the town since it had been overrun in 1940. However, one story highlights the lengths the crews went to in order to reduce the risk of loss of civilian life.

Art De Breyne was a first-generation Canadian who still had many relatives living in Belgium; as it happens his mother originally came from Durham, only a few miles from where the young De Breyne was stationed at Middleton St George. His bomb aimer was Sgt Jack Friday who, by chance, had relatives living in Louvain. Both men were therefore even more apprehensive than usual and determined to be as accurate as possible. The long journey down the length of England passed off without a hitch and De Breyne then turned east and brought the heavily laden Lancaster over the already burning town of Louvain, some 7,000ft below, at a little after half past midnight. De Breyne was unable to pick out the TIs from the fuzzy multicoloured glow below, intensified by a considerable ground haze, and called the navigator, Flg Off Body, forward to see if he could locate them. Under fire De Breyne methodically circled the target several times before calling a halt to the proceedings and turning for home with his destructive load still on board. One person who, perhaps, had good grounds to thank him for that decision was Hortense Damon, who had helped two of 419 Squadron's downed airmen in July 1943 and was now enduring the harsh conditions of the women's prison just 200 yards from the railway tracks, having been arrested for her Resistance activities. Several bombs did hit the jail but Hortense's luck held and she escaped unscathed.

Although 419 Squadron now enjoyed an unexpected ten-day break in operations, training flights continued as usual and on 16 May one of these ended in disaster. KB701, the aircraft recently flown by De Breyne over Louvain, was in the hands of Plt Off J.E. McMaster on a routine cross-country training flight when it smashed into a hillside at Potter House farm on Helmsly Moor near RCAF Wombleton. All the crew, which included men from Canada, Britain and America, died in the crash. Investigations later revealed that the pilot had simply strayed beneath the recommended safety height in conditions of low cloud base and drizzle. Death could be as simple as that.

On 22 May, while 428 Squadron mined the sea off St Malo, 419 Squadron was shocked to receive orders to attack Dortmund in the Happy Valley, in the first attack on the city in a year. The attack fell mainly on the south-eastern districts of the town and Wg Cdr Pleasance was among several crew members who reported that the raid lacked concentration, on account of somewhat scattered marking caused by the PFF releasing the markers at 19,000ft, too high for a good degree of accuracy. It is interesting to note that to an inexperienced eye, that of Flg Off J.M. Calder, the raid seemed to have gone well, with the whole town in flames. Although the flak was generally considered to have been a little below the Ruhr's traditionally fearsome level, the massive amount of searchlight activity was not. Bob Packer's aircraft was coned twice:

It was a perfectly clear night, a night in which a searchlight is at its best. The Germans took full advantage of this. They had what must have been every searchlight in the Ruhr burning. It was an amazing sight, a sight that really shakes your morale somewhat. It seemed impossible to get through but it had to be done so we did it. Weaving without ceasing right into the heart of the Ruhr and out again must have been a tremendous strain on the pilot but we got to the target, dropped our bombs and got out again.

The level of casualties associated with raids on the German heartland also returned, with 18 Lancasters, or 4.8 per cent of the attacking force, being brought down. One belonged to 419 Squadron. Plt Off C.E.G. Patterson and his crew, all of whom were at least half way through their tour, fell victim to a night-fighter and plunged to their deaths near Mönchengladbach.

Two nights later another German target was on the briefings board. The border town of Aachen was a key junction in the main rail links between Germany and France, and damage to the two main marshalling yards would cause serious disruption to the rail network. Given that the town was German, a greater number of bombers than usual, some 442, were dispatched to the target, all heavily laden with high explosive. The PFF marking was a little below par but both the yards and the town sustained heavy damage, in spite of the use of dummy markers to distract the bombers. There was much heavy flak and several night-fighters were seen at work in the bomber stream over the Eindhoven and Aachen areas. Once again 419 Squadron did not escape unscathed. WO D.M. Robson's Lancaster was shot down at Tilburg-Kronsstraat in Holland. Sgt W.D. Lillico, a New Yorker in the RCAF, was the only survivor of the crash. Unfortunately he succumbed to his wounds two days later.

Dennis Bowe, who like most flight engineers, was British, was on his first operation and it was almost his last. A new arrival on the squadron, he was rounded up to fly as a spare bod in Sqn Ldr 'Jimmy' Stewart's Lancaster. Although the flight to the target was quite quiet, the bomber was later attacked by enemy aircraft on no fewer than three separate occasions, the last attack being made by an intrepid intruder over Goole. The bomber made it home minus several chunks, most notably from the starboard tail section.

On the same night fifteen of 428 Squadron's Halifaxes put in attacks on the coastal defences and batteries at Trouville on the Normandy coast. Encountering very little opposition and making the most of the clear conditions, the crews delivered their ordnance with considerable accuracy and brought home some splendid target photographs. Thick cloud greeted four more Halifaxes a few miles along the coast as they mined the waters off Le Havre.

The final night of the month saw 428 and 419 Squadrons operating together. Their target was a radio-jamming station at Mont Couple on the French coast, a target that was known to be heavily defended. However, the flak, bad though it was, proved not to be the main problem for the crews: it was the weather. The bombers had to plough through severe electrical storms and the buffeting was so bad that a couple of crews turned for home, unable to find a safe passage through. Plt Off Carter of 428 Squadron took off a little before 22:00 hours and headed south. Even before reaching York, he ran into a terrible thunderstorm and turned north again towards Doncaster to avoid it. Having found what he thought was the edge of the storm, Carter turned the Halifax south once more but very soon ran into the storm once again and the aircraft almost fell out of the sky on account of heavy icing. With no chance of making it to the target on time he headed north once more and landed at his home station. One of his fellow squadron members, Plt Off Hawthorn, pithily commented in his report that there was as much water inside his Halifax as outside of it.

WO Forsberg did not get that far. Having just hauled the heavily laden Halifax into the air, Forsberg, to his horror, suffered an engine failure. He immediately slammed the throttles forward and with the engines screaming he managed to coax the wallowing Halifax high enough to clear the trees dotted around the locality. With his temperature gauges climbing off the scale, Forsberg gained enough height to be able to jettison his bomb-load over the sea before returning to carry out a perfect landing back at the station. Plt Off Gouthrea, also of 428 Squadron, was not quite so lucky. On take-off, his Halifax flew into an air pocket that caused the bomber to lurch downwards, slamming the starboard wheel down hard on the tarmac. The Halifax bounced back up into the air but the undercarriage had buckled and the wheel could not be retracted. Frantic efforts by the crew managed to achieve only the worst of all outcomes, a wheel that was neither fully up nor fully down but jammed solid. Gouthrea decided to head for the nearest airfield and crash-landed successfully at Dalton, where 'every emergency appliance was used'. The crew escaped largely unscathed but the bomber was not so lucky, being badly damaged.

The raid itself proved successful and all Middleton's aircraft brought home excellent photographs to show 'our aircraft, at least, had bombed the target well', in spite of the Master Bomber's instructions being indistinct at best and inaudible at worst. A further seven of 428 Squadron's Halifaxes were deployed for a spot of gardening in the well-tended gardens off Dunkirk, Lorient and St Nazaire. These crews too encountered foul weather, which played havoc with their radar and W/T sets, but managed to carry out their duties successfully. Although 428 Squadron's main duties had involved gardening, which was hardly headline-grabbing stuff, Wg Cdr McLeish was undoubtedly correct when he wrote as a summary to the month: 'From all reports the crews can feel a considerable pride in the results achieved.'

June 1944, which was destined to be one of the most crucial months of the whole war, began quietly with no operational flying at Middleton St George. Then 428 Squadron kicked off the month's tally with yet more gardening, still using the Halifaxes while the squadron was gradually converting to Lancaster Xs. In crystal clear conditions a sortie to Le Havre was described as 'probably the most successful the squadron has ever had. There was absolutely no reaction from the Hun.' Presumably the Hun felt he had more important fish to fry that night but 24 hours later, when another ten bombers repeated the procedure, they came under heavy fire from flak ships stationed to catch the unwary 3 or 4 miles off the coast. Fortunately, 428 Squadron's long run of sustaining no casualties continued and all the crews returned home safely.

In the early hours of the 5th 419 Squadron swung back into operation, dispatching fourteen aircraft to attack the coastal batteries around Calais, some of which had been shelling convoys passing through the Channel and the area around Dover itself for several years. Flying through drizzle and broken cloud at 7,500ft, the crews were relieved to spot a solid concentration of red markers and 'the preponderance of bombs were seen [sic] to burst on the red markers, which, if they were properly placed, should result in a successful attack'. As it turned out the markers were on target and the batteries suffered a heavy bombardment, a fate not shared by batteries further along the coast where cloud prevented accurate marking and bombing.

Flg Off Glen Bassett of 428 Squadron recalls a long-awaited and highly emotional sight:

It was an uneventful night until we crossed the coast a little west of Portsmouth and the Isle of Wight, just as the sun was rising over the horizon. Suddenly our pilot yelled 'Bloody hell, look to starboard!' That meant port for me as I was the rear gunner. And down there before my eyes was the D-Day invasion fleet, hundreds of ships and craft of all kinds.

It was a once-in-a-lifetime sight, a glimpse of the greatest seaborne invasion force in history. Both 428 and 419 Squadrons were involved in two attacks that night, the first on the heavy gun batteries at Merville, just north-east of Caen, and then at Longues, further west along the coast near Arromanches. On both occasions thick cloud swallowed up the PFF markers, leaving only a faint dull glow to aim at; indeed, several crews, fearful of causing friendly-fire casualties, chose not to bomb and brought their bombs home. No fewer than four aircraft were attacked by night-fighters but these were all driven off by the prompt and punchy actions of the gunners. The 428 Squadron log records the feelings of the crews at this time: 'D-Day at last! The boys were very pleased to think that last night's attack was a prelude to the invasion.' Meanwhile 6 Group records stated that 'radios are working overtime, an atmosphere of expectancy pervades the camp. However, underneath all the elation there is the realisation by all personnel that there is a long, hard struggle ahead and plenty of work to be done.' Middleton St George was proud that 'their two squadrons were "in" on the invasion from the start' but there was little time for celebration or self-congratulation.

THE BATTLE OF NORMANDY

The very next night Middleton St George put up one of its largest-ever forces, a headache for and a tribute to all the efforts of the ground crews. Twenty Lancasters from 419 Squadron and seventeen Halifaxes from 428 Squadron were sent to smash the bridges, railway lines and road junctions in the important bottleneck town of Coutances on the western side of the Cherbourg peninsula. It was not an easy night for the crews, who had to contend with patchy cloud and confusing instructions from the Master Bomber. His initial instructions were to bomb the white markers but this was then countermanded and the target swapped to the greens, then to the reds and finally to overshoot the yellows. The result was an unhappy one, with far more indiscriminate destruction than intended; 65 per cent of the buildings in the town were either destroyed or damaged and over 300 civilians were killed. Once again there were several reports of combats with night-fighters, but for Bob Packer and his 419 Squadron crew the greatest danger came from his own side: 'We very nearly got shot down by a Halifax in front of our kite over the target. There was a lot of this sort of thing going on. The gunners [were] getting rather shaky. We were diverted due to bad weather, so we could not get back to base.' In fact 419 Squadron ended up at RAF Colerne in Wiltshire, and 428 Squadron at RAF Westcott in Buckinghamshire, returning to Middleton St George the following morning. Awaiting them was a message from Harris, their Commander in Chief, congratulating the crews on their operations against the coastal batteries, which, he said, had done much to ensure the invasion went as well as it had.

On 7 June all the aircraft returned to Middleton St George but on the 8th it was time to take to the night skies once again. Eleven Lancasters from 419 Squadron headed south to join the 100-strong force heading for Acheres and its marshalling yards. Crossing the coast in the Dieppe area at just 7,000ft, the force came under fire from both heavy and light flak units, supported by a number of well guided searchlights. The red TIs were easily visible and appeared well concentrated and on target but the smoke from the bomb bursts prevented accurate assessment of the results; indeed, Flg Off R.N. Wilson felt the visibility was sufficiently poor to bring back his bomb-load. As this was a slightly deeper penetration into enemy territory, there was more time for the Luftwaffe to react and it used all the time available to maximum effect. No fewer than four of 419 Squadron's aircraft came under aerial assault. The pilot of W for William was forced to abandon his final run-in as the aircraft came under fire from a Ju88, which pressed home its attack to just 150 yards. Rear gunner Sgt Stuart returned fire throughout and tracer was seen to enter the assailant's cockpit before it broke off and headed downwards. An official claim was made for a damaged. T for Tare, piloted by Flg Off W.M. Lacey, suffered a very similar attack just before the target was bombed, but escaped unscathed. Just after turning for home, the Lancaster was singled out for no fewer than four successive attacks by a lone Fw190 but on each occasion the German pilot was thwarted by violent evasive manoeuvres and was driven off by concentrated fire from the mid-upper and rear gunners. G for George had an unusual encounter with an Me110, which followed the Lancaster perfectly throughout two complete corkscrews but for some reason chose not to open fire. Rear gunner Sgt E.L. Vince opened up for all he was worth and submitted a claim for a damaged as tracer strikes were clearly seen on the enemy aircraft. The greatest success of the night fell to gunners Sgt W.F. Mann and Sgt P.F. Burton, flying in X for X-ray. The Lancaster had just left the target area and set course for home when a Ju88 was spotted three-quarters of a mile away, clearly silhouetted against a full moon. It turned to attack and at 600 yards rear gunner Sgt Mann gave his pilot, Flg Off W.J. Anderson, the instruction to corkscrew to starboard and then opened fire with Sgt Burton joining in. At 400 yards the Ju88 broke away on fire and a short time later the crew noted a large explosion on the ground. This was the first time a Canadian-built Lancaster had downed an enemy aircraft, and this incident was mentioned in both Burton's and Mann's citations for the DFM in October.

With 428 Squadron still gardening, 419 Squadron dispatched fourteen Lancasters to attack the airfield at Le Mans in an attempt to hinder any aerial counter-attack on the still-vulnerable beachheads. Coming in low at just a few thousand feet, the crews were forced to fly through considerable amounts of multicoloured tracer criss-crossing the night sky before visually identifying the target and releasing their loads on the markers, which were seen to straddle the main runway. For Bob Packer, a veteran of over thirty operations, it was a memorable night:

We bombed in the face of intense flak and it was the first time I had ever seen the target, that is, the actual buildings. I could see huge hangers with holes in the roofs and the runways all full of craters from previous bombings. Our aircraft was hit as if with a gigantic hammer, which was, in fact, the 1,000-pounders being dropped on the airfield. I would have hated to have been down there. Coming out of the target we had two fighter attacks in quick succession but evaded both.

So, fortunately, did all the other crews and all returned safely to their base in the north-east.

After just a few hours' sleep the crews of both squadrons found themselves preparing for operations that night. For 428 Squadron the day began badly when O for Oboe failed to return from a cross-country practice flight. Shortly after take-off the port outer engine had failed and the pilot, Flg Off J. Martin, struggling to keep the aircraft under control, ordered his crew to bale out while they could. Martin stayed at the controls and attempted a crash-landing near Caxton Hall, a few miles north of York. The Halifax, the last one written off by a Main Force squadron, broke up on impact and burst into flames. Fortunately, Martin was hauled alive out of the wreckage and rushed to York's military hospital, where he received long-term treatment for serious burns, a broken ankle and fractures to four vertebrae. The remainder of the squadron had completely uneventful gardening trips to Brest, Lorient and St Nazaire before being diverted to land at Colerne.

Ten Lancasters of 419 Squadron joined the force bound for the railway junction at Versailles-Matelots. For Wg Cdr Pleasance in E for Easy his night's work was almost very short indeed. Just as the wheels of the Lancaster left the ground, both port engines cut out. Only his sharp reactions and some very nifty airmanship prevented the heavily laden Lancaster from smashing into the ground and killing all on board. Pleasance coolly put his knowledge of the local area to good use as he took advantage of the low ground to give flight engineer Plt Off M.D. McGill time to sort out the problem. Never climbing higher than 200ft, Pleasance covered some 20 heart-stopping miles before a sweating McGill managed to coax the engines back to life. After all this, Pleasance elected to catch up with the others from 419 Squadron and continue with the operation. McGill was awarded a DFC for his skill and efficiency and Pleasance a bar to his DFC for his determination and superb airmanship. The operation itself turned out to be successful with the Master Bomber, who was described as presiding 'over the affair like a women's club chairman at a social tea', keeping the attack on target and offering useful advice 'interspersed with such expressions as "nice going, boys" and "wizard prang"'. In spite of several near-misses, all the crews made it home safely.

The night of 12/13 June is a memorable date in the annals of the RCAF for it was during this night's attack on the railway yards at Cambrai that WO Andrew Charles Mynarski, a mid-upper gunner in 419 Squadron's A for Able, won the Victoria Cross, 6 Group's only one of the war. Patchy cloud and an indecisive Master Bomber, who was shot down by a Ju88 during the bombing period, conspired to make the bulk of the bombs fall across the southern part of the town and only a fraction on the yards themselves. Fighter opposition was very heavy, with attack following attack both en route to and from the target. Bob Packer, on his 35th and final operation, noted that the Germans directed their fighters into the area and

aircraft started to go down all around us. Over the target area, which was lit up like day, we could hear the Master Bomber giving directions; we saw his aircraft, then saw a Ju88 on his tail. The next thing we saw was a huge explosion in the sky and the Master Bomber gave no more instructions. With no markers visible, we had to bomb in the light of flares so we let our bombs away and headed for home at a speed faster than I have ever seen before. Our ground speed must have been about 350 to 400mph. We did not intend to give the Germans a chance to get us on our last trip. All the way back kites were going down behind.

Plt Off Andrew Mynarski was awarded a posthumous Victoria Cross for his actions during an attack upon Cambrai on 12 June 1944. He was 6 Group's sole VC recipient. *(PL 38261 DND)*

Three of them belonged to Packer's squadron. One was A for Able, flown by Flg Off Art De Breyne. At about 00:15 hours on 13 June rear gunner Flg Off Pat Brophy shouted a warning that a Ju88 was coming in to attack from behind and below. A second or two later cannon shells from the fighter crashed into the port wing and fuselage, setting it on fire. De Breyne immediately ordered his crew to bale out of the bomber, the inside of which was in a state of burning chaos. The British flight engineer Sgt Roy Vigars tripped over the unconscious bomb aimer, Sgt J.W. Friday, on his way to the hatch. Not sure if he was alive or not, Vigars pulled Friday's parachute cord, his foot preventing the silk from billowing out, and pushed him unceremoniously out of the hatch, following him out straightaway. Friday regained consciousness in Amiens hospital four and a half days later, while his saviour Vigars landed safely to spend the rest of the war as a POW. W/Op WO Jim Kelly and navigator Flg Off Bob Brodie landed together near Varennes and were discovered by a woman who gave them food and shelter while she contacted a local Resistance member. The pair were moved to a house in Henencourt where they remained until mid-July, when their position was compromised by their loquacious hostess. The men were moved several times before returning to Varennes. Unfortunately, on 23 July several members of the Resistance whom they had met were arrested by the Gestapo, and the Canadians, now joined by several other aircrew, were hurriedly taken to hide in the woods and fields outside the town. There they remained until early August, when they were taken, somewhat bedraggled and hungry, to a large château at Senlis-le-Sec, where they stayed until they were liberated by Allied troops at the end of the month.

Art De Breyne held the mortally wounded Lancaster steady for as long as he could before, thinking that everyone had baled out, he jumped out of the hatch. Unknown to him, the rear gunner, Flg Off Pat Brophy, had become trapped in his turret. The hydraulic power for the turret had failed when the port engine was put out of action, leaving Brophy dependent on the manual rotation gear. To his horror, when he applied pressure on the handle, it came away in his hand, effectively entombing him in the turret. Mynarski, making his way to the rear escape hatch, noticed Brophy's desperate plight and gradually made his way through the flames towards the turret. As he did so, all his clothing up to his waist caught fire but he continued to batter away at the door with an axe he had picked up en route. Mynarski could not budge the door more than a couple of inches and Brophy, realising how little time there was left, frantically gestured to his friend that enough was enough and that he should escape while he could. Reluctantly Mynarski turned and headed back through the flames towards the hatch where, his clothes aflame, he turned to face his comrade, stood to attention and saluted. Several Frenchmen saw Mynarski fall to earth, his clothes and parachute blazing furiously. He died shortly afterwards, having given up any realistic chance of survival in the burning bomber.

By chance, Brophy survived the impact, being thrown clear as the Lancaster skied along having come to earth in an almost perfect belly-landing. More amazing still, he was largely uninjured and managed to walk to nearby Pas-en-Artois, where he was picked up by some Frenchmen who put him into the hands of the Resistance. He was back in Britain by September and immediately informed the authorities of Mynarski's selfless courage. The award of the Victoria Cross followed on 11 October 1946.

'Great excitement today as our first daylight operation was ordered with everyone jockeying for a position on the battle order.' This description, taken from 428 Squadron's record, captures the enthusiasm for this operation, a potent symbol of changing times and

The 'Mynarski' Lancaster, one of only two airworthy Lancasters in the world, maintained at the Canadian Warplane Heritage Museum, Mount Hope, Ontario, as a memorial to the losses suffered by the RCAF. (Author)

Allied air power. The target on 15 June was Boulogne harbour, where a number of light German naval vessels had assembled in addition to the usual E-boat flotilla, for operations against the invasion fleet and supply routes. Flying south over England, the bombers picked up a heavy escort of fighters, roughly on a one bomber/one fighter ratio, to form a 600-strong aerial armada. Not surprisingly, the Luftwaffe opted not to offer any resistance, leaving the defence of the port to the flak batteries, which were rapidly overwhelmed. The bombers encountered the same problems by day as they had so often by night: cloud partially obscured the TIs, which appeared well scattered over the harbour area. Nevertheless, the damage caused to the port area was immense and about 25 vessels were sunk or badly damaged; unfortunately, around 200 civilians lost their lives in what turned out be the heaviest raid of the war on the French town. Happily 428 and 419 Squadrons suffered no losses.

The following night both squadrons made a rare foray into German airspace to attack the synthetic oil plant at Sterkrade. For many, new to the skies over Germany, it was to be a sobering experience. The oil plant was smothered deep beneath a thick blanket of cloud stretching right up to 13,000ft, which easily swallowed up the PFF's ground markers, leaving the crews little to aim at. Although some bombs did find their way into the plant area, most of the bombing was scattered, with Flg Off J.M. Stevenson for one noting that 4,000lb bombs were visible exploding over an area 6 miles long. For the Germans it was a much better night. Some 32 bombers were blown out of the sky, either by the fighters or by the heavy flak defending the plant. Two of these belonged to 419 Squadron, the Lancasters of Flg Off D. Morrison and Flt Lt E.S. Smith.

Lt Joe Hartshorn USAAF earned a DFC for his determination to carry the fight to the enemy. Just as he settled G for George into the bombing run, a flak shell exploded directly beneath the port wing and at the same time the Lancaster came under fire from an unseen assailant. Hartshorn quickly corkscrewed to port as a second aircraft, an Me410, came to within 225 yards before being driven off by rear gunner Sgt E.L. Vince with its port engine trailing flames. As it was, the Lancaster had sustained damage to its fuselage, tail plane, bomb doors, rear turret, windscreen and astrodome; the navigator, Flg Off C.E.T. Hamilton, had also been wounded in the arm and leg. Nevertheless, Hartshorn dragged his aircraft back towards Sterkrade, enabling the bomb aimer, Flg Off A.L. Delaney, to attack the target, only a little behind schedule, before setting course for home.

On a cool and dismal midsummer's day, twenty-one Lancasters from 419 and 428 Squadrons joined a strong force attacking the V1 site at St Martin-l'Hortier, the first time that the squadrons had attacked such a target. As weather conditions over northern France were poor, the take-off time was postponed twice, leaving the crews in an uncomfortable state of limbo for the day. The Lancasters finally began to roll down the runway at 17:30 hours to join up with a strong escort of Spitfires over southern England. The evening light proved to be of little value as a thick layer of impenetrable cloud was smothering the target, obscuring some of the lighter green coloured markers. Nevertheless, all the crews bar one had picked up the markers by the second time around and, guided by an efficient Master Bomber, delivered an accurate and concentrated attack. The Luftwaffe did not put in an appearance and all the

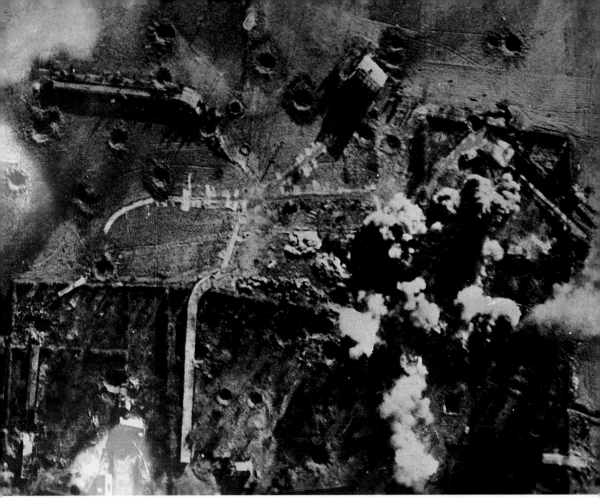

A V1 flying bomb site under attack in Northern France. In the summer of 1944, 419 and 428 Squadrons took part in several such attacks that proved to be remarkably effective. *(Imperial War Museum C 4430)*

crews returned safely in time for a quick foray to the local pub before closing time. Significantly, the crews found it no more difficult to attack other V1 sites at Bienteques and Bamieres by night a few days later. They and the crews of 428 Squadron's last operational Halifaxes, returning from another mining sortie, could, for once, see the purpose of their mission, having observed 'several flying bombs when going into the target area' en route to cause mayhem in Britain.

The summer weather closed in for the last few days of this momentous month, which had been the busiest on record for the men and women stationed at Middleton St George. Indeed, in the north-east it was so poor that it precluded even routine training flights. The thick fog and drizzle lasted into July and one massive 30-minute downpour left the meteorological section paddling in several inches of water. The weather abated sufficiently on 4 July to allow an attack on the railway yards at Villeneuve St Georges to go ahead; many men wished it had not as 6 Group lost nine of the 102 aircraft involved, four of them coming from Middleton St George alone. The aircraft had to contend with heavy cloud cover all the way and, on the orders of the Master Bomber, came down beneath the cloud to attack the target. Although there was little in the way of flak, the night-fighters operating in the area were too numerous to count and were responsible for all Middleton's losses.

Sadly 428 Squadron suffered its first loss since 23/24 April when Q for Queenie was brought down at 00:42 hours near La-Mailleraye-sur-Seine. For 419 Squadron the night showed a triple loss, but an unusually high 17 out of the 21 downed men survived and of these seven managed to evade capture to wait for liberation by the Allied armies. Flg Off L.W.A. Frame, flying J for Jig, had just bombed the railway yards when a twin-engined night-fighter piled in from dead astern and put the rear turret and port inner engine out of action and set the fuel tanks alight. As soon as it became clear that the fire was spreading out of control, the crew baled out and landed safely, three into almost immediate captivity and four to eventual freedom. Frame came down near the village of Fays and was quickly taken to a house in Barbizon, where, over the next four days, he was joined by his navigator, Flg Off W.C. Watson, flight engineer Sgt P.P. Barclay, and two other 419 Squadron members who had come a-cropper on the same operation, Flg Off C.A.D. Steepe and Flg Off G. Murphy. This group remained in the house until the arrival of American troops on 23 August. Flt Sgt J. Morris, Frame's mid-upper gunner, landed near Melun and at daybreak was spotted by a lady who took him to an empty house and told him to stay there. Morris waited with growing impatience but on the fourth day he was visited by an English-speaking girl from the Red Cross, who led him to another house in Melun. Here he once again waited for developments. After spending several days cooped up in the house, he was taken by train to Paris, where he remained, moving houses periodically, until the city's liberation by Allied troops in mid-August.

Flg Off J.M. Stevenson was the only member of his crew to evade capture when H for How was shot down in unusual circumstances near Chartainvillers. With 13 minutes to go before reaching the target, a Ju88 bored in from dead astern, cannons blazing. The mid-upper gunner Sgt J.T. Pett and rear gunner Sgt W.R. Gibson returned fire and saw their tracer enter the nose and port wing of their assailant. At any rate, the German pilot broke off the attack, diving down to port. Gibson recounts what happened next:

About three minutes later I saw a Fortress II on our starboard quarter at 800 yards. I noticed that it had a black nose and no turret. As it edged over to a position dead astern at 700 yards I gave the order to corkscrew and the Fortress followed us through all the combat manoeuvres. When I opened fire at 500 yards, tracer entered the nose of the Fortress, which banked at 90 degrees and fell away starboard quarter down.

Whatever scheme the Fortress was involved in, it was not seen again but it had, perhaps, passed on the location of the Lancaster as the unfortunate crew suffered no fewer than three more attacks in the ensuing minutes, one of which set the entire port wing ablaze. Flg Off Stevenson immediately gave the order to bale out, being himself the last one out, landing safely near Sgt Gibson. The pair covered an estimated 18 miles during the night before sleeping in a wheat field for much of the next day. About 17:00 hours the pair approached a farmer, who gave them their first food in quite some time before taking them to another farmhouse, where they met up with their W/Op, WO L.F. Head. Over the next few days several other downed airmen joined them. On 12 July the six young men were driven to

Paris by the son of a local doctor and distributed in pairs around several hotels on the outskirts of the city. On the afternoon of 14 July Stevenson and his navigator, Flg Off J.E. Prudham, were visited in their room by an American who claimed to have come from Barcelona to make arrangements for them to cross the Pyrenees to Spain. The pair instantly became suspicious of his manner and the nature of his questions, and refused to talk to him beyond making the blandest of comments. The American eventually left, saying that they would be taken by car to another location soon as part of their homeward journey. When the car turned up a couple of hours later, the two airmen were suspicious but reassured by the sight of the driver, who was the same young man that had brought them to Paris. They got in and travelled only a short distance before stopping – at the Gestapo headquarters. After questioning, the pair were taken to Fresnes, the notorious jail on the outskirts of Paris, where they met up with the other airmen. On 15 August, as the Allied troops were within a whisker of Paris, the airmen were taken by truck to the Gare L'Est and crammed into already overloaded box cars for transportation to Germany. Stevenson and two French officers, toiling with only the most primitive tools, managed to make a hole in the wooden floor of the crowded wagon and dropped on to the tracks below while the train was trundling along at about 25mph on the morning of the 18th. The trio succeeded in avoiding serious injury in this risky manoeuvre and set off towards Mezy-Moulins, where arrangements were made for Stevenson to go to Château Thierry, where he hid above a shop until the Americans arrived on 28 August. It was a happy conclusion to a remarkable and courageous evasion.

The third 419 Squadron Lancaster lost over Villeneuve was U for Uncle, piloted by Flg Off C.A.D. Steepe. Shortly after releasing its bomb-load over the railway yards the Lancaster was ripped apart by flak and the fuselage quickly became a raging inferno. So intense was the heat inside the aircraft that the front escape hatch expanded and buckled, making it impossible to force it open. In desperation Flg Off W.J.L. Thompson, the bomb aimer, grabbed an axe and battered a hole through the nose large enough for a man to pass through, thereby saving his own life and those of Steepe and the navigator, Murphy. Sgt B.A. Reaume, the only other member of the crew to escape from the burning bomber, exited from the rear hatch and remembered nothing else until he came to in a field, in pain from a dislocated knee joint and burns to his face and feet. Flg Off Thompson landed in Fontainebleau Forest with wounds to his leg, side and arm, but was still able to hobble along. For the next 48 hours he struggled along the paths in the forest and neighbouring countryside, hiding by day and travelling by night, and boldly passing German troops who did not catch on to who he was. Eventually, worn down by the pain of his wounds, he stopped at an isolated farmhouse and asked for help. The inhabitants said they had no medical supplies to give him and suggested he should give himself up to the Germans. Disappointed but unable to go on any longer, he did so. He was taken to the hospital at Fontainebleau where he was treated but also sharply interrogated before being moved to Boujon Hospital in Paris. There, on 6 July, he was told that he was well enough to be transferred to a POW camp in Germany. In order to avoid this, he deliberately exacerbated the injury to his knee by over-exertion. The ploy worked and a fortnight later he played the same painful trick again and managed to extend his stay until the Resistance took over the hospital a few weeks later. He eventually made it back to Britain in early September.

The attack on 4 July had proved to be Middleton's mostly costly for quite some time, with four aircraft lost and several more damaged, most notably 419 Squadron's O for Oboe, which successfully bombed the railway yards in spite of being set on fire and losing an engine in an unfriendly encounter with another Lancaster's rear gunner. As if that were not enough, as the Lancaster limped home it suffered four brushes with night-fighters. To add insult to injury, upon touching down at Middleton the tail wheel tyre and one of the main tyres burst, making it a somewhat hair-raising landing. The pilot and flight engineer, Flt Sgt J.A. Phillis and Sgt N. Norman respectively, were awarded DFMs for their courage and skill in the air.

On 5 July 428 Squadron dispatched half a dozen crews to mine the seas off Brest, Lorient and St Nazaire. It was to be the last gardening trip for some time for what was affectionately nicknamed 'The Herring Fleet'. As they came in to land that morning, 419 Squadron was preparing to take off to attack the well-defended V1 site at Siracourt, a good illustration of the round-the-clock campaign now being waged. The following evening Bomber Command carried out the first of several attacks made in direct support of the ground forces, struggling to break out of the main bridgehead. The Canadian First and British Second Armies were badly bogged down by dogged German resistance around Caen and it was clear that something big would be needed to dislodge the Wehrmacht from its well-fortified positions. Harris was called upon to provide the 'something big', but given the proximity of thousands of Allied soldiers, it would also need to be very accurately delivered. The attack was timed to begin in mid-evening when visibility was still good. The two aiming points were well marked by Oboe-equipped Mosquitoes and the attack was carefully controlled by the Master Bomber, Wg Cdr S.P. Daniels of 35 Squadron. The 467 bombers, a dozen of which came from 419 Squadron, dropped no less than 2,276 tons of high explosive on to the German positions, raising a huge cloud of smoke and dust to several thousand feet. By the time the crews landed, jubilant at the success of this novel type of attack and delighted at being able to do something to help their own countrymen, a message from Second Army was already waiting for them. 'Heavy bomber attack just taken place. A wonderfully impressive show and was enormously appreciated by the army. The army would like its appreciation and thanks sent to the crews.' No Allied troops were killed in the close-quarter bombing and Bomber Command had successfully added another string to its bow, its considerable accuracy proven to a wide and appreciative audience. That said, the raid caused the Wehrmacht less trouble than expected as it had few units in the areas targeted and its determined resistance continued.

The next four targets were all V1 launch and storage sites in northern France, two of them attacked by day, Mont Candon and Thiverny, and two by night, Bois des Jardins and Acquet. Oddly enough, the latter attacks were far more successful. Reeling under the weight of numerous sustained attacks, the German defences over France were beginning to crumble and there was no opposition to speak of to challenge the might of Bomber Command.

The 18th was to prove one of the longest for the crews of 419 and 428 Squadrons, with Middleton St George mounting two major attacks on the same day. In the first seventeen

Caen lies in ruins on 9 July 1944 following the heavy raids in support of the Allied breakout from the Normandy beachhead. *(Imperial War Museum B 6714)*

aircraft from 419 Squadron and nine from 428 Squadron joined over 900 others in an operation to smash five fortified villages in the Caen area as part of Operation Goodwood, the British Second Army's gigantic armoured thrust to break out from the beachhead. The crews rated the target marking as 'par excellence' and the Master Bomber, Sqn Ldr E.K. Cresswell, was praised for his cool work, methodically switching the attack from one target to another as required. The bombing was extremely accurate and concentrated, tearing great chunks out of 16th Luftwaffe Field Division and 21st Panzer Division. Bomber Command dropped over 5,000 tons of high explosive and the USAAF added another 1,800. The bombers, roaring in at between 5,000 and 9,000ft in almost never-ending waves, seemed to fill the early morning summer sky and provided those who witnessed the attack with an unforgettable sight. The *Daily Mail* the next day carried the headline 'Caen: mightiest air blow of all time launches the great offensive' and its correspondent Courtney Edwards provided an eyewitness account:

It was terrifying to watch. Using the air weapon as a mighty bulldozer, thousands of British and American bombers today battered the German lines. It was a terrifying spectacle. I hope I shall never be called upon to witness anything like it again. Try to recall the most violent thunderstorm you have ever seen, multiply that by one hundred, add an earthquake and you may have some idea of what the German troops on the other side of the river [Orne] went through this morning.

The air raid was a major factor in Goodwood's initial success. All the 419 and 428 Squadron crews returned home jubilant, having been able actually to see the results of their efforts and knowing they had made a direct and beneficial contribution to the campaign being waged in Normandy.

Barely 13 hours after the crews had clambered stiffly out of their bombers, many of them were climbing aboard ready to attack the synthetic oil plant at Wesseling in the heavily defended Happy Valley. The twenty-eight crews, fourteen from each squadron, were all too aware that this target would be a totally different proposition from the one attacked that morning. In order to thwart the potent defences, the top brass at Command HQ came up with a novel plan. The aircraft crossed the English coast at 9,000ft as normal before dropping to just 2–3,000ft for the flight across Occupied Europe, only climbing to 12–14,000ft within 50 miles of the target; the process was reversed on the return journey. This unusual flight plan certainly confused the German controllers as only one aircraft was lost from the 194 taking part. The raid itself was a spectacular success with both the marking and bombing being bang on target. German records reveal that over a thousand bombs landed within the works' compound, wreaking considerable havoc and disrupting production for some time. Nevertheless, the fearsome reputation of the extensive Ruhr defences was fully justified according to the crews and several bombers sustained damage from flak or fighters, often having been lit up like prima donnas on stage by the numerous dazzling searchlights.

Attacks on the V1 sites at L'Hey and Anderbeck, both successful and concentrated, provided a welcome interlude before German targets appeared on the ops board once again. The first of these was the port of Kiel and it was to be Bomber Command's first major attack on a German city in two months. Over 600 aircraft pounded the city in a whirlwind 25-minute onslaught, badly damaging both the port area and the crucial U-boat yards, as well as the infrastructure of the city in general. It turned out to be the port's heaviest assault of the war and it was achieved for the loss of just four Lancasters, so successful were the Command's new radar counter-measures, known as Mandrel.

For the ground crews at Middleton St George 24 July was a busy day as they worked flat out to bomb-up and make ready fifteen aircraft from both squadrons for an attack on Stuttgart. Once again the summer weather was not kind and the crews came across an unbroken layer of cloud shielding the city below and no particular results could be ascertained. Among the 21 bombers lost that night, some 4.6 per cent of the attacking force, was that of Flt Sgt J.A. Phillis of 419 Squadron. Phillis, who, along with Sgt R.G. MacKinnon, managed to evade capture, reported that his Lancaster was hit by rocket projectiles which set the fuselage ablaze, somewhere near Luxembourg. Almost immediately the Lancaster went into a violent spin and it was only with the greatest difficulty and after some considerable time that Phillis, MacKinnon and the only other survivor, Flt Sgt W.M. Devine, managed to drag themselves out of the escape hatch. By the time Devine emerged from the burning aircraft, he estimated it was at barely 1,000ft above the blacked-out French countryside.

In addition, 428 Squadron also suffered a loss that night, although all of the crew in this instance escaped unscathed. Flg Off C.M. Corbet's Lancaster was accidentally rammed in mid-air by another unidentified bomber while en route to the target. The collision wrecked the bomb bay area, the undercarriage and the propeller tips on the starboard side, which caused the inner engine to overheat and eventually burst into flames. The flight engineer, Sgt Enfield, the only Briton in the crew, immediately activated the Gravener extinguisher, which quickly doused the flames, enabling the bomber to limp towards home. Corbet decided to head for the emergency strip at Woodbridge in Suffolk, and as he approached he ordered the rest of the crew to don their parachutes in case the opportunity to use them arose. Somewhere along the line the wires became crossed and the rear gunner, Sgt J. Sanduluk, not only donned his parachute but promptly baled out too, landing safely in the English countryside. The rest of the crew stayed with the Lancaster and put their trust in their skipper, who, as it turned out, repaid their faith by pulling off a textbook emergency landing.

The inconclusive nature of the attack put Stuttgart back on the board the following night. For some reason the details of the route, timings and tactics were late in coming through from Group HQ with the result that some of the Lancasters took off from Middleton St George a little later than scheduled, with some navigators still working out their figures. Several 419 and 428 Squadron Lancasters flew a more direct route than planned in order to make up lost time. The bombers were so heavily laden that the undercarriage of 419 Squadron's P for Peter actually struck a fence post some 50 yards beyond the end of the runway as it clawed its way laboriously into the night sky. Over the cloudy city 419 Squadron's Lt Hartshorn USAAF felt he had to make sure of his target and dipped beneath the cloud for a better view. Similarly Flt Lt H.H. Smith courageously circled the city, in spite of the obvious dangers, for some 25 minutes before finally identifying the target to his satisfaction. Both actions displayed an admirable devotion to duty and a strong desire to do the job properly. In spite of considerable amounts of flak and several brushes with prowling night-fighters, 419 and 428 Squadrons suffered no losses.

However, 6 Group as a whole was not to be so lucky on its next outing to Hamburg, its first serious raid since the great aerial battle fought exactly a year before. The heavy flak barrage and swarms of night-fighters both in and out of the target are accounted for 22 of 6 Group's aircraft, some 9.4 per cent of the Canadian force taking part and the largest loss on a single operation sustained during the war. Whereas 431 Squadron based at Middleton St George's satellite station Croft lost five of its seventeen aircraft, the squadrons based at Middleton got off lightly with 428 Squadron sustaining the only loss of the night. Flg Off T. 'Mac' Magill and his crew were never seen again after taking off from Middleton St George at

22:36. Magill was a well known character and one of the longest-serving officers on the strength; sadly, he was on his 40th and final operation prior to screening. Flying as his W/Op that night was Flt Lt B.L. Smith, the Squadron Signals Leader, who had won the DFM while serving in the Middle East with 37 Squadron; a Briton, Smith was one of the original 'Ghosts' but he had been fully accepted as an honorary Canadian by a succession of young men passing through the squadron. By contrast Flg Off R. Parsons, flying as second dickey, was on his first operation, having only joined the squadron the previous day. Such are the vagaries of war.

The seamless and almost timeless routine continued. If July had been busy, no one noticed anything significantly different in August and with V1s still hammering Britain daily, there was a palpable buzz among the crews when the next targets were revealed. On the 2nd Middleton St George dispatched a whopping forty-one aircraft, twenty-one from 419 Squadron and twenty from 428 Squadron, to attack the V1 storage depot at Bois de Cassan. Unusually, as it seemed to the crews, there was little to hinder their vision apart from the huge plumes of smoke and dust hurled skywards by the force of the explosions. The Middleton St George-based squadrons themselves delivered over 250 tons of high explosive in a concentrated and accurate attack, guided by a Master Bomber who was reported to be 'very clear and in complete control of the situation'. Photographic evidence supported this positive assessment of the attack. To the surprise of the crews, who thought there was little left to hit, Bois de Casson was again selected as the target for the next day. Once again, conditions were favourable and the sixteen aircraft from each squadron based at Middleton St George had no problem in identifying the target nor in following the Master Bomber's directions. 'It seems that the whole target area was carpeted' was how the station record put it.

The next day's work turned out to be an attack on a limestone hillside above the River Oise at St Leu d'Esserent, in which tunnels had been constructed to house V1s. Over 450 bombers, of which thirty-eight came from Middleton St George, were dispatched to pound the area in the hope of collapsing the tunnels or at least disrupting the rail and road links in the immediate area. The site was well defended by flak positions, which put up a heavy and intense barrage, damaging several aircraft. One of these was 419 Squadron's B for Baker under the command of Flg Off J.F. Tees, whose Lancaster lost both port engines to flak over the target. The bomber lost almost 7,000ft in altitude before the inner engine was coaxed back into life. Now flying relatively slowly and at only 9,000ft, the bomber was a prime target for the Germans' traditionally impressive light flak barrage. To the great relief of the crew, half a dozen Spitfires hung back to protect the stricken bomber and to divide the enemy's fire, while others screamed down to engage the flak units more closely and succeeded in considerably reducing their lethal activities. Tees managed to coax the Lancaster further up into the sky and plodded homewards, eventually executing a beautiful landing in spite of a puncture in one of the tyres. In recognition of his skill in bringing his aircraft and crew home, Tees was awarded an immediate DFC.

There was to be no let-up. On the following day fifteen Lancasters from each of 419 and 428 Squadrons joined a massive 1,000-plus force on their way to pound five separate targets around Normandy in support of the Allied ground forces. Although visibility was excellent, with nothing more than a slight summer haze to contend with, the crews were acutely aware of the close proximity of the soldiers, many of whom were Canadian, to the target area. As a result only 660 bomb aimers felt sufficiently certain to let their bombs go, whatever the instructions of the Master Bomber. As it turned out, everything went well with the targets receiving a severe bashing without loss to the troops. This operation marked the completion of a second tour for 428 Squadron's CO, Wg Cdr G. McLeish. This popular and experienced officer was replaced by Wg Cdr Chester Hull, a graduate of the Royal Military College and the son of an air commodore.

For a good number of crews no more than 16 hours elapsed between returning from the raid in the Caen area and setting off for an evening attack, this time on an important oil storage depot at Foret de Chantilly. Conditions were good and there was sufficient light to identify the target visually, and for once there was little room for doubt regarding the outcome. As 419 Squadron's Flg Off Calder stated, 'there is no doubt we hit what we went after'; huge columns of oily black smoke, stretching up over two and a half miles into the sky, were eloquent witness to that. On the return journey many crews at a distance of some 50 miles could still see the flames leaping high into the air and massive explosions covering the target area. In spite of an unusually nasty flak barrage, all thirty-two Lancasters from Middleton St George returned more or less intact. Such was the pace of events that well within 24 hours the hard-pressed ground crews had managed to make ready a total of thirty-eight Lancasters, all serviced, refuelled and bombed-up. Seventeen of them belonged to 428 Squadron and these were tasked to bomb a V1 site at Coulonvilliers. At the same time 419 Squadron dispatched twenty bombers to attack a similar target in Acquet, which had barely escaped the attentions of Bomber Command on the first day of the month. The strain upon all concerned was immense.

Coming off the back of a night attack on the oil storage tanks at La Pallice, 11 August was one of the great days in the wartime history of Middleton St George as it saw the visit of King George VI, Queen Elizabeth and Princess Elizabeth. An investiture was held at which, among others, the COs of 419 Squadron and 428 Squadron, Wg Cdr Pleasance and Wg Cdr McLeish respectively, were decorated, and 419 Squadron also received its squadron crest. The events of this memorable day will be described later. The following day Middleton St George received another visit from a distinguished person, no less than MRAF Lord Trenchard, who informally inspected the station and addressed the crews.

Even so, there was little time for rest and reflection for on the night of 12 August ten Lancasters from 419 Squadron and eleven from 428 Squadron were scheduled to attack a cloudy Brunswick. It was to be an unusual and experimental raid, deliberately denying the crews the use of PFF and leaving them to rely solely on the use of H2S. Dependent upon the flickering and indistinct images on the H2S screen, the crews offloaded their bombs as accurately as they could and several large red glowing patches were seen developing beneath the cloud. The station log summarised the crew reports as 'general opinion favours a good attack, well spread over the city with a fair-sized concentration in the centre'. German records largely concur, denoting the attack as 'a heavy raid', with bombs falling in the centre and

Stadpark areas, killing a total of 99 people. However, 419 Squadron's Flg Off Kent was less optimistic, noting that in his opinion some bombs had landed on Hildesheim, a town over 20 miles away; German records also concur with the observant Kent. The results of the raid as a whole were out of line with those of raids directed by PFF, evoking little surprise. Like most other towns in Germany, Brunswick was well protected by flak units and they hurled up a heavy predicted barrage. Several night-fighters were also spotted operating in the area and one of these accounted for Flg Off J.A. McGregor's 428 Squadron Lancaster which came down near Winsen on the River Aller shortly after midnight. The shattering attack from the Ju88 was over in a matter of seconds but it left the bomber on fire and with damaged controls. The aircraft went into a spin, as McGregor recounts: 'I was thrown to the starboard side. The aircraft stalled and spun again and I was then in the nose. At the next stalled spin I was thrown clear.'

While this was going on, seven crews from 428 Squadron took off to blast a German troop concentration and road junction just north of Falaise. Five aircraft from 419 Squadron were due to follow but the second to take off became bogged down in the mud just off the runway while taxiing, blocking enough of the runway to prevent the other three bombers from squeezing past. The rest pressed on to find the target clearly marked in red and green and, guided by a Master Bomber, and with no opposition to speak of, the crews had no problems in putting in a good attack, leaving them 'unanimously of the opinion that the attack was successful'.

On the clear and sunny morning of the 14th orders were received for another Battle Area Target. Eighteen Lancasters from 419 Squadron and nineteen from 428 Squadron were to form part of an 800-plus force which was to pound seven German troop concentrations and strongpoints ahead of the 3rd Canadian Division near Falaise. The crews at Middleton St George were in high spirits, keen to help their fellow countrymen struggling in the green fields of Normandy. Unfortunately, the day was to have a tragic outcome. The crews had been thoroughly briefed, and it had been rammed into them that the Canadian soldiers were positioned not far from the actual target and that a high degree of accuracy was essential. The crews map-read their way to the target and began their timed runs from the moment they crossed the coast; in addition Oboe-guided markers were dropped at each target and the attack on each target was also controlled by a Master Bomber and a deputy. It seemed that all that could be done to ensure both accuracy and the safety of the ground troops had been done. However, even the best laid plans can go wrong and this one did.

The instructions issued by the Master Bombers caused considerable confusion as aircraft bound for other targets found that they could pick up several transmissions, and the puzzled crews were unable to sort out which instructions applied to them and which did not. The situation was made worse by the usual smoke and debris which blotted out much of the view of the ground. Sqn Ldr Don Lamont of 428 Squadron recalls that his crew 'had quite a discussion about where to bomb but decided to stay with the timed run'. Successive waves of bombers struggled with these problems, having to make on-the-spot decisions that could mean life or death for those below. Even worse was to follow. As the Canadian soldiers realised the disaster that was unfolding that summer's afternoon, they hurriedly sent yellow flares arching high into the sky, and set off yellow ground markers, their signals for the presence of friendly forces. Owing to a breakdown in communications between Bomber Command and the Canadian army commanders, yellow was also the colour of the TIs to be bombed that day. Shortly before a quarter past three, two aircraft from 428 Squadron, amid all the confusion, conflicting instructions, smoke and multicoloured pyrotechnics, released their loads on a quarry at Haut Mesnil, where elements of 12th Canadian Field Regiment were stationed. Approximately seventy more aircraft followed their lead, causing heavy casualties. At Haut Mesnil and the other Canadian areas which were bombed in error, 65 men were killed and more than 300 were wounded or missing. The wonder was that the casualty figures were not even greater. When news of the tragedy filtered home, the crews were devastated. Bob Marshall, an experienced gunner with 428 Squadron, summed it up: 'It was a sad day for us, particularly when the trip was a milk-run. There was no enemy opposition; it was one of the very few trips I experienced without being shot at.'

The recriminations went right to the top but in the cold light of day it is clear that both military hierarchies took what precautions they could to ensure the safe execution of the attack; it is equally clear that in the fog of war errors will happen – a point brought forcefully and tragically home to British soldiers serving in the recent Gulf Wars. Nevertheless, the official Court of Enquiry held in London inevitably found several individual crews culpable and these were broken up, reassigned to other duties and some members demoted or reprimanded.

For the crews stationed at Middleton St George, much of the controversy was carried on both above their heads and in the future. It was business as usual the following day. Fifteen aircraft from both 419 and 428 Squadrons joined a mighty 1000-plus force in attacking several Luftwaffe airfields. Their target was the airfield at Soesterberg in Holland and they arrived over it in mid-afternoon. Accompanied by a veritable swarm of fighters, the bomber crews enjoyed the sunny conditions and were able to identify the airfield from several miles away. The usual clouds of thick smoke, debris and dust erupted, greatly reducing effective observation, but the Master Bomber skilfully switched targets on the airfield to ensure the destruction of most of the buildings and much of the runway.

The flak gunners on the ground did, however, give an excellent account of themselves, hurling up large quantities of explosives. WO A.P.A. Jakeman later recalled:

The last bomb had just gone when we were hit. The aircraft immediately went into a spiral dive. . . . I gave the order to bale out and the engineer, who was in the bomb aimer's compartment dropping Window, reached up with my chute. Meanwhile I was trying to regain control before feathering the engines. However, in a matter of seconds, before I could trim, it was in a violent spin.

Jakeman had not even had time to unbuckle his belt before he was blown free by an enormous explosion, only regaining consciousness as he fell through the air. Quickly deploying his parachute, he gently returned to mother earth with barely a scratch. The flight engineer, Sgt S.W. Wright, was the only other survivor.

The men and women at Middleton St George had also had an eventful afternoon, witnessing a fine piece of flying by WO A.C. Weston of 419 Squadron. Almost immediately after take-off, the port inner engine had begun to belch out clouds of thick black smoke, requiring it to be feathered. A minute or two later the starboard inner began to follow suit, leaving Weston with a difficult decision: to head out to sea to jettison the bomb-load safely and pray the engines would hold out, or to turn for home and attempt a landing with a full bomb-load, full fuel tanks and ropey engines. He chose the latter and, watched by a large and anxious audience, pulled off a textbook landing.

The attack switched back to Germany with the port of Stettin being hit hard on 16 August and another northern port, Bremen, 24 hours later. The only hindrance to visibility was a thin layer of haze and this did nothing to prevent the PFF from marking the target very accurately. An exceptionally heavy and concentrated raid followed with the whole city seemingly ablaze beneath the bombers. Towering plumes of thick, black, oily smoke stretched up into the sky almost as far as the aircraft themselves as oil storage tanks in the port area exploded. The light from the fires lit up the streets of the city and the sheets of flame were visibly mirrored in the waters of the River Oder. The whole of the city centre and most of the north-western districts of the city simply ceased to exist in recognisable form as the massive fires, described in German records as firestorms, engulfed building after building; although over 1,000 bodies were recovered, 300 from one public shelter alone, many more simply disappeared amid the flames and ashes. The flak defences were initially active but were completely overwhelmed in the later stages of the attack; although several aircraft sustained damage, only a single bomber was brought down. By plain misfortune, that one belonged to Plt Off C.M. Corbet of 428 Squadron. Hit by flak, the Lancaster soon caught fire and once it became clear that the flames were beyond control, Corbet gave the order to bale out. All succeeded in doing so except for one of the gunners, Flt Sgt R.E. Good, who had been mortally wounded by shrapnel and was unable to make it to the escape hatch. The sad demise of Corbet's crew put a serious dampener upon the party planned to celebrate 428 Squadron's 2,000th sortie of the war. The honour of flying that landmark sortie fell to Plt Off A.J. Carter, who had recently been awarded the DFC.

The long and tiring run of operations was broken by the lousy British summer weather and the crews did not fly operationally again until the night of 25/26 August, when they attacked the large Opel works in Russelsheim. The entire assault lasted just 10 minutes but considerable damage was caused to both the town and the main factory area, although the overall halt in production was a bare two days on account of the company holding a large reserve stock of parts.

Although conditions were generally good, it was a difficult night for many crews. Flt Sgt Robert Maxwell, a 20-year-old from Toronto serving with 428 Squadron, was on his first operation as skipper, having previously flown operationally only as second dickey. While still some 40 miles short of Russelsheim, his Lancaster was suddenly blasted by flak, the explosion mortally wounding Sgt P. Recabarren, the flight engineer working alongside him; the W/Op, Sgt Fearby, was also wounded by flying shrapnel, and Maxwell himself was hit in the leg. To cap it all, the starboard outer engine was also put out of commission. In spite of all this, Maxwell made the decision to press on to the target, only to find when he got there shortly after 01:00 hours that an electrical fault prevented the bombs from being released. Nothing daunted, Maxwell remained over the target until the load could be dropped manually. Only then did he turn for home, struggling all the way to maintain stability and height. Without the benefit of any wireless aids, the Lancaster drifted a little off course, eventually crossing the English coast near Portsmouth. Maxwell decided to land at the first available airfield, Thorney Island. Two days later he was recommended for a well deserved Conspicuous Gallantry Medal.

The victim of flak or, perhaps, a mid-air collision, 419 Squadron's Y for Yoke, captained by Flg Off M.D. Witwer, did not make it home. In his report written after his release from a POW camp, Witwer described what happened after the Lancaster was hit:

The nose went down and I could not pull it out. Told crew we had been hit. Then we went into a violent spin. Controls seemed stiff, intercom went U/S. I shouted for the crew to bale out . . . was thrown against the roof and knocked unconscious. Woke up in the air, pulled my chute and within 20 seconds landed in a tree about 30 miles east of Mannheim.

Although Witwer records seeing two of his crew bale out of the front hatch, he was in fact the only survivor.

Sadly 419 Squadron suffered four more fatalities that night when E for Easy, commanded by Flg Off W.A. Milner, crashed upon return to Boscombe Down, having been diverted there on account of poor weather conditions further north. Sgt L. Weston, the mid-upper gunner, recounted what happened when E for Easy began its final approach:

The fog had closed in and obscured the landing lights. We were the ninth aircraft to attempt to land. The pilot approached the field when permission was given but was unable to see the flare path, so an overshoot was made. Almost immediately all four engines cut and the aircraft started to hit tree tops. I could feel the air rushing into the cabin, so surmise that the Perspex panel in the nose had been stove in . . . The pilot pulled the aircraft up and the engine appeared to cut in momentarily and then cut out again. He suddenly banked sharply to port (to avoid trees) and shouted to everyone to hold tight. I felt a crash and was unconscious for a few minutes. I then made my way out of the wreckage.

Indeed, wreckage was all there was left as the aircraft had broken in two, trailing torn metal over a wide area. An inquiry later found that the aircraft had simply run out of fuel at a critical moment, leaving Milner with little room for manoeuvre and absolving him posthumously from any blame for the crash.

An attack on Mimoyecques near Calais on the 27th was the Middleton squadrons' final contribution to Operation Crossbow, the operation intended to counter the very real threat from the indiscriminate V-weapons. The raid, carried out in clear conditions, was particularly successful, all the more so since intelligence later reported that the site, partly buried beneath a chalk ridge, had also housed another new terror weapon, the V3, an enormous, long-range gun designed to pound London and south-eastern England. Perhaps as a result of this, the local defences were a little sharper and more active than usual, damaging a number of aircraft.

No aircraft were lost over enemy territory but 419 Squadron's K for King crash-landed only a few miles from Middleton St George. WO L.M. McDonald had just hauled his heavily laden Lancaster into the air when one of the starboard engines coughed and lapsed into silence. McDonald, with a nifty bit of flying, managed to keep the wallowing aircraft in the air but two minutes later the other starboard engine came out in sympathy with its neighbour. With insufficient power and height in a Lancaster fully loaded with high explosive and fuel, there was nothing the pilot could do to defy the laws of gravity any longer. The aircraft crashed at Appleton Wiske. Miraculously, everyone on board emerged from the wreckage under their own steam, more or less unscathed. The same could not be said for the Lancaster, which was written off.

CHAPTER 7

The Last Lap

THE ASSAULT ON GERMANY

September turned out to be a far quieter month, with 6 Group operating on just twenty occasions; the crews at Middleton St George took part in a dozen of them. The aircrew in particular were worn out after the almost daily attacks mounted in August and the break enforced by the dismal late summer weather was not unwelcome. It was not until the 6th that Middleton St George was called upon, dispatching eighteen Lancasters from 419 Squadron and sixteen from 428 Squadron to attack the ship and U-boat yards in Emden. This was the first attack on the port since June 1942 and, as it turned out, it was also the last of the war. The attack was to be made in daylight with Spitfires providing a strong escort in the initial stages and American long-range Mustangs taking over further on. In the event, the fighters were not needed but the flak gunners, making full use of the clear conditions, put up a fearsome and accurate barrage, damaging eleven of the bombers from Middleton.

The bomb aimer in one of these aircraft was Flg Off A.L. Lakeman of 419 Squadron. On the run-up to the target a near-miss sent shrapnel hurtling through the Lancaster and some of it lodged in the young man's head. Despite his painful injuries, Lakeman continued to give directions to his pilot and dropped the bomb-load on the target. For his cool courage and determination, he was awarded an immediate DFC. Lakeman's bombs contributed to a concentrated and devastating attack in which the U-boat yards, Nordsee Werke, and the shipbuilding yards, Berkamer Kleinbohn, suffered serious damage. In addition, several ships in the harbour were sunk or damaged and the town itself was described as being 'a mass of flames', clearly visible to the crews well over 100 miles away. Neither 428 nor 419 Squadron, now under the command of Wg Cdr Hagerman, previously the A Flight Commander, following the screening of Wg Cdr Pleasance, suffered any losses that day.

On the morning of 10 September orders came through for a maximum effort from both squadrons as part of a series of massive attacks on the port of Le Havre, still in German hands. Almost a thousand bombers were assigned to pound the garrison into submission. The patchy cloud drifting over the target did not prevent the crews from being able to identify their targets, several gun emplacements, visually. Most TIs were noted to be clustered around the various targets and any out of position were pointed out by a vigilant and efficient Master Bomber, mindful of the proximity of friendly forces stationed around the French town. Once again the Luftwaffe did not make an appearance and the flak defences were weak and seemed to peter out as the raid went on, allowing all of the enormous force to return home without sustaining a single loss.

A night attack on 11/12 September was called off but orders were received on the morning of the 12th for a daylight raid on the synthetic oil plant in Dortmund. There was little time to prepare the eighteen Lancasters from 419 Squadron and fourteen from 428 Squadron and the ground crew worked at a furious pace to make the deadline. The aircrew too had to hurry, especially the navigators, who received no fewer than three changes of route, the last shortly before take-off. In the event several crews had to lose time over the North Sea in order to arrive as scheduled. Conditions were ideal for bombing over Dortmund and the Master of Ceremonies was on the ball, and his reported comment of 'Come on you Canucks, and let's see what you can do' appears to have spurred the crews on. Certainly Flg Off Sparling, an experienced campaigner with 419 Squadron, was moved to say in his report 'that this is the most concentrated bombing I have ever seen'. Although the thick black oily smoke prevented accurate assessment of the results, the massive explosions rising up to 2,000ft into the air seemed good enough for most of the men there. Dortmund's flak defences were formidable and a dozen of Middleton's aircraft sustained damage.

The most amazing story of the day belonged to 428 Squadron's Z for Zebra, flown by Flt Lt Russell Curtis, an American serving in the RCAF. Curtis was in the process of lining up his aircraft for the final run in when the Lancaster took a hit that killed the rear gunner, Flg Off J.J. Flood, and left Curtis with a compound fracture of the skull. With Sgt J.W. Rose RAF, the flight engineer, wiping the blood from his eyes, Curtis managed to keep the bomber level and on track long enough for the bomb aimer, Plt Off Dougal McGillivray, to drop the load over the oil plant. He then passed out, leaving McGillivray to coax the ailing aircraft back to Britain, assisted by Rose, who dealt with all technical problems and helped with the navigation. Eventually they arrived over the emergency landing strip at Woodbridge, ready to carry out a wheels-up landing. As they approached, McGillivray, who had never landed any aircraft before, let alone a battered Lancaster, was ordered by the control tower to go around again and try a wheels-down landing. Their second approach was also aborted as a badly damaged Halifax was given priority, forcing McGillivray to go round yet again. The third time proved lucky and the bomber touched down more or less intact. It was a remarkable feat of flying and courage. Curtis, who had already been awarded a DFM, was awarded a DSO, as was McGillivray.

It was a cloudless night over Kiel on the 15th and, apart from a slight ground haze, conditions were excellent for bombing. The attacking force made full use of this lucky break to deliver a heavy blow to the port. Although the flak and searchlight activity was considered moderate it was more than enough for a distinguished non-combatant flying with 428 Squadron that night. Sqn Ldr J.G. Edwards had invited the station's Catholic padre, Father Philip Lardie, to join his crew for the night in order to see what the men in his care went through when on operations. Although Lardie had already taken part in the raid on Falaise the month before, this was to be his first raid against a heavily defended German target. Throughout the bombing run Lardie stood between the pilot and the flight engineer, watching the flak, the searchlights weaving right and left, the photoflashes going off and the markers and bombs exploding far below in a spreading carpet of flames. All went well until the rear gunner spotted a night-fighter closing in and shouted to Edwards to begin corkscrewing. As he did so, the unfortunate padre found himself alternately banging his head on the canopy or rolling around the floor, frantically trying to grab hold of something solid. The violent manoeuvre succeeded in shaking off the night-fighter and the Lancaster returned home without further interference, leaving Lardie to sum up his night. 'I wasn't looking for thrills but a better understanding of what it meant to fly on operations – and afterwards I had an entirely different outlook. I felt much closer to the airmen.' Most of the men greatly appreciated the gesture and respected the padre for undertaking the operation voluntarily but it was strictly against regulations. It was no surprise when Wg Cdr Hull came across Lardie sitting reading a newspaper in the mess the next day and, putting his hand on his shoulder, said, 'Padre, you're screened!'

Two days later, on 17 September, eighteen Lancasters from each of 419 and 428 Squadrons joined almost 750 other bombers in an attack on a number of positions in the Boulogne area, prior to a ground attack. Anxious not to repeat the dreadful errors of the Falaise raid, the crews were warned to take particular care with accuracy and to act on any instructions given by the Master Bomber. As the weather was quite good, the Master Bomber was able to see that the early markers had drifted short of the aiming point and redirected the crews accordingly. In any event, the results were good enough to persuade the German garrison that it was all over for them and they surrendered shortly afterwards. It was a perfect example of the efficacy of tactical heavy bombing.

There followed three major attacks on Calais and another on Cap Gris Nez before the end of the month. The German garrison was still firmly ensconced in this important port, somewhat ironically the nearest to southern England, and a good dose of high explosive from Bomber Command was deemed the most effective way of shifting it. Consequently, on 20 September some 646 aircraft, of which thirteen came from each of 419 and 428 Squadrons, were designated to blast German positions in and around the town. The early evening sky was clear over Calais and the bombers were largely untroubled by the desultory flak and had time to drop their loads accurately on the well laid red markers. The skies cleared again on the morning of the 25th, the day on which direction of Bomber Command passed from SHAEF back to the Chief of Air Staff, to allow the second operation against Calais. The squadrons, each fielding twenty Lancasters, had been briefed to use a technique new to them, known as offset marking. This had evolved to prevent the markers being obscured beneath the cloud of dust and smoke that a major attack hurled up into the air. Instead the markers were deliberately offset and a timed and directed run was made from them to the target. Unfortunately the crews found Calais partly hidden beneath large patches of cloud and the usual Oboe-directed sky markers proved less than accurate on this occasion, resulting in scattered bombing patterns. Some audacious crews came down beneath the

2,000ft cloud base in an attempt to drop their bombs more accurately but flew into a maelstrom of light flak which accounted for the seven Lancasters and one Halifax lost in the raid. Fortunately none belonged to the squadrons based at Middleton St George.

There was a repeat performance the next day when a 700-plus force attempted to hammer the Germans in and around Calais into submission. Clear skies and excellent visibility greeted the crews on this occasion and, again deploying the offset technique, the bombing was far more concentrated and accurate than the previous day. Flg Off Errington, for example, of 419 Squadron noted in his report 'a perfect circle of bomb bursts in the target area' and there is little doubt that the various targets were hard hit. The cumulative effects of this tremendous pounding took their toll on the German garrison and it surrendered to Canadian troops a few days later.

Next up was the Ruhroel AG synthetic oil plant in Bottrop in the heart of the infamous Happy Valley. For this raid 419 Squadron contributed an impressive twenty-two Lancasters and 428 an even more impressive twenty-four Lancasters, representing sterling efforts by the ground crews, both setting squadron records. The crews were scheduled to take off at 7:00 hours, and had been promised at the briefing, held at the ungodly hour of 02:00 hours, a strong fighter escort but few of the crews even caught a glimpse of the fighters in among the thick cloud and clag. Arriving over the target area the majority of crews could see nothing beneath an almost solid layer of cloud and even the Oboe-directed red sky markers were quickly swallowed up by the cloud. The Master Bomber ordered those crews unable to locate any markers to bomb on dead-reckoning or to attack any secondary target they could find in the Ruhr Valley. One or two crews were lucky enough to find a break in the cloud; 419 Squadron's Flt Lt J.P. Barlow came across just such a break that seemed to run parallel to the valley and flew along the length of it. Suddenly a large factory hove into view and Barlow promptly ordered his bomb aimer to drop their load on to it. The target photo revealed that the factory was indeed the primary target, and that their bomb-load had landed slap bang on top of it. However, for most the station log summed it up: 'The results of this attack were practically impossible to assess owing to adverse cloud conditions.'

The reception the bombers received from the flak was as hot as anticipated and several aircraft were damaged by the shrapnel from near-misses, none more so than 419 Squadron's P for Peter, captained by Flg Off J.A. Anderson. A seasoned and experienced campaigner, Anderson was leading one of the crews thwarted by the murky conditions over the target area. Rather than simply letting his bomb-load go in the general area, he decided to orbit in the hope of locating a break in the cloud, despite the heavy flak. His CO, Wg Cdr D.C. Hagerman, picks up the narrative:

At the beginning of the orbit, the aircraft was repeatedly hit by shell fragments and both the port outer and inner engines were put out of action. The port outer was also set on fire, the hydraulic system was rendered unserviceable and the controls damaged to such an extent that [Anderson] had to call on the assistance of two members of his crew to pull manually on the rudder controls. With complete disregard for the heavy opposition and the difficulty in controlling his crippled aircraft, Flt Lt Anderson completed the orbit and made a steady bombing run, enabling the Air Bomber to attack the target very accurately.

Shortly after leaving the target, it was found that the starboard inner engine had also been badly damaged and was giving less than half power. Through superb planning, crew cooperation and flying skill, Flt Lt Anderson successfully flew his crippled aircraft back to this country with full power only from the starboard outer, half power on the starboard inner, and made a masterly landing without causing further damage to his aircraft or crew.

Hagerman submitted this report as a recommendation for Anderson to be awarded the Victoria Cross. Though many in the know felt his magnificent exploits were worthy of the highest honour, the powers that be did not. Instead, on 21 December 1944 Anderson was awarded a DSO, a rare distinction for a man of his rank.

Several of the crews spotted something sinister that morning. Flying towards Germany, Ron Cassels, a navigator with 428 Squadron, was called forward by his pilot 'to look at three vapour trails in the eastern sky. They went straight up and we had a good look at them as it was just before sunrise. We didn't have any idea what they could be as they were perpendicular and went very high. It was afterwards that we realised that we had seen the trails of three V2s being launched against London.' It was a sharp reminder that there was still lots of life in their tough and resourceful foe and that there was still a great deal of flying to be done before there could be any general relaxation and rest. At least there was one major cause for celebration: for the first time since the two squadrons began operating side by side at Middleton St George, neither squadron had suffered any operational losses for a calendar month.

Aircraft based at Middleton had not been sent to Norway since the famous raids on the *Tirpitz* in 1941–2 but on 4 October forty Lancasters were tasked to attack the enormous U-boat pens in the harbour area of Bergen. Having lost their main Atlantic bases in France, a good part of the still potent U-boat fleet had moved further north to Norway. The crews found the area clear that morning and many were able to identify the targets visually, enabling some very accurate bombing. Flg Off A.M. Roy and his 419 Squadron crew, for example, were awarded a much-prized target token in recognition of their accuracy. Records from Bergen confirm 6 Group's assessment that the target had been well blasted but added that the bombs had little effect on the massive reinforced concrete pens themselves. Collateral damage was remarkably limited given the scale of the attack, a testimony to the efforts of the crews, but by a stroke of ill luck the loss of life at the two places where there were civilian casualties was substantial. A total of 34 people lost their lives when a local factory was hit and 2 teachers, 17 air raid workers and 60 schoolchildren were killed when the basement in which they were sheltering took a direct hit from a stray bomb. Such was the price paid by the innocent for the defeat of Hitler and Nazism. Nor was this the only price paid that autumn morning: Flg Off G.R. Duncan and his crew failed to return from the operation. Initially it was thought they had vanished without trace, probably into the North Sea, but a shepherd, Basil Oliver, found wreckage on a remote Northumberland hillside near Rothbury and it was quickly identified as belonging to 419 Squadron. There were no survivors from this crash, which took place no more than 15 minutes' flying time from Middleton St George and safety.

In the early afternoon of Sunday 6 October the crews filed into the briefing room to find out where they would be heading that evening. There was always a certain tension in the air when the curtain was pulled back to reveal the target and route, and this occasion was no different. The red ribbon this time led to Dortmund, which everybody knew was no soft target. The whole airfield was buzzing with activity as men and women worked hard to make ready a 'maximum effort' force of twenty-three Lancasters from 428 Squadron and twenty-two from 419 Squadron. Indeed, it was 6 Group's biggest effort of the war, launching no fewer than 293 bombers into the night sky over Germany. Another milestone was reached when U for Uncle, flown by Flg Off P.D. Griffiths, lifted off the runway; it was 419 Squadron's 3,000th operational sortie of the war. Many of Middleton's aircraft carried a high percentage of incendiaries and it was reported that in the clear conditions individual streets could be clearly distinguished by the crews in the light of the raging fires below. Dortmund suffered a heavy blow that night, with great swathes of the city being reduced to rubble. Nevertheless, the flak and searchlight batteries were still putting up a very active defence, damaging a number of aircraft, and night-fighters were observed operating in considerable numbers.

Flt Lt J. Anderson found his 419 Squadron Lancaster coned by searchlights for 5 minutes in spite of pulling every stunt in the book to shake them off. Shortly after, he was obliged to put his aircraft through its aerobatic paces again after brief encounters with first an Fw190 and then a Ju88. Flg Off G.R. Pauli of 428 Squadron was just one minute away from his 20:25 attack time when his mid-upper gunner, Sgt W. Harper, spotted an Me410 streaking in from the starboard quarter above. Pauli immediately began to corkscrew and Harper and rear gunner Sgt A.E. Scott loosed off over 200 rounds at the night-fighter, forcing it to break off the attack and look for easier prey elsewhere in the crowded sky. Many of the crews landed away from home but at least all made it back safely.

A few nights later Flt Lt J. Anderson, no stranger to dire straits, once again brought his Lancaster home bearing the deep scars of battle. P for Peter was hit by flak on the run-in to Bochum, causing severe damage to the electrical system and H2S and putting both turrets out of action. To cap it all, the battered electrical system decided to switch the navigational lights on and resisted all attempts to turn them off, thereby inviting attack from all and sundry. No sooner had the bombs been released than a Ju88 tore in with its guns and cannon blazing. Anderson shoved the Lancaster's nose down and headed for the cloud below and succeeded in shaking off his assailant. Nevertheless, the crew of P for Peter had to endure a further four brief but terrifying attacks before making it home. Daylight revealed the true extent of the punishment P for Peter had taken: incredulous ground crews logged no fewer than 167 distinct holes in the Lancaster's wings and fuselage. The mental strain placed on crews by such events, exacerbated by the knowledge that they would have to do it all again and again, was immense and it is remarkable just how well the overwhelming majority of aircrew stood up to such a punishing routine.

There came a slight break in operations and the crews had a little time to relax, and in spite of the lousy weather life on the station had its moments. Quite a crowd, for example, rapidly assembled on the 12th to watch a Wellington from 82 OTU drop in to make an emergency landing. Plt Off L. Morrison had been on a routine training sortie over the North Sea when one engine unexpectedly spluttered to a standstill. Anthony Sarson, the WAG on board, takes up the story:

> As we also had no brakes or flaps, the crew took up crash-landing stations and, as the skipper hadn't had instruction on single-engine landings, he kept the speed up to make sure we made the runway at Middleton St George. Our tail-wheel never did touch the runway and we went through the barbed wire entanglement and on out into a newly ploughed farmer's field. We had arrived on a special day. The station was having a Victory Loan dance that evening and after the dance I spent two hours in the control tower chatting with the WAAFs on duty.

It could easily have been so different.

The following day saw an attack on Duisburg scheduled then scrubbed, but an attack timed for just after first light on the 14th did go ahead. This enormous operation, codenamed Hurricane, was organised and executed in conjunction with the US Eighth Air Force and was intended to demonstrate to the people of the Ruhr the air superiority and massive striking capacity of the Allied bomber force. A total of 1,013 British bombers were sent to blast Duisburg, and shortly afterwards a similar number of American bombers pounded Cologne.

As 428 Squadron navigator Ron Cassels recalls:

> We had barely got to bed on the night of the 13th when we were awakened and told there was a navigation briefing at 01:00 hours, meals at 02:00 and main briefing at 03:00. There was a certain amount of grumbling as to how long we would be up until it was scrubbed. But it didn't get scrubbed and 428 Squadron sent twenty-two Lancasters to attack the rail yards and docks at Duisburg. We were off at 06:04, and our bombing time was 08:48, three minutes after the raid had started.

It was not an easy journey, as the crews had to cope with stronger than expected winds of 80 knots and heavy icing, with the temperature at the bombing height of 21,000ft being 'minus 46°C'. To cap it all, the visibility, even in daylight, was dreadful as a layer of thick cloud all but blocked any view of the ground 4 miles below, compelling the Master Bomber to give the order 'Free Hand', instructing the crews to bomb wherever they could locate in Duisburg.

Although there was little in the way of fighter intervention, a massive barrage of predicted heavy flak greeted the bombers, causing damage to several of the aircraft based at Middleton St George. For example, 419 Squadron's V for Victor, under the command of Plt Off Mansfield, suffered severe damage, forcing Mansfield to put down at Woodbridge. His mid-upper gunner, Sgt G.E. Norell, was immediately taken to hospital in Ipswich with a compound fracture in his right arm and shrapnel wounds. His squadron colleague Flg Off A.M. Roy also enjoyed a lucky escape, sadly not one shared by the rest of his crew. C for Charlie was on its run-in when there was a burst of flak just ahead of the bomber, then, as Roy later recalled, a second flak shell exploded at the starboard wing tip, knocking a piece off the wing, holing the aileron and setting both the starboard engines on fire. The aircraft shuddered as if stalling and dropped away in a spiral dive to starboard. . . . The crew was ordered over the intercom to bale out. I believe the starboard wing tank exploded. I was apparently blown out of the aircraft. Came to about 5–6,000ft and pulled the chute ring. I do not remember hitting the ground but when I came to again there were flak gunners around me.

There were no survivors from the loss of 428 Squadron's NA-T, flown by Flt Lt W.H. Janney. Ron Cassels watched what happened to the Lancaster, which was 'about 100 yards to our right and just above us. Just as they opened the bomb doors the aircraft exploded and disappeared. They must have received a direct hit which exploded the cookie. They certainly never knew what happened.'

The inhabitants of Duisburg were in for a further shock that day. The weary crews, who had been up all night, began landing at Middleton a little after midday to be greeted by the news that there was to be a navigator's briefing at 14:00 hours and a general briefing an hour after that. At these briefings it was announced that they would be going back to Duisburg that evening to finish off the job properly; over a thousand bombers were dispatched to see that it was. The hard-working ground crews were pushed to the limit to turn their aerial charges around but by that evening they had added a total of forty aircraft to Bomber Command's Order of Battle. This time the crews were faced with far more benign flying conditions and well-broken cloud allowed accurate marking of the city by the PFF. The cumulative effects of having 9,000 tons of bombs exploding and burning in the city in one day were immense. Crews reported an area 3 square miles in size burning out of control and visible for up to 200 miles on the return journey. The experienced Sqn Ldr McGuffin, an original Mooseman now on his second tour, rated it as 'the best attack ever seen' and most of the comments recorded by the crews, bone-weary as they were, followed in much the same enthusiastic vein. All of the Middleton St George aircraft returned safely in spite of the still active flak defences.

The shattered crews shuffled off to their beds, many of them having completed two major operations, tough ones at that, within the previous 30 hours. Many were forcibly awoken far earlier than they expected and given the news that ops were on again that night. Five Lancasters from 419 Squadron and ten from 428 Squadron were scheduled to carry out what was to be Bomber Command's final major attack of the war on the port of Wilhelmshaven. Neither 419 nor 428 Squadron suffered any losses that night, though the crews were less than pleased to be diverted to RAF Tempsford on their return on account of fog closing down their home station.

On 23 October Harris sent his bombers back to one of the most frequently attacked targets, the industrial city of Essen. There had not been a major raid on the city for over six months and Harris was keen to make sure that any industrial recovery was nipped in the bud. To ensure that this was the case, Bomber Command dispatched 1,055 heavy bombers, the largest total sent in a single attack during the war to that date. Between them 419 and 428 Squadrons provided a total of forty-three Lancasters for the attacking force, which had to endure dreadful flying conditions en route, encountering thick icing, heavy rain and massive electrical storms, with St Elmo's Fire putting on a spectacular pyrotechnic display for the crews. Upon their arrival over the target, the crews were disappointed to discover that the city was protected by an impenetrable shield of cloud and industrial murk. Once again, the PFF had to fall back on Wanganui sky marking, which, although well backed up, appeared a little scattered. Even so, the 4,500 tons of mainly high explosive offloaded on Essen caused massive damage; almost 1,500 buildings were reported as destroyed or damaged and 662 people lost their lives. As confirmation of just how much the balance of the air offensive had altered over the previous few months, it should be noted that Bomber Command lost just eight aircraft to the famed Ruhr defences on this occasion. Unfortunately one of them belonged to 419 Squadron, in the hands of the A Flight commander, Sqn Ldr W. McGuffin, an experienced pilot who was well into his second tour. Whatever the cause of the Lancaster's demise, there were no survivors.

A follow-up raid on Essen the next day was scrubbed early on but a daylight raid on the city the following day went ahead. The smaller force of 771 aircraft was due over the target in late afternoon but the daylight made little difference as cloud conditions remained very helpful to the enemy. There were two separate designated aiming points, J and G, though in practice the sky marking was not sufficiently accurate to be able to distinguish very well between the two. In fact the attack proved very successful and effectively dealt the death blows to Essen as a significant industrial centre; Krupps, for example, was badly hit and reduced to a state of virtual paralysis and several sections of it did not make any further contribution to Germany's war effort. Although the flak defences made a brave showing, they too had passed their peak efficiency and only four bombers were lost. By a further misfortune one belonged to 428 Squadron, that of Flg Off F.S. Raftery, an American serving in the RCAF, which was brought down over the city.

Cologne was the next city to be hammered. As the eighteen aircraft from each squadron lined up ready to take off and join the other 700 or so aircraft in the bomber stream, the weather seemed marginal at best and the meteorological reports were predicting wall-to-wall cloud over the already hard-hit city. They were right. As the two waves of bombers roared in, many of the crews were unable to locate any PFF markers at all in the murk below. To make matters even trickier, the Master Bomber was inaudible to many crews. Nevertheless, a dull red glow was plainly visible beneath the cloud and most did all they could, piling their capacity loads into the fires below; smoke from the inferno that was Cologne was spotted rising up in towering columns to 20,000ft. Enormous damage was caused and well over 2,000 buildings and premises were recorded by German officials as being damaged or destroyed. Some 630 residents lost their lives that night. In spite of the pounding, Cologne could still mount a vigorous defence and a large amount of predicted heavy flak put up in a loose barrage hounded the bombers all through the attack. This was almost certainly responsible for bringing down the Lancaster piloted by Flt Lt A.N. Nelligan a few miles from the city. There were no survivors.

Two days later the crews assembled at briefing to be told that their target would once again be Cologne. Twenty Lancasters from each squadron provided only a small part of the massive 900-plus bomber force, intended to deliver around 4,000 tons of high explosives and incendiaries on to a different area of the still-smouldering city. Indeed, 6 Group had chosen to sacrifice fuel for bombs and provision was made from the outset for the aircraft to land away from home in southern England. Initially the Lancasters, struggling to gain height, met with potentially lethal problems with ice but once they had climbed up through the thick cloud, the night was as clear as a bell. This enabled the crews to enjoy the rare sight of the other bombers bathed in strong moonlight and silhouetted against the snowy white clouds. All on board spent several tense hours anxiously scanning the sky for prowling fighters and were more than a little relieved when the Luftwaffe failed to put in a significant appearance. However, Flt Lt Bell's 419 Squadron crew did report having observed 'about six jet-propelled aircraft just short of the battle line, travelling in the direction of the bomber stream'; fortunately these did not come into action against the men of 419 and 428 Squadrons.

In spite of the heavy flak barrage, the PFF markers were well concentrated and the Main Force had little difficulty in dropping their loads in and around them. Much of the bombing was centred on the residential suburbs, and in some districts these were all but razed to the ground, dehousing and disrupting the lives of many essential industrial workers. Amazingly the Command did not lose a single aircraft in the attack. Within 24 hours Cologne was pounded heavily again but the Middleton squadrons were not involved.

Both 419 and 428 Squadrons had operated at record levels in terms of numbers and serviceability during October, often putting more than forty aircraft on to the Order of Battle. It had been a hard month for those men and women who laboured selflessly to support the aircrew in their vital and more glamorous work. The events of 27/28 October are typical of the pressures they worked under. Operations were declared on for the 27th and the station swung into action to get ready in time; briefings were prepared and held, thirty-two aircraft were checked and bombed-up, and a thousand and one other tasks carried out – only to receive an order in the late afternoon calling the whole thing off. The rest of the day was spent undoing their work. At 10:00 on the 28th orders were received to have eighteen Lancasters from each squadron ready for take-off by 11:30 hours. Separate briefings were rapidly prepared for all trades within the aircrew while outside the ground crews worked frantically to meet the deadline. Shortly before 11:30 orders were received putting back the take-off time, initially by some 70 minutes, enabling all involved to catch their breath and grab a sandwich and a mug of tea. Little wonder that the official record comments on 'an exceptionally fine effort on the part of the ground crews'.

Both squadrons based at Middleton St George put up nineteen aircraft for take-off shortly after 17:00 hours on 1 November, bound for Oberhausen. As the Lancasters climbed higher into the night sky many experienced severe icing and met with unexpectedly strong tail-winds that pushed them on to the target area well ahead of schedule. The Luftwaffe responded to this attack more vigorously than it had to others that autumn and several combats were reported; one of these involved U for Uncle of 419 Squadron flown by Flg Off R. Cox.

At 20:35 the Lancaster, flying straight and level at 20,500ft, had just dropped its load when shrapnel from a near-miss damaged the mid-upper turret and punctured both main tyres. Seven minutes later the Lancaster shuddered as cannon shells and machine-gun bullets

Armourers prepare small bomb containers for loading into a 419 Squadron Halifax. In the background can be seen a long-range fuel tank, which was fitted into the forward section of the bomb bay. This suggests a distant target for the night ahead – perhaps Berlin. *(Author)*

from an Fw190 riddled the fuselage, shot up the intercom and hydraulic systems and knocked out the port inner engine. The explosion of another shell bodily blew Sgt J. Wilkins, the mid-upper gunner, clean out of his turret, dumping him unceremoniously on the floor below, shaken but unhurt. Cox immediately corkscrewed starboard and the rear gunner, Flt Sgt R.A. Toane, gamely returned fire, even although he was almost blinded by the blood streaming down his face from a head wound and was hampered by wounds to his arm and leg. Nevertheless, the damage had been done. A fire had broken out behind the pilot's seat and it was only put out with considerable difficulty by the W/Op, Flg Off L.W. Sitlington, and the navigator, Flg Off S.B. Lindsay, both of whom had been wounded and suffered burns. As the stricken bomber limped across the Belgian coast, the starboard inner engine packed up, forcing Cox to turn inland once more with a view to crash-landing on land rather than in the sea. Before he could find a suitable place to put down, the port inner engine spluttered back to life and Cox swung the Lancaster westward once more and headed out over the North Sea. Without the benefit of navigational aids, Lindsay succeeded in guiding his skipper to Manston, the nearest emergency airfield. The three wounded men were immediately taken to hospital for treatment. Cox, Lindsay and Sitlington were later awarded the DFC for their skill and determination and Toane the DFM for his.

The following night saw Bomber Command assemble a force just eight aircraft shy of a thousand to pound Düsseldorf, in what turned out to be the city's final major raid of the war. As the vast armada approached the city in mid-evening, it was met with an intense barrage of predicted heavy flak, supported by about fifty searchlights. To add to this lethal pyrotechnic display, prowling night-fighters released their flares above the bomber stream to create a real-life Dante's inferno. The bombers ploughed on to find Düsseldorf cloud-free and hidden by nothing more than a light industrial haze. The northern part of the city took the brunt of the massive bombardment and over 5,000 houses were destroyed or damaged, along with 25 industrial premises; at least 678 people lost their lives and more than 1,000 were injured. Sadly, nineteen bombers failed to return, one of which belonged to 428 Squadron. There were no survivors when Flg Off J. Holtze's Lancaster came down in Germany, most probably a victim of the heavy flak over the city.

Two nights later, on 4 November, thirty-two bombers from Middleton St George took to the already dark skies a little after 17:00 hours, bound, along with more than 700 others, for the industrial town of Bochum. The crews realised that it was going to be a hard night when the first clashes with the Luftwaffe took place only a few miles out into the North Sea. Although neither 419 nor 428 Squadron lost any crews on this sortie, this was achieved only by the grace of God, as 419 Squadron's E for Easy, under the command of Flg Off L.A. Blaney, came under heavy attack first by an Me110 and then, just seconds later, by an Me109. The Me110 opened fire from the port quarter at 400 yards, trading blows with rear gunner Flt Sgt D.M. Lanchot until cannon shells wrecked his turret and wounded him in the face and arm. The Me109 bored in from starboard, opening fire at just 250 yards, trading shots this time with Sgt R. Altham in the mid-upper turret. While strikes were seen on both German aircraft, it was clearly the Lancaster that came off worst in the encounter, sustaining severe damage to the starboard wing, elevators and tail unit. Fortunately, there were no more attacks and Blaney managed to reach the English coast, setting the bomber down at Woodbridge. Lanchot, who had remained vigilant at his post throughout, in spite of his wounds, was awarded a DFM.

There was also cause for celebration in 428 Squadron when Ben Rakus, the rear gunner in Plt Off Walker's crew, was officially credited with shooting down an Me262 fighter, the first such claim made within the squadron. Walker recalled:

An Me262 was spotted by the W/Op off to one side and above at a range of about 1,200 yards. It looked like a blot trailing vapour and according to our rear gunner Ben Rakus it was moving faster than anything he had ever seen. Ben gave me the order to corkscrew and the jet shot over to our other side before closing in to 500 yards. We took further evasive action while Ben went to work with his guns hitting the jet along the fuselage and wings, giving it another burst as it peeled over and dived towards the ground, where several crew members saw it explode.

The attack itself went very well, with mostly clear skies allowing clearly visible and accurate marking and some visual identification of the river and built-up areas. As a result the attack was both concentrated and devastating, leaving an area of 2 square miles blazing furiously. The glow of the flames was visible for the best part of 100 miles. In this, the last major raid on the town during the war, in excess of 4,000 buildings and industrial premises were destroyed or damaged and almost 1,000 residents killed. The Battle of Germany was on with a vengeance.

A little over 24 hours later each squadron based at Middleton St George was preparing to dispatch sixteen aircraft on a daylight raid on the Nordstern synthetic oil plant at Gelsenkirchen, 7 miles north-east of Essen. As the station log records, 60mph winds and winter conditions made this task neither easy nor pleasant: 'Bombing-up in rain and high wind all night, conditions at their very worst for the men, who did an excellent job.' There were no losses among the Middleton aircraft that night, although Plt Off Noel's 428 Squadron Lancaster came as close to becoming a 'loss' as ever one could without actually being lost. Ron Cassels, the navigator in the crew, tells the story:

> We did have a good scare because of the blind bombing. Bill reported an aircraft with bomb doors open, directly above us. As he talked, they dropped their bomb-load which straddled us; the 4,000lb cookie went down our starboard rear and the string of six 1,000 and six 500 pounders passed on our port bow. We were unable to identify the aircraft. We wondered how often this happened at night when it was too dark to see the bombs going past or see the other aircraft.

On the afternoon of 16 November it was back to supporting the war on the ground with fifteen bombers from each squadron joining over 1,150 others to attack three towns, Düren, Heinsburg and Jülich, in support of the US First and Ninth Armies; a little later another 1,239 American bombers blasted the same areas, effectively completing the absolute destruction of the three towns and severing the German lines of supply and communication. Both 419 and 428 Squadrons were assigned to Jülich and the crews, mindful of the tragic results of some of the army support operations carried out in Normandy, were delighted and relieved to find the cloud over the target area well broken so that they could identify the target visually. An accurate and concentrated display of marking, combined with crisp instructions from the Master Bomber, made for a devastating demonstration of precision bombing. Unfortunately the US attack was far less successful, as the tanks and infantry found the waterlogged ground heavy going and the advance quickly foundered and petered out.

Whenever possible between operations, various test flights and training exercises were carried out. One such exercise, on 24 November, ended in tragedy. Y for Yoke, under the command of Flg Off R.G. Mansfield, had taken off in the late afternoon to carry out a cross-country exercise, and at 18:12 hours was contacted by RT and instructed to carry on to the Bradbury Bombing Range to execute a practice attack. At 19:15 the sergeant in charge of the bombing range reported seeing a 'great flash' and said that Y for Yoke had not yet arrived. The wreckage of the Lancaster was found at Sands Farm near Sedgefield in County Durham. Jean Green, a WAAF driver stationed at Middleton St George, played a very poignant role in the sad events. She remembered 'joking and larking with them' when she took them to the plane before they took off, and, once the crash had been reported:

> I drove there in a Jeep, I couldn't drive fast enough, we hurtled through on the roads. When we got there I had to stay in the Jeep but the plane was still blazing and the whole sky was lit up. The armoury officer was very concerned because of the bomb dump at

Bradbury. He said that if they didn't get the fire under control and the Bradbury bomb dump went up there wouldn't be any of Sedgefield left.

The 20-year-old WAAF was sent back to the station to collect a lorry to pick up the bodies.

When I got back with the lorry, stretchers and flags, they opened the gates and I was allowed on to the site. They brought the six bodies (the seventh was never recovered), covered with flags, and put them in the vehicle. I then had to take them to the morgue and I cried all the way back. They were lovely boys. I got 24 hours' leave after that and I went home to bed and just slept.

All the crew were well known at Middleton St George as they had been with 419 Squadron for some time and had completed over twenty sorties. Their loss, so close to home, hit everyone hard. By a cruel irony notice of the award of a DFC to Plt Off Mansfield for bravery on the recent attack on Duisburg came through two days later. A post-crash investigation revealed that there had been a fire on board prior to the crash but the cause was not pinpointed. A memorial service, attended by Col J. David OMM, CD of the Canadian Air Force, several veterans of 419 Squadron and a couple of hundred local people, was held in St Edmund's Church, Sedgefield, on 19 June 1994. Four Canadian Air Force fighters made a fly-past in honour of the five Canadians, one American and one British airmen who died that midwinter night.

An oil target, the refinery at Castrop Rauxel, and a transportation target, the railway yards at Neuss, on the western edge of the Ruhr, were attacked in between spells of bad weather. The final attack of the month came on its last day. The crews were awoken at the unearthly time of 02:30 hours to allow for the various briefings and necessary preparations for a 07:30 hours take-off. The crews were actually in their aircraft ready and waiting when the order came through calling off the operation. Having screwed up their courage and prepared themselves mentally for the ordeal to come, the young men were usually none too pleased when this sort of thing happened. They were even less happy a couple of hours later when briefings were called for 13:00 hours. The target was Duisburg. The take-off did not go smoothly. KB744, second in line to take off, bogged down en route to the start line, having run off the hard track. It required frantic activity on the part of the ground crews to drag it back on to the runway in time for it and the rest of the force to take off. It was an inauspicious start for crews who were already tired and feeling the pressure. By the time the aircraft crossed the enemy coast they were bathed in bright moonlight and, feeling rather vulnerable, the crews keenly scanned the skies for night-fighter activity, all the time expecting the worst. However, apart from some tell-tale vapour trails high above, the armada attracted little attention and made it to the target without interference. The city was entirely hidden beneath an impenetrable layer of cloud when the bombers arrived a little after 20:00 hours, necessitating the use of sky markers, this time red flares with yellow stars, giving the Germans little chance of deploying dummy markers. A large dull red glow gradually spread across the city beneath the cloud, leading 6 Group records to conclude: 'All crews believe the attack to be successful, basing their claim on the very good concentration of aircraft on the bomb run, the good marking and the resulting explosions and fire.'

Keen to carry out their orders fully, Flg Off C.D.P. Williams and his bomb aimer Flt Sgt S.M.K. Light had to improvise when an electrical failure robbed them of the use of the intercom and bomb sight just before the crucial moment. Standing by the jettison toggle, the only means of releasing the bomb-load, Light was unable to see outside the aircraft, so when Williams, peering out of the cockpit, judged the aircraft to be over the target area, he gesticulated wildly with his arm as a signal for Light to pull the toggle. The results of this crude bomb aiming are not known but it was the best solution possible in the dangerous and hostile skies over the target.

December began operationally on the night of the 2nd when 419 and 428 Squadrons contributed fifteen aircraft each to a 500-plus force sent to attack Hagen in the Ruhr Valley. The weather was dire throughout and posed a far greater danger to the bombers than either the spasmodic flak or the few night-fighters bold enough to brave the conditions of 10/10ths cumulonimbus cloud billowing up as far as 18,000ft. The accompanying heavy icing caused serious problems. Indeed, 419 Squadron's E for Easy, under the command of Flg Off B.D. Hyndman, almost instantly iced up at one point, resulting in a rapid loss in altitude, falling from 16,000 to 3,000ft, at which point the pilot managed to regain control as the ice broke away, bashing noisily into the fuselage. His colleague Flg Off F.G. Dawson made the final bombing run on three engines, having lost the port outer to problems caused by the icing.

The icing was also responsible for the loss of 428 Squadron's O for Oboe, one of only two aircraft lost in the attack. Not far into France, the pilot, Flg Off Bob Laturner, successfully evaded a brief attack made by an Me410 before encountering freezing rain, which compounded the rapidly forming icing. Laturner quickly realised that the heavily laden Lancaster would not remain airborne for long and, as gunner Sgt Thomas Walton remembers, he shouted the order, 'Emergency jump . . . jump!' Walton himself recalls working frantically to take down the flight engineer's seat in order to bale out more easily. The engineer, Sgt M. Hempseed RAF, and the navigator, Flg Off M.S. Sucharov, lost their lives but the others landed near Le Havre and were back in Britain within three days. In the meantime, Laturner had managed to locate an airfield and chose to try to land the ponderous Lancaster, still fully loaded with fuel, a 4,000lb cookie and eleven 500lb bombs. As the wheels touched down they buckled and gave way, sending the Lancaster skidding along at 100mph in a cacophony of tortured metal and sparks. Amazingly, there was no fire and Laturner emerged with nothing more than a cut forehead.

Most of the crews were diverted on their return to Britain, which was not usually a popular occurrence. However, this time Ron Cassels and his 428 Squadron crew found themselves on the USAAF's B-17 base at Mendlesham, where they were assigned beds, issued with full personal kit and served a meal of steak and hash browns, washed down by fresh orange juice – luxuries unknown in wartime Britain. They were not too disappointed when repairs to their flak-damaged Lancaster were judged to need a couple of days to complete.

Two nights later the weather was scarcely better for the thirty-two aircraft that took off from Middleton St George bound for Karlsruhe. An unusual feature of the attack was, for the

A pilot and navigator check their load of 500lb general purpose bombs destined for a target in the Ruhr in the winter of 1944. The H2S dome is visible to the rear of the bomb bay. *(Department of National Defence PL 40683)*

first time since March 1942, the inclusion of bumph, or propaganda leaflets, among the general bomb-load. Their effect is unknown but ACM Harris was reported to believe that such leaflets, far from undermining the enemy's morale, were a positive bonus to the Germans, supplying them with a free and much-needed source of toilet paper. The following night it was the turn of the marshalling yards in Soest. The flying conditions en route were dreadful, as 419 Squadron's Flg Off Anderson reported: 'At briefing Met. was known to be very poor but we never realised that weather conditions like those we flew through could exist. We flew nearly the whole trip through stratus and cu-nim clouds and had several near collisions.' Indeed, there was more than near-misses: Flt Lt M.A. Shewfelt and his 428 Squadron crew were lost when their aircraft collided with one from 426 Squadron near Rugby. The fully loaded bombers exploded on impact with the ground, leaving no chance for survivors.

The remainder pressed on, unaware of the tragedy, and found that conditions improved markedly over the target, which Flg Off Beggs of 419 Squadron described as 'a glowing mass of molten lead', visible from the air 100 miles away. Flg Off Anderson reported: 'we encountered heavy flak in both barrage and unseen predicted form. Our instruments were icing up and we sustained major air frame damage to the extent of 17 large holes . . . returned to base on three engines, the port inner having been damaged by flak.'

The weather, still the Command's Achilles heel, was to play a key role in the next operation, an attack on Osnabruck's railway yards. The crews once again faced the towering cumulonimbus masses, rising right up to their average flying altitude of 21,000ft. Flg Off Anderson again made a detailed comment in his report: 'Those were six and a half hours of the worst flying weather I have ever experienced. From base we climbed up to 23,000ft, trying in vain to avoid heavy icing cloud that covered England and the Continent. We iced up badly and the stuff made a weird sound as it was flung off the prop tips and hit the fuselage. Flew all the way there and back on instruments.' It is an indication of the determination of the crews involved that only one from Middleton St George returned early and then only when the pilot, Flt Lt D.B. Hunter, lost the use of all his instruments en route to the target; it was only with great difficulty that he made it home safely. The flak defences were active and there was ample evidence of night-fighter combats as far west as the Dutch coast. Ron Cassels, a navigator with 428 Squadron, and his crew noted tracers flashing through the sky around them. His pilot

decided no one was going to attack us from below and kept going down. It was very dark and thus we were flying low level on instruments. At the Zuyder Zee we were so low that I went forward to lend another pair of eyes to watch for windmills. We were bucking a 60-knot head-wind so it seemed to take forever to reach the North Sea. All the way, Jack [rear gunner] kept reporting air-to-air tracer and aircraft blowing up.

In fact just eight bombers were lost from the 453 taking part, though many others suffered damage.

No more operations were carried out from Middleton St George for the next nine days, although operations were planned, mounted and scrubbed on no fewer than six of the days.

This meant a continuation of the gruelling work rate endured by the ground crews, working in such harsh winter conditions that rum was issued to sustain the men. The air crew too were unable to relax and it was almost a relief when the attack on the IG Farben synthetic oil and chemical works near Ludwigshafen actually went ahead. Unusually for that time of the year, the conditions over the target were excellent and the crews could see a heaving carpet of every conceivable hue far below as each Lancaster added its 12,000lb load, shattering the works.

The flak over the city was ferocious but the closest shave of the day came from a most unexpected source. At around 18:45 hours 419 Squadron's J for Jig, skippered by Sqn Ldr C.M. Black, came under fire from a B-17 Flying Fortress. When it was first spotted, the B-17, an unusual aircraft to find in the area at night, was a little above and to the port of the Lancaster but gradually it moved to starboard until it was almost dead ahead. Just as Black lifted the Lancaster's nose to avoid its slipstream, the B-17 opened up from its starboard waist and rear gun positions. Black immediately climbed hard to port but was unable to avoid the hail of 0.5in bullets that slammed into the Lancaster's nose and badly shredded Flt Sgt B.L. McKinnon's right foot. The B-17 was then swallowed up by the darkness and its hostile action was never satisfactorily explained. Black's night continued to get worse as his Lancaster was badly buffeted by flak several miles west of the target. He was mightily relieved when he eventually crossed the English coast and put his battered aircraft down on the emergency runway at Woodbridge. McKinnon was immediately taken to the Ipswich and East Suffolk Hospital, where he remained on the 'dangerously ill' list for the best part of a week.

The weather remained at its awful worst, with heavy clouds, strong winds and electrical storms. Nevertheless, Bomber Command had little option but to operate as best it could for a few days earlier Field Marshal von Rundstedt had unleashed Germany's last major offensive of the war, successfully driving the American forces back through the Ardennes region of Belgium. Bomber Command was called upon to provide both direct tactical and strategic support for the ground forces. The thirty-two Lancasters from 419 and 428 Squadrons formed almost a quarter of the force dispatched to attack the Nippes marshalling yards at Cologne, which were being used to move supplies in support of the German offensive. The crews did not hold out much hope for a successful raid as they ploughed through acres of storm clouds, often able to see little from their wet, misted and iced cockpits and turrets; they were right. Stronger than expected winds helped to fragment the attacking force and many of the crews could not locate any markers, compelling them to rely on ETA or simply to add their bomb-loads on to the dull glow below, barely visible through the cloud. Nevertheless, several large explosions were noted and a number of bombs did hit the railway yards, destroying areas of track, a repair facility and around 40 wagons.

In spite of it being the festive season, orders came through for an attack to be mounted on Lohausen airfield near Düsseldorf on Christmas Eve. The crews were awoken at 05:00 hours and, as the weather was cold, damp, pitch black and very very foggy, they expected the operation to be scrubbed at any minute. To their amazement it was not, even though the pilots had to be guided around the taxiways by ground crews. All along both edges of the runway dozens of men were frantically painting thick white lines to act as markers for the pilots. It required a great act of faith to release the brakes and hurtle down the runway, heading with increasing speed into a white mass of cotton wool. However, almost as soon as the heavily laden Lancasters hauled themselves into the air, the crews found themselves bathed in bright sunshine and looking out at a dazzling blue sky.

The bombers, flying in a loose 'gaggle' formation, had no difficulties in locating and identifying the airfield visually. The red and green TIs were seen to fall directly on target and the various hangers, workshops, runways and grass areas were soon smothered beneath tons of high explosive which kicked up dust and debris far into the air. Flg Off Vatne of 419 Squadron summed up the attack succinctly in his report: 'no aerodrome there now'. Nevertheless, the target was no pushover and the flak crews in their turn made the most of the clear midday conditions, throwing up a tremendous barrage. Many of the bombers sustained flak damage and three bombers were lost over the target, one of which was J for Jig from 419 Squadron. It was over the airfield when a shell exploded directly beneath the starboard wing, dislodging the outer engine from its housing and setting fire to the inner one. The pilot, Flg Off T.H. Cowan, immediately realised that the stricken Lancaster was doomed and gave the order to bale out. The crew, apart from the mid-upper gunner, Sgt F. Hector, had baled out when, to his surprise, Cowan managed to gain some sort of control over the aircraft and he and Hector decided to stick with it a little longer in the hope of reaching, or at least going some way towards, Allied-held territory. However, their optimism soon faded and they took to their parachutes over Venlo. All of the crew were captured on landing but Flg Off R.W. Hale was dreadfully unfortunate, being executed later the same day. A postwar investigation failed to establish why or by whom.

The remaining 419 and 428 Squadron aircraft returned safely to British shores and were much annoyed to find themselves ordered to land at bases further south as Middleton St George was still fogged in. Christmas Day barely dawned over the north-east of England, removing from the disappointed crews the last vestige of hope of spending even part of the day 'at home'. While the official log records the extraordinary kindness shown to many of the stranded crews by the station at which they had landed so unexpectedly, it was not the same for everyone. Ron Cassels of 428 Squadron and his crew ended up at RAF Wethersfield, a Stirling glider-tug station in Essex. As they wearily climbed down from their aircraft, the crew noticed the general lack of activity around the airfield. Their worst fears were confirmed when their driver cheerfully explained that nearly everyone had gone home on leave, with only a skeleton crew left behind to keep it ticking over. The crew did not make it back to Middleton St George until 27 December and were less than thrilled to hear about the wonderful Christmas fayre and celebrations they had missed. Their spirits were raised a little later when their bombing photographs earned them a target token, signed by AVM McEwen himself.

The Christmas spirit did not last long and there was no let-up in the run-up to the end of the year. Orders were received to mount an attack on the railway yards at Opladen, north of Cologne. It cost the lives of two crews, those of Flg Off F. How of 419 Squadron and Flg Off E.W. Page of 428 Squadron, both lost without trace. Then came an evening attack on the Scholven synthetic oil plant near Buer in the northern Ruhr Valley. This cost the lives of all but two of the crews of Flg Off R.A. McVicar and Plt Off R.E. Adams. The next evening, 30 December 1944, both 419 and 428 Squadrons launched fifteen Lancasters to attack the

Kalk-Nord railway yards near Cologne, which was once again smothered beneath thick cloud, forcing the PFF to deploy sky markers on positions located by Gee and Oboe. It was impossible to assess the damage caused at the time but German records show that the yards and surrounding autobahn were thoroughly plastered, causing severe disruption to all forms of transportation in the area. The flak defences were not what they once were but they were still capable of giving the young airmen a terrifyingly rough ride. Ron Cassel's 428 Squadron crew had taken off from Middleton St George at 17:15 and had had a fairly routine flight until 'about 35 minutes before the target we really got peppered with flak. There was no warning and four shells exploded just under the aircraft. The blast tossed the Lanc as if it were a basket ball.' For the next 9 minutes the bomber was bounced around the night sky, buffeted by successive near-misses, until eventually it flew out of range and everything went quiet.

A quick damage check revealed that the H2S set had gone U/S and that one engine was overheating, so it was quickly feathered. Being so close to the target area and not too far behind schedule, the crew elected to press on and successfully attacked the railway yards before turning for home. It was only much later, over England, that the full extent of the damage became apparent as Cassels recounts:

I had to use the biffy [the Elsan toilet] and I started to the back in the dark. I had reached the end of the bomb bay and noticed lights on the floor of the plane. This was most unusual and I stopped to try to figure out where they were coming from. As I watched I suddenly realised it wasn't lights but the moon shining on the tops of the clouds below. There was a huge hole in the bottom of the plane where the H2S scanner was located. The H2S had gone blank because we had left the scanner in Germany. I changed my mind about going to the Elsan and returned forward.

Events took another turn for the worse when another engine began to overheat and had to be feathered, leaving the Lancaster to limp home on just two engines. Having made it back to Middleton St George, they discovered that one of the tyres had also been hit, leaving Norman Noel, the 24-year-old pilot from Cape Breton island, with the heavy responsibility of putting the Lancaster down safely on just two engines and one wheel, still unsure of what other damage it might have sustained. Noel succeeded in controlling the large bomber on its final approach, guiding it to land on its good tyre before the other hit the ground, dug in and caused the aircraft to slew around, quickly coming to rest in the soft grass outfield. Daylight revealed just how good a piece of flying the landing had been for 'there were some big holes in the wings, some of the trim tabs were missing. The starboard elevator was a bare shaft and the rudder was half missing'. In total, the amazed crew counted over 160 holes in the aircraft, including one several feet long and 3 or 4 feet wide where the H2S scanner was supposed to have been. Not surprisingly, Lancaster NA-J never flew on operations again, although it was repaired in time to make the long flight back to Canada with 428 Squadron in June.

This spectacular landing was watched by dozens of men and women, each with their heart in their mouth, and with it Middleton St George's operational year came to an end. While many had hoped not to be still fighting the war by this time, there had been much to be proud of in 1944. The number of operational sorties flown from the station had more than doubled, the tonnage of ordnance dropped had increased similarly, aircraft serviceability rates had improved markedly and losses had more than halved. It was with justifiable pride and pleasure that the young men and women stationed at 64 Base listened to the New Year message from Prime Minister MacKenzie King:

> To officers and other ranks of the Canadian Bomber Group. My warmest congratulations on the occasion of its second anniversary. Canada is very proud of the skill and daring displayed by the Canadian Bomber Group and its magnificent record. I send you the heartfelt good wishes of the Canadian people together with my own personally for continued marked success in the coming year.

Nevertheless, as the men and women of all ranks danced in the NAAFI to the music of the Black Outs band, few gave much thought to the year ahead. If they had, it would have had a most sobering effect: V1s and V2s were still coming down regularly all over England, the ground lost during the unexpected Ardennes offensive was only just beginning to be regained, the crossing of the formidable Rhine was still ahead, German resistance could only be expected to stiffen in defence of their homeland and the Luftwaffe and flak defences were still sufficiently potent to wreak havoc, death and destruction in the skies over Germany. There was clearly still a lot of war to be fought in 1945.

For 419 and 428 Squadrons that fighting began on 2 January when thirty-one Lancasters took off for a long penetration into Germany, the target being the symbolic heart of Nazi Germany, Nuremburg. The huge force encountered little resistance and arrived over the city to find it bathed in moonlight and obscured by nothing more than a light haze. The red and green TIs were clearly visible and the Main Force had no problem in dropping their loads accurately, gradually moving the focus of the attack on the instructions of the Master Bomber. It was, in the parlance of the day, 'a really good prang'. German records show that this estimation was absolutely correct; the city centre was largely destroyed, as were large areas in the south and north-east of the city, and over 400 industrial premises suffered a similar fate, including the MAN engineering works and the Siemens factory. In all some 1,838 people were recorded as being killed in this devastating attack.

None of the Lancasters from 419 and 428 Squadrons met with any problems on the return journey and all was well until 419 Squadron's Z for Zebra entered the circuit over the airfield. As Flt Lt A.G.R. Warner gave instructions for the undercarriage to be lowered, the warning light lit up indicating that only one wheel was down and locked. A careful visual check found nothing amiss and Warner decided to make an ordinary landing, believing the activated warning light to be an electrical malfunction. Everything seemed fine until the last moments before touchdown. Warner takes up the story: 'I think we must have lost the flap on our round-out, because even though we were well above stall speed there was a "clunk" and we sank and hit runway 240 a hell of a smack – the worst landing I ever made.' The bomber bounced magnificently before remaining earthbound but failed to stop before the end of the runway, overrunning by some 50 yards. 'This was my twenty-second op, I was fully familiar with the regulations that a "bogged" aircraft had to wait to be towed away. But I was also aware that we were in direct line with incoming aircraft.' Warner decided to try to get back on to the perimeter track and out of danger but as he swung round his starboard outer propeller made contact with a trench digger parked there by workmen. In seconds Z for Zebra became a blazing inferno and Warner recalls the moment clearly. 'I can remember, as though it just happened, thinking what a helluva way to go, in a fire, sitting on the ground, at your own base.' It did not happen that way and he quickly scrambled out of the aircraft and, together with the rest of his crew, ran as fast as he could towards the ditch the machine had conveniently dug. From the comparative safety of the ditch, they watched the remaining fuel ignite with a huge oomph and a spectacular firework show as the tracers, Verey cartridges and suchlike went off amid the flames. One brave soul, it was reported, climbed into the blazing wreckage in order to rescue any trapped crew members and was somewhat upset to find that he had risked his life for nothing; the crew had been so busy taking cover that they had not noticed him going on board and had therefore had no opportunity to prevent him from doing so. The incident, not in itself such a newsworthy event, received a good deal of publicity as the aircraft involved was KB700, the 'Ruhr Express', the first Canadian-built Lancaster. It was on its 49th operation and due to be retired for posterity upon completion of its 50th sortie.

Hannover was left burning from end to end on 5 January but the attack was far more costly than many of the recent raids, with 31 bombers, or 4.7 per cent of the attacking force, failing

The burnt-out wreckage of KB700 'Ruhr Express' following its collision with some construction equipment upon its return from attacking Ludwigshafen on 3 January 1945. *(Department of National Defence PL 45597)*

Winter 1944–5. Clearing snow and ice from the wings of a Lancaster. Strenuous efforts were made to keep the Middleton St George open and operational at all times. *(Department of National Defence PL 41650)*

to make it home. One of these belonged to 419 Squadron. Plt Off N.D. Mallen and his crew were flying at 20,000ft over the Dutch–German border when at 21:17 hours they came under accurate fire from a four-engined aircraft they immediately identified as a Lancaster. This, as the crew clearly thought they were under attack, corkscrewed and quickly vanished from sight. The damage, however, had already been done. The .303 bullets had smashed into the cockpit area, rendering several of the instruments U/S and, more vitally, into both inner engines which began to stream fuel. Mallen, on only his second operational sortie, hauled the Lancaster round and set course first for Brussels and then for an emergency airfield at Juvincourt. Having made it that far, he was dismayed to find the airfield closed on account of thick fog. More in hope than anything else, he decided to make for Manston but when it became apparent that the Lancaster was not going to make it that far, he ordered his crew to look for any suitable open space they could pick out beneath the patchy cloud. One was soon located and with the crew all at their crash positions, Mallen eased the Lancaster down into a field 2 miles from Guise, near the road to St Quentin. The crash-landing was just that but all of the young men were able to extricate themselves from the wreckage, though four were taken to hospital suffering from cuts, bruises and sprains. Although none of the men ever flew operationally again, the results of this friendly fire incident could have been far worse.

Heavy snowfall on the 8th, 9th and 10th defeated even the best efforts of the available machinery and of a veritable army of men and women to keep the runway open and the station operational. When normal flying resumed, the airfield was busy catching up with its routine test and training flights. One of these took off at 17:49 on the 13th to carry out a cross-country exercise. Plt Off W.S. McMullen and his 428 Squadron crew had almost completed the flight when the Lancaster's port inner engine caught fire. The flames, fanned by the slipstream, quickly spread across the wing, sealing the aircraft's fate, even though it was only a couple of miles from Middleton St George. Passing over Darlington, John Feeley, the mid-upper gunner, recalled his skipper giving the order to bale out, adding, 'It's only me for it. There are thousands below.' As the rest of crew baled out, MacMullen remained at the controls, grimly struggling to keep the bomber in the air long enough to clear the town; he succeeded, the aircraft eventually coming down near a barn at Lingfield Farm.

Mary Waddington who lived on the farm recalled the incident some forty years later: 'I remember being in the kitchen and this big ball of flame came past the window. We saw it coming towards the house and we all rushed further inside.' The first fire engine from Darlington ended up in a ditch, having taken the entrance to the farm too quickly, leaving the second one to contain the blaze as best it could until the RCAF fire crews arrived. The barn burned for several hours. Les Dennis also remembered the event well, telling the *Northern Echo* in 1995:

It was a Saturday night and my wife and I were listening to the radio at home at 55 Lingfield Lane. It must have been about 8.50 p.m. because it was a music hall show hosted by Vic Oliver and he was about to come on as the last turn. We used to see the bombers take off most nights from Goosepool at Middleton St George and hear the droning noise from the air but that night it was such a noise I said to my wife, 'That one must be low.' Next we heard a bang and I went to the back door and saw the plane on fire in the fields. I knew the farmer and never gave it a thought and ran out over the hedge and 100 yards across the field. I was wearing a brand-new pair of brown suede shoes and they were ruined. The wreckage was so close to the farmhouse that the side of the barn caught fire. The front part of the plane just scattered, it was a mass of debris. There were two tail fins and a few yards of fuselage standing absolutely perfect in the ground. The bullets were going off like firecrackers all around but you don't think about the danger. I asked the farmer what I could do and he asked me to get the horses out of the stable. The luckiest thing was there were no bombs on it. Our houses were lightly built government prefabs so there would have been a bit of damage. To this day, I can see the crew coming down in their parachutes, lit up by the flames of the plane, and going to land over towards Middleton St George. There would have been about five of them in echelon.

Indeed, there were and only one, mid-upper gunner Flt Sgt E.D. Dykes, sustained any injury, twisting his ankle. Plt Off William MacMullen, a native of Toronto, did not receive any official recognition of his selfless bravery, but his sacrifice has been honoured by the people of Darlington. Lingfield Lane was renamed MacMullen Road and in May 1986 a large stone memorial was placed near the crash site, commemorating the young Canadian's courageous act.

Councillor J. Anderson on 7 May 1986 unveiling the memorial to Plt Off William McMullen who died while guiding his stricken Lancaster away from the built-up area of Darlington, County Durham, on 13 January 1945. The nearby road is named after him. *(Northern Echo)*

Operations, however, carried on as normal and the following day orders were received to mount an attack on the Leuna synthetic oil refinery at Merseberg, west of Leipzig. As so often happened in winter, a layer of heavy cloud and murk lay over the target like a grey blanket and initial reports as to the success of the first attack were far from encouraging. However, in Albert Speer's postwar interrogation, he rated this raid on Leuna as one of the most damaging of the war. Certainly the importance of the oil refinery was underlined by the ferocious defence put up by both night-fighters and potent flak batteries. Ten aircraft failed to return that night, two of them from 419 Squadron. Flt Lt G.O. Tedford and his crew took off at 18:42. Heading for home at 01:05 hours, the Lancaster was raked from beneath by machine-gun and cannon fire which caused the aircraft to catch fire and break up immediately. The only survivor was the navigator, Flg Off J.Q. Eddy, who later described what happened as he attempted to follow the order to bale out: 'The plane seemed to go out of control and I was tossed around furiously, ending up facing aft, with the "G" very heavy. The Perspex bulge blew out and with much difficulty I pulled myself up to it and jumped out. I landed in trees with a cut over my right eye.'

W for William, piloted by Flg Off N.R. Vatne, was one of the very first aircraft over the Leuna plant and seemed to attract more than its fair share of attention from the flak defences. For several minutes the Lancaster was buffeted by a series of near-misses, with red-hot shards of shrapnel tearing through the aircraft. For a while it looked like they might get away with it until the flight engineer, Sgt B. Mitchell, called out that they were losing fuel from both tanks. Vatne, immediately after the bombing, hauled the bomber round, aiming to get as close to Allied lines as possible. Uncertain as to how great the actual fuel loss was, the crew eagerly ticked off the miles, with each minute in the air bringing them around 3 miles closer to home. However, it gradually became apparent that the fuel supply was dwindling far faster than the number of miles to be covered and Vatne gave the order to bale out. He flew straight and level at 12,000ft as the crew carried out a textbook evacuation, and as Flt Sgt E. Chatwin passed by his skipper he noted that he was making the final preparations for his own departure. The crew came down between Trier and Koblenz, close to but still well on the wrong side of the battle line, and were all quickly rounded up by German troops. For some reason – perhaps he tried to keep the Lancaster in the air for just a few more miles – Vatne failed to make it out of the aircraft and went down with it to his death.

Middleton St George was unusually busy and crowded on 17 January as twenty-eight USAAF B-24 Liberator bombers had been diverted there, and all required refuelling and servicing before they could head south to their base. The ground crews had an extremely busy day, working on aircraft with which they were unfamiliar, outside in midwinter. The station log records that this unexpected work 'placed a severe strain on the servicing sections', but adds with a touch of pride, 'all aircraft were serviced' and departed on time. The Americans were lucky to get away as the weather quickly clamped down, putting an end to flying for several days. By the 20th temperatures had plummeted to just 6°F (–14°C), causing severe problems across the station, especially in the WAAF quarters where all the pipes froze and remained frozen for several days; snow lay an even foot deep across the airfield.

It took another week before conditions improved sufficiently to allow an operation to be mounted. Fourteen aircraft from 419 Squadron, now led by Sqn Ldr M.E. Ferguson following the posting of Wg Cdr Hagerman, on completion of his second tour, to command the Flight Engineers' School at St Athan, and fifteen from 428 Squadron formed part of a massive two-stage assault on Stuttgart. They were to take part in the first stage of the attack, bombing the railway yards at Kornwestheim, a little to the north of the city proper. At the briefing it had been pointed out to the crews that a high degree of accuracy would be necessary in the attack as two Allied POW camps were in the vicinity. As if this was not enough to put the crews on edge, news reached the station just as the briefing was ending that conditions were likely to deteriorate both over the station and over the target. Indeed, shortly after the crews had taken off at 17:40 reports came through that one of 428 Squadron's Lancasters had crashed at Elton Hall, on the outskirts of Stockton on Tees, a few miles away. The crew, led by Plt Off H.L. Clark, had taken off just before 14:30 to carry out a cross-country training exercise but on their return had been unable to locate the airfield in the darkness and midwinter low-level murk. Trying to get beneath the cloud in order to fix their position, the bomber came too low and ploughed into the ground, killing five of the six men on board; the sixth, Flt Sgt Crabb, got away with only a broken femur.

The rest of the crews pressed on towards Stuttgart, anxiously observing the build-up of stratocumulus cloud. To make matters worse, the marking was up to 6 minutes late and then scarce and difficult to pick up, forcing many crews to orbit the area under sporadic fire. Ron Cassels, a navigator with 428 Squadron, describes what his crew did:

It was a bright clear night with scattered clouds and as we approached it was easy to see the target. Just before Mac was going to bomb a cloud drifted across obscuring the target so we went around again. As we did the orbit Wimp [the pilot] asked everybody to watch for aircraft as we left and re-entered the stream of bombers. The same thing happened on our second run and we went around again and as we approached for the third time the target markers burned out so we brought the bombs home.

Several others, acting on the Master Bomber's instructions not to bomb on Gee positioning alone, followed suit. The bombing that did take place was scattered but caused substantial damage to various parts of the city. Sadly 428 Squadron lost Sqn Ldr H.L. Kay, on his first sortie as flight commander, and all but two of his crew.

The rest of the crews made it back to England to be greeted by the news that the Met. reports had got the second part of their forecast right too. All the aircraft were diverted to stations further south, where they stayed for three or four days until the dreadful winter conditions abated sufficiently to allow them to return. Indeed, Middleton St George was a very busy place on 31 January as no fewer than thirty-five B-17s and six B-24s were themselves diverted to the airfield just as it reopened. Although a building to accommodate 280 airmen had only recently been completed, several freezing empty Nissen huts had to be pressed into service to deal with the 356 visiting Americans. The ground crews, mindful of their responsibilities to keep their own squadrons operational, worked round the clock to patch up and refuel the US bombers, dispatching them on time the next day.

For 428 Squadron's Ron Cassels and his crew the mid-evening attack on Ludwigshafen on 1 February was a special one as it was the last operation of their tour. He described their attack:

We were on at H-hour and bombed on Gee and Mac [bomb aimer] could see the glow of the TIs through the clouds and said we were right on. Timing was good, 12 seconds early. On leaving the target we dropped 4,000ft to gain speed and held the speed as long as we could. We weren't worried about gas mileage and really pushed Z for Zombie back to Middleton. We landed after 7 hours and 15 minutes. As were first back the truck was waiting for us and we were out of debriefing before the next plane hit the circuit.

Then it was off to the party to polish off the barrel of beer that they had earlier clubbed together to buy, fervently praying they would still be around to enjoy it. Plt Off D.W. Storm DFM, mid-upper gunner in Flt Lt Halket's crew, was also celebrating that night after being credited with shooting down an Me410 over the blazing target.

Operations were on again the very next day. Owing to the vicissitudes of the weather, the take-off time was postponed no fewer than six times, each occasion adding to the nervous strain on the crews. Shortly after 20:15 hours the twenty-seven bombers began to move along the taxiways and line up at the end of the runway before accelerating hard and gradually climbing into the darkness towards Wiesbaden. The strongest protection for this famous spa town, which had never been bombed before, lay not in the sporadic flak or limited searchlight defences but in the cloud which was banked up in layers to a height of 20,000ft. Little could be ascertained from the air of what was happening 4 miles below but as it turned out the raid caused considerable damage to the town and its railway station.

Losses overall were light but the squadrons based at Middleton St George lost three aircraft that night. The first, 428 Squadron's NA-L, did not make it as far as its Rhineland target but turned for home with serious engine problems. The Lancaster slowly but surely limped westwards, eventually joining the circuit over the station shortly after half past midnight. Struggling to keep the Lancaster steady and under control, Flt Lt V.M. Gadkin began his approach but could not coax the bomber down and overshot the runway. While trying to gain height to go round for another attempt, the unfortunate pilot lost power and control and the bomber came down in fields between Longnewton and Elton, a few miles from the airfield, killing two of the gunners. The second, NA-I, also of 428 Squadron and piloted by Flt Lt D.E. Berry, was lost when it disintegrated over Wiesbaden, presumably as a result of a direct hit by flak. A very similar fate befell 419 Squadron's N for Nan, which had already turned for home when it was hit by an isolated burst of flak. The captain, Plt Off B.W. Martin, immediately gave the order to bale out. Rear gunner Flt Sgt W.J. McTaggart landed only 300 yards from the blazing wreckage and was captured almost at once. Unusually the German troops took him to see the burning remains of the bomber, which had become the funeral pyre of his six friends.

On 7 February orders were received to mount a very popular type of operation, one in direct support of the ground troops. There were two targets that night, the towns of Kleve and Goch, with 419 and 428 Squadrons being assigned to the latter. These towns had been strongly fortified and were believed to be held in force and stood square in the path of Lt Gen Horrocks' XXX Army Corps. At the briefings it was stressed that accuracy was vital, given the nature of the target and the proximity of British and Canadian troops. When the bombers arrived over the target they found it covered by cloud but were surprised when the Master Bomber decided to take advantage of the virtual absence of flak and ordered the crews to descend below the cloud base, which was at just 5,000ft.

The attack opened very well but such was the thick smoke and airborne debris that the Master Bomber had to call off the raid at 22:17 after only 155 of the 464 aircraft had dropped their loads. Nevertheless, considerable damage had been done and two days later each station involved in the attack received a copy of the following message: 'Harris from Crerar. Reports indicate that the very powerful support given to the 1st Canadian Army by Bomber Command on 7/8 February was of usual super quality. Request that you advise all crews of our appreciation.' Fortunately 419 and 428 Squadrons did not lose any aircraft that night, but the Luftwaffe probably did. Plt Off R.S. Grant, flying as rear gunner in 419 Squadron's H for Harry, watched as a Ju88 homed in on and then shot down a Halifax some 2,000ft above before dropping a further 1,000ft to dispatch another. Grant realised that the night-fighter would pass close to his own aircraft and he waited until it came within 200 yards before opening fire. He and the mid-upper gunner, Plt Off R. Andrews, both observed hits on the port engine and wing before the Ju88 broke off in a steep dive. A claim for a damaged was upheld, though both gunners thought it was at least a probable.

Two scheduled attacks on Dortmund were called off but on 13 February orders came through for what has since become the most controversial raid of the war, the attack on Dresden. There was nothing, however, to mark this attack as anything unusual for the crews, except perhaps that the location of the city and the deep penetration it involved increased the risks they faced. Many pages of authoritative books have been devoted to either condemning or affirming the decision to attack Dresden, and perhaps there was no single pressing reason for the attack. However, there is little doubt that in February 1945 the city was a target that had become strategically and politically worthwhile to attack as part of Operation Thunderclap, a joint British and American plan intended to cause overwhelming dislocation and disruption to military, civil and communication facilities in a localised area. Several targets were selected, including Berlin, Leipzig, Chemnitz and Dresden, and it was purely a matter of chance that Dresden was the first to be attacked and that freak conditions, similar to those that occurred in Hamburg in July 1943, conjoined to make the attack so devastating. Devised and approved at the highest levels, even beyond Harris as AOC-in-C Bomber Command, it was for the crews just another night's work in a long and dangerous war.

At Middleton St George the intelligence officer simply revealed the target at the briefing as usual and added that the Soviet Marshal Koniev had called for the attack as the city was being used a military centre. He pointed out that the civil authorities were already under pressure from the military and refugee traffic passing through and that the raid would cause a complete collapse in control, which in turn would aid the Soviet advance. The crews had listened to similar explanations before and paid no more or less attention than usual. The focus of their attention was very much on what was to come for them.

The first attack was due to have been carried out by the USAAF but this was scrubbed on account of bad weather. The weather did not put off 5 Group, which attacked the city some 3 hours before the second wave, which included the aircraft from 419 and 428 Squadrons. The crews had no difficulty in locating the target as the blazing fires were visible from over 60 miles away, drawing in the bombers like a magnet; by the time the second wave left, having dropped their predominantly high explosive, not incendiary, loads, the fires were visible through the patchy cloud over 150 miles away. Many crews reported being able to pick out the streets and buildings by the glare and concluded 'this was the best attack they had ever seen'. The destruction wrought is impossible to quantify, given the subsequent US raids on the 14th and 15th, but it was certainly immense. Flt Sgt F. Bramley gave a typical contemporary view in an interview with Canadian journalist Sqn Ldr Les Powell: 'After the terrific beating, I doubt if it will get up off its knees in time to do Hitler any good. The result was that when we left the fires were more intense than ever. I doubt if many of the Nazis below will need much anti-war education after this is over.' It was a laudable, fully justifiable and pugnacious approach to Bomber Command's offensive.

It is important to note that on the morning after the attack it was considered a totally non-controversial success, remembered by the young crewmen only in as much as something

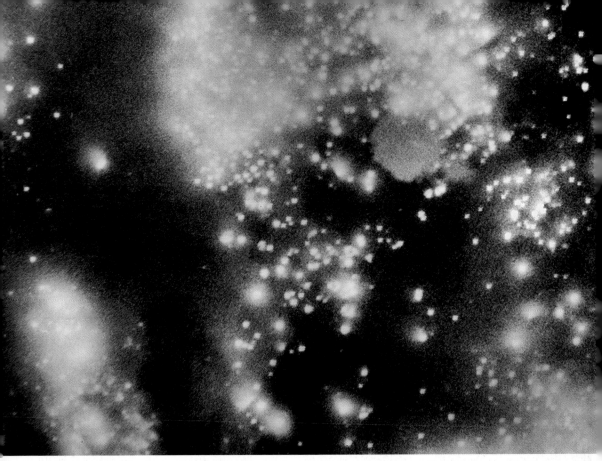

A still from an RAF Film Production Unit film of the attack upon Dresden on 13/14 February 1945. *(Imperial War Museum C 4971)*

unusual had occurred to them. For David Lambroughton of 419 Squadron it had a special significance as it was his first operation:

> Briefing was the high point of suspense prior to take-off. It was usually given by an Intelligence Officer from Group HQ. The target for tonight is Dresden. My first op and what a target! I was second pilot, this being my first operational trip. I learned a bit too. On leaving the city in flames, we headed for the UK. First pilot suggested I take over. OK. Within 15 minutes first pilot noted two bursts of flak following us and said 'to starboard quick'! Sure enough, the third burst of flak exploded on our original track – predicted flak!

Another new skipper, Plt Off J.W. McGregor of 419 Squadron, would remember the night because, short of fuel, he put down at Laon-Anthier airfield. There an A-26 Douglas Invader collided with it, ripping off the Perspex nose. McGregor then endured a brief but blowy trip to Juvincourt, where RAF ground crew quickly straightened out the damage. Bad weather meant it was the 19th before the Lancaster finally made it back to Middleton St George.

Operation Thunderclap continued with another two-stage, 500-plus raid on Chemnitz, some 35 miles south-west of Dresden, on the night of 14 February. Middleton St George contributed nineteen Lancasters, which took off in the late afternoon and set course for the long haul to south-eastern Germany. The attack was nowhere near as effective as the one the previous night, though not for want of trying. Patchy stratocumulus cloud stretched right up to 20,000ft and did much to hamper the bombing, as did below-par marking. None of the bombers based at Middleton St George was lost but 419 Squadron's N for Nan did account for an unidentified twin-engined assailant. Flg Off C.J. Widdlecombe's novice crew spotted a white flare dropped dead astern of their Lancaster and mid-upper gunner Sgt S.E. Kronyak and rear gunner Flg Off W.G. Cotter almost immediately picked up the outline of the fighter only 400 yards away and closing rapidly. Cotter at once gave the instruction to corkscrew starboard and both gunners opened up simultaneously. The fighter did not get a chance to open fire but nose-dived out of sight; the crew observed an explosion on the ground a few seconds later. Their claim was upheld.

Harsh winter weather now forced a break in operations but the station remained busy, especially for the ground crews. In a better patch of weather on 18 February twenty-three Halifaxes from 427 and 429 Squadrons were diverted to Middleton, each requiring servicing and two the replacement of an engine. Working outside, the men toiled hard to finish the work but there was in fact little hurry as the Halifaxes were unable to leave until the weather improved on the 20th. Wg Cdr M.W. Gall, 428 Squadron's CO, had a lucky escape that afternoon when both port engines packed up at 2,000ft shortly after take-off. He managed to

The fires are still burning fiercely in Dresden following the massive attacks of the previous night. *(Imperial War Museum C 4973)*

coax the wallowing Lancaster towards the base but overshot and was brought to an abrupt halt some way beyond the runway by an inconveniently placed clump of mature trees. The crew emerged very shaken but unhurt.

Six hours later, a little after 21:00 hours, twenty-eight heavily laden Lancasters roared down the runway and into the night sky, bound for Dortmund. Conditions were typically dire with heavy stratocumulus cloud smothering the target. A few minutes short of the target Flg Off L.A. Blaney's Lancaster of 419 Squadron was hit in quick succession by two bursts of flak. Blaney immediately gave the order to bale out but the process went far from smoothly. The front hatch initially jammed and it took the combined efforts of three crewmen to shift it before they were able to get out. Two others made it through the rear hatch without any problem but the rear gunner, Flt Sgt R. Althan, could not open the door to his turret as it had frozen solid. It seemed an eternity before he succeeded in prising open the door just wide enough for him to squeeze through but his trials were still not over. As he pushed himself through the narrow gap his right foot became jammed, leaving him dangling upside down from a nose-diving bomber, trailing flames all around him. After a few painful seconds the slipstream tore him free and he was able to parachute to safety, albeit with a mighty sore leg and mild burns. Blaney, like so many pilots before him, was unable to get out in time.

A final attack was made on an oft-visited target, Duisburg, on the night of 21 February. By contrast, the next target for the Middleton squadrons was Pforzheim, which had never been attacked by Bomber Command before. For this raid 419 Squadron contributed thirteen Lancasters and 428 Squadron twelve to the 350-plus force which made its way to the small city, 15 miles south-east of the better-known Karlsruhe. They arrived over the target area at around 20:00 hours and the next 22 minutes must have seemed a volcanic eternity for those below. Crystal clear skies and an unusually low attack height of 7,500–8,500ft gave the crews a panoramic view of the city so that the PFF markers, as accurate as they were, were scarcely necessary. Some 1,825 tons of bombs pounded the city centre and the crew inside the aircraft could actually feel the blast from the 4,000lb cookies exploding beneath them and smell the smoke from the fires below. The crews rated the attack as a complete success and German records and postwar analysis reveals just how right they were: 83 per cent of the city had been gutted and around 17,500 people killed, the third highest casualty total in a single raid, behind only those sustained in the Dresden and Hamburg firestorms. Pforzheim had largely ceased to exist as a productive and coherent community.

Four days later, on 27 February, orders came through for an attack on Mainz, this time in daylight. This type of raid still held some attraction as a novelty and many of the crews enjoyed being able to see what was going on around them; it made a welcome change from their usual isolation in darkness. They were heartened too to see their loose gaggle of Lancasters and Halifaxes more than amply protected by a strong fighter escort. As 450-odd Bomber Command crews crossed the Franco-Belgian border, they passed a large formation of US Eighth Air Force B-17s and their escorts returning from a mission over Germany. The young men in both formations could not have failed to be impressed by the awesome array of airpower now ranged against the German war machine. For the Canadians and Britons in 419 and 428 Squadrons, the attack on Mainz turned out to be little different from any night-time attack as 10/10ths stratocumulus cloud, with tops up to 10,000ft, completely blanketed the city. However, it was Mainz's most destructive raid of the war; much of the central and eastern areas of the city were virtually levelled and around 1,200 people lost their lives.

As the calendar turned to March 1945, it was becoming increasingly obvious that the end was very clearly in sight but also that it had not yet arrived. The novelty of the daylight raids began to wear a little thin when orders were received to bomb Mannheim and then to attack the bridges over the Rhine in Cologne in order halt movement to and from the front line only a few miles to the west of the city. Aircraft from both 419 and 428 Squadrons were to form part of the first wave of the attack, and once again they headed east, well protected by a large fighter screen. Cologne was a familiar target but one that was rarely attacked in daylight, and as they approached shortly before 10:00 hours the crews were able to pick out the Gothic cathedral, the river and the bridges through the widening gaps in the cloud and attacked accordingly. Curiously a number of Middleton's crews reported picking up a female voice, with only the faintest trace of an accent, instructing the crews to bomb the yellow markers; these decoy tactics were ignored. Harder to ignore was the vicious predicted heavy flak that still showed little sign of weakening nor of running short of ammunition. Flg Off Jack Birt compiled the following dispatch for CBC:

This Friday fliers from our Canadian Group took part in the most dramatic attack of the year so far. Starting early in the morning they joined other units of RAF Bomber Command, streamed far across the continent, and pounded the war-torn German city of Cologne by daylight . . . [It] was a tactical job that may speed the advance of General Simpson's 9th US Army now pounding towards the outskirts of this Rhineland city. Whatever was left of Cologne certainly copped it today.

The inaugural edition of the less widely circulated *Middleton St George News* carried the story of the courageous act of 419 Squadron's Flg Off Lambroughton during this attack:

Returning from a daylight raid on Cologne Flg Off Lambroughton in B Flight sighted a Lancaster, badly damaged and flying on two engines, which left it without power to operate the turrets, bumping along behind the stream. Flg Off Lambroughton slowed down his Lanc and acted as an escort to the crippled kite as far as the English coast. He then proceeded to base and landed some time after the other crews. Wg Cdr Ferguson commending the crew said that Flg Off Lambroughton showed personal keenness and thoughtfulness to take it upon himself to aid a fellow in trouble and to provide cover for a kite, irrespective of the fact that the kite and crew were unknown to him.

A further operation against Chemnitz was called for but soon scrubbed on 4 March but the same operation was laid on for the following day and went ahead, though in very marginal conditions for those squadrons based in the north-east of England. The weather at the time of take-off, around 16:30 hours, was described by the meteorological section as '7/10 to 10/10 variable stratocumulus cloud, base between 2,000 and 3,000ft in layers to 8,000 to 9,000ft.

Thin medium layers between 10,000 and 20,000ft. Freezing level 5,000ft. Icing index moderate.' The conditions were a little worse over North Yorkshire and within minutes of take-off from Linton three of 426 Squadron's Halifaxes had crashed on account of a rapid build-up of ice. One of them, beyond the control of its skipper, Flt Lt I. Emerson, came down in York itself, killing several civilians. Two of 420 Squadron's Halifaxes and two more from 425 Squadron followed suit just minutes after leaving Tholthorpe.

The 419 and 428 Squadron crews, having taken off a few miles further north, had managed to climb a little higher and, although they still experienced considerable icing, they missed the worst of it. Flying conditions en route remained marginal and as the aircraft arrived over the target a little before 22:00 hours the thick layers of cloud were as dense as ever, making even the usual dull red glow below barely visible. Matters were made even worse by unforeseen strong winds and navigator Jim Gunn of 428 Squadron recalls some tense exchanges with the flight engineer over the wind speed and fuel consumption, resulting in the crew adopting the most direct course possible for base, irrespective of the original flight plan. Other returning crews reported heavy icing conditions over England, and perhaps it was the lethal combination of icing and flak damage that brought 419 Squadron's L for Love down north-east of Aylesbury in Buckinghamshire, with the loss of all on board. The grim reaper had still not finished. Flg Off W. Mytruk and his crew had successfully dropped their load over Chemnitz at 21:54 hours and had reached the Belgian border on their way home when the Lancaster began to collect large amounts of ice. Very quickly Mytruk began to lose control of the bomber and, as the aircraft began to plunge earthwards, he gave the order to bale out. Three of the crew did not make it but Mytruk, although injured, and the three others survived. The attack had cost Middleton St George two aircraft and 6 Group as a whole seventeen, not far short of 10 per cent of their contribution to Bomber Command's activities that night. It was a sharp reminder of the untamed powers of nature the crews faced each time they took to the skies.

Then on 11 March came Bomber Command's final but largest attack on Essen, once the heavy industry capital of Germany. No fewer than 1,079 bombers, of which thirty were from Middleton St George, pounded the city through a dense layer of cloud, raising an enormous pall of smoke, silent witness to the death of the city. The defences, once among the most feared in Germany, were but a pale shadow of their former selves and posed little threat to the massed ranks of bombers.

The following day Bomber Command set a new and never surpassed record for the largest number of aircraft dispatched to a single target as 1,108 Lancasters, Halifaxes and Mosquitoes dropped a record 4,851 tons of bombs on Dortmund. The young men in the aircraft were left in no doubt as to the success of the attack, with even experienced crews gazing in awe at the gigantic mushroom of grey-black smoke, some 4 to 5 miles wide, that bubbled up through the cloud. Operations were on again the next day, though when news of the loads and the objective came through at 12:40 many were left scratching their heads at the target named, Zweibrucken. A quick look at the map revealed that it was a town in Bavaria. It had not been attacked by Bomber Command before nor, as it turned out, was it destined to be again. German records reveal the massive extent of the damage wrought by the 230 heavy bombers;

every public building was either destroyed or damaged and likewise 80 per cent of all housing. What remained of Nazi Germany was being systematically reduced to rubble.

It was still not all one-way traffic. Reaching the oil production centre of Hagen about 20:30 on 15 March, the crews soon discovered that the Ruhr defences still packed a formidable punch, hurling thousands of deadly shells high into the night sky. Flak caused damage to several of the Middleton-based aircraft but it was the night-fighters that accounted for the losses sustained that night. Although they arrived too late to intercept the bomber stream en route to the target, they wrought havoc among the bombers returning home, some determined pilots pressing home their attacks as far west as Reading in Berkshire. A Ju88 accounted for the Lancaster flown by Flt Lt J.D.C. Craton of 428 Squadron not long after the crew had turned for home. Five of the experienced crew, all on their second tour of operations, went down with the aircraft, though the two survivors were back in the UK by the end of the month. A similar fate befell 419 Squadron's N for Nan, flown by Flt Sgt C.W. Parrish, which came off second best in an encounter with a night-fighter near Mönchengladbach at 20:45 hours. The aircraft came down near Fishln, taking with it four of the crew; two of the three survivors were back with 419 Squadron in a matter of days but the third, air gunner Sgt E. Bristow, was held in hospital at East Grinstead for several weeks, receiving specialist care for his injuries. K for King, piloted by Flt Lt M.W. McLaughlin, was 419 Squadron's other loss that night. It was attacked and shot down several miles behind Allied lines and only four of the crew managed to bale out before the bomber exploded in mid-air.

None of the survivors from the downed 419 Squadron crews was able to identify their assailants but it is possible that they were victims of the feared Me262 jet aircraft, which are known to have been operating that night. Indeed, another of 419 Squadron's bombers, under the command of Flg Off D.B.R. Lambroughton, endured the attentions of not one but two of them on his flight home. At 21:09 hours rear gunner Flt Sgt A.M. Dennis sighted an Me262 flying dead astern and slightly above his Lancaster at a range of 1,000 yards. As the Me262 rapidly closed to 600 yards, Dennis gave the instruction to corkscrew starboard and simultaneously opened fire, trading shots with the German pilot. For a few minutes it looked as if the German had been thrown off the scent but then Dennis noticed it back in its previous position, this time supported by another on the starboard fine quarter above. Clearly working together, the pair screamed in to the attack, opening fire again at 600 yards. Dennis blasted back at the aircraft approaching from the rear and his crew mate Flt Sgt B.K. Dwyer opened up on the other one. In seconds the Me262 had flashed past and swept out of sight. Coordinating their efforts once more, the pair put in another attack 6 minutes later but were again thwarted and driven off by the combined alertness and firepower of Dennis and Dwyer, after which they disappeared, perhaps seeking easier prey.

Orders were received on the 22nd to carry out a daylight attack on the marshalling yards at Hildesheim, a town a dozen or so miles south-east of Hannover. This was another new target for Bomber Command as it put the final touches to its demolition of Germany's transport and industrial infrastructure. Flying in perfect conditions, the crews were able to map-read their way to the target, which was readily identified by its autobahn and railway junctions. Within a matter of minutes the railway yards had been pulverised, as had some

263 acres or 70 per cent of the surrounding town. A towering column of thick black smoke, 3 miles high, stood in mute testimony to the death of the town and some 1,645 of its residents. Flt Lt J.F. Hadley of 428 Squadron in KB777 had successfully bombed the target and had just turned for home when the Lancaster was hit by flak. The port inner engine burst into flames and the massive air-flow quickly caused the fire to engulf a good section of the wing. Two US P-51 Mustangs closed in to offer support to the stricken bomber, which was steadily losing height as Hadley battled to reach Allied lines. When it became clear that the Lancaster was not going to make it, Hadley gave the order to bale out but it appears that only four of the crew managed to do so successfully before the aircraft ploughed into the ground, killing Hadley and the two other men on board.

No sooner had the Lancasters come to a halt on their bays in the late afternoon when the ground crews swarmed all over them in order to turn them around for another operation that night. At 01:00 hours new orders were received, necessitating changes in the bomb- and fuel loads. Once again, the men set to, working flat out to meet the deadlines given; once again, they need not have bothered. Successive postponements were made until the operation was finally called off the following morning. Operations were listed on the following morning for another daylight raid on what was left of Nazi Germany's oil production plants, this time the Mathias Stinnes benzol plant near Bottrop. It was hardly worth the effort as much of the ordnance did little but churn up the surrounding fields.

With the long-awaited announcement that Allied forces had successfully established a bridgehead across the Rhine, it was clear that the war really was now entering its final phase. Nevertheless, there was no let-up for the young crews of Bomber Command. The railway yards at Hannover were attacked and then, on the final day of the month, the Blohm und Voss shipyards in Hamburg, where new, long-range U-boats were being manufactured. Both suffered massive destruction. For some reason the leader of the third wave of bombers, which included those from 419 and 428 Squadrons, miscalculated his time over target and arrived some 10 minutes late. After several raids without interference from enemy fighters, it was sheer bad luck that on this day the Luftwaffe managed to get its act together and mount a sustained and heavy attack. To make matters even worse for the young men in the lumbering bombers, their assailants were thirty heavily armed Me262 jet fighters. The German pilots, an elite and experienced group, rapidly closed and opened fire with their four 30mm cannons and R2M rockets, ripping their way through the formation. The gunners hunched up in the turrets of the bombers did their best to return fire but they were hopelessly out-gunned and found it all but impossible to hold their sights on the jets as they flashed past at speeds in excess of 500mph. There was only ever going to be one result in this unequal contest: the third and final wave, made up of 6 Group aircraft, lost five Lancasters and three Halifaxes within a handful of minutes, without inflicting any identifiable damage on the Me262s.

Two of the downed Lancasters belonged to 419 Squadron. The all-Canadian crew in H for How, skippered by Flt Lt H.A. Metivier, was lost to a man but three men managed to get out of Q for Queenie, skippered by Flg Off D.S. Bowes, before it crashed at 09:07 near Hiltfeld. D for Dog of 428 Squadron very nearly followed suit after being attacked at 19,000ft over the target area. The Me262's pilot anticipated the bomber's corkscrew to starboard and stuck with it, opening fire and closing in to within 200 yards, blasting great chunks out of the Lancaster. Fortunately the German pilot then broke off his attack and did not return, leaving the battered bomber and its badly shaken crew to make their way home in comparative peace. There was little answer to the Me262s in the air and the young men on both sides knew it.

Several attacks were planned then cancelled as Bomber Command searched for worthwhile targets, their choice often being restricted by the fast-moving and fluid situation on the ground. As a result no one was taking bets when, at 11:00 hours on 4 April, the station received orders to mount an attack that night. The target was the Leuna oil plant at Merseburg, one of the last large synthetic oil plants still capable of production and still in German hands. A little after 18:00 hours that evening, no fewer than thirty-two Lancasters started up their engines and trundled to the end of the runway, pausing a moment before thundering away and climbing slowly into the sky. The crews realised that the conditions prevailing were far from favourable, with dense layers of cloud billowing up to 10,000ft and unpredicted strong winds. Nevertheless, several large explosions were noted shortly before 23:00 hours and photo-reconnaissance confirmed that some fresh damage had been caused to the plant. However, there was no getting away from the fact that the attack was, as the station log put it, 'not a good one'.

The next day was given over to spit and polish for a double celebration. With the AOC RCAF Overseas, AM G.O. Johnson, and AOC 6 Group, AVM C.M. McEwen, in attendance, a full parade was held on the station to mark the 21st anniversary of the foundation of the RCAF and to present to Wg Cdr M.W. Gall the official crest of 428 Squadron. Once over, it was back to business.

Once the slight frost and early mist had cleared, 8 April blossomed into a brilliant fine spring day. Orders came through for an operation that night and for about the first time in 1945 the ground crews were able to work outside in relative comfort. The crews' briefings revealed the target as the Blohm und Voss shipyards in Hamburg, which were still striving to turn out the new super U-boats. The shipyards, already pounded by a US aerial armada earlier in the day, took a great hammering which finally knocked them out of commission. The city's flak defences were still strong enough to inflict significant damage on the bomber force and the threat posed by night-fighters was also still very real, especially the marauding Me262s that were spotted in the target area. Once again 419 Squadron's D for Dog, flown by Flg Off D. Lambroughton, came under attack from one, which bored in from the fine starboard quarter and opened fire at 600 yards. Rear gunner Flt Sgt A. Dennis spotted the danger but did not have time to get his sights fixed on the fighter before it screamed off into the darkness. Lambroughton immediately corkscrewed and was quickly enveloped by a conveniently placed layer of cloud. The crew, shaken but uninjured, made it back to Britain without further interference and, like most of the Middleton-based crews that night put down at RAF Wing.

However, 419 Squadron's V for Victor was not so fortunate. Not long after the aircraft had crossed the English coast on the outward leg of the trip, the starboard inner engine began to play up, cutting out intermittently and sending out showers of sparks and bursts of flames.

The skipper, Flg Off H.R. Cram, an experienced pilot on his second tour, reckoned that it might right itself and decided to press on to Hamburg. Once the Lancaster was free of its bomb-load, Cram feathered the engine and turned for home, gradually losing height. About half an hour later the starboard outer packed up and burst into flames, presumably on account of increased temperature or flak damage. The Graviner system managed to put the fire out at once but with both starboard engines U/S, it was only a matter of time before the aircraft would fall from the sky. Cram and his flight engineer, Flt Sgt J.T.R.E. Cave RAF, worked hard to coax the Lancaster towards Allied lines but when its altitude had dropped to just 2,500ft, the crew realised that it was now or never for baling out safely, whichever side of the lines it was on. The crew carried out an orderly evacuation and, to their delight, six of them floated to earth behind Allied lines. The seventh, Sgt E.K. McGrath, was not so fortunate. However, he landed undetected just the wrong side of the lines and was able to make his way to friendly territory without mishap. All returned to Middleton St George within a few days.

The weather continued to hold fair and the 10th was another lovely spring day. The crews received orders to make the long haul to the Engelsdorf railway yards in Leipzig in daylight, a route and penetration that would have been unthinkable only a few months earlier. The bomber stream was largely untroubled as it headed deep into south-eastern Germany and the conditions were so clear that the navigators had no difficulty map-reading their way to Leipzig. The bomb aimers too had the rare luxury of actually seeing their target clearly and certainly made the most of the opportunity. Sqn Ldr Les Powell, reporting for CBC, gave this account:

> In the longest daylight raid ever made by Lancasters and Halifaxes of this Bomber Group, our aircraft, in an all-Canadian show, yesterday struck a devastating blow to the important marshalling yards of the historic central German city of Leipzig and the twin attacks [6 Group Halifaxes attacked the yards in the suburb of Monchau] are described as exceptionally successful. The Canadians left the railway yards with smoke billowing up so high that it was seen by the returning fliers for more than 100 miles. There was no doubt in their minds as to the success of the attack as most of the bombing was done visually.

The crews' views were valid, and vital rail traffic to the crumbling Eastern Front was severely disrupted and curtailed.

The Deutsche Werke U-boat yards in Kiel were still managing to turn out U-boats, which in turn were still sinking Allied ships. Unfortunately the attack on the night of 13/14 April did little to hinder production; much of the bombing hit the Elmschenhagen suburb of the city, a couple of miles inland, as the whole area was blanketed by a thin but unbroken layer of low-lying cloud. There was still a considerable amount of flak over the city and either this or the fighters observed at work in the area accounted for 419 Squadron's M for Mike, flown by Flt Sgt C.C. MacLaren, and its entire crew. Whatever the cause of its demise, no trace of the Lancaster and its seven-man crew has ever been found. These young Canadians were to be the last members of their squadron to be killed on operations during the war.

The 428 Squadron crew led by Flg Off D.M. Payne was more fortunate. Payne had just initiated his bomb run when his Lancaster was blasted by a near-miss. Shell fragments tore through the outer skin of the Lancaster and several lodged in Payne's legs, left arm and hand. In spite of the pain, he held his course and completed his run. As he turned for home, flak struck again, knocking out three of his engines. Payne managed to coax the Lancaster westwards for a few miles before the last remaining engine gave up the ghost, leaving him the unenviable task of ditching in the North Sea without power and in pitch darkness. In a superb act of airmanship, Payne succeeded in setting the Lancaster down on an even keel, giving sufficient time for the crew to get out and climb into the dinghy. However, when everyone had clambered in to the small dinghy, it was found that Flt Sgt Vardy, one of the gunners, was missing. In the circumstances, there was nothing the other battered survivors could do to find him and his body was never recovered. Payne himself had smashed his head on the windscreen on landing and was drifting in and out of consciousness, only partly aware of the seriousness of their situation. Three of the other crewmen were also injured, but to a lesser extent. The navigator, Flg Off G.C. Riley, took charge of the situation and

organised the sailing of the dinghy, as well as attending to the injuries of the crew. With coolness, calm courage and splendid example he kept up the spirits of the crew by reading passages from a pocket Bible and by organising diversions such as card games. He was instrumental in preventing the crew from drinking sea water when the fresh water supplies were running low and he organised the distribution of emergency rations on an economical basis. Eventually, the dinghy grounded on some sand flats near Bremerhaven and the crew were taken prisoner.

The men had been at sea for twelve days and the citation for Riley's MBE concluded 'without this officer's direction, guidance and example, it is doubtful if the members of his crews would have survived this very trying ordeal'. Payne was awarded a DFC for his determination and skill shown during the attack and ditching.

On 16 April 419 and 428 Squadrons bombed the railway yards at Schwandorf in eastern Bavaria, halting traffic there for the remainder of the war. Following that for several days the aircraft sat ready, bombed- and fuelled up, with nowhere to go. Quite simply, Bomber Command was fast running out of suitable and worthwhile targets within the ever-decreasing Nazi-held Germany. However, on the morning of 22 April orders were received to join a massive 750-plus force to blast the south-eastern suburbs of the port of Bremen, prior to the final assault to be carried out by XXX Army Corps. It was an unusual and red letter day at Middleton St George, and one that was almost ruined by the postponement of take-off from 06:30 hours to first 14:00 hours and then 15:50 hours. On 17 April a new and special Lancaster had been delivered to Middleton St George: the 300th Lancaster X built by the Victory Aircraft Company at Malton, Ontario. Since 419 Squadron had received the very first one built, the 'Ruhr Express', it seemed only right and proper that the same squadron should also receive this milestone aircraft, especially as the opportunity to use it operationally was obviously slipping away. It had been christened 'Malton Mike' in honour of AVM 'Black

The final attack: Wangerooge, 25 April 1945, when 482 aircraft bombed the coastal gun batteries. *(Department of National Defence PL 144281)*

Mike' McEwen, AOC 6 Group, and he, together with a film crew, came to Middleton St George to watch its inaugural operational take-off.

As it turned out, its first operation was far from spectacular and Sqn Ldr Les Powell, who covered the event for CBC, had his work cut out to make his story match the high expectations of those back in Canada, awaiting this much-trumpeted event:

It was a thrilling sight to look out of the pilot's cabin and see the vast array of heavy bombers – many of them Canadian-built – join the ever-growing stream. It reminded me of a swarm of angry hornets, hurrying to attack an enemy. Up above the clouds, the sun shone brightly and through occasional breaks in the fleecy whiteness, we saw the waters of the North Sea, then the coast of Holland. Across the flooded fields we sped without opposition until we reached the target when bursts of heavy flak – well predicted – greeted us.

Unfortunately, by the time the 6 Group aircraft had arrived over the target, the Master Bomber had already called a halt to the bombing. Such was the scale of the smoke and debris that it had become impossible to judge accurately the fall of the bombs; and with British troops stationed all around preparing for the attack, it was too dangerous to continue. Given the uninspiring, if understandable, end to the proceedings, the best Powell could conclude was 'the crew was high in its praise of the new aircraft. The veteran skipper Sqn Ldr Jack Watts of Hanley, Saskatchewan, claimed it flew like a charm and was a pleasure to handle.' After visiting the official jettisoning zone, 'Malton Mike' and its associates landed safely at Middleton St George.

On 25 April, a typically dull, cloudy and mild spring morning, the ground crews were busy making their final checks and the crews their final preparations for the day's operation. They could not have known it, but this was to be the last time that they would carry out this well rehearsed routine. The curtain fell on Middleton St George's operational career in the Second World War after the attack on the island of Wangerooge. The powerful coastal batteries on this island at the end of the Frisian chain controlled the sea lanes into the ports of Bremen and Wilhelmshaven, which the British were keen to open up as quickly as possible in order to bring in much-needed supplies to the troops still involved in heavy fighting in the area.

Fifteen Lancasters from each squadron lined up for a mid-afternoon take-off and as they headed east across the North Sea towards the island the sky cleared, providing excellent visibility. The crews could see, from miles away, the smoke and debris billowing up from the island, hurled high into the sky by the earlier waves of bombers. They could also see a considerable amount of flak from the adjacent islands of Spiekerooge and Langerooge exploding all around the bomber stream. Occasionally fighters, including Me262s, were observed but the Spitfires, no fewer than ten squadrons of them, kept the predators at bay. The crews were unanimous in their opinion that 'this is . . . considered a very successful attack', though at the end of the war it was discovered that the batteries, despite being hit repeatedly, were ready for action once more within a matter of hours, stationed as they were within enormous concrete emplacements. Although the flak caused some damage to the bombers, only one was shot down, but sadly mid-air collisions accounted for no fewer than six aircraft, four of which came from 431, 408 and 426 Squadrons in 6 Group. All twenty-eight Canadians on board lost their lives. By chance the last bomber from the Group to land after the attack was D for Dog of 428 Squadron, piloted by Flg Off D.R. Walsh. Thus at 20:36 hours on 25 April 1945, as the Lancaster rolled down the runway, carefully taxied around the perimeter, slowly came to a halt and closed down its engines, the operational war of Middleton St George came to an end.

CHAPTER 8

The End of the Line

The men and women stationed at Middleton St George had, of course, no way of knowing that their part in the war in Europe was now over, and the routine of training and test flying continued as normal. One of these flights on 30 April 1945, sickeningly close to the end of the war, brought about the station's final fatalities. Flt Lt W.G. Campbell that morning took up 428 Squadron's KB879 NA-Y and headed south-west, flying over the peaceful English countryside. He and his crew of five Canadians and one Scotsman had no inkling that there was anything wrong and no distress signals were made before, at 11:54, the Lancaster broke up in mid-air, the pieces plummeting to earth at Hixon, a few miles east of Stafford. All the men on board were killed.

Both the Middleton-based squadrons missed out on the joyful sorties carried out between 26 April and 7 May as part of Operation Exodus, the collection and return by air of thousands of ex-POWs. They were likewise not included among the squadrons detailed to execute Operation Manna, the dropping of over 6,500 tons of foodstuffs into the German-occupied area of western Holland. Rumour was rife, much of it postulating a heavy involvement in the war in the Far East alongside the USAAF. By early May it had been confirmed that 419 and 428 Squadron would join 405, 408, 420, 425, 431 and 434 Squadrons to form the RCAF's contribution to Bomber Command's 'Tiger Force', carrying out attacks against strategic targets in Japan.

Shortly after VE-Day on 8 May, a joyous day full of celebration but marred by heavy rain for the best part of the day, the station log records a 'confused mass of instructions starting to arrive' regarding supplies and a proposed early return of the aircraft to Canada. Extensive exercises were carried out over the sea in order to give much-needed practice in transatlantic flight and navigation, which was a whole new ball-game for most crews. The rather complicated plans for the departure of 419 and 428 Squadrons gradually began to take shape over the next few days. A forward party of essential ground crew was to fly to Lagens in the Azores ahead of the Lancasters, which were to join them there a few days later. Overhauled and refuelled, the aircraft would then head towards Canada and land at Debert in Nova Scotia, from where the crews would go on leave awaiting orders regarding their role in Tiger Force. This plan swung into action at 10:00 hours on 22 May 1945, when RCAF Transport

ACM Sir Arthur Harris and AVM 'Black Mike' McEwen attended the ceremony to mark the return of the squadrons to Canada at the end of May 1945. It was Harris's first and only visit to the station, a mark of the significance of the occasion. *(Department of National Defence UK 21881)*

KB739 of 428 Squadron completed 56 operational sorties and is pictured here upon its return to Dartmouth, Nova Scotia, on 8 June 1945. *(Department of National Defence PL 36550)*

Command Dakotas took off from Middleton St George carrying the forward party under the command of Wg Cdr L.L. McKinnon DSO, DFC, on the first leg of their journey to RAF St Mawgan in Cornwall.

The departure of the two squadrons on 31 May 1945 was a much grander and more formal occasion. The station log baldly summarised it.

At 10:00 hours an impressive ceremony took place at the beginning of 024 runway in connection with the departure of the first 15 aircraft flying from the station to Canada. ACM Sir A.T. Harris KCB, OBE, DFC, AOC-in-C Bomber Command, attended and delivered an excellent talk on the successes of the Canadians in 6 Group and Bomber Command. AM Y.O. Johnson CB, MC, AOC-in-C RCAF Overseas, and AVM C.M. McEwen CB, MC, DFC, also spoke to the aircrew. All major press reporters were in attendance, as were those of the BBC.

The take-off was excellent . . . No technical snags developed on take-off, however, KB884 returned early due to faulty trim. This was adjusted and after an air test the aircraft was declared serviceable.

It was a rare event for Harris actually to visit a station and his presence at Middleton St George to watch 428 Squadron's Flt Lt S.V. Eliosoff's Lancaster, the first to leave for home, take off is a measure of the significance attached to the Group's departure after a job well done. Initially sceptical, and with some justification, of the Canadian Group's effectiveness at a time when all-out efficiency was an absolute necessity, Harris appears to have been won over. On 1 April 1945 he had signalled 6 Group HQ:

> On this 21st anniversary of the RCAF I take the opportunity of congratulating 6 Group RCAF on its great contribution to the Bomber offensive. In the last war the RAF owed much to the gallant Canadians who fought in its ranks and now in this war the RCAF fighting beside us has put the seal on our comradeship in arms.

Now, as the crews were departing, he told them: 'you leave this country, after all you have done, with a reputation that is equal to any and surpassed by none.' High praise indeed.

The remainder followed in batches with far less fanfare over the next few days until, by 4 June, they had all gone. The rest of the Canadian personnel quickly followed suit. The station was not quiet for long, however. Within days, Middleton St George had reverted to RAF control to become No. 13 OTU, Fighter Command, flying Mosquitoes, and it remained in RAF hands until 1963, when it became surplus to requirements and was sold off to become Teesside International Airport. The 419 and 428 Squadron crews never flew operationally again, for

The survivor: Lancaster X KB889, once assigned to 428 Squadron, is now a static exhibit at the Imperial War Museum, Duxford. *(DUX 2006-29-44)*

although they were officially incorporated into Tiger Force in mid-July and commenced training in Canada, the dropping of the atomic bombs on Hiroshima and Nagasaki a few weeks later, perhaps the ultimate enactment of the strategic air offensive, put paid to all the plans.

Once again, a victorious government deemed that it had no further use for well equipped and well trained fighting units. Both 419 and 428 Squadrons were disbanded and passed into history on the same day, 5 September 1945. The three Canadian squadrons that had been based at Middleton St George, 419, 420 and 428, did at least have a history to be proud of. They had taken a full part in every aspect of the strategic bomber offensive, taking the war to the German industrial cities, transportation systems and oil refineries, preparing the way for D-Day, mining the seas to great effect and providing support to the ground troops as required. Flying from Middleton St George, they had completed almost 8,000 operational sorties, sustained the loss of a little under 200 aircraft and suffered over 1,000 casualties. It had been a long and hard war for the young men so far from home, but they had always, in the parlance of the day, pressed on regardless and ultimately had gained the victory.

CHAPTER 9

The Reasons Why

S ir Arthur Harris once answered the charge levelled at him by his critics during the war
that 'bombing can never win a war' with the remark, 'Well, we shall see. It hasn't been
tried yet.' Time proved that his critics were right and Harris was wrong, but it was not
for want of trying on his part or that of his dedicated crews from around the Empire and
Commonwealth. Bombing might not have won the war against Germany but it went a long
way towards achieving the Allies' overwhelming victory.

It has long been fashionable to criticise the strategic air offensive, to dismiss it as
ineffective and to brand the crews as villains or, worse, murderers. It was not until the last
decade of the twentieth century that the pendulum began to swing back a little bit the other
way. It is not the purpose of this book to dissect the offensive and analyse its results beneath a
metaphorical microscope, but it is only fair to the men and women who served in the
Command to make a few pertinent observations.

First and foremost, Britain and her Empire were at war, fighting for their very survival. At
the time Middleton St George was completed and opened in January 1941, that survival was
very much in doubt. Driven out of France, the Low Countries and Norway, and facing serious
threats in North Africa, the Balkans and the Far East, Britain was being blasted from one end
to the other by 'the Blitz'. Tens of thousands of Britons had been killed, others had lost their
loved ones, their homes, their livelihoods and their neighbourhoods, and had had their lives
shattered and turned upside-down. With much of the army battered and ill-equipped, and
working flat out to defend the British Isles from invasion, and with the Royal Navy stretched
thinly across the globe and unable to participate directly in the continental war, who else but
Bomber Command could take the war to the enemy and carry out overtly offensive
operations? This was to remain the case until at least the end of 1942 and well into 1943,
when the North African and Italian campaigns began to pay dividends. It also goes a long
way to explaining the public's support for Bomber Command and its offensive – a support
boosted by the German attacks on Britain during 1942 and 1943 and ultimately by the
deployment of V1 and V2s, which continued to cause death and destruction as late as March
1945. The urge to hit back when threatened is a strong one and not easily suppressed. Few in
Britain during the war saw any need to even try.

A wrecked factory building at the massive Krupps armaments works in Essen in 1945. *(Imperial War Museum CL 2383)*

This active defiance and offensive spirit did much to underpin Britain's claims to be down but not out in the early years of the war, especially in the USA where Roosevelt was in need of any ammunition he could muster in his battle against the isolationists in his country. Later on it gave Churchill the means to pacify Stalin, who was desperate for the second front. However, the strategic air offensive's real value lies beyond the political spin-offs, important though they were; it lies in the pure military and economic nitty-gritty of total war. In the United Kingdom the two best-known operations carried out by Bomber Command are the Dambusters raid in May 1943 and the attack on Dresden in February 1945. These raids, so very different in their aims and methodologies, typify the breadth of Bomber Command's activities. Less than half of all sorties carried out were mounted against cities and 'area targets'; the rest were attacks against specific targets or types of targets. Thus Bomber Command laid over 50,000 sea mines (419 and 428 Squadrons, for example, became specialists in this line of work), attacked U-boat yards and carried out numerous operations against German naval surface units such as the *Scharnhorst*, *Gneisenau* and *Tirpitz*. The Command also did much to pave the way for the successful invasion of Europe in June 1944 and often intervened tactically on behalf of the Allies, including the USSR, until the end of the war.

The Command attacked cities and factories involved in German aircraft production, railway and road transportation and oil production. This resulted in less efficient industrial dispersal, the redirection of resources into otherwise unnecessary areas such as underground factories, acute shortages and increased immobility of goods and manpower. This, combined with the massive dislocation to day-to-day routine civic life and amenities, the destruction of public buildings and private housing, led to a capping of war production, in spite of the Herculean efforts made by the Nazi regime. Such efforts would have borne far more fruit – much to the detriment of the Allies – without the effects of the offensive, ably and decisively supported by the USAAF. An overwhelming majority of the Germans interviewed after the war by the Allied authorities stated that they had found the incessant raids the hardest single cross to bear during the war.

With a keen and wary eye on the morale of the German people, the Nazi government was forced to devote more and more resources to the protection of the Fatherland. By 1942 German anti-aircraft personnel numbered 439,000 and by 1944 this number had almost doubled to 889,000. Civil defence workers topped 1,200,000. Flak defences swallowed up almost 15,000 heavy cannons and over 40,000 lighter guns; in 1944 almost 20 per cent of all ammunition manufactured went straight to the flak guns around the Reich. By 1 January

The beautifully maintained Commonwealth War Graves Commission memorial at Runnymede in Surrey, where the names of the over 20,000 missing aircrew are recorded. *(Commonwealth War Graves Commission)*

1944 68 per cent of all German fighters manufactured went to home defence duties and by October this had risen to 81 per cent, thereby robbing the Wehrmacht of vital air support and greatly weakening its ability to function effectively in modern battle.

One final and often-overlooked consequence of the strategic offensive was to limit the scale of the German aerial assault on Britain. By the beginning of 1944 only 20 per cent of German aircraft production was given over to bombers, eventually forcing the Germans to rely on the more temperamental, less accurate and less effective V1 and V2s; indeed, from 1943 onwards Bomber Command had played a significant role in countering the threat from these technologically advanced weapons, making repeated attacks on the Peenemünde facility and the V-weapon sites. It had been foreseen as early as the 1920s that, in the coming war, the side which was able to withstand the pounding and hang on the longest in this dreadful campaign of civilian and social attrition would prevail. Bomber Command's efforts over Germany did much to spare the people of Britain from enduring this harsh test in full.

When put against all the above, the heavy price paid by the men and women of Bomber Command – some 55,500 were killed on operations or in training – appears as something of a bargain. Just like their better-known counterparts in Fighter Command, when push came to shove they delivered the goods, time and again, often against daunting odds. For that, we, in succeeding generations, should be very grateful.

APPENDIX 1

The Creation of an Air Force

On 11 November 1918 the Royal Air Force had 22,647 aircraft on its books, operating in 188 active squadrons. Within two years that figure had shrunk to around 2,000 aircraft and only 17 operational squadrons. The world's largest and most powerful air force, built up almost from scratch in just a few hectic years, had been reduced to a mere shadow of its former grandeur and potency, the inevitable result of misguided cutbacks and the quest for an over-generous peace dividend. The RAF's loss, however, was to prove Canada's gain.

In 1918 Canada did not have any form of national air force at all, though many Canadians had served with great distinction in the RFC and RAF during the war. A nation of only 8,000,000 people, with no credible enemy within striking range, Canada was one of many countries which did not see the need for an irrelevant postwar luxury like an air force. However, in 1919 the RAF offered and dispatched 16 aircraft and $170,000-worth of spare parts to Canada free of charge. In the following year a further 100 aircraft followed, free to a good home.

With no real use for them, nor any organisation to make use of them, the Canadian authorities simply put them into storage and left them there. It was not until the potential uses of aircraft in the vast open spaces of Canada began to become gradually more apparent that the government began to be lobbied by ex-flyers who were keen to set up some sort of national air force. Persuaded mostly by the commercial and social opportunities afforded by better communications with the many remote communities in the country, the government was won over and on 1 April 1924 the Royal Canadian Air Force officially came into being.

In spite of its grand title, the RCAF, like its British counterpart, struggled for survival and by 1928 there were still just 936 service personnel. As the Great Depression bit deep into the North American economy, the RCAF was deemed to be one extravagance that Canada could almost do without. As a result the total manpower of the fledgling force was slashed by a massive two-thirds. As the economy gradually recovered, so did the fortunes of the RCAF and on the eve of war it comprised 4,061 members, of whom just 235 were pilots and 298 regular officers. These were mustered nominally in some 20 squadrons, of which 8 were regular and 12 auxiliary; all were seriously understrength and equipped with outdated, almost vintage, aircraft. It was a matter of considerable embarrassment to the Canadian government that there were far more Canadian pilots serving in the RAF than in the RCAF. Nevertheless, with the outbreak of war in September 1939, Canada made ambitious plans to play a full part in the Allied air campaign.

From the outset it was clear that the Canadian government did not intend to shirk its perceived duty to Britain, nor let the opportunity to consolidate its nationhood go by. On 10 September 1939, in response to King George VI's call for the Empire to take up arms, the Canadian Prime

Minister MacKenzie King made a broadcast to the nation that proudly stated: 'Canada has already answered that call. There is no home in Canada and no man, woman or child whose life is not bound up in this struggle.' The question was not whether to join a conflict several thousand miles distant from Canada's shores, but rather how Canada could make the greatest impact upon and the most useful contribution to that conflict.

Canada had suffered appallingly in the First World War, sustaining over 60,000 casualties. The acclaimed attack on Vimy Ridge in August 1917 alone had cost 9,937 men killed or wounded; in the first two weeks of November 1917 a further 15,634 were added to the grim total in the second Battle of Passchendaele. Such losses did much to fuel the heartfelt passions displayed during the crisis over conscription, which came close to tearing Canada apart, the British Canadians largely supporting the measure and the French Canadians opposing its introduction. MacKenzie King, who had undertaken the first of his three terms of office in 1921, when the scars of war were still very much deep and open, had no wish to find his country in a similar position in the current war. As it turned out, he did in 1944, when the issue of conscription for service raised its ugly head once again and the country split along much the same lines as it had done in 1917.

The Canadian government, therefore, turned its gaze to the fledgling RCAF. If it could be manned by volunteers, then the need for conscription could be pushed aside; furthermore, such a force held out the prospect of limited casualties and, with the benefits of modern technology and firepower, enabled Canada to punch far above its weight. Even so, the plans to expand the RCAF in line with these aspirations were necessarily highly ambitious and to bring them to fruition would take some time. It was clear to AVM G.M. Croil, who had been Chief of Air Staff since 1938, when the RCAF finally became independent of army control, and to Ian MacKenzie, the Minister of Defence, that Canada would have to rely heavily on Britain to arm and maintain this new force, at least for the foreseeable future. With such support in place, it was hoped that Canada would be able to make the worthwhile and identifiable contribution to the war effort it felt commensurate with its status as a nation within the British Empire.

The British government, while being delighted by the prompt and purposeful Canadian response, took a radically different view of how Canada might best help the war effort, especially in the air. As early as 6 September the British government sent a telegram expressing its doubts about the RAF's ability to meet its manpower requirements if the air war intensified as predicted. As a result, the telegram continued, it was thought more effective for Canada to concentrate on training airmen for service with the RAF rather than building up complete units of her own. Canada was, after all, thousands of miles from the centre of operations and, as such, an ideal area for training. As a sop to Canadian aspirations, the telegram added that if and when it was felt that sufficient aircrew were available for service, RCAF contingents could be formed from the surplus. Given the flow of aircrew necessary to match the predicted wastage, this seemed an aspiration unlikely to be fulfilled.

The proposals infuriated MacKenzie King, who stated his government's position most clearly:

> It is the desire of this government that the Canadian Air Force units be formed as soon as sufficient trained personnel are available overseas for this purpose, such squadrons to be manned by and maintained with Canadian personnel at the expense of the Canadian government. Owing to the shortage of service equipment in Canada, Canadian squadrons overseas would require to be completely equipped by British authorities at Canada's expense.

The British responded by dispatching Lord Riverdale, a prominent industrialist with considerable interests in and experience of doing business in Canada, to Ottawa in October 1939 to try to broker a suitable deal. The negotiations were far from smooth and there were a number of clashes over each nation's perceptions of the other's role and status. To the British it was as plain as a pikestaff: Canada was keen to help and, as the lesser partner, should fall in line with British requests and proposals. To the Canadians, on the other hand, it was equally plain that their government was offering its support voluntarily and that they could expect its views to be taken into account. MacKenzie King fumed: 'It is amazing how these people have come out from the old country and seem to think that all they have to do is to tell us what is to be done.'

Essentially, by the early autumn the British had put a twin-track proposal on the table in Ottawa. The first was an overall Empire Air Training Scheme, whereby elementary flying schools would be set up clear of the operational theatres in each Dominion according to its capacity: the Canadian component of this was intended to feed into the system a staggering 20,000 aircrew a year. The second was a plan whereby aircrew would serve with the RAF, notwithstanding their country of origin, with the provision that, at some unspecified date in the future, circumstances permitting, some national units might be formed to serve under the aegis of the RAF.

While the Canadian authorities were content to have their country become a vast training airfield, it would, as Croil wrote in an official memo on 23 November, 'be detrimental to Canadian prestige as a nation to restrict its official air effort to Home Defence and Training'. Croil continued to press for a firm commitment from the British to set up an RCAF Overseas Force, under the command of an RCAF Overseas Headquarters. MacKenzie King, ever an astute politician, lent his support to this and insisted that as a 'prerequisite to signature' by his government, 'Canadian personnel from the training plan will, on request from the Canadian government, be organised in RCAF units and formations in the field.' The Canadians held their ground – far more tenaciously than either the Australians or the New Zealanders – and eventually won the point, having their view enshrined in Article XV of the British Commonwealth Air Training Plan (BCATP) Treaty. Even with the main points agreed, the wrangling over the details dragged on for several months and necessitated a number of revisions. There was, however, a large gap between aspiration and reality and it was far from clear exactly how Canada was to meet all its military commitments.

By June 1940 some 16,000 Canadians were serving in the RCAF, with about a thousand more volunteering each week. However, a recruit is not an airman and it was clear that it would take some time to train them to operational levels. The government did not feel it could wait for this process to produce results and felt compelled to make an immediate gesture and get its foot in the door in Britain. The most economical and effective contribution it could make would be the deployment of a fighter squadron, albeit one equipped by the RAF. The Officer Commanding the contingent of pilots, Gp Capt G.V. Walsh, arrived in Britain on 3 March 1940 and by early June 1 Squadron RCAF (later renumbered as 401 to avoid confusion with the RAF's own 1 Squadron) was operational at Middle Wallop, flying Hurricane Is. After a short spell at Croydon the squadron moved to Northolt in early August, from where it operated throughout the Battle of Britain, claiming a total bag of 29 aircraft destroyed.

Buoyed by this success and still irritated by the fact that there were still more Canadians serving in the RAF than in the RCAF, the Canadian government kept up the diplomatic pressure on the Article XV issue. In the winter of 1940/1 a new agreement was pieced together by Sir Archibald Sinclair, the British Secretary of State for Air, and J.L. Ralston, the Canadian Defence Minister. This allowed for many hundreds of Canadians to be gradually clawed back from the RAF to form the backbone of a 25-squadron Canadian overseas force. Progress over what became known as Canadianisation remained painfully slow, partly owing to obfuscation on the part of the Air Ministry, which was keen not to lose much-needed aircrew, and partly owing to the unwillingness of many Canadians to leave friends and RAF units in which they felt perfectly at home, in spite of the better conditions and pay offered by the RCAF. Many agreed with the view espoused by AOC 4 Group, AVM C.R. Carr, himself a New Zealander in the RAF:

> They must leave the crews they have been working with and start afresh with strangers . . . I feel that your Canadians miss a lot by being posted direct to RCAF squadrons. In RAF squadrons, they mix and operate with English personnel and personnel from other Dominions and all get to know and respect each other. The various personnel gain a great deal from this association and assimilate fresh ideas from many parts of the world, which broadens their outlook.

The level of Canadianisation in Canadian-designated squadrons remained a live issue throughout the war. For example, 405 Squadron in July 1942 had only 50.3 per cent Canadian aircrew. By December 1943 the corresponding figure in Canadian-designated squadrons as a whole had clawed its way up to 66.8 per cent, but even at the end of March 1945 the figure was just 88.2 per cent. The figures were far lower when the national origin of the ground crews was taken into account.

By the spring of 1941 Canada's Air Minister C.G. Power and Britain's Under Secretary of State for Air H.H. Balfour had thrashed out the details of an agreement whereby Canada would be able to set up a semi-autonomous Bomber Group within Bomber Command as its major contribution to the air war. In the end, after much wrangling and several false starts, the RCAF did indeed get its own bomber force, 6 Group, eventually mustering some 15 bomber squadrons overseas. All of these were formed in Britain, the first being 405 Squadron on 23 April 1941, and manned if not entirely by Canadians then by BCATP graduates. The squadron flew its first operational sortie on the night of 12/13 June, its Wellingtons attacking the railway marshalling yards at Schwerte. No. 419 Squadron, later based at Middleton St George, was the third squadron to be formed, coming into existence at Mildenhall in Suffolk on 15 December 1941 under the command of Wg Cdr John 'Moose' Fulton DFC, a native of Kamloops, British Columbia, who had transferred to the RCAF following a successful tour with the RAF. This squadron made its first operational sortie on 11 January 1942 on a raid against the port of Brest. When 420 Squadron, also based for a time at Middleton St George, came into being on 19 December 1941, and with six more squadrons on the drawing-board, the RCAF, backed by an assertive government in Canada, pressed hard for the establishment of an independent Bomber Group. To the newly appointed AOC-in-C Bomber Command, Sir Arthur Harris, who saw far more merit in operational efficiency than political expediency, this was, as yet, an unrealistic option. As a result he posted all of the squadrons to 4 Group, based in the most northerly part of eastern England, and assigned a number of Canadian officers to 4 Group Headquarters to learn the ropes in preparation for the formation of a new Group.

New squadrons were created as the resources became available over the next few months, with 425 Squadron, a francophone unit intended to encourage the hitherto sluggish French–Canadian enlistment, being formed on 22 June 1942, 426 Squadron on 15 October, 427, 428 and 429 Squadrons all on 7 November 1942 and 431 Squadron a few days later. Three more squadrons, 432, 433 and 434, were added the following year as the final Canadian contribution to Bomber Command.

On New Year's Day 1943 the RCAF and the Canadian government finally achieved their goal when 6 (RCAF) Group, the only designated single nationality Group in the Command, proudly took its place in the line under the command of AVM G.E. Brookes. It had been a long, tortuous and bumpy road, what with the massive diversion of resources to the BCATP, the wrangling over funding and the ever-thorny question of Canadianisation, but dogged resolve and perseverance eventually won through. There was many a smile on the faces of the senior Canadian officers in Britain when 6 Group Headquarters received a congratulatory telegram from Harris: 'A happy birthday and a prosperous New Year to No. 6 RCAF Group. As individuals and as RCAF squadrons, you have done fine work already. As the RCAF Group, I know you will maintain and even surpass your own high standards. We are proud to have you with us. Hail Canada! Hail Hitler, with bombs!'

There was, however, still much to be done. Indeed, in spite of his cheerful and supportive public stance, Harris had expressed some reservations about the RCAF's readiness to participate fully and effectively in the air offensive. Although he never doubted the Canadians' spirit or commitment, he did question their experience, particularly in terms of command. With a relatively inexperienced team to support him, a great deal rested on the shoulders of the Group's commander, AVM Brookes. He had served in the RFC during the First World War and had subsequently joined the RCAF on its inception in April 1924, but his only operational command had been SASO Eastern Air Command in the early days of the war. With the eyes of an expectant government and nation upon him, not to mention the critical eyes within Bomber Command, Brookes did not have long to learn his trade thoroughly.

Brookes had not even had an easy time in setting up his headquarters. His first choice in Northallerton, North Yorkshire, in the summer of 1942 came to nothing because the building could not be fitted out with the necessary communications equipment. On 1 September he succeeded in requisitioning Allerton Hall, a rambling and sombre 75-room Gothic edifice about 15 miles north of York. Work upon 'Castle Dismal', as it became known, began in the autumn but such was the scale of the alterations necessary to make it function as a headquarters that it was far from ready by the time 6 Group became operational on 1 January 1943. At one stage the Harrogate Fire Service was making daily visits to fill the water storage tanks hastily erected in the grounds of the house.

Brookes was also informed that the proposed new 6 Group airfields at Piercebridge, West Tanfield, Easingwold and Strensall were being scrubbed on account of a chronic shortage of building materials and labour. This meant that 6 Group comprised stations at Dalton, Dishforth, East Moor, Leeming, Topcliffe, Middleton St George and its satellite Croft. It was to the last pair that, at one minute past midnight on 1 January 1943, the honour fell to become the first operational bases of the new Group, the potent symbol of a mature nation. Brookes saw in the New Year and celebrated the birth of his new command with a dozen or so officers enjoying a few drinks in his office. The young men and women under his command, many of them from Canada and stationed in North Yorkshire and County Durham, many thousands of miles from home, partied a little more vigorously but remained mindful of the fact that it would be back to business as usual in the morning. Whatever the changes in command, for them there was always another sortie to prepare for and carry out, always another aircraft to service or bomb-up, always another radio to check or parachute to pack, always another meal to cook or guard to stand. Always another day in a long, long war.

The Squadrons

76 SQUADRON RAF

Motto: Resolute
Crest: A lion passant, guardant, in front of the white rose of Yorkshire
Formed: 15 September 1916, Ripon, North Yorkshire. Disbanded 13 June 1919, Tadcaster.
Re-formed 12 April 1937, Finningley. Disbanded 22 April 1940, Upper Heyford, Oxfordshire.
Re-formed 12 April 1941, Linton-on-Ouse. Disbanded 31 December 1960, Luqa, Malta.
Middleton St George: 4 June 1941–17 September 1942
Aircraft flown at Middleton St George: Handley Page Halifax I

78 SQUADRON RAF

Motto: Nemo non paratus (Nobody unprepared)
Crest: Heraldic tiger rampant and double queued
Formed: 1 November 1916, Harrietsham, Kent. Disbanded 1919. Re-formed 1 November 1936,
Boscombe Down, Wiltshire. Disbanded 30 September 1954, Fayid, Egypt. Later re-formed and
still in service.
Middleton St George: 7 April 1941–20 October 1941. Transferred to Croft (a satellite station)
10 June 1942–18 September 1942.
Aircraft flown at Middleton St George: Armstrong Whitworth Whitley V, Handley Page Halifax I

419 (MOOSE) SQUADRON RCAF

Motto: Moosa Aswayita (Beware of the Moose)
Crest: A moose attacking
Formed: 15 December 1941, Mildenhall, Suffolk. Disbanded 5 September 1945, Yarmouth, Nova
Scotia. Re-formed and still in service.
Middleton St George: 11 November 1942–31 May 1945
Aircraft flown at Middleton St George: Handley Page Halifax II, Avro Lancaster X

420 (SNOWY OWL) SQUADRON RCAF

Motto: Pugnamus finitum (We fight to the end)
Crest: A snowy owl with wings elevated
Formed: 19 December 1941, Waddington, Lincolnshire. Disbanded 5 September 1945, Debert, Nova Scotia. Later re-formed and disbanded.
Middleton St George: 16 October 1942–16 May 1943
Aircraft flown at Middleton St George: Vickers Wellington III and X

428 (GHOST) SQUADRON RCAF

Motto: Usque ad finem (To the very end)
Crest: A death's head in a shroud
Formed: 7 November 1942, Dalton, North Yorkshire. Disbanded 5 September 1945, Yarmouth, Nova Scotia. Later re-formed and disbanded.
Middleton St George: 4 June 1943–31 May 1945
Aircraft flown at Middleton St George: Vickers Wellington X, Handley Page Halifax II and V, Avro Lancaster X

APPENDIX 3

Losses Sustained by Squadrons at Middleton St George

76 SQUADRON

DATE	TARGET	AIRCRAFT	CAPTAIN	KILLED	PoWs/ EVADERS
23/6/41	Kiel	Halifax L9492	Plt Off W.K. Stobbs	5	1
21/7/41	Training	Halifax L9533	Plt Off L.R. Blackwell	6	over UK
24/7/41	La Pallice	Halifax L9529	Flt Lt A. Lewin	4	3
	La Pallice	Halifax L9517	Plt Off J.F.P.J. McKenna	7	0
	La Pallice	Halifax L9494	Sqn Ldr W.R. Williams	0	7
5/8/41	Karlsruhe	Halifax L9516	Sgt T.A. Byrne	1	6
13/8/41	Berlin	Halifax L9530	Flt Lt C.C. Cheshire	2	5
	Berlin	Halifax L9531	Sgt C.E. Whitfield	5	2
	Berlin	Halifax L9562	Sgt J. McHale	7	0
29/8/41	Frankfurt	Halifax L9518	Sqn Ldr R. Bickford	2	over UK
13/9/41	Brest	Halifax L9567	Plt Off R.E. Hutchin	1	over UK
12/10/41	Bremen	Halifax L9561	Flt Sgt E.B. Muttart	1	7
31/10/41	Dunkirk	Halifax L9602	Flt Sgt C.S. O'Brien	7	0
30/11/41	Hamburg	Halifax L9604	Sgt G.R. Herbert	0	over UK
30/12/41	Brest	Halifax L9615	Plt Off D.S. King	7	0
30/3/42	Tirpitz	Halifax R9453	Sqn Ldr A.P. Burdett	7	0
10/4/42	Essen	Halifax R9484	Flt Sgt J.H. Lambeth	7	0
12/4/42	Essen	Halifax R9487	Sgt K.F. Lloyd-Jones	6	1
27/4/42	Dunkirk	Halifax R9487	Sgt P.C. Morris	4	3
3/5/42	Hamburg	Halifax R9451	Sgt J.B. Williams	4	2
8/5/42	Warnemünde	Halifax R9456	Plt Off H.B. Moorhouse	6	0
19/5/42	Mannheim	Halifax W7660	Flt Sgt W.F. Anderson	0	7
29/5/42	Gennervilliers	Halifax W1065	Plt Off J.D. Anderson	7	0
1/6/42	Essen	Halifax W1064	Sgt T.R.A. West	2	2, 2 evaded

DATE	TARGET	AIRCRAFT	CAPTAIN	KILLED	PoWs/ EVADERS
3/6/42	Bremen	Halifax R9457	Flt Sgt J.W. Stell	5	2
	Bremen	Halifax W1035	Plt Off J.A. Philip	6	0
20/6/42	Emden	Halifax W1114	Plt Off H. Norfolk	3	4
24/6/42	Training	Halifax W7661	Sgt J.H.G. Bingham	6	over UK
25/6/42	Training	Halifax R9482	Sgt A. Aston	5	over UK
25/6/42	Bremen	Halifax W7747	Sgt J.E. Meyer	7	0
19/6/42	Vegesack	Halifax W770	Flt Sgt W.L. Belous	2	over UK
26/7/42	Hamburg	Halifax R9485	Sgt E.J. Butt	3	4
31/7/42	Düsseldorf	Halifax B3195	Plt Off W.R. Waite	1	over UK
9/8/42	Osnabruck	Halifax W1106	Sgt W.A. Wilson	7	0
18/8/42	Training	Halifax V9992	Flt Sgt D. Gillies	7	over UK
1/9/42	Saarbrücken	Halifax W1244	Plt Off H.G. Sherwood	1	6
8/9/42	Frankfurt	Halifax W1128	Sgt J.E. Nicholson	7	0
16/7/42	Essen	Halifax R9365	Plt Off A.C. Campbell	7	0
Total				165	63

78 Squadron

DATE	TARGET	AIRCRAFT	CAPTAIN	KILLED	PoWs/ EVADERS
8/5/41	Bremen	Whitley T4147	Sgt L. Thorpe	5	0
16/5/41	Cologne	Whitley Z6493	Plt Off J.A.T. Garrould	5	0
28/5/41	Kiel	Whitley Z6484	Sgt A.T. Copley	5	0
8/6/41	Dortmund	Whitley Z6571	Sgt D.R. Simm	5	0
16/6/41	Cologne	Whitley Z6492	Plt Off D.S.W. Lake	5	0
18/6/41	Bremen	Whitley Z6560	Flt Sgt V.H. Marks	5	0
	Bremen	Whitley Z6661	Plt Off T.C. Richards	5	0
29/6/41	Bremen	Whitley Z6664	Sgt R.S. Green	5	0
2/7/41	Cologne	Whitley Z6558	Sgt A. Jepson	5	0
8/7/41	Hamm	Whitley T4209	Sgt W.M. McQuitty	4	over UK
	Hamm	Whitley Z6555	Sgt D.W. McLean	5	0
16/8/41	Cologne	Whitley Z6577	Sgt T.A. Sherman	5	0
	Cologne	Whitley Z6752	Sgt J. Malet-Warden	5	0
	Cologne	Whitley Z6823	Flt Lt J.A. Cant	2	3
24/8/41	Düsseldorf	Whitley Z6466	Sgt W.G. Rogers	5	0
	Düsseldorf	Whitley Z6742	Plt Off Fransden	1	over UK
27/8/41	Mannheim	Whitley Z6508	Plt Off K.W. Davies	5	0
6/7/41	Hüls	Whitley Z6881	Plt Off F.B. Thorpe	5	0
29/9/41	Stettin	Whitley Z9126	Sgt R.W. Bird	5	0
19/6/42	Emden	Halifax BB200	Flt Sgt M. Crowe	7	0
25/6/42	Bremen	Halifax W1067	Flg Off J. Whittingham	2	4
26/7/42	Hamburg	Halifax W1184	Flg Off C. Mitchener	7	0
5/8/42	Bochum	Halifax W1180	Sgt J.C. Stevens	3	4

DATE	TARGET	AIRCRAFT	CAPTAIN	KILLED	PoWs/ EVADERS
6/8/42	Duisburg	Halifax W1237	Flg Off J.M. d'Ursel	7	0
11/8/42	Mainz	Halifax W1061	WOII W.E. Lunan	2	4, 1 evaded
	Mainz	Halifax W1115	Sgt E.G.S. Monk	2	5
	Mainz	Halifax W1233	Flt Sgt J. Fleetwood	7	0
	Mainz	Halifax W1245	Flg Off D.A. Kingston	5	2
28/8/42	Saarbrücken	Halifax W7809	Sgt J.A.B. Marshall	7	0
8/9/42	Frankfurt	Halifax W7782	Flt Lt P. Tippetts-Aylmer	3	2, 2 evaded
10/9/42	Düsseldorf	Halifax DT491	Plt Off C.J. Stevenson	7	0
Total				146	24, 3 evaded

420 (SNOWY OWL) SQUADRON RCAF

DATE	TARGET	AIRCRAFT	CAPTAIN	KILLED	PoWs/ EVADERS
15/10/42	Cologne	Wellington X3808	Flt Sgt L.E. White	5	0
9/11/42	Hamburg	Wellington Z1679	Sgt W.S. Beale	5	0
21/1/43	Minelaying	Wellington BJ966	Sgt J.J. Gergley	6	0
29/1/43	Lorient	Wellington DF615	Plt Off E.J. Stanton	5	0
	Lorient	Wellington DF626	Sgt D.R. Sanderson	4	over UK
13/2/43	Lorient	Wellington BK330	Plt Off L.G. Gibson	5	0
26/2/43	Cologne	Wellington BK468	Sgt H.A. Hanson	5	0
1/3/43	Training	Wellington Z1274	Flt Sgt P.E. Townsend	5	0
5/3/43	Essen	Wellington HE280	Plt Off R. Graham	6	0
12/3/43	Essen	Wellington HE690	Sgt G.H. Cooke	1	4
13/3/43	Minelaying	Wellington BK296	Sgt C.H. Tidy	5	0
29/3/43	Bochum	Wellington X3814	Sgt R.L. Brandon	5	0
	Bochum	Wellington MS484	Plt Off B.A. Grant	4	1
8/4/43	Duisburg	Wellington MS479	Plt Off W. Walkinshaw	5	0
10/8/43	Frankfurt	Wellington HE422	Plt Off C.W. Jackson	1	over UK
14/4/43	Stuttgart	Wellington HE550	Sqn Ldr F.V. Taylor	2	1, 2 evaded
	Stuttgart	Wellington HE863	Sgt P.G. Cozens	5	0
16/4/43	Mannheim	Wellington HE682	Sgt L.M. Horahan	4	1
26/4/43	Duisburg	Wellington HE 693	Sgt E.L. Newbury	5	0
Total				83	6, 2 evaded

419 (MOOSE) SQUADRON RCAF

DATE	TARGET	AIRCRAFT	CAPTAIN	KILLED	PoWs/ EVADERS
9/1/43	Minelaying	Halifax W7857	Sgt F.H. Barker	7	0
3/2/43	Hamburg	Halifax DT630	Flt Sgt J.D. McKenzie	4	3
18/2/43	Minelaying	Halifax DT639	Flt Sgt B.A. Levasseur	7	0

DATE	TARGET	AIRCRAFT	CAPTAIN	KILLED	PoWs/ EVADERS
1/3/43	Berlin	Halifax DT641	Plt Off A.J. Herriott	7	0
5/3/43	Essen	Halifax DT646	Sgt L. Bakewell	1	5, 1 evaded
27/3/43	Berlin	Halifax DT634	Flg Off C.E. Porter	1	6
28/3/43	St Nazaire	Halifax BB283	Sgt R.F. Becket	7	0
3/4/43	Essen	Halifax DT617	Plt Off P.D. Boyd	7	0
8/4/43	Duisburg	Halifax BB327	Sgt J.H. Morris	6	1
20/4/43	Stettin	Halifax JB912	Plt Off T.E. Jackson	1	7
28/4/43	Minelaying	Halifax JB923	Sgt G.K. Smallwood	7	0
4/5/43	Dortmund	Halifax W7817	Plt Off C.J. Vaillancourt	1	6
	Dortmund	Halifax DT794	Flg Off W.G. Elliot	7	0
12/5/43	Duisburg	Halifax JB791	WOI G.A. McMillan	2	5
	Duisburg	Halifax JB861	Flt Sgt J. Palmer	7	0
13/5/43	Bochum	Halifax DT672	Sgt G. Adams	7	0
	Bochum	Halifax JD113	Sgt W.H.S. Bucknall	4	3
23/5/43	Dortmund	Halifax JB862	Sgt A.S. Green	6	1
29/5/43	Wuppertal	Halifax JB793	Sgt F.E. Winegarden	4	3
	Wuppertal	Halifax JB805	Sgt P.S. Johnson	7	0
11/6/43	Düsseldorf	Halifax JD143	Flg Off W.J. Boyce	3	5
12/6/43	Bochum	Halifax DT616	Sgt B.D. Kirkham	0	7
21/6/43	Krefeld	Halifax W1271	Sgt D.R. Pearce	7	0
24/6/43	Wuppertal	Halifax JD147	Flt Lt B.N. Jost	3	4
	Wuppertal	Halifax JD214	Sgt G.V. Neale	0	7
	Wuppertal	Halifax JD258	Sgt R. Whitfield	7	0
28/6/43	Cologne	Halifax JD215	Plt Off H.W. Fowler	7	0
3/7/43	Cologne	Halifax JD159	Plt Off A.H. Bell	3	5
13/7/43	Aachen	Halifax BB323	2/Lt B.J.J. Furey	1	6
25/7/43	Essen	Halifax JD256	Sgt L. Chapman	7	1
2/8/43	Hamburg	Halifax DT798	Sgt J.S. Sobin	4	3
9/8/43	Mannheim	Halifax JD257	Flg Off M.T.R. Ludlow	7	0
17/8/43	Peenemünde	Halifax JD158	Flg Off S.M. Heard	8	0
	Peenemünde	Halifax JD163	Sgt J.M. Batterton	7	0
	Peenemünde	Halifax JD458	F/SGT S.T. Pekin	7	0
31/8/43	Berlin	Halifax JD270	Sgt W.D.L. Cameron	4	3
	Berlin	Halifax JD331	Flt Lt J.D. Corcoran	3	4
	Berlin	Halifax JD464	Flg Off R. Stewart	3	4
5/9/43	Mannheim	Halifax JD210	Flg Off J.A. Studer	7	0
	Mannheim	Halifax JD410	Sgt F.B. Allan	6	1
16/9/43	Modane	Halifax LW240	Flt Lt A.N. Quaille	0	4, 4 evaded
23/9/43	Mannheim	Halifax JB791	Sgt R.T. Griffiths	7	0
	Mannheim	Halifax JD457	Sgt J. Kelly	7	0
29/9/43	Bochum	Halifax BB376	Plt Off J.R. Symons	7	0
4/10/43	Frankfurt	Halifax JD204	Flg Off W.H. Hamilton	4	3
	Frankfurt	Halifax JD463	Sgt A.R. Tare	6	1 evaded
22/10/43	Kassel	Halifax JD382	Wg Cdr G.A. McMurdy	5	3
18/11/43	Mannheim	Halifax LW239	Flg Off E.G. Fogg	7	0

DATE	TARGET	AIRCRAFT	CAPTAIN	KILLED	PoWs/ EVADERS
	Mannheim	Halifax LW328	Flt Sgt A.L. Sedgwick	1	6
22/11/43	Berlin	Halifax LW231	Sgt W.L. Hunter	7	0
26/11/43	Stuttgart	Halifax LW242	Sgt S.E. Clarke	7	0
29/12/43	Berlin	Halifax LW282	Flt Sgt R.L. Thompson	0	7
20/1/44	Berlin	Halifax DT731	Flt Sgt I.V. Hopkins	0	7
	Berlin	Halifax HX162	Plt Off H.L. Bullis	2	5
21/1/44	Magdeburg	Halifax JD420	Flt Sgt V.L. Hawkes	1	6
	Magdeburg	Halifax JD466	Flt Lt A.G. Hermitage	7	0
28/1/44	Berlin	Halifax JD119	Flt Sgt F.H. Palmer	8	0
12/2/44	Minelaying	Halifax HR 910	Flt Lt D.D. Laidlaw	7	0
15/2/44	Berlin	Halifax JD456	Plt Off J.A. Parker	7	0
19/2/44	Leipzig	Halifax JD114	Flt Sgt D.K. Macleod	7	0
	Leipzig	Halifax LW327	Flg Off L.T. Lucas	3	4
25/2/44	Minelaying	Halifax JD200	Flg Off A.L. Warren	7	0
29/3/44	Vaires	Halifax HR 912	WOII J. Greenage	7	0
18/4/44	Minelaying	Halifax JD202	Plt Off J.D. Quinn	7	0
22/4/44	Laon	Halifax HX189	Flg Off C.A. Thomas	1	2, 4 evaded
27/4/44	Montzen	Halifax JD954	Plt Off R.A. McIvor	7	0
1/5/44	St Ghislain	Lancaster X KB711	Plt Off J.C. McNary	2	6
12/5/44	Leuven	Lancaster X KB710	Plt Off H.I. Smith	7	0
	Leuven	Lancaster X KB713	Plt Off B.F. Edwards	7	0
15/5/44	Training	Lancaster X KB701	Flg Off S.G. McMaster	7	0
22/5/44	Dortmund	Lancaster X KB717	Plt Off C.E.G. Patterson	8	0
24/5/44	Aachen	Lancaster X KB706	WOI D.M. Robson	6	1
12/6/44	Cambrai	Lancaster X KB714	Flg Off R.N. Wilson	7	0
	Cambrai	Lancaster X KB726	Flg Off A. de Breyne	1	2, 4 evaded
	Cambrai	Lancaster X KB731	Flg Off W.M. Lacy	5	2 evaded
16/6/44	Sterkrade	Lancaster X KB728	Flg Off D. Morrison	7	0
	Sterkrade	Lancaster X KB734	Flt Lt E.S. Smith	5	1, 1 evaded
4/7/44	Villeneuve	Lancaster X KB718	Flg Off L.W. Frame	0	3, 4 evaded
	Villeneuve	Lancaster X KB723	Flg Off C.A.D. Steepe	3	1, 3 evaded
	Villeneuve	Lancaster X KB727	Flg Off J.M. Stevenson	0	6, 1 evaded
24/7/44	Stuttgart	Lancaster X KB719	Flt Sgt J.A. Phillis	4	1, 2 evaded
7/8/44	Caen	Lancaster X KB755	Flg Off B.D. Walker	7	0
25/8/44	Russelheim	Lancaster X KB708	Flg Off W.A. Milner	4	over UK
	Russelheim	Lancaster X KB775	Flg Off H.D. Witwer	6	1
4/10/44	Bergen	Lancaster X KB745	Flg Off G.R. Duncan	7	0
9/10/44	Bochum	Lancaster X KB754	Plt Off A.I. Cohen	6	1
14/10/44	Duisburg	Lancaster X KB800	Flg Off A.M. Roy	6	1
23/10/44	Essen	Lancaster X KB776	Sqn Ldr W. McGuffin	7	0
28/10/44	Cologne	Lancaster X KB712	Flt Lt A.N. Nelligan	7	0
24/11/44	Training	Lancaster X KB785	Flg Off R.G. Mansfield	7	0
6/12/44	Osnabruck	Lancaster X KB779	Flg Off B.D. Hyndman	7	0
24/12/44	Lohausen	Lancaster X KB715	Flg Off T.H. Cowtan	1	6
27/12/44	Opladen	Lancaster X KB738	Flg Off F.W. How	7	0

DATE	TARGET	AIRCRAFT	CAPTAIN	KILLED	PoWs/ EVADERS
29/12/44	Scholven-Buer	Lancaster X KB753	Plt Off R.F. Adam	6	1
	Scholven-Buer	Lancaster X KB765	Flg Off R.A. McVicar	6	1
13/1/45	Leuna	Lancaster X KB769	Flt Lt G.O. Tedford	6	1
	Leuna	Lancaster X KB799	Flg Off N.R. Vatne	1	6
2/2/45	Wiesbaden	Lancaster X KB750	Flg Off B.W. Martin	6	1
4/5/45	Bonn	Lancaster X KB787	Flt Lt J.B. Barlow	7	0
20/2/45	Dortmund	Lancaster X KB804	Flg Off L.A. Blaney	2	5
5/3/45	Chemnitz	Lancaster X KB845	Flg Off C.L. Reitlo	7	0
7/3/45	Dessau	Lancaster X KB797	Flg Off B.T. McVeill	5	2
15/3/45	Hagen	Lancaster X KB814	Flt Sgt C.W. Parish	4	3 evaded
	Hagen	Lancaster X KB870	Flt Lt M.W. McLaughlin	3	over Allied lines
20/3/45	Heide	Lancaster X KB786	Flg Off R.W. Millar	6	0
31/3/45	Hamburg	Lancaster X KB761	Flt Lt H.A. Metivier	7	0
	Hamburg	Lancaster X KB869	Flg Off D.S. Bowes	4	3
13/4/45	Kiel	Lancaster X KB866	Flt Sgt C.C. Maclaren	7	0
Total				541	187, 30 evaded

428 (GHOST) SQUADRON RCAF

DATE	TARGET	AIRCRAFT	CAPTAIN	KILLED	PoWs/ EVADERS
9/7/43	Gelsenkirchen	Halifax V DK229	Sqn Ldr F.H. Bowden	1	5, 1 evaded
13/7/43	Aachen	Halifax V DK228	Flt Lt W.G. Weeks	7	0
	Aachen	Halifax V DK 257	Flt Lt D.S. Morgan	2	4, 1 evaded
	Aachen	Halifax V ED209	Plt Off W.D.F. Ross	0	5, 2 evaded
29/7/43	Hamburg	Halifax V DK239	Sgt D.H. Bates	6	1
2/8/43	Hamburg	Halifax V EB212	Plt Off V.T. Sylvester	8	0
	Hamburg	Halifax V EB274	Sgt M. Chepil	8	0
17/8/43	Peenemünde	Halifax V DK230	Flt Lt G.W. Ianson	7	0
	Peenemünde	Halifax V DK238	Sgt W.W. Blackmore	2	5
	Peenemünde	Halifax V EB211	Sgt J.F. Sheridan	7	0
23/8/43	Berlin	Halifax V DK267	Flt Sgt H.A. Read	1	4, 2 interned Sweden
27/8/43	Nurnburg	Halifax V EB216	Sgt A.L. Mitchell	4	3
31/8/43	Berlin	Halifax V DK249	Sgt B.R. Harrison	7	0
	Berlin	Halifax V DK233	Sgt J.D. Este	3	4
6/9/43	Munich	Halifax V DK196	Sgt W. Brown	1	6
15/6/43	Montlucon	Halifax V LK913	Wg Cdr D.W. Smith	0	4, 4 evaded
22/9/43	Hannover	Halifax V LK635	Flg Off H.E. McRae	7	0
	Hannover	Halifax V LK914	Flg Off K.W. Jones	6	1
23/9/43	Mannheim	Halifax V DK271	Flt Lt H.F. Davis	4	3

DATE	TARGET	AIRCRAFT	CAPTAIN	KILLED	PoWs/ EVADERS
	Mannheim	Halifax V EB207	Plt Off W.A. Hadden	7	0
27/9/43	Hannover	Halifax V JB968	Flg Off R.H. Sherback	7	0
	Hannover	Halifax V DK270	Sgt R. Wilson	4	over UK
	Hannover	Halifax V EB215	Sgt J.E. Farmer	6	1
	Hannover	Halifax V LK915	Flg Off M.G.Whalley	5	2
3/10/43	Kassel	Halifax V EB213	WO F.B. Edwards	6	2
	Kassel	Halifax V EB214	Sgt K.A. McArthur	2	5
4/10/43	Frankfurt	Halifax V LK931	Flt Sgt J. Harkins	0	5, 2 evaded
22/10/43	Kassel	Halifax V LK908	Sgt E.J. Sykes	1	over UK
3/11/43	Düsseldorf	Halifax V LK954	Flg Off R.G. Eaton	8	0
19/11/43	Leverkusen	Halifax V LK950	Flt Sgt Hawthorn	1	over UK
	Leverkusen	Halifax V LK956	Flt Sgt H.C. Shepherd	0	4, 3 evaded
22/11/43	Berlin	Halifax V LK906	Sgt J.M. Jacob	7	0
25/11/43	Frankfurt	Halifax V LK969	Sqn Ldr J.R. Beggs	1	6
26/11/43	Stuttgart	Halifax V JN966	Flt Sgt R.M. Buck	7	0
20/12/43	Frankfurt	Halifax V EB252	Plt Off W.J. Armour	7	1
	Frankfurt	Halifax V LK928	Flt Sgt J.L. Keighan	6	1
20/1/44	Berlin	Halifax V LK739	Flt Sgt F.F.E. Reain	0	1, 6 evaded
21/1/44	Magdeburg	Halifax V DK237	Flt Sgt R.E. Terry	1	6
19/2/44	Leipzig	Halifax II JD271	Flg Off A.W. Wolverton	7	0
17/4/44	Minelaying	Halifax II JN973	Plt Off G.W. Lillico	7	0
20/4/44	Lens	Halifax II JD113	Flt Lt C.G. Ford	1	5, 1 evaded
21/4/44	Minelaying	Halifax II JP199	Sqn Ldr F. McGuigan	2	over UK
23/4/44	Minelaying	Halifax II LW285	Flg Off W. Blake	1	6 evaded
4/7/44	Villeneuve	Lancaster X KB756	Plt Off W.C. Gay	2	2, 3 evaded
28/7/44	Hamburg	Lancaster X KB759	Plt Off T.E. McGill	8	0
12/8/44	Braunschweig	Lancaster X KB758	Flg Off J.A. McGregor	5	2
15/8/44	Soesterberg	Lancaster X KB749	WO A.P. Jakeman	5	2
16/8/44	Stettin	Lancaster X KB751	Flg Off W. Fairgrieve	6	1
18/8/44	Bremen	Lancaster X KB743	Plt Off C.M. Corbett	1	6
29/8/44	Stettin	Lancaster X KB709	Flg Off L.S. Plunkett	7	0
14/10/44	Duisburg	Lancaster X KB780	Flt Lt W.H. Janney	7	0
25/10/44	Essen	Lancaster X KB737	Flg Off F.S. Rafferty	6	1
2/11/44	Düsseldorf	Lancaster X KB752	Flg Off J. Holtze	7	0
2/12/44	Hagen	Lancaster X KB766	Flg Off L.A. Turner	2	over Allied lines
5/12/44	Soest	Lancaster X KB768	Flt Lt H.A. Shenfelt	7	0
27/12/44	Opladen	Lancaster X KB798	Flg Off E.W. Page	7	0
13/1/45	Training	Lancaster X KB793	Plt Off W.S. McMullen	1	over UK
28/1/45	Training	Lancaster X KB763	Plt Off H.L. Clark	5	over UK
	Stuttgart	Lancaster X KB770	Sqn Ldr H.L. Kay	5	2
2/2/45	Wiesbaden	Lancaster X KB725	Flt Lt V.M. Gadkin	2	over UK
	Wiesbaden	Lancaster X KB792	Flt Lt D.E. Berry	6	1
5/3/45	Chemnitz	Lancaster X KB778	Flg Off W. Mytruk	3	over Allied lines

DATE	TARGET	AIRCRAFT	CAPTAIN	KILLED	PoWs/ EVADERS
15/3/45	Hagen	Lancaster X KB 846	Flt Lt J.D.C. Craton	5	2 evaded
22/3/45	Hildesheim	Lancaster X KB 777	Flt Lt J.F. Hadley	3	4
13/4/45	Kiel	Lancaster X KB 784	Flg Off D.M. Payne	1	6
30/4/45	Training	Lancaster X KB 879	Flt Lt W.G. Campbell	7	0
Total				283	111, 32 evaded

Select Bibliography

The literature on Bomber Command is vast. Below is a selection of useful and relevant books.

Greenhous/Harris/Johnston/Rawling. *The Crucible of War: the Royal Canadian Air Force at War 1939–45* (University of Toronto Press, 1994)

Milberry/Halliday. *The Royal Canadian Air Force 1939–45* (Canav Books, Toronto, 1990)

Dunmore/Carter. *Reap the Whirlwind* (McClelland & Stewart, Toronto, 1991)

Anon. *The Royal Canadian Air Force Overseas* (OUP, Toronto, 1944–9)

Harris, Sir A.T. *Bomber Offensive* (Collins, 1947)

Harris, Sir A.T., ed. S.Cox. *Dispatches on War Operations* (HMSO, 1985)

Middlebrook/Everitt. *Bomber Command War Diaries* (Midland Publishing, 1985)

Chorley, W.R. *Bomber Command Losses* (Midland Publishing, 1992–2003)

Chorley W.R. *To See the Dawn Breaking* (Privately published)

Richards, D. *The Hardest Victory* (Hodder & Stoughton, 1994)

Sawyer, Gp Capt T. *Only Owls and Bloody Fools Fly at Night* (Goodall, 1985)

Waite, R. *Death or Decoration* (Newton Publishing, 1991)

Renaut, M. *Terror by Night* (William Kimber, 1982)

Cassels, R. *Ghost Squadron* (Ardenlea Publishing, Winnipeg, 1991)

Brown, D. *Aerodromes in North Yorkshire* (Stockton-on-Tees, 1996)

Index